CURRENT RESEARCH ON OCCUPATIONS AND PROFESSIONS

Volume 6 • 1991

CURRENT RESEARCH ON OCCUPATIONS AND PROFESSIONS

A Research Annual

Series Editor: HELENA Z. LOPATA
Center for the Comparative Study
of Social Roles
Loyola University of Chicago

Volume Editor: JUDITH A. LEVY
School of Public Health
University of Illinois
at Chicago

VOLUME 6 • 1991

 JAI PRESS INC.

Greenwich, Connecticut   *London, England*

Volumes 1-3 published as: Research in the Interweave of Social Roles

CONTENTS

v

PART III.   PROFESSIONAL IDEOLOGY AND SOCIAL CONTROL

PART IV.   PROFESSIONAL DOMINANCE IN A CHANGING
MEDICAL ENVIRONMENT

INTRODUCTION

Consensus exists among scholars that the current medical environment is undergoing great change that will have long-range effects on the occupations that it encompasses. Less agreement exists, however, as to the shape and direction that occupations have taken in managing the forces and consequences of this change. The papers in this volume are organized around examining this issue along two lines. At the institutional level, they examine how occupations and their practitioners develop and use proactive strategies to promote and maintain their self-interests. At the interactional level, selections in this volume explore the effects of health work in a changing medical environment on the lived experience, personal choices, and well-being of those delivering and receiving care.

Part I of this volume examines how current trends in the health care sector affect the opportunity structure of a medical career. In contrast to earlier decades when the average physician engaged in solo practice based on fee-for-service, the nascent physician of today confronts a practice environment that requires higher financial investment to become established, potentially fewer rewards, increased competition from other practitioners, and greater medical diversification. An overconcentration of physicians in certain specialties and geographic locations also limits the range of practice opportunities. Meanwhile, when compared to their older counterparts, greater diversity appears to exist among young physicians both in life-style preferences and the willingness to assume a heavy work load. Olson's analysis of factors influencing physicians' employment decisions examines how neophyte practitioners weigh such considerations in planning and executing their professional roles.

Over the last decade, the career decisions that Olson examined increasingly were made by women. Within the health care sector, many previously male-dominated occupations such as medicine have experienced and likely will continue to attract an influx of women among their ranks. Speculations about the effects of occupation "tipping" suggest that an increase in the ratio of females to males within a profession produces a more supportive social environment that can translate into greater power and opportunity for women. Yet, as Lorber's analysis demonstrates, despite a proportional increase in their numbers, women physicians continue to confront a "glass ceiling" of social barriers restricting access to positions of greater authority and higher rewards. According to Lorber, this ceiling will remain in place as long as existing forms of institutionalized sexism and informal norms of discrimination persist.

Part II turns to the stresses, interactional negotiations, and moral dilemmas that arise as health care providers, caregivers, and patients act out their respective roles. Caregiving occupations are organized around time schedules that require frequent trade-offs between the demands of getting work accomplished and meeting patients' affective needs. Litt's study of the collegial obligations and normative rules that define and reinforce the division of labor among residents in surgical training highlights this point. Her analysis attests to the stress of delivering humanistic medicine within an organizational structure designed to maximize efficiency. Compromises in personal and professional principles occur when residents are forced to choose between meeting their bureaucratic responsibilities and handling the problems of patients who need help.

Along similar lines, Marshall, Barnett, Baruch, and Pleck focus on the stresses of caregiving as experienced by social worker and licensed practical nurses. As they note, caregiving as an occupation is physically exhausting and emotionally draining. Strain occurs as caregivers worry over the social dilemmas of taking responsibility for others. Such providers commonly question their training and ability to meet the needs of their patients or clients. The author's analysis builds on and extends the Job Strain Model as a theoretical perspective for understanding how various job characteristics of caregiving produce occupational stress and its consequences. Their findings reveal that the rewards of helping others can moderate the negative effects of job demands.

Turning to the fears and emotional impact of illness as experienced by patients, Robboy and Goldstein's research calls attention to the steady stream of medical emergencies that routinely occur among long-term, continuous-use ventilator patients. The authors identify and point to the tactics and strategies that caregivers use to cope with and manage the continual episodes of patient crises that threaten their staff well-being and daily routine. Meanwhile, patients are shown to be in a state of constant panic that their ventilator equipment will fail despite continual reassurance of the low probability of such an event.

Part of the work of staff entails helping patients gain a sense of control over their lives and bodies.

The practical and ideological conflicts involved in empowering during crisis event is central to Simond's analysis of the social relations in an abortion clinic. Drawing on personal experience as a volunteer in a gynecology and abortion clinic, her analysis compares the medical practitioner's view of abortion as both a physical and moral event with that held by counseling staff. Reflections on her own experience as a staff member and observer within this interactional context are interwoven throughout the analysis. In the process, readers are given an insider's view of the ideological tensions and human dilemmas of abortion as a socially constructed act.

In analyzing the verbal interchange that occurs between patients and physicians, Waitzkin also offers readers a first-hand view of the influence of the medical model on defining and constructing patients' illness experience. In analyzing the structure of medical text to determine how patients and doctors deal with problems of living, Waitzkin shows that patient complaints often have their roots in the contextual sources of personal troubles that include social class, race, age, and the organization of family and work. The language of medicine and the role of the physician as an agent of social control does not encourage the expression of these contextual concerns or any movement toward change. Thus, medical discourse ideologically reinforces the status quo and the role of the physician as agent of social control can be seen as reaching far beyond the boundaries of the sick role.

Part II explores the relationship between professional ideology and social control as used by occupations to advance their position. In this regard, Langton's work calls attention to how ideological adaptation to environmental competition produces a diversity of professional identity within a particular occupation. Using historical analysis to identify tactics in occupational survival, she argues that nurse-midwives have developed at least three professional identities in response to changes in the informal and institutional arrangements of childbirth. These three identities, she argues, have been created and sustained through the development of matching ideologies that promote congruent social constructions of occupational control over the birthing process. In selecting between the three identities, the prevailing strategy among contemporary nurse-midwives, as promoted by its primary organizational body, has been to accept an occupational identity subordinate to the more powerful profession of obstetrics. This accommodation, however, demands tht nurse-midwives also accept and promote obstetrics' ideology at the partial cost of its own body of theory and knowledge.

Practitioners who developed the theory and practice of sensory integration as a body of knowledge within the profession of occupational therapy have paid similar dues in their fight for a position in the medical marketplace. Arluke begins his analysis by reminding readers that medicine's position of professional power partly was derived through the production and control of an esoteric body of knowledge. Presumably, other occupations can improve their status by developing and promoting a similar, idiosyncratic knowledge-base. Arluke's analysis traces the conceptual evolution of sensory integration and the strategic maneuvers of its proponents to gain acceptance for its ideology within occupational therapy and other related professions. As appears true for nurse-midwives, the survival and acceptance of sensory integration within the mainstream of medicine has been accomplished at negative costs. Although now widely practiced by a wide range of health care occupations, this success has occurred through co-optation of its knowledge-base, compromises in ideological principles, and the debasement of its core expertise. Arluke concludes that the institutionalization of knowledge as a strategy of professional advancement may have undesirable consequences for occupations with limited power.

The tension between promoting occupational self-interest while simultaneously remaining loyal to professional principles is also the focal point of Harrison's account of the nationwide, four-month strike by over 8,000 physicians that occurred in Israel in 1983. As Harrison notes, unionism and the right to militant, collective bargaining counters the basic ideological tenets upon which professions launch their claims to privileged status, highly valued rewards, and the right of self-governance. His analysis of the events, moves, and countermoves by various players over the course of the strike indicates that professionals can successfully draw upon militant tactics to promote occupational rewards but at the possible loss of some level of autonomy and social standing.

Part IV focuses on the retention of professional autonomy as an on-going concern among health care occupations jockeying for positions in a rapidly changing environment. According to the professional dominance explanation of occupational stratification, organized medicine historically has used the properties and privileges of a profession to strategically control and limit the work and rewards of other occupations. Hafferty and Wolinsky outline the nature of this struggle by reviewing the arguments and evidence that support or refute this perspective's utility for understanding the contemporary organization of health care. Their work points to the complexity of the current debate and warns against the pitfalls of unintentionally misusing concepts and constructs when comparing occupations.

In addressing the professional dominance debate, Elkind notes that the training and practice of medicine from 1910 to 1980 can be viewed within a temporal framework that differentiates between four distinct sociotechnical periods: the General Practice Era (1910-1939), the Specialty Era (1940-1958), the Scientific Era (1959-1968), and the Community/Family Practice Era (1969-1979). Drawing on data from a statewide study of the attitudes and self-reported behaviors of Maryland physicians, Elkind establishes that the attitudes and behaviors of the physicians that she studied differed significantly across these generational units. She concludes that variations in the degree of importance that physicians assign to maintaining the rights of professional autonomy and self-regulation have their roots in the differing socialization processes and practice environments encountered across generations of practitioners. Thus, concerns about controlling their work environment or being superordinate to other professions is not uniform across all ages or cohorts of physicians.

The study by Gross and Budrys of physicians in prepaid practice also supports this finding. They found that physicians who elect or choose by default to practice in large, bureaucratic organizations typically are pleased to relinquish some, but not all, aspects of the professional control traditionally associated with the physician's role. Contrary to arguments in the literature suggesting that physicians uniformly resent any loss of autonomy and control over their work, the physicians in this sample were aware of and willing to make trade-offs. They reported having made a conscious choice to accept an organizational arrangement that demanded greater accountability and supervision but which freed them from many of the burdensome pressures of administrative decision making.

In summary, the studies contained in this volume lend new insight and offer additional evidence attesting to the dynamic nature of professions and the proactive maneuvers of their practitioners and organizational bodies in directing and managing the forces of social change. Through the work of the various authors, a picture of the professions emerges in which occupational members both individually and collectively contribute to both the enlargement and erosion of control over the organization of work and its rewards. From this standpoint, professions are always in proactive or reactive process. The challenge for research is to chart and analyze variation in the goals, stages, strategies, and consequences of a particular course. The authors who contributed to this volume have done a splendid job in tackling this assignment.

Judith A. Levy
Volume Editor

PART I

ENTRY AND GATEKEEPING IN MEDICINE

FACTORS INFLUENCING EMPLOYMENT DECISIONS OF YOUNG PHYSICIANS

Lorayn Olson

ABSTRACT

With the array of patient care arrangements now available to young physicians, how physicians make employment decisions in the early stages of their careers is problematic. Using data from a nationally representative study of young physicians, factors that influence a physician's employment decisions were analyzed using regression analysis. Personal autonomy and future income potential are the strongest predictors of the percentage of time spent self-employed. For the percentage of time spent in nonpatient care activities, the strongest positive predictor variable was the importance given to the factor of "opportunity to pursue professional interests" and the strongest negative predictor variable was the factor "future income potential."

Current Research on Occupations and Professions, Volume 6, pages 3-23.
Copyright © 1991 by JAI Press Inc.
ISBN: 1-55938-236-8

INTRODUCTION

Recently, the health care delivery system has been changing rapidly. As new practice arrangements have emerged, a growing number of physicians are working as employees or treating patients in group practices. At the same time, the number of physicians providing prepaid patient care has increased. Moreover, many physicians assemble a package of practice arrangements, often incorporating some nonpatient care activities as part of their professional activities. The array of patient care arrangements now available to young physicians poses the question of how physicians make employment decisions. While recent changes in the health care system have affected all health care professionals, the ways in which physicians in the early stages of their careers make employment decisions have been particularly complicated by these added considerations. Using a nationally representative sample of young physicians, factors that might influence a physician's employment decisions are considered.

While there are various theories to explain how the provision of medical care has changed in recent decades, and what that means for individual physicians (Friedson 1984, 1985, 1986; Haug 1976; McKinlay and Stoeckle 1988; Starr 1982), there is consensus that the medical profession and medical care are undergoing great change. Due to the changing medical practice environment, young physicians are facing decisions regarding various aspects of medicine that simply have not been considerations in the past. It is now more difficult for a physician to establish a solo practice due to the cost of starting a practice (particularly the high cost of new technology) and rising medical student debts (Starr 1982, p. 425). Increased competition, or at least the perception of a current or impending physician oversupply (Hafferty 1986), may also play a role in how physicians make employment decisions, causing the guaranteed income of a salaried position to be more appealing. Simultaneously, there has been growth in the number of group practices (from 6,371 in 1969 to 15,485 in 1984; Havlicek 1985, p. 5), in the sizes of individual group practices, corporate practice of medicine, and the provision of prepaid medical care. At the same time that there has been increased medical specialization, the provision of medical care has diversified.

On the other hand, the physician population is changing in several respects that could shape how young physicians make employment decisions. Between 1970 and 1985, the total number of physicians grew by 65.5% while the total number of women physicians increased nearly 217.8% (Roback, Mead, and Randolph 1986, p. 12). At the same time, a higher percentage of the younger physicians have employed spouses (according to the Socioeconomic Monitoring System, 52.4% of those under age 40 compared with 47.7% of those 40 and older; Center for Health Policy Research 1988). These demographic changes suggest that young physicians may put more emphasis on life style considerations, resulting in larger proportions of young physicians choosing a salaried position with a predictable schedule (and the possibility of part-time and intermittent work).

Female physicians are more likely than their male counterparts to favor salaried practice (Bobula 1980) and to work fewer hours per week and fewer weeks per year. Silberger, Marder, and Willke (1987) suggest that female physicians want to maintain greater geographic mobility or spend more time in activities outside the profession than men, making the high costs of opening a private practice prohibitive. Differences by sex also exist in medical specialty. While the top five specialties for both men and women physicians in 1985 included Internal Medicine, Family Practice, Psychiatry, and Obstetrics/ Gynecology, for women physicians, Pediatrics was the other top specialty while for men physicians it was General Surgery (Roback et al. 1986, pp. 47-48). To the extent that the employment priorities of women physicians differ from those of their male colleagues, the employment characteristics of this younger generation of physicians will differ from those of older physicians.

While female physicians are generally thought to be more concerned than male physicians about balancing personal goals and family responsibilities with the demands of a medical career, others have argued that life style concerns are on the minds of most young doctors, regardless of gender. It has been pointed out that male newcomers to medicine do not work as many hours as earlier generations nor will such a high percentage enter solo practice, making it impossible to separate gender from age effects with respect to life style considerations. While it has become more difficult for young physicians to establish solo, fee-for-service practice, it is quite possible that, given a choice of practice arrangements, many young physicians would not choose this option. It is now acceptable, and certainly quite possible, to deviate from certain practice characteristics that previously were taken for granted. For example, while in previous years very long working hours were considered the norm for practicing physicians, a more balanced life style, including fewer and more predictable work hours, is now possible. Starr suggests that, "Young doctors may be more interested in freedom from the job than freedom in the job, and organizations that provide more regular hours can screen out the invasions of private life that come with independent professional practice" (Starr 1982, pp. 445-446). The prevalence of two wage-earner households, accounting for 44.5% of the male physicians under age 40 (Center for Health Policy Research 1988), might result in a greater emphasis on a balanced lifestyle.

YOUNG PHYSICIANS' EMPLOYMENT DECISIONS

Possibly because employment decisions are relevant to the issue of physician distribution, numerous studies examine how physicians choose their medical specialty and practice location (Ernst and Yett 1985). With the recent growth in prepaid care and the number of salaried positions, physicians must also consider additional aspects of medical care when making employment arrangements. Nonetheless, a paucity of research exists on how physicians are making these practice arrangement decisions.

Borus (1982, p. 593), in a search of the literature, found "few reports of studies examining the actual period of transition from training to practice, the decision-making process by which post-residency practice choices are made or organized efforts by medical educators to help residents explore how they might apply their training in alternative practice situations." He reports on 33 residents graduating from the Massachusetts General Hospital-Harvard Medical School Psychiatry Residency Training Program in 1976, 1977, and 1978. Nine items were ranked in terms of their relative influence on practice choice decisions as follows: opportunities for professional growth and stimulation; opportunities for peer-professional relationships, including time for family and other personal pursuits; academic status; location; opportunities to help others; esteem of professional colleagues; income; and practice stability. While this is an interesting study, unfortunately it includes only residents in one specialty at one medical school and does not show how the professional outcomes of these residents might be related to the importance that they attach to each of these decision-making factors.

Using data from the 1978 American Association of Medical Colleges survey of senior medical students, Cuca (1979) looked at specialty and career plans. She found that while half of the women expressed an interest in private practice, 21.2% of the women compared with 8.7% of the men preferred a salaried clinical position. This research suggests that gender, likely due to heavier family responsibilities and less mobility, affects employment status outcomes. Gender roles represent only one of many factors that enter into the employment decisions that physicians make, but these have not been adequately examined in light of how the practice environment has been changing in recent years.

Perhaps the most enlightening research on this topic addressed the choice between solo and group practice. Goodman and Wolinsky (1982) analyzed (1) the relative importance of expected earnings; (2) individual preferences for a predictable practice schedule; (3) opportunities for developing personal associations and professional contacts with colleagues; (4) a more structured approach to the quality of care through more direct and immediate peer regulations, and personal autonomy in the delivery of health care; (5) individual attributes including country of medical school graduation, board certification, and age; and (6) market characteristics measured by hospital bed ratio and per capita income. Based on an analysis by Freeman (1978) of the occupational choices of persons with initially high income, Goodman and Wolinksy hypothesized that physicians would make career decisions that offer the greatest nonpecuniary rewards, with expected earnings being only marginally important in evaluating the options of solo and group practice. They indeed concluded that among the individual preference variables, only the earnings potential measure proved nonsignificant in predicting physicians' practice mode choices. The importance of autonomy was the most significant factor in the choice with the factor being significantly related to whether or not a physician opted for solo rather than group practice. Location was also more important to physicians selecting solo rather than group practice. The choice of group practice was also significantly related to the predictability of a practice schedule, maintenance of professional contacts, and the quality of medical care delivered. Younger physicians had a higher probability of entering group practice, possibly due to an inability to finance a solo practice or a preference for fewer nights and weekend days spent on call. Indeed, according to the AMA Physician Masterfile, in 1985, only 21.5% of patient care physicians under age 40 were in self-employed solo practice compared with 40.6% of patient care physicians age 40 or older (Division of Survey and Data Resources 1985).

In addition to concerns that traditionally have influenced physicians' employment choices, the employment decisions now encompass employment status (self-employed or employee) and the type of reimbursement for care (prepaid or nonprepaid). Previous research has not considered how attitudinal factors, in addition to background characteristics, influence how physicians entering the medical profession make decisions regarding these additional aspects of employment.

This paper will examine how a new generation of physicians, in many ways different from earlier generations, make employment decisions in a more varied medical practice environment. Factors in professional employment decisions regarding the new multiplicity of employment opportunities are analyzed using a nationally representative sample of young physicians. First, we will analyze the relative importance of a dozen factors that can play a role in employment decisions. This will show what predispositions young physicians have at the outset. Second, we will look at how physicians in the early stages of their medical careers are distributing their professional time, as an employee or self-employed, providing prepaid and nonprepaid care, and in nonpatient care activities. Next, we will analyze how factors influencing employment decisions, in conjunction with demographic characteristics, determine how many hours are devoted to professional endeavors and how they are distributed. While we have physicians' self-reports of importance accorded various employment factors for the year of the survey and the first year in practice, these are the physicians' perceptions of what factors have been important and, to a certain extent, could be rationalizations for their current situation. It is difficult to sort out the factors that would be accorded importance regardless of medical practice possibilities available to young physicians from those factors that represent rationalizations of previous employment decisions. The extent to which young physicians have misperceptions of characteristics of various employment opportunities is also unknown. Nonetheless, this study of physician employment provides us with some clues as to how physicians attempt to manage and make sense of their place in a rapidly changing practice environment.

METHODS

In 1985, the American Medical Association's Ad Hoc Committee on Young Physicians conducted a survey of young physicians (Department of Survey Design and Analysis 1985). The survey was designed to determine the current needs and concerns of young physicians by studying relevant demographic, practice, and attitudinal information. The young physician population was defined as physicians who were younger than 40 years old and had graduated from medical school after 1969.[1]

A random sample of 3,000 was selected from the population of 131,301 young physicians. A mail survey with telephone follow-up of nonrespondents yielded a response rate of 51.0%. The respondents were representative of the sample with respect to age, sex, geographic region, medical specialty, and major professional activity. Since there was an overrepresentation of AMA members, the descriptive statistics below are weighted by AMA membership to more accurately reflect the distribution of the young physician population. The regression analyses are computed using unweighted data.[2]

These data were merged with information from the Record of Physicians' Professional Activities (PPA), a rotating census of the U.S. physician population conducted by the American Medical Association, and from the AMA Physician Masterfile. The PPA Census collects information regarding how many hours physicians spend in various professional activities, employment arrangements, and specialties as well as other background information such as hospital affiliation, race, and professional address. Using the PPA, data on the number of hours worked during a typical week were added. From the AMA Physician Masterfile, data on the respondent's sex, self-designated practice specialty, and country of medical school graduation were added.

Measures

The respondents were asked to indicate which 3 of 12 factors were most important in influencing their employment decisions currently and during the first year in practice. There is great variability in income derived from medical practice. The AMA's Socioeconomic Monitoring System has shown that while the mean 1985 net income (after expenses, but before taxes) for patient care physicians was $113,000, it varied from $83,800 for employed physicians to $124,500 for self-employed physicians and by medical specialty from $77,000 for pediatricians to $155,400 for surgeons (Gonzalez and Emmons 1986, p. 104). Since this difference is likely to be an important employment consideration for some physicians, monetary considerations were measured by these variables: future income potential, guaranteed income, and professional liability costs. Variables reflecting the physicians' perceived ability to provide adequate patient care included quality of care, personal autonomy, and opportunity to pursue professional interests. With the view that there is increased competition among physicians becoming more commonplace, perceived opportunity structures were considered by the following items: opportunity to join existing practice, availability of hospital privileges, and lack of better alternative. Life style factors are represented by questions concerning location preference, convenience of work hours, and family influence.

RESULTS

With each responding physician indicating the top three factors influencing current employment decisions, the ranking of the factors was as follows:[3]

- location preference   42%
- personal autonomy   39%
- quality of care considerations   36%
- future income potential   36%
- opportunity to pursue professional interests   35%
- convenience of work hours   23%
- guaranteed income   21%
- family influence   21%
- opportunity to join existing practice   11%
- professional liability costs   8%
- availability of hospital privileges   7%
- lack of better alternative   6%

Location preference, which has long been influential in physicians' practice choices, was cited most often as one of the three most important in influencing these young physicians' employment decisions. Personal autonomy, traditionally associated with solo practice, was also indicated frequently as an important factor.

There is considerable debate regarding whether or not salaried positions necessarily mean that physicians' autonomy is diminished. Salaried positions actually may free physicians from the administrative and business aspects of medical practice so that they are able to concentrate exclusively on patient care (Prybil 1974; Zako 1976; Phillips and Dorsey 1980; Friedson and Mann 1971; Engel 1969; Luft and Trauner 1981). Here we are not evaluating the degree of autonomy associated with each practice arrangement, but rather the importance that personal autonomy plays in employment decisions.

Given the hypothesis that this generation might place great importance on life style matters, it is remarkable that convenience of work hours and family influence ranked only sixth and eighth, respectively, out of twelve factors. All three variables that measure attentiveness to patient care issues (personal autonomy, quality of care considerations, and opportunity to pursue professional interests) ranked higher than these two life style considerations. Only location preference, a variable that has been very important in employment decisions for previous generations, was rated highly with respect to employment decisions. Perhaps most notably, "lack of a better alternative" was checked least often and "opportunity to join existing practice" and "availability of hospital privileges" were not often ranked as the most important influences. Evidently, despite much discussion of an impending physician oversupply and increasing competition, these young physicians perceive that they have some control in their selection of an employment arrangement.

The respondents were asked the percentage of professional time spent in five categories:

- self-employed prepaid practice
- self-employed nonprepaid practice
- employee prepaid practice
- employee nonprepaid practice
- nonpatient care activities

The choice of self-employed or employee status (or a combination of both) can act as a proxy for a decision regarding degree of control over many employment aspects. Choosing to provide prepaid or nonprepaid patient care (or some combination of both) signifies a decision about control over patient care determination and other practice characteristics. Physicians were queried regarding both sets of options.

The relative ranking of characteristics of medical practices that might not have played a role in decisions made by older physicians when they entered medical practices were evaluated in conjunction with more traditional choice determinates (i.e., location preference and personal autonomy). Convenience of work hours, guaranteed income, and family influence might characterize the importance young physicians give to life style considerations. Professional liability costs also have come to play an increasingly important role in medical care as they now consume a high proportion of practice expenses. Accounting for 4.6% of practice revenues in 1985 (Gonzalez and Emmons 1986, p. 12), they are considered here as a potential predictor of employment outcomes.

Only 31.1% of the physicians spent 100% of their time in one type of professional activity. Half (50.6%) divided their time between two types of activities and 18.2% were involved with three, four, or five activities. Since the young physicians assemble a package of activities, these doctors are not easily categorized into distinct types of employment. One alternative is to treat the category in which the physician spends the plurality of his or her time as the major professional activity. This approach, however, discards pertinent information. The secondary activities of a physician may consume a substantial amount of time or the number of hours spent in those activities may grow as a physician's career progresses. For this reason, the percentages of time spent in each type of activity are considered here.

Table 1 shows the average percentage of time spent in five categories. (Here the patient care hours have been grouped, first by employment status and again by method of payment). On average, during the first year in practice, 36% of the physicians' time is spent in self-employed patient care compared with 49% of the time spent as an employee. Between the first year in practice and the current year, there is a shift in employment status; a greater portion (49%) of time is spent in self-employed practice compared with 37% as an employee. During the first year in practice, almost three-quarters (72%) of the time is spent in nonprepaid patient care compared with 14% of the time spent in prepaid patient care. These percentages remain unchanged during the current year. The figure of 14.3% of the time spent in nonpatient care activities during the first year in practice increases only slightly to 15.0% in 1985.

Table 1.   Average *Percentage Of Time* Spent
in Professional Activities During
First Year in Practice and Current Year

	Mean	*Median*
First Year in Practice		
Self-Employed Patient Care	36.4	0
Employee Patient Care	49.2	50
Prepaid Patient Care	13.5	0
Nonprepaid Patient Care	72.2	90
Nonpatient Care Activities	14.3	5
Current Year		
Self-Employed Patient Care	48.5	56
Employee Patient Care	36.6	10
Prepaid Patient Care	13.5	0
Nonprepaid Patient Care	71.5	90
Nonpatient Care Activities	15.0	5

Using regression analysis, we examined the relationship of the employment decision influences, along with some control variables (years in practice, sex, medical specialty, and country of graduation), with some measures of professional activities. These included the percentage of time spent self-employed, the percentage of time spent providing nonprepaid patient care, the percentage of time spent in nonpatient care activities, and the number of hours worked per week.

Looking first at priorities influencing employment decisions during the first year in practice, Table 2 shows that the statistically significant predictors of the percentage of time spent self-employed were personal autonomy, future income potential, availability of hospital privileges, opportunity to join an existing practice, opportunity to pursue professional interests, graduation from a U.S. medical school, and guaranteed income. The first four of these variables were positively correlated with self-employment and negatively associated with employee status. On the other hand, guaranteed income, as an employment influence, and graduation from a U.S. medical school were negatively correlated with self-employment and positively correlated with employee status. The opportunity to pursue professional interests was negatively correlated with each employment status.[4]

Payment method is another dimension of patient care. Turning to the percentage of time spent in prepaid care and in nonprepaid care, Table 2 shows that future income potential, the opportunity to join an existing practice, personal autonomy, and location preference are positive predictors of the percentage of time spent providing nonprepaid care. Two factors—the opportunity to pursue professional interests and convenience of work hours—were negatively correlated with the percentage of time spent in nonprepaid patient care. As for the percentage of time spent in prepaid care, the strongest positive predictor variables were convenience of work hours, guaranteed income, and professional liability costs. The importance of personal autonomy, the opportunity to join an existing practice, and the opportunity to pursue professional interests were the strongest negative predictors.

While 39.5% of the respondents did not spend any of their professional time in nonpatient care activities, and only 1.6% of respondents spent 100% of their professional time in nonpatient care activities, many did spend some hours in nonpatient care activities. Seventeen percent spent more than 20% of their time and 6.5% spent more than 50% of their time in nonpatient care activities. The regression analysis shows that some of the other factors are statistically significant predictors of the percentage of time spent in nonpatient care activities. In this instance, opportunity to pursue professional interests and graduation from a U.S. medical school are positively correlated with the percentage of time spent in nonpatient care activities while future income potential and the opportunity to join an existing practice were negatively correlated with this activity.

Table 2. Regression Analysis of Percentage of Time Spent in Three Types of Employment During First Year in Practice (Using Employment Decision Influences)

| | Percentage of Professional Time | | | | | |
| | Self-Employed Patient Care | | Nonprepaid Patient Care | | Nonpatient Care Activities | |
	Unstdz. Coeff.	Stdz. Coeff.	Unstdz. Coeff.	Stdz. Coeff.	Unstdz. Coeff.	Stdz. Coeff.
Constant	27.14		67.02		11.82	
Years in Practice[a]	.38	.03	.43	.04	.02	.003
Sex[b]	−1.19	−.01	−2.32	−.02	−.04	−.001
Primary Care Specialty[c]	3.44	.04	−1.91	−.03	−.37	−.008
Country of Graduation[d]	−7.70	−.07*	−3.12	−.03	4.81	.08**
Guaranteed Income[e]	−6.85	−.07*	−2.14	−.03	−1.96	−.04
Future Income Potential[e]	17.14	.18***	11.27	.15***	−7.73	−.16***
Convenience of Work Hours[e]	−4.75	−.04	−6.07	−.07*	.67	.01
Professional Liability Costs[e]	−.03	−.0001	−6.93	−.04	−1.06	−.01
Personal Autonomy[e]	28.48	.29***	7.70	.10**	−1.28	−.03
Location Preference[e]	5.16	.06	6.03	.09**	−2.62	−.06
Family Influence[e]	4.30	.04	2.52	.03	.54	.01
Lack of Better Alternative[e]	6.47	.04	−1.48	−.01	−1.23	−.02
Quality of Care Considerations[e]	−5.00	−.05	1.88	.03	−.95	−.02
Available Hospital Privileges[e]	12.89	.08**	5.37	.04	−.71	−.01
Join Existing Practice[e]	7.62	.07*	12.31	.15***	−6.75	−.13***
Pursue Professional Interests[e]	−8.73	−.09**	−8.37	−.11***	13.52	.29***
R^2		.18		.11		.17
F		18.57***		10.14***		17.31***
Number of Respondents		1362		1362		1362

Notes: $* p < .05$; $** p < .01$; $*** p < .001$.

[a] Year entered practice (after completing residency program)—1985.

[b] 1 = female, 0 = male.

[c] 1 = family practitioners, general practitioners, pediatricians, obstetricians, gynecologists, and internists (excluding subspecialists in internal medicine), 0 = all other specialties.

[d] 1 = graduate of a U.S. medical school, 0 = graduate of a foreign medical school.

[e] 1 = checked, 0 = not checked.

13

Since many young physicians take an HMO, locum tenens, or other salaried position when they first begin medical practice, fully intending to remain in such a position only until they establish their own practice, it is important to examine how the relative importance of employment influences might change during these early years. Are the factors influencing employment decisions during the early years of practice identical to those important during the first year in practice? Personal autonomy and future income potential are again statistically significant. With respect to employment status, personal autonomy, future income potential, and the availability of hospital privileges are again positively correlated with self-employment and negatively correlated with employee status. Now, location preference, the number of years in practice, professional liability costs and quality of care considerations are positively correlated with self-employment and negatively correlated with employee status. The opportunity to join an existing practice is no longer a strong predictor. It is not evident whether liability costs has become a more important factor influencing employment decisions because the issue becomes more important as physicians become older, more established practitioners or because in 1985, professional liability costs became more salient for all physicians, regardless of the number of years in practice. The opportunity to pursue professional interests and graduation from a United States medical school are negative predictors of percentage of time spent self-employed (see Table 3).

As for the percentages of time spent providing prepaid and nonprepaid care, in addition to the variables statistically significant during the first year in practice, guaranteed income and the sex of the physician are statistically significant. Both of these variables are positively correlated with prepaid care and negatively correlated with nonprepaid care. Since guaranteed income was an important influence for only one out of five young physicians, one would not expect, on this basis, an overwhelming number of young physicians to opt for provision of prepaid patient care. The strong correlation between being female and providing a higher percentage of prepaid patient care is another matter. The increasing percentage of medical students and residents who are women could indicate that with the increasing percentage of women physicians, more physicians will be providing prepaid patient care. The availability of hospital privileges is negatively correlated with provision of prepaid care. Convenience of work hours is no longer statistically significant.

With respect to the percentage of time spent in nonpatient care activities, the opportunity to pursue professional interests and future income potential remain the two strongest predictors. Again, as for the first year in practice, the opportunity to pursue professional interests is a positive, statistically significant factor only with respect to nonpatient care activities. Sex and location preference become significant predictors (positively and negatively, respectively) of the percentage of time spent in nonpatient care activities. Given concerns regarding competition in

Table 3. Regression Analysis of Percentage of Time Spent
in Three Types of Employment During 1985   (Using Employment Decision Influences)

| | Percentage of Professional Time | | | | | |
| | Self-Employed Patient Care | | Nonprepaid Patient Care | | Nonpatient Care Activities | |
	Unstdz. Coeff.	Stdz. Coeff.	Unstdz. Coeff.	Stdz. Coeff.	Unstdz. Coeff.	Stdz. Coeff.
Constant	27.93		70.29		11.19	
Years in Practice[a]	1.35	.09***	.35	.03	.16	.02
Sex[b]	−4.74	−.04	−7.42	−.08**	3.21	.05*
Primary Care Specialty[c]	1.36	.01	−3.14	−.05	1.06	.24
Country of Graduation[d]	−8.15	−.07**	−4.62	−.05	4.13	.07**
Guaranteed Income[e]	−2.86	−.03	−9.15	−.11***	1.09	.02
Future Income Potential[e]	15.66	.16***	10.52	.15***	8.10	−.17***
Convenience of Work Hours[e]	−4.01	−.04	−5.71	−.07	1.81	.03
Professional Liability Costs[e]	13.20	.08**	2.63	−.02	.30	.004
Personal Autonomy[e]	27.77	.30***	7.88	.11***	2.34	−.05
Location Preference[e]	10.11	.11***	6.59	.10**	−3.37	−.07*
Family Influence[e]	5.21	.05	−1.35	−.02	1.31	.02
Lack of Better Alternative[e]	9.38	.05	3.92	.03	−6.20	−.07*
Quality of Care Considerations[e]	5.53	.06*	3.65	.05	−3.34	−.07**
Available Hospital Privileges[e]	9.57	.05*	6.74	.05	−.29	.003
Join Existing Practice[e]	2.68	.02	10.13	.10***	−4.84	−.07*
Pursue Professional Interests[e]	−9.70	−.10***	−7.85	−.11***	12.88	.27***
R^2		.18		.12		.16
F		17.99***		11.85***		15.88***
Number of Respondents		1362		1362		1362

Notes: * $p < .05$; ** $p < .01$; *** $p < .001$.
[a] Year entered practice (after completing residency program)—1985.
[b] 1 = female, 0 = male.
[c] 1 = family practitioners, general practitioners, pediatricians, obstetricians, gynecologists, and internists (excluding subspecialists in internal medicine),
    0 = all other specialties.
[d] 1 = graduate of a U.S. medical school, 0 = graduate of a foreign medical school.
[e] 1 = checked, 0 = not checked.

15

medicine, it is interesting that the factor of "lack of a better alternative" is negatively correlated with the percentage of time spent in nonpatient care activities as well as for the percentage of time spent as an employee. Evidently the idea that physicians are accepting employee status only as a default is not upheld by the physicians' view of how they make employment decisions.

Using PPA data, we are able to look at the relationship of these same factors with the total number of hours worked per week. The number of years in practice, personal autonomy, location preference, and future income potential were positively correlated and convenience of work hours and being female negatively correlated with the number of hours worked (see Table 4).

Table 4. Regression Analysis of Hours Worked During a Typical Week (Using Employment Decision Influences)

	Unstdz. Coeff.	*Stdz. Coeff.*
Constant	39.67	
Years in Practice[a]	1.62	.20***
Sex[b]	−4.69	−.07*
Primary Care Specialty[c]	2.46	.05
Country of Medical School[d]	.90	.01
Guaranteed Income[e]	1.25	.02
Future Income Potential[e]	3.18	.07*
Convenience of Work Hours[e]	−4.30	−.08*
Professional Liability Costs[e]	2.45	.03
Personal Autonomy[e]	5.21	.11**
Location Preference[e]	3.33	.07*
Family Influence[e]	2.98	.05
Lack of Better Alternative[e]	1.84	.02
Quality of Care Considerations[e]	1.71	.03
Available Hospital Privileges[e]	1.15	.01
Join Existing Practice[e]	3.59	.05
Pursue Professional Interests[e]	2.41	.05
R^2		.08
F		6.76***
Number of Respondents		1219

Notes: * $p < .05$; ** $p < .01$; *** $p < .001$.

      [a]Year entered practice (after completing residency program)—1985.

      [b]1 = female, 0 = male.

      [c]1 = family practitioners, general practitioners, pediatricians, obstetricians, gynecologists, and internists (excluding subspecialists in internal medicine), 0 = all other specialties.

      [d]1 = graduate of a U.S. medical school, 0 = graduate of a foreign medical school.

      [e]1 = checked, 0 = not checked.

Next we considered the importance of some more general items. The young physicians were asked to rank (using a scale of 1,2,3,...8, where 8=most important and 1=least important) eight items regarding their importance to them currently and five years from now. In terms of their average scores, the items are ranked as follows for the current year:[5]

- enjoying a balanced lifestyle   6.7
- having financial security   6.4
- continuing educational growth   6.1
- establishing and building your practice   6.0
- being active in community affairs   4.0
- completing the certification process   3.3
- assuming a leadership role in organized medicine   3.1
- seeking different type of employment   2.3

This group of variables does not tell us as much as the previous set of variables which focuses more on employment decisions. There are, nonetheless, some intriguing results. Looking first at work hours, having financial security, in terms of relative importance, was negatively correlated with the number of hours worked during a typical week. This suggests that physicians are motivated to put in long hours for reasons other than financial gain. Indeed, "seeking different type of employment," while not statistically significant, was negatively correlated with the number of hours spent in professional activities. Two demographic variables, years in practice and sex, were stronger predictors of the number of hours worked. Presumably, as a physician's patient load expands, the number of work hours increases. The effect of family demands on many female physicians' practice characteristics, detailed in previous research, is demonstrated again here (see Table 5).

As for self-employment, Table 6 shows that establishing and building a practice, the number of years in practice, having financial security, and being in a primary care specialty were positively correlated while there was a negative correlation with the relative importance given to continuing educational growth, assuming a leadership role in organized medicine, and seeking a different type of employment. Except for assuming a leadership role in organized medicine, the percentage of time spent employed was correlated with each of these variables in the opposite direction. Seeking different types of employment and completing the certification process were positive predictors for the percentage of time spent as an employee, suggesting that the greater the amount of time spent providing patient care as an employee, the greater the likelihood that a physician will be changing his or her employment status.

For the percentage of time spent in nonprepaid patient care, there was a positive correlation with establishing and building a practice and being active in community affairs and a negative correlation with being a female

Table 5.   Regression Analysis of Hours
Worked During a Typical Week
(Using General Influences)

	Unstdz. Coeff.	Stdz. Coeff.
Constant	54.33	
Years in Practice[a]	2.12	.26**
Sex[b]	−6.80	−.10*
Primary Care Specialty[c]	2.83	.06
Country of Graduation[d]	−1.20	−.02
Establishing Practice[e]	.76	.07
Seek Different Employment[e]	−.82	−.07
Completing Certification[e]	−.17	−.02
Active in Community Affairs[e]	−.04	−.03
Leadership Role in Organized Medicine[e]	.22	.02
Having Financial Security[e]	−1.56	−.10*
Enjoying a Balanced Lifestyle[e]	−.40	−.03
Continuing Educational Growth[e]	.87	.06
R^2		.10
F		6.25**
Number of Respondents		703

Notes: * $p < .01$;   ** $p < .001$
[a]Year entered practice (after completing residency program)—1985.
[b]1 = female, 0 = male.
[c]1 = family practitioners, general practitioners, pediatricians, obstetricians, gynecologists, and internists (excluding subspecialists in internal medicine), 0 = all other specialties.
[d]1 = graduate of a U.S. medical school, 0 = graduate of a foreign medical school.
[e]1 = 1, 2, 3, . . . 8, where 1 =least important and 8 = most important.

physician and assuming a leadership role in organized medicine. The only statistically significant predictor for the percentage of time spent in prepaid patient care was sex. There is a positive correlation with being a female physician.

The demographic variables were not a good predictor of the percentage of time that physicians spend in nonpatient care activities. Of the eight items, assuming a leadership role in organized medicine and continuing educational growth were positively correlated and establishing and building your practice and enjoying a balanced lifestyle were negatively correlated.

Table 6. Regression Analysis of Percentage of Time Spent
in Three Types of Employment During 1985 (Using General Influences)

| | Percentage of Professional Time | | | | | |
| | Self-Employed Patient Care | | Nonprepaid Patient Care | | Nonpatient Care Activities | |
	Unstdz. Coeff.	Stdz. Coeff.	Unstdz. Coeff.	Stdz. Coeff.	Unstdz. Coeff.	Stdz. Coeff.
Constant	16.73		66.66		24.87	
Years in Practice[a]	2.83	.18**	.75	.06	-.01	-.002
Sex[b]	-2.40	-.02	-13.64	-.15**	3.71	.06
Primary Care Specialty[c]	6.73	.07*	-2.73	-.04	-1.40	-.03
Country of Graduation[d]	-2.89	-.02	1.04	-.01	3.04	.05
Establishing Practice[e]	5.39	.26**	3.15	.21**	-2.45	-.26**
Seek Different Employment[e]	-1.80	-.07*	-.91	-.05	-.18	-.02
Completing Certification[e]	-1.01	-.06	-.11	-.01	-.12	-.02
Active in Community Affairs[e]	1.67	.06	1.58	.08*	-.53	-.04
Leadership Role in Organized Medicine[e]	-1.98	-.08*	-2.63	-.14**	2.03	.17**
Having Financial Security[e]	2.73	.09*	-.72	-.03	-.61	-.05
Enjoying a Balanced Lifestyle[e]	.56	.02	.08	.04	-1.16	-.09*
Continuing Educational Growth[e]	-4.31	-.15**	-.99	-.05	1.22	.09*
R^2	.16		.09		.13	
F	11.51**		6.38**		8.96**	
Number of Respondents	742		742		742	

Notes: * $p < .05$; ** $p < .001$.

[a] Year entered practice (after completing residency program)—1985.

[b] 1 = female, 0 = male.

[c] 1 = family practitioners, general practitioners, pediatricians, obstetricians, gynecologists, and internists (excluding subspecialists in internal medicine),
0 = all other specialties.

[d] 1 = graduate of a U.S. medical school, 0 = graduate of a foreign medical school.

[e] 1 = 1, 2, 3, . . . 8, where 1 = least important and 8 = most important.

CONCLUSION

Despite a rapidly changing practice environment, in many ways less favorable to physicians, these young physicians give indications that they were able to take a positive approach to employment decisions during their first year in practice and in 1985. The effect of market factors and increasing competition have been debated. Here we have looked at physicians' perceptions of how they make employment decisions. Perhaps most striking, from a list of 12 factors influencing employment decisions, "lack of a better alternative" ranked last. This suggests that physicians are actively evaluating their preferences and matching them to an appropriate employment arrangement, or at least perceive that they are.

People sometimes reinterpret and reconstruct their pasts to justify their present circumstances and to give their lives some appearance of continuity. Given this tendency for rationalization in reporting why they are where they are, some respondents may be selectively recalling what led them into certain decisions or they may come to believe in reasons that do not coincide with their contemporaneous outlook.

Given the tendency to characterize young physicians to be more concerned than older physicians with life style considerations, the relative low importance given to work hours and family influence is one of the most notable findings of the survey. Recent AMA qualitative research confirms this result (Division of Survey and Data Resources 1990). It is possible that the demands of practicing medicine make it difficult to put life style considerations above practice-related characteristics. It is also conceivable that, while these life style considerations are very important, many young physicians have put them "on hold" while working to establish a practice.

This explanation coincides with the shift from employed to self-employed practice between the first year in practice to the current year. Some physicians appear to assume employed positions only temporarily before settling into self-employed practice. Given this possibility, it is even more remarkable that "lack of a better alternative" ranked lowest of twelve factors influencing employment decisions. Presumably, while some of these physicians eventually practice medicine on a self-employed basis, they are not discontent to spend a portion or all of their time in an employed position early in their careers. This seems to be an adjustment to a new medical climate made by this generation of physicians.

This analysis has shown that different sets of factors are useful predictors of different types of employment. For example, of the factors considered, "personal autonomy" was by far the strongest positive predictor of percentage of time spent self-employed. "Assuming a leadership role in organized medicine" and "opportunity to pursue professional interests" were the strongest positive predictors of the percentage of time spent in nonpatient care activities.

One limitation of the present research is that the survey did not collect information regarding satisfaction with current employment status. Some of the respondents may not have "landed" in their chosen employment arrangement. The relative strength of "seeking different type of employment" as a predictor of percentage of time spent employed suggests that employee status might be only temporary or that there might be more job changes among employed physicians. It would be interesting, also, to determine whether or not the process of making employment decisions differs by demographic characteristics and varies from one cohort to another.

ACKNOWLEDGMENTS

An earlier draft of this chapter was written as part of the study of The Practice Patterns of Young Physicians, supported through grants from the Robert Wood Johnson Foundation to the American Medical Association Education and Research Foundation.

The views in this chapter are those of the author and no official endorsement by The American Medical Association is intended nor should be inferred. The author would like to thank Judith A. Levy, Rachel A. Rosenfeld, Roger L. Brown, Norbert W. Budde, Penny Havlicek, Kevin Kenward, John D. Loft, William D. Marder, and Mary Lou S. White for helpful comments on earlier drafts of this chapter and Ann Marie Weaver for technical assistance.

NOTES

1. Physicians in residency training, inactive physicians, osteopaths, and physicians whose major professional activity is unknown were excluded.

2. The following formula was used to calculate the weights:

$$\text{Weight} = \frac{\text{Population of Physicians with AMA Membership Status}}{\text{Total Population of Physicians}} \times \frac{\text{Total Number of Respondents}}{\text{Number of Responding Physicians with AMA Membership Status}}$$

3. As for the ranking of these factors during the first year in practice, there were a couple of differences. "Opportunity to join an existing practice," "quality of care considerations," and "guaranteed income" were checked second, third, and fourth most often, and "professional liability costs" was checked the least.

4. Since the results for the percentage of time spent as an employee are generally the mirror image of those for the percentage of time spent self-employed, these results are discussed but not presented in a table. The same presentation of results is used for the analysis of percentage of time spent providing nonprepaid and prepaid patient care.

5. The respondents were asked to rank the items with 1=most important and 8=least important. For analysis purposes, the scale was reversed. Because of the complexity of this question, it was omitted from the follow-up phase of the survey. With respect to five years from now, "completing the certification process" fell to the bottom of the list.

REFERENCES

Bobula, J.D. 1980. "Work Patterns, Practice Characteristics, and Incomes of Male and Female Physicians." *Journal of Medical Education* 55: 826-833.

Borus, J.F. 1982. "The Transition to Practice." *Journal of Medical Education* 57: 593-601.

Center for Health Policy Research. 1988. *Socioeconomic Monitoring System Core Survey 1988.* Chicago: American Medical Association.

Cuca, J.M. 1979. "The Specialization and Career Preferences of Women and Men Recently Graduated from United States Medical Schools." *Journal of American Medical Women's Association* 34: 425-435.

Department of Survey Design and Analysis, Division of Survey and Data Resources. 1985. *Survey of Young Physicians Report.* Prepared for the American Medical Association's Ad Hoc Committee on Young Physicians. Chicago: American Medical Association.

Division of Survey and Data Resources. 1985. AMA Physician Masterfile 1985 Year-End File. Chicago: American Medical Association.

_____. 1990. *Response to American Medical Association Communication Vehicles.* Unpublished. Chicago: American Medical Association.

Engel, G.V. 1969. "The Effect of Bureaucracy on the Professional Autonomy of the Physician." *Journal of Health and Social Behavior* 10: 30-41.

Ernst, R.L. and D.E. Yett. 1985. *Physician Location and Specialty Choice.* Ann Arbor, MI: Health Administration Press.

Freeman, R.B. 1978. *The Market for College-Trained Manpower.* Cambridge, MA: Harvard University Press.

Friedson, E. 1984. "The Changing Nature of Professional Control." *Journal of Health and Social Behavior* 27: 358-369.

_____. 1985. "The Reorganization of the Medical Profession." *Medical Care Review* 42(1): 11-35.

_____. 1986. "The Medical Profession in Transition." In *Applications of Social Science to Clinical Medicine and Health Policy,* edited by L. Aiken and D. Mechanic. New Brunswick, NJ: Rutgers University Press.

Friedson, E., and J.H. Mann. 1971. "Organizational Dimensions of Large Scale Medical Practice." *American Journal of Public Health* 61: 786-795.

Gonzalez, M.L., and D.W. Emmons, eds. 1986. *Socioeconomic Characteristics of Medical Practice 1986.* Chicago: American Medical Association.

Goodman, L.J., and F.D. Wolinsky. 1982. "Conditional Logit Analysis of Physicians' Practice Mode Choices." *Inquiry* 19: 262-270.

Hafferty, F.W. 1986. "Physician Oversupply as a Socially Constructed Reality." *Journal of Health and Social Behavior* 27: 358-369.

Haug, M.R. 1976. "The Erosion of Professional Authority: A Cross-Cultural Inquiry in the Case of the Physician." *Milbank Memorial Fund Quarterly* (Winter): 83-106.

Havlicek, P.L. 1985. *Medical Groups in the U.S. 1984.* Chicago: American Medical Association.

Luft, H., and J. Trauner. 1981. *The Operations and Performance of Health Maintenance Organizations: A Synthesis of Findings from Health Services Research.* San Francisco: University of California School of Medicine, Institute for Health Policy Studies.

McKinlay, J.B., and J.D. Stoeckle. 1988. "Corporatization and the Social Transformation of Doctoring." *International Journal of Health Services* 18(2): 191-205.

Phillips, R., and J. Dorsey. 1980. "A Look Inside: Some Aspects of Structure and Function in Forty Prepaid Group Practice HMOs." *The Group Health Journal*: 16-31.

Prybil, L. 1974. "Characteristics, Career Patterns and Opinions of Physicians Who Practice in Large Multi-Specialty Groups." *Medical Group Management* 21: 22-26.

Roback, G., D. Mead, and L. Randolph. 1986. *Physician Characteristics and Distribution in the U.S. 1986 Edition*. Chicago: American Medical Association.

Silberger, A. B. W., D. Marder, and R.J. Willke. 1987. "Practice Characteristics of Male and Female Physicians." *Health Affairs* (Winter): 104-109.

Starr, P. 1982. *The Social Transformation of American Medicine*. New York: Basic Books.

Tarlov, A.R. 1988. "The Rising Supply of Physicians and the Pursuit of Better Health." *Journal of Medical Education* 63: 94-107.

Zako, L.R. 1976. "My Year With an HMO Was One Year Too Many." *Medical Economics* 53: 79-85.

CAN WOMEN PHYSICIANS EVER BE TRUE EQUALS IN THE AMERICAN MEDICAL PROFESSION?

Judith Lorber

ABSTRACT

This paper will discuss the role of women physicians in American medicine in the 1980s and 1990s, and will argue that the bureaucratization of medical practice and the increasing control of medical decisions by the government and other third-party payers will not impact equally on all members of the American medical profession. As in the past, while all physicians may have equal (albeit lesser) authority over and responsibility for their patients' treatment, women physicians will continue to be unequal in their control over medical resources and priorities. The two-tiered stratification within the medical profession allows all physicians to work; thus, women's training is not wasted, nor can the profession be accused of open discrimination. The policy-making positions of great authority, however, are still held by members of the socially dominant group (in the case of U.S. medicine, middle-class white men).

Current Research on Occupations and Professions, Volume 6, pages 25-37.
Copyright © 1991 by JAI Press Inc.
All rights of reproduction in any form reserved.
ISBN: 1-55938-236-8

INTRODUCTION

By virtue of their medical degree, all physicians are supposed to be equal in their authority over and responsibility for patients' treatment. In the 1940s, Hall (1946), in a study of the medical community in Providence, Rhode Island, found that a physician's policy-making power and access to medical resources depended on whether or not the physician was a member of the local medical elite. To become part of the inner elite, a physician had to have the sponsorship of an established member. A second circle, not quite as favored with good hospital affiliations and referrals of patients, were what he called "friendly outsiders." Most of the women physicians in the community were friendly outsiders—that is, not members of the inner circle.

Other groups of physicians in the United States, regardless of the quality of their work, have not been sponsored for membership in the inner circles of the medical profession by their colleagues (Starr 1982). These have been the members of groups with disfavored social characteristics—Jews, Catholics, Blacks, and those with foreign medical educations. Solomon (1961), in his study of medical practices in Chicago, found, however, that Jews and Catholics were able to develop their own medical communities, with patient referrals and hospital affiliations. Through federal funding, Blacks had Howard Medical School and tax-supported hospitals to work in (Moldow 1987). Black women physicians had no medical community of their own, and white women physicians, after the 1930s, were never more than "friendly colleagues" to the men of any group—WASP, Jewish, Catholic, or Black.

Today, women physicians in the United States are approaching a substantial minority—about 30% of all practicing physicians. While they have an active association—the American Medical Women's Association—and caucuses in specialty associations, as well as conferences and a journal, they have not developed their own colleague networks or hospitals, despite advice to that effect from radical feminist physicians (Howell 1975). All-women clinics were run by advocates of the women's self-help movement, which relegated the women physicians on their staff to minor, legally necessary roles (Ruzek 1978). Women physicians, therefore, unlike men physicians with devalued social characteristics, have had few places to show their leadership capabilities.

American women physicians are, of course, no longer subject to the formal discrimination that discouraged application to medical school, denied them internships and residencies, and tracked them into specialties that tended to be less lucrative and prestigious. Neither are they openly barred from staff appointments in good hospitals, from membership in group medical practices, or from heading laboratories and services. However, as in other professions, there has been a "glass ceiling" on their upward mobility. Women physicians who aspire to the very visible top tier of positions hit invisible barriers when they try to attain them. As a result, women physicians rarely direct large, prestigious services, are rarely heads of teaching hospitals, and are almost never heads of large medical centers. For example, when the University of California named Mary A. Piccone its first woman head of a teaching hospital and medical center, it was unusual enough to warrant a newspaper story ("SUNY Aide Gets California Post," 1988).

This paper will discuss the role of women physicians in American medicine in the 1980s and 1990s, and will argue that the bureaucratization of medical practice and the increasing control of medical decisions by the government and other third-party payers will not impact equally on all members of the medical profession. As in the past, while all physicians may have equal (albeit lesser) authority over and responsibility for their patients' treatment, physicians continue to be unequal in their control over medical resources and priorities.

My argument is that as in other professions, there is a "glass ceiling" on women physicians' upward mobility. They are kept from top-level positions, I will argue, through the subtle process of a kind of colleague boycott—not keeping them out entirely, but not including them in ways that allow them to replace the senior members of the medical community. This process is the "Salieri phenomenon"—a combination of faint praise and acceptable denigration of their abilities to lead which delegitimates women physicians' bids to compete for positions of great authority.[1] The reason men are so reluctant to allow women into the inner circles, I contend, is their fear that if too many women become leaders, the profession will "tip" and become women's work— and men will lose prestige, income, and authority.

Stratification within the medical profession allows all holders of certification to work; thus, their training is not wasted, nor can the profession be accused of open discrimination. The policy-making positions of great authority, however, are still held by members of the socially dominant group, and it is their values and priorities that prevail.

THE "GLASS CEILING"

The "glass ceiling" has been reported for every male-dominated profession and occupation that American women have entered in increasing numbers in the last twenty years (e.g., Adelson 1988; Berg 1988; Blum and Smith 1988; Goldstein 1988). Women are kept out of the top positions by sexism that is ingrained in men's attitudes and built into the structure of career mobility (Reskin 1988). If a woman becomes a mother, she is out of the running for top positions, even when she works 12- hour days and weekends, because professions are structured on the concept of the professional's total devotion to the career (Lorber 1984). But professions are happy to have hard-working professional employees who will not compete with dominant-group men for the power, privilege, authority—and income—that being at the top means.

The process of creating these companies of professional unequals was beautifully summed up by a front-page story titled, "Women in the Law Say Path is Limited by 'Mommy Track'" (Kingson 1988), which argued that in the prestigious law firms in the United States, women who took advantage of flexible working hours, child care, and lenient maternity leave were out of the running for the competition for partnership. According to the article, women lawyers feel that "the highest barriers . . . are the ones that cannot be legislated away. They are the traditional attitudes that reflect a double-edged sexism, attitudes that say a man must give everything to his career or be considered weak, and that a woman cannot give everything to her career and still be a good wife or mother."

Why are men physicians so reluctant to allow substantial numbers of women into the elite inner circles or to support the ambitions of more than a select safe few for leadership positions? Competition is one reason. Yet other men are competitors, too. Catholic and Jewish physicians, once also subject to discriminatory quotas in American medical schools, are more successfully integrated than women into the prestigious ranks of the profession. I argue that male physicians feel the profession will become feminized—will "tip"— if too many women are heads of medical centers, chiefs of prestigious services, and directors of policy-making bodies. Just as whites seem to fear neighborhood tipping when too many blacks move in, male physicians in the United States may be afraid that if too many women become leaders of the profession, the profession will become women's work—and the men in it will lose prestige, income, and their control over access and resources (cf. Carter and Carter 1981), and their masculine differentness (Reskin 1988).

PRESERVING GENDER DIFFERENCE

In an address to the 1987 Berkshire Conference on the History of Women, Kessler-Harris (1988) said of comparable worth that it "challenges the legitimacy of gender lines. It purports to de-legitimize one element of the market pattern—namely, sex. The end result would be to equate female and male workers; to threaten a male worker's sense of self, pride, and masculinity; and to challenge the authority of the basic institutions that touch all aspects of social and political life" (p. 245). To pay women and men equivalently would, Kessler-Harris points out, raise the value of "those presumed qualities of womanhood— nurturance, community, and relational abilities" (pp. 245-246). The same erosion of gender differences would occur if women and men were equally to be found at the top levels of the prestigious professions. To promote women and men physicians equivalently would mean that those presumed qualities of womanhood—nurturance, community, and relational abilities—were as valuable to those in positions of authority as they are to those who give primary care (and, of course, bedside care). However, the American medical profession today is far from a true company of equals, and prevalent informal discriminatory practices against women indicate that it is never likely to be one.

THE CURRENT CLIMATE IN
THE MEDICAL PROFESSION

A study of the career development of 176 women and 106 men, who were recent medical school graduates, found that as medical students, in postgraduate training, and in practice, women perceived more career hindrances than men did (Cohen, Woodward, and Ferrier 1988). According to Cohen et al., "[t]he primary disadvantages perceived by women during both medical school and postgraduate training are sexist attitudes and behavior and being taken less seriously than men" (p. 151). Of the 78 women reporting a gender disadvantage in practice, 31% felt they were taken less seriously than men, and 21% reported overt sexism.

A study done in the early 1980s (Grant 1988), based on interviews with 173 men and 97 women medical school seniors from five successive graduating classes of a major midwestern medical school, found that male doctors on the medical school faculty and on the staffs of teaching hospitals still feel free to be openly sexist towards women medical students. Some of the older men, especially those with physician daughters, were great supporters of their women students, so they seemed to exhibit both ends of spectrum. Since both the sexism and the support women physicians get from older male physicians early in their careers fades as they advance, it is more important to look at their future colleagues—their fellow students and the residents a few years ahead of them—to predict whether the medical profession will change substantially in the direction of real gender equality.

Here, the data were more disturbing. In many ways, the male residents were the source of the most sexism—teasing women students, subjecting them to endurance tests and sexual harassment.

> Several [of the women students] suggested that it was the residents, only a few years ahead of the women students in their careers, who felt the most threatened by the women students. One student felt the problem was particularly acute in obstetrics/gynecology and pediatrics, areas where women are the primary consumers of medical services and where many patients now explicitly request treatment by women doctors (Grant 1988, p. 115).

Some men students said they were the victims of reverse discrimination because of patients' preferences for women physicians. They also expressed resentment at what they felt were the effects of affirmative action in allowing less qualified women to be accepted to medical school—in actuality, the admission credentials of the men and women students were virtually equal. Male classmates were likely to attribute blame to the women targets of gender discrimination, and, according to the women students, to sometimes join in the teasing, and to be generally oblivious of subtle sexism. However, the higher the class ranking of the man, the more likely he was to have been aware of gender discrimination toward women classmates.

So, unless this school is atypical, what researchers have found in other settings is true in medicine—as more women enter an occupation, and as they are increasingly successful as competitors, there is less support from their male peers and immediate superiors (South, Bonjean, Markham, and Corder 1982; Zimmer 1988). That is, while established and very secure men can treat women colleagues as equals, those who see them as formidable competitors will use social weapons to keep them down.

Some of these weapons are described by Benokraitis and Feagin in *Modern Sexism* (1986): condescending chivalry, supportive discouragement, friendly harassment, subjective objectification, radiant devaluation, liberated sexism, benevolent exploitation, considerate domination, and collegial exclusion. What is in actuality structured and institutionalized sexism is often transformed into women's seemingly free choices to limit their ambitions, not work too many hours, and put their families before their professions. Forgotten are the nasty remarks about women as assertive competitors, the hostility to women who become mothers, and the dismal marriage and divorce statistics for well-educated and successful women; ignored are the long hours and hard work women actually put into their jobs (Bielby and Bielby 1988; Weisman and Teitelbaum 1987).

WOMEN PHYSICIANS' FUTURE PLACE

Where women physicians supposedly fit best into American medicine in the 1980s and 1990s is very clear if we heed some influential policymakers. It is as salaried workers in third-party-payment group practices and HMOs (Bowman and Gross 1986; Ehrensing 1986; Kroser 1987; Lanska, Lanska, and Rimm 1984; Lisoskie 1986; Lorber 1987a).

The more bureaucratized practice of medicine will not create a company of equals any more than did solo, fee-for-service medicine. The bureaucratization of medical practice and the increasing control of medical decisions by the government and other third-party payers will not impact equally on all members of the medical profession. As in the past, while all physicians may have equal (albeit lesser) authority over and responsibility for their patients' treatment, physicians will continue to be unequal in their control over medical resources and priorities, and women physicians are likely to be more unequal than others. Even those who ascend to top positions of authority are likely to get positions of lesser power than those held by their male peers. The woman physician who was appointed to head the University of California Medical Center, for instance, was not given the additional position held by her male predecessor—that of vice chancellor for administrative and business services at the campus where the medical center was located, a position which gave him greater control over allocation of resources.

A stratified structure of practice will continue. When American medicine was predominantly solo-fee-for-service, the profession was stratified through limited access to elite medical schools and teaching hospitals and lucrative specialties. Now that it is more bureaucratized, the profession is stratified through limited access to policy-making positions in HMOs, hospitals, insurance agencies, and city, state, and national governments (Freidson 1983). Instead of inner circles, friendly colleagues, and boycotted loners, the profession is stratifying into powerful administrators, policymakers, and rank-and-file professional employees (Freidson 1986, pp. 134-157). As in the past, when their numbers were few, women will be heavily overrepresented for the duration of their careers in positions where they have discretion and autonomy in their treatment of patients but where they do not control budgets, allocate resources, or determine the overall direction of the organizations for which they work. The need for reliable, hard-working, nonrebellious professionally satisfied rank-and-file professional employees will be neatly solved, as will the problem of what to do about the increasing numbers of women physicians.

If women physicians do not advance in significant numbers from rank-and-file professional employees to management positions, they will not be any more equal in the medical profession than in the past. For, according to Freidson (1986), the "power to allocate resources determines the particular kind of work that can be done and limits the way work can be done" (p. 154).

What resources does management allocate that are so crucial to professional work? According to Freidson (1986), these are: size of professional staff, caseload, and who is to be serviced—"the critical variables are the number and type of tasks performed in a working day, the number and type of cases to be handled, and the supportive resources to be made available to aid performance—the rules of eligibility that determine, for example, task flow, equipment, space, and assisting personnel" (p. 169). Physicians who cannot control how many patients they see and with what problems, and have little say in the allocation of supporting resources, are likely to end up doing routinized work. For example, an Israeli study found that primary care women physicians in national health service clinics with heavy case loads were least accepting of patients' initiatives and physician-challenging behavior (Shuval, Javetz, and Shye 1989). The most accepting were hospital-based specialists with lighter case loads, who were most likely to be men.

While American women physicians who form their own group practices can shape them to be responsive to patients' needs and sensitive to feminist issues

(Candib 1987, 1988), those who work for larger third-party-payment HMOs as rank-and-file employees cannot. More important, women physicians without high-level administrative positions as chiefs of service in hospitals or deans of medical schools are unlikely to make any impact on the delivery of services or the production and dissemination of knowledge (cf. Freidson 1986, pp. 185-230).

The important questions in assessing whether or not all types of physicians (by race, religion, social class, gender, and philosophy of practice) have equal opportunities to shape the profession are, according to Freidson (1986, pp. 185-186):

> Who . . . creates, sustains, and alters the official framework of professional activities— the credential system that establishes staffing standards for employers and standards for the content of professional training? And who establishes the standards that define the substance of what is acceptable professional work? Who negotiates with the state to secure the official adoption of professional standards across work settings?

Not numbers but strategic and central positions in the elite sector translate into the power to transform professional practice (Martin 1985; Martin and Osmond 1982; South, Bonjean, Corder, and Markham 1982).

WILL THE FUTURE REPLICATE THE PAST?

In the nineteenth century, hospitals and clinics run by American women physicians used the extant technology, but structured the delivery of care "with a heart" (Drachman 1984; Morantz and Zschoche 1980; Morantz-Sanchez 1985). Women physicians were more alert to the potential for the spread of post-partum infection and to the social difficulties of unmarried mothers. Moldow's (1987) history of black and white women physicians in Washington, D.C., at the end of the nineteenth century describes the female medical community there. Denied access to the dispensaries and clinics that gave novice doctors clinical experience and contacts, white women physicians set up four medical infirmaries. They were run for mostly women and children patients, and offered free and low-cost care. Only one, the Woman's Clinic, was completely staffed by women, and it was the only one that survived the rise of the scientifically oriented, better-equipped university hospitals, which became, in Moldow's words, "no-woman's land."

Moldow shows that the closing of the doors of the medical community to women happened before the findings of the Flexner Report were published in 1910. Both Flexner's recommendations that most of the American medical schools should be closed, and the escalating discrimination against women and blacks by established white medical men, were reactions to that era's "oversupply" of physicians. The project of professionalization, high-minded as it may have seemed, was rooted in fear of competition.

Women appeared to be gaining ground in the medical profession just when their male colleagues were growing concerned about overcrowding in the field. Physicians in the nation's capital—as elsewhere—began to take action to limit the number of graduating doctors in order to sustain a fair income and a high level of status within the profession. Women were primary targets among those considered superfluous (Moldow 1987, p. 15)

After World War I, when women got the vote in the United States, they helped to pass the Sheppard-Towner Act, which, in 1921, set up state and federally funded parental and child health centers throughout the country. These centers were staffed by women physicians and public health nurses, and they offered low-cost medical services and preventive care and education in maternal and child health. By 1929, in the face of the desperate need of its members for paying patients during the Depression, the American Medical Association, headed by men in solo, fee-for-service practice, led the fight to deny further funding to the Sheppard-Towner clinics (Costin 1983).

Today, in the late twentieth century, although women physicians are again a significant minority of obstetricians and gynecologists and are sought out by clients as private practitioners and by administrators as valuable additions to group practices, they are in positions of authority only in their own solo or small group practices, where they are able to work differently from men physicians (Candib 1987, 1988; Lorber 1985). In training in hospitals, where few women physicians determine curriculum and where teaching physicians and senior residents tend to be men, they must suppress any criticism and work in standard, high-technology ways (Harrison 1983; Scully 1980). The high rates of routinized amniocentesis (Rothman 1986) and hysterectomy (Fisher 1986) and the use of in vitro fertilization in couples where the woman has a normal reproductive system but the man is infertile (Lorber 1987b) are some examples of the effects of the continued domination of male doctors in American medicine. These procedures, not incidentally, can be quite profitable.

In sum, the structure of medical practice in the United States since the late nineteenth century has been stratified, and physicians have filled positions in that structure not randomly, but according to their race, religion, social class, and gender. The lines of discrimination may shift somewhat, but the battle of the dominant white male majority to maintain control over access, resources, and patients has not changed. Black, Catholic, Jewish, and working-class male physicians have become more integrated into the medical profession, but women physicians are still vulnerable—and *not* because they limit their ambitions and practice hours and put their families first. If that were true, men physicians would have nothing to worry about.

It is rather the opposite—American women physicians are formidable competitors for private patients and group-practice appointments because patients feel they offer a different practice style; they successfully compete for institutional and federal funding of clinical research; they do not turn down the chance to head services. But they are vulnerable because the current structure of American medicine will be used against them.

In the mid-nineteenth century, free-for-all medicine allowed women an equal chance to compete, and American men physicians fought bitterly (and unsuccessfully) to keep them out of medical schools, medical associations, and hospitals. When the structure of medical practice changed, it was used against women, as a means of exclusion. The same is true today. In the 1960s, when American medicine was opening to greater access for patients and more varied practice styles, and money was freer, the doors of medical schools and hospitals opened to women. Now that eligibility for medical services is tightening and money is scarce, control over access, resources, and paying patients is again a battle ground (Hafferty 1986; Lanska, et al. 1984; Rushing 1985). This time, because of anti-discrimination laws, American women physicians cannot be subject to 5% quotas, but there will continue to be unacknowledged gender discrimination in men's efforts to hold onto their dominant position.

If the medical profession in the United States loses its dominance in the delivery of health care services somewhere in the next 25 years, the profession is likely to tip into a women's profession. The tipping may be blamed on the influx of women, but the sequence goes in the other direction: As a profession becomes one of high demand for services that are moderately remunerated and increasingly government-regulated, it loses its attractiveness to high-status men, leaving an occupational niche that is filled by high-status women and lower-status men.

Current medical school enrollments already reflect this pattern. Over the past five years, the proportion of white male first-year students has declined by 13% (Jonas and Etzel 1988). However, the administrators and policymakers are likely to continue to be white men because the number of minority male physicians is small. Despite being a substantial proportion of the American medical profession, women physicians are unlikely to become a substantial proportion of the leadership because of a combination of institutionalized and informal sexist practices. The structure of work and family life still does not allow women with family responsibilities to add overtime administrative responsibilities or policy committee work to their allocated client contact hours (Ehrensing 1986). Women who remain single or enter into childless dual-career marriages could be formidable competitors for men (Hunt and Hunt 1982), but as I have argued, informal discriminatory practices are likely to present equally formidable barriers to their rise to the top.

In sum, as the medical profession in the United States comes to resemble the more bureaucratized systems of other countries (Elston 1977, 1980; Lapidus

1978; Shuval 1983), the two-tier system will solidify—women physicians will do general practice, family medicine, and primary care; white men physicians will allocate resources and make policy.

ACKNOWLEDGMENTS

Versions of this paper were presented at the American Sociological Association Annual Meeting, Atlanta, Georgia, August 1988, and at the Centennial of Johns Hopkins Medical Institutions, Baltimore, Maryland, June 1989. The writing of the paper was supported by PSC-CUNY Grant No. 666-206.

NOTE

1.   In Peter Shaffer's play, *Amadeus* (1980), Mozart's lack of social graces gives Salieri, the court composer and gatekeeper of musical patronage, the opportunity to block the young musicians' career advancement, not by direct opposition, but by lukewarm support. The effects of sponsorship and other processes of informal career advancement for women physicians are discussed at length in Lorber (1984).

REFERENCES

Adelson, A. 1988. "Women Still Find Bias in Engineering." *New York Times* (March 8).
Benokraitis, N.V., and J.R. Feagin. 1986. *Modern Sexism: Blatant, Subtle, and Covert Discrimination.* Englewood Cliffs, NJ: Prentice-Hall.
Berg, E.N. 1988. "The Big Eight: Still a Male Bastion." *New York Times* (July 14).
Bielby, D., and W.T. Bielby. 1988. "She Works Hard for the Money: Household Responsibilities and the Allocation of Work Effort." *American Journal of Sociology* 93:1031-1059.
Blum, L., and V. Smith. 1988. "Women's Mobility in the Corporation: A Critique of the Politics of Optimism." *Signs: Journal of Women in Culture and Society* 13:528-545.
Bowman, M. and M.L. Gross. 1986. "Overview of Research on Women in Medicine—Issues for Public Policymakers." *Public Health Report* 101:513-520.
Carter, M.J., and S.B. Carter. 1981. "Women's Recent Progress in the Professions or, Women Get a Ticket to Ride After the Gravy Train Has Left the Station." *Feminist Studies* 7:477-504.
Candib, L.M. 1987. "What Doctors Tell About Themselves to Patients: Implications for Intimacy and Reciprocity in the Relationship." *Family Medicine* 19:23-30.
————. 1988. "Ways of Knowing in Family Medicine: Contributions from a Feminist Perspective." *Family Medicine* 20:133-136.
Cohen, M., C.A. Woodward, and B.M. Ferrier. 1988. "Factors Influencing Career Development: Do Men and Women Differ?" *Journal of the American Women's Medical Association* 43:142-154.
Costin, L.B. 1983. "Women and Physicians: The 1930 White House Conference on Children." *Social Work* (March-April):108-114.
Drachman, V. 1984. *Hospital with a Heart.* Ithaca, NY: Cornell University Press.
Ehrensing, R.H. 1986. "Attitudes Towards Women Physicians: a Multispecialty Group Practice Perspective." *The Internist* 27(March):17-18.

Elston, M.A. 1977. "Women in the Medical Profession: Whose Problem?" Pp. 115-138 in *Health and the Division of Labor*, edited by M. Stacey et al. London: Croom Helm.

————. 1980. "Medicine: Half our Future Doctors? Pp. 99-139 in *The Careers of Professional Women*, edited by R. Silverstone and R. Ward. London: Croom Helm.

Fisher, S. 1986. *In the Patient's Best Interest*. New Brunswick, NJ: Rutgers University Press.

Freidson, E. 1983. "The Reorganization of the Profession by Regulation." *Law and Human Behavior* 7:279-290.

————. 1986. *Professional Powers*. Chicago: University of Chicago Press.

Goldstein, T. 1988. "Women in the Law Aren't Yet Equal Partners." *New York Times* (February 12).

Grant, L. 1988. "The Gender Climate in Medical School: Perspectives of Women and Men Students." *Journal of the American Medical Women's Association* 43:109-110, 115-119.

Hafferty, F.W. 1986. "Physician Oversupply as a Socially Constructed Reality." *Journal of Health and Social Behavior* 27:358-369.

Hall, O. 1946. "The Informal Organization of the Medical Profession." *Canadian Journal of Economics and Political Science* 12:30-41.

Harrison, M. 1983. *A Woman in Residence*. New York: Penguin.

Howell, M.C. 1975. "A Woman's Health School?" *Social Policy* 6(September/October):340-347.

Hunt, J.G., and L.L. Hunt. 1982. "The Dualities of Careers and Families: New Integrations or New Polarizations?" *Social Problems* 29:499-510.

Jonas, H.S., and S.I. Etzel. 1988. "Undergraduate Medical Education." *Journal of the American Medical Association* 260:1063-1071.

Kessler-Harris, A. 1988. "The Just Price, the Free Market, and the Value of Women." *Feminist Studies* 14:235-250.

Kingson, J.A. 1988. "Women in the Law Say Path is Limited by 'Mommy Track.'" *New York Times* (August 8).

Kroser, L.S. 1987. "The Growing Influence of Women in Medicine." Pp. 109-137 in *Future Practice Alternatives in Medicine*, edited by David B. Nash. New York and Tokyo: Igaku-Shoin.

Lanska, M.J., D.J. Lanska, and A.A. Rimm. 1984. "Effect of Rising Percentage of Female Physicians on Projections of Physician Supply." *Journal of Medical Education* 59:849-855.

Lapidus, G. 1978. *Women in Soviet Society*. Berkeley, CA: University of California Press.

Lisoskie, S. 1986 "Why Work Fewer Hours?" *Journal of the American Medical Women's Association* 41:73, 90.

Lorber, J. 1984. *Women Physicians: Careers, Status, and Power*. New York and London. Tavistock.

————. 1985. "More Women Physicians: Will it Mean More Humane Health Care?" *Social Policy* 16(Summer)50-54.

————. 1987a. "A Welcome to a Crowded Field: Where Will the New Women Physicians Fit In?" *Journal of the American Medical Women's Association* 42:149-152.

————. 1987b. "*In Vitro* Fertilization and Gender Politics." *Women and Health* 13:117-133.

Martin, P.Y. 1985. "Group Sex Compositions in Work Organizations: A Structural-Normative Model." Pp. 311-349 in *Research in the Sociology of Organizations*, edited by S. Bacharach and S. Mitchell. Greenwich, CT: JAI Press.

Martin, P.Y., and M.W. Osmond. 1982. "Gender and Exploitation: Resources, Structure, and Rewards in Cross-Sex Social Exchange." *Sociological Focus* 15:403-416.

Moldow, G. 1987. *Women Doctors in Gilded-Age Washington: Race, Gender, and Professionalization*. Urbana and Chicago: University of Illinois Press.

Morantz, R.M., and S. Zschoche. 1980. "Professionalism, Feminism, and Gender Roles: A Comparative Study of Nineteenth Century Medical Therapeutics." *Journal of American History* 68:568-588.

Morantz-Sanchez, R.M. 1985. *Sympathy and Science: Women Physicians in American Medicine.* New York: Oxford University Press.

Reskin, B.F. 1988. "Bringing the Men Back In: Sex Differentiation and the Devaluation of Women's Work." *Gender & Society* 2:58-81.

Rothman, B.K. 1986. *The Tentative Pregnancy.* New York: Viking.

Rushing, W.A. 1985. "The Supply of Physicians and Expenditures for Health Services with Implications for the Coming Physician Surplus." *Journal of Health and Social Behavior* 26:297-311.

Ruzek, S.B. 1978. *The Women's Health Movement.* New York: Praeger.

Scully, D. 1980. *Men Who Control Women's Health.* Boston: Houghton Mifflin.

Shaffer, P. 1980. *Amadeus.* New York: Harper & Row.

Shuval, J.T. 1983. *Newcomers and Colleagues: Soviet Immigrant Physicians in Israel.* Houston, TX: Cap and Gown Press.

Shuval, J.T., R. Javetz, and D. Shye. 1989. "Self-Care in Israel: Physicians' Views and Perspectives." *Social Science and Medicine.*

Solomon, D. 1961. "Ethnic and Class Differences Among Hospitals as Contingencies in Medical Careers." *American Journal of Sociology* 61:463-471.

South, S.J., C. M. Bonjean, W. T. Markham, and J. Corder. 1982. "Social Structure and Intergroup Interaction: Men and Women of the Federal Bureaucracy." *American Sociological Review* 47:587-599.

South, S.J., C.M. Bonjean, J. Corder, and W.T. Markham. 1982. "Sex and Power in the Federal Bureaucracy: A Comparative Analysis of Male and Female Supervisors." *Work and Occupations* 2:233-254.

Starr, P. 1982. *The Social Transformation of American Medicine.* New York: Basic Books.

"SUNY Aide Gets California Post." 1988. *New York Times* (August 3).

Weisman, C.S., and M.A. Teitelbaum. 1987. "The Work-Family Role System and Physician Productivity." *Journal of Health and Social Behavior* 28:247-257.

Zimmer, L. 1988. "Tokenism and Women in the Workplace: The Limits of Gender-neutral Theory." *Social Problems* 35:64-77.

PART II

LAY AND PROFESSIONAL ENCOUNTERS

HUMANISM AND PROFESSIONALISM:
CONFLICTING RESPONSIBILITIES
IN SURGICAL TRAINING

Jacquelyn Litt

ABSTRACT

Based on a field study of surgery training, this paper examines how the social relations of teamwork—the division of labor and the normative structure of collegiality—limit surgical residents' responsibilities for patients' emotional concerns and their opportunities to attend to them. I argue below that residents' healing activities derive largely from how they negotiate collegial obligations in teamwork. The organization of teamwork rests on a suspension of patients' emotional concerns, institutionalizes a depersonalization and dehumanization of patients, and creates—in routine yet consequential ways—antagonism between the needs of patients and those of residents. While participation in this process constrains the possibilities for humanistic care, it signifies residents' ethical expression of professionalism.

Current Research on Occupations and Professions, Volume 6, pages 41-60.
Copyright © 1991 by JAI Press Inc.
All rights of reproduction in any form reserved.
ISBN: 1-55938-236-8

INTRODUCTION

Surgeons, in popular imagination, symbolize all that is meritorious and all that is problematic in medical care. While regarded as heroes—bravely investigating, probing, and cutting the hidden realms of the body to effect seemingly miraculous cures—they are also viewed as callous technicians, who demonstrate little regard for the person beneath the scalpel.

Undergoing surgery produces this paradox of intimacy, reverence, and depersonalization in deeply felt ways. In the experience of being a surgical patient, anxiety over being dependent on others, and the attack on privacy that virtually all patients undergo, combine with a sense of oneself as an object dissected by a team of largely anonymous practitioners. Awakening in an unfamiliar setting, possibly feeling more weakened than on entering the hospital, separated from community and kin, and frequently concerned or even panic-stricken over a life-or-death prognosis—surgical patients experience awe and dread, thankfulness and helplessness.

In the routine course of their work, surgical residents see more suffering, grief, and tragedy than many lay people encounter in a lifetime. Yet they maintain a striking silence about this suffering, an implicit and shared ethos that such matters are better left undiscussed. This "structured silence" (Light 1979; Bosk and Frader 1980; Haas and Shaffir 1984), around what Fox (1980) calls the "human condition problems" of medicine, leaves residents virtually alone to manage the existential angst of healing. And in their everyday work, residents designate a secondary, even marginal, place to the emotional and support-giving aspects of the surgeon's role.

Surgical residents, however, are not unfeeling people. Many realize that patients want and often need support, compassion, and sensitivity. Yet the organization of their work all but requires them to disregard patients' emotional needs and to dismiss sentiment and psychological support for healing and the healer's role.

Based on a case study of surgery training,[1] this paper examines how the social relations of teamwork—the division of labor and the normative structure of collegiality—limit surgical residents' responsibilities for patients' emotional concerns and their opportunities to attend to them. I will argue that residents' healing activities derive largely from how they negotiate collegial obligations in teamwork. The organization of teamwork rests on a suspension of patients' emotional concerns, institutionalizes a depersonalization and dehumanization of patients, and creates—in routine yet consequential ways—antagonism between the needs of patients and those of residents. While participation in this process constrains the possibilities for humanistic care,[2] it signifies, as we shall see, residents' ethical expression of professionalism.

METHOD

Data from this study are drawn from five months (some 1,500 hours) of fieldwork and intensive interviews with surgical residents. It was conducted in an Eastern inner-city teaching hospital with a 600-bed capacity. The fieldwork took place from mid-March through May 1984 and from mid-December 1985 through February 1986.

The Department of Surgery has four surgical services: two general surgery, one cardiac, and one transplant. The general surgical services, where I did my fieldwork, are divided into two services, one with 16 attendings, one with 17. Attendings specialize in a range of abdominal procedures and in breast, colorectal, vascular, and thoracic surgery. Field notes used in the paper are drawn from both general services. All names are pseudonyms.

The program has 38 residents, 11 women and 27 men. Each of the two general surgery services has 6 residents (the number can vary), ranging from intern to chief (fifth-year resident, rotating position) and two or three medical students. Throughout the year, residents from family medicine, obstetrics and gynecology, and rehabilitation medicine rotate through the services.

My observations were directed toward explicating the routine features of the residents' workday: What tasks are residents responsible for? How is teamwork organized? How is work divided between residents and attending physicians? As I recognized the task structure's significance in circumscribing residents' responsibilities, I focused on discerning the opportunities for humanistic care that the task structure affords. My in situ and post hoc interviewing was intended to discover how residents understand the organization of labor, their responsibilities, and the implications of these responsibilities for patient care.[3]

MEDICAL EDUCATION AND PATIENT CARE

The transformation of the lay outsider into the professional insider involves more than a mastery of medical knowledge and techniques. As Hughes (1971) states, it also includes "initiation into a new role . . . and learn[ing] to play the role well" (p. 399). Adopting the insider role occupies a central place in medical training. Like all strangers seeking inclusion in a foreign setting, medical recruits must discover prevailing systems of rights and responsibilities and acceptable forms of self-presentation. Being subordinates, however, they are particularly vulnerable to breaches of acceptable action. Indeed, studies of medical training indicate that learning and following rules of etiquette are of enduring concern to trainees (Becker, Geer, Hughes, and Strauss 1961; Miller 1966; Bosk 1979).

It is not surprising that trainees suffer over learning to master the social techniques of the role: Those in authority measure suitability for inclusion in the professional community largely by assessing residents' execution of their social responsibilities. Bosk (1979), in his study of how surgical error is defined and managed in training, demonstrates that acquiescence in the corporate, normative rules of role relations, more than technical competence, signals for attendings a resident's reliability, trustworthiness, and commitment to patient care. The test of becoming an insider is normative compliance.

Yet becoming an insider, or learning to play the role well, results, according to Hughes (1971), in "a separation, almost an alienation of the student from the lay medical world" (p. 399). Immersion in medical rationales of healing and illness supplants the understandings of the naive (and increasingly distant) past conceptions that trainees once held. Light's (1980) examination of delimited definitions of therapeutic success in psychiatry, and Abbott's (1981) explication of the different bases of public and professional determinations of physician prestige are among the many studies testifying to the difference between professional and lay perspectives. Numerous sociological studies of medical education examine how trainees experience this transformation from outsider to insider, the mechanisms through which it is done, and its implications for the kinds of physicians our medical institutions produce.[4]

The distancing from lay conceptions of patient care during medical training forms an important barometer of the movement from outsider to insider. A model of physician responsibility that incorporates compassion and emotional support opposes the predominantly biomedical and technological bases of healing and professional identity that endure in medical culture. Physicians' prestige (Abbott 1981) and identity (Bucher and Stelling 1977) are rooted in the mastery of narrowly defined technical complexities as well as in problems of the human condition. However, physicians are masters only of the technical complexities. To what extent and how medical training fosters such attitudes has been the object of much attention. Trainees' peer groups are identified as a primary arena where such socialization occurs, since it is in peer relations that trainees learn and practice norms of healing.[5]

The Columbia University Medical School's Research Project (Merton, Reader, and Kendall 1957) was one of the first studies to explicate the significance of medical-student culture to trainees' identity. As part of Columbia's research projects on medical training, Fox's studies (1957; Fox and Lief 1963) have had an important influence on the study of socialization. They portray a student culture that reflects faculty ideals of compassion, service, and humanitarianism. Adopting the values and ideals of their faculty role models, students learn the corpus of scientific materials and develop a set of collectively reinforced responses to manage the enduring uncertainty and emotional dilemmas that they will routinely encounter as physicians. The shared responses to these problems—gallows humor, intellectualization, a focus on the scientific dimension and probabilistic reasoning—give students the necessary distance from the tribulations of uncertainty and emotionalism while providing support, fellowship, and new understandings of action. Students balance these distancing mechanisms, however, against concern for delivering "sensitive, understanding care" (Fox 1957, p. 12). In the process, they undergo "anticipatory socialization" to the physician's role and internalize the professional characteristics and motivations that will serve as guides to practice.

Becker et al. (1961) find a very different picture of student culture. They suggest that the self-sacrificing, altruistic, and humanitarian students represent the mythical, rhetorical stance of the medical profession—not actual, empirical behavior. Contemporaneous with the Columbia studies, they analyze the underside of medical-student culture: the strategies that students collectively develop to satisfy their own interests at the unintended emotional expense of patients. Instead of encountering students wedded to faculty standards of conscientiousness and service, the study identifies a student culture explicitly developed against the "unrealistic" demands of faculty. As students evolve collective coping mechanisms to master the vast material and techniques to be learned and to deal with the seemingly unmanageable ward demands, they lose the idealism with which many entered medical school, undergo a diminished appreciation of and interest in the expressive aspects of the healer's role, and become less concerned with patient comfort than with protecting their own time and their image among superordinates.

The studies' conflicting characterizations of medical trainees arise partly because of the different theoretical perspectives that each brings to the data and because of the different problems and strategies they analyze. Fox, like those from the Columbia studies, examines the psychodynamic responses to medical work, or the latent yet socially constructed devices that students develop to manage the existential conditions of healing (see also Fox 1989; Light 1979, 1980). Becker et al. analyze the constant sorting and re-sorting of strategies as students respond, largely in their own interests, to the work-load pressures of the student role. However divergent their perspectives, both of these early studies recognize the effects of workplace and student culture on socializing trainees to insider's systems of relevance.

Later studies of specialty training, conducted since the late 1960s, also acknowledge the importance of student culture for shaping rationales of responsibility.[6] According to these studies, residents' shared experiences, the socially constructed and reinforced responses to the pressures of training, and the camaraderie that peer groups develop figure largely in the dehumanizing and often antipathetic attitude toward patients that residents exhibit.[7]

Not unlike the findings in Becker et al. (1961), the studies by Scully (1980) of obstetrics/gynecology residents and by Mizrahi (1986) of training in internal medicine indicate that residents during training are driven by the limits of their skill and experience to maximize their opportunities for clinical practice—with the result that they come to resent patients for making competing demands.

Scully claims that residents' clinical inexperience creates a collective "hunger for surgery" that they satisfy by prowling among new "cases" for potential learning experiences. Preoccupied with mastering their trade, residents have little time or inclination to treat patients with compassion or dignity.

Mizrahi (1986) attributes much of residents' hostility toward patients to the battlelike conditions of residency. The constant record-keeping and scut work, large patient loads, time pressures, and psychological and social isolation forge a sense of group allegiance while fostering antipathy and instrumentalism toward patients. In Mizrahi's view, the peer group and student culture serve primarily as a refuge for trainees, offer a means of renewal, and provide an identity in an otherwise degrading and dehumanizing work setting.

> As residents became alienated and isolated from more and more groups of people, a strong sense of solidarity and camaraderie developed so that the most salient reference group and the primary socializer became colleagues rather than faculty whose participation was, by design, and default, limited (p. 219).

Despite these investigators' sustained attention to peer-group and student culture, we still know remarkably little about the work process within which resident culture develops and the mechanisms of social control that peer groups exert. It appears from previous research that the peer group occupies a central position in socialization primarily because it provides an emotional resource and a place for trainees to fraternize. By locating the development of resident culture and resident-patient relationships in the psychological anxieties, social frustrations, clinical inexperience, and work overload of training, however, these studies divert attention from how the organization of labor affects the structure of peer relations and their consequences for patient care.[8]

By following residents in the routine of their daily work, my field study explores resident culture, and its implications for healing activity, by investigating the conditions that structure peer allegiance. I explore why everyday work occurs as it does, the relationship between work design and norms of peer allegiance, the prominence of peer responsibility in constructing views of professionalism, and the implications for patient care. The analysis will show that peer allegiance develops as more than emotional resources or as social pleasantries (although it can be both). Peer bonds must also be seen as institutionalized within the team-based labor process, and as maintained, enforced, and legitimated by the norms of collegiality—both of attendings and fellow residents—that regulate teamwork. It is the structure of teamwork bonds and responsibility that conflicts with residents' ability to offer patients compassion and support.

The paper begins with an analysis of attending physicians' expectations—for, as we shall see, attendings control the work protocols that residents develop and the nature of the resident-patient relationship.

ATTENDINGS' DEMANDS AND PATIENT CARE

Surgical decision making follows hierarchical lines and is tightly controlled by attending physicians (Seeman and Evans 1961; Burkett and Knafl 1974; Bosk 1979). Because clinical judgment, experience, and theoretical reasoning guide decision making, and because surgical intervention has identifiable and sometimes fatal consequences, attending physicians require residents to defer to and carry out their orders, turn to superordinates (attendings or senior residents) in situations of uncertainty, and receive permission to implement nonroutine procedures.

Beyond that, attendings expect residents to assume collective responsibility for the service. Residents are responsible not for an individual attending's patients but for all patients on the service (on average, 70) and for all attendings affiliated with that service. Residents are expected to monitor medical data about each patient's condition—lab values, tube drainage, vital signs, medications—and to know about and report any "significant" or nonroutine changes in the patient's well-being. Moreover, attendings expect residents to be prepared to discuss this information at any point during the day; it is a normative error not to know the information.[9] Failure to be prepared brings a variety of disciplinary responses: Residents are not allowed to operate as scheduled; they are admonished before other residents (and sometimes other attendings); they are subjected to increased scrutiny by attendings; and, as Bosk (1979) indicates, their career trajectories can be damaged.

This overarching moral system maximizes medical safety, for it ensures that attendings have the information needed to make surgical-management decisions and that attendings and their patients are protected from the possible ignorance, sloppiness, or inadequacy of any particular resident. Under this system, physicians with greater skill are kept informed of patients' conditions; patients are monitored by a team rather than an individual, securing that complications, problems, or mistakes not detected by one resident will be by another; and residents restrain their heroic impulses. Controlling safety in this way depends on a resident's willingness to follow proprieties of decision making and information control and admit their uncertainty and mistakes.

The moral system and its centrality in regulating technical care explain why, according to Bosk (1979), committing a normative error constitutes the most serious mistake a resident can make. Technical errors reveal temporary and normal deficiencies in a resident's level of training. Normative errors breach social expectations of the resident's role relations with colleagues, reveal deficiencies in a resident's willingness to learn from technical shortcomings, and demonstrate a disregard for conscientious surgical management. Thus, the structuring of residents' responsibilities is as much a symbolic examination of their moral readiness to be trustworthy colleagues as of technical skill.

However effective this moral surveillance system may be in supervising technical care, it eliminates (albeit inadvertently) moral responsibility for the humanistic aspects of care. In fact, rationales of ethical performance constrain resident-patient relationships; residents have little discretion in shaping their interactions with patients, enjoy little autonomy in constructing their healing behavior, and have limited opportunities to develop relationships with patients that are based on compassion and sensitivity.

Embedded in attendings' expectations of residents' collective responsibility is an assumption that residents are essentially interchangeable—not technically, of course, because they vary in rank and skill, but interpersonally. To be prepared with medical data on all patients and to monitor clinical safety in ways that meet faculty expectations, residents must follow all patients on the service and therefore cannot develop ongoing relations with a select group of patients. Attendings' expectations of collective responsibility create a normative conflict for residents in which they must choose between developing continuity and rapport with patients and satisfying the expectations that work will be handled and monitored collectively. A third-year male resident explains the significance and penalty of deviating from the norm:

> If I end up taking care of Dr. Smith's patients, which is what happened, Dr. Abrams [may] want to round with me. And because I'm free [i.e., not in the operating room], I have to go. I know from [card] rounds a couple of bits but I really don't know Dr. Abrams' patients; then Dr. Abrams is gonna be pissed off. And that's exactly what happened.... [During the annual review of residents] Dr. Abrams [who is also the director of residency training] said I should sleep an hour less each night if I want to see some patients more than others.

Thus, developing continuity with and responsibility for patients—conditions that allow a personal and human approach to healing—bear little relevance to the successful discharge of residents' responsibility. They can actually threaten a resident's capacity to satisfy attendings' tests of reliable and scrupulous surgical management.

Another level of attendings' expectations constrains the resident-patient relationship even further. Not only do attendings feel formally responsible for how medical intervention proceeds; they also perceive a professional mandate to perform the social duties that intervention creates: telling patients about pathology reports and proposed treatment; informing families and patients about progress, prognoses, and operative efficacy; educating patients and families about discharge plans and instructions; and allaying patients' fears and uncertainties.[10] While residents are expected to monitor and transmit to their superordinates any dissatisfaction or questions raised by patients or families, attendings tightly control the exchange of information communicated to patients. Violating the rules governing this chain of communication constitutes yet another normative breach and presents yet another normative conflict for residents. As a third-year resident, Dr. Morgan, explained:

> I try to avoid the situation where the patients ask questions about their conditions. I don't want trouble with the attending. I act friendly. It's a rough spot. You don't want the patient to say to the attending, "Well, Dr. Morgan said . . . "

Attendings' control over both the clinical and the social aspects of healing validates a medically defined conception of residents' responsibility and spawns antagonism between residents and patients: Residents are responsible for managing patients' concerns and questions only to the extent that they do not interfere with obligations to attendings. Residents' relationships with patients, then, are bound by their superordinates' and patients' conflicting systems of relevance. It is only by satisfying the former that a resident properly executes the surgeon's role.

Attendings' influence on the resident-patient relationship, however, extends more routinely to the work protocols that residents develop as a corporate body to meet attendings' expectations. Although attendings give little thought to how residents organize work patterns, they implicitly communicate that they expect residents to organize work collectively and to demonstrate allegiance to the team's work standards. In fact, fulfilling attendings' demands depends ultimately on a resident's successful participation in the team. And because an individual resident's success depends on a coordinated work effort, it is in the context of their team responsibilities that they are routinely, consistently, and forcefully taught to honor the collective standards of work. These team responsibilities, like attendings' demands, require residents to develop a task-based and narrowly medical responsibility for patients that further limits their discretion in relationships with patients.

RESIDENTS' WORK AND PATIENT CARE

Surgical residents manage the service of patients as a corporate body; they treat the entire caseload of patients as a team and divide work according to the task rather than the patient. The morning rounding process reveals this shared responsibility. Rounds begin about 6:15 a.m. Surgical beds are located in five places around the hospital, and consultation patients are housed in various wards. Residents do not see patients as a group; they split up and see patients individually. The chief resident sees the patients in the Intensive Care Unit and usually has to go to the operating room at 7:30, thus leaving no time to see other patients on the wards. The remaining residents divide rounds "geographically," go to a different location each morning, and return to the same patient every two or three days. This organization of treatment is rationalized by pointing to the efficiency it creates for detecting problems and for completing work:

> There are two philosophies of rounds. One is to see the same patients every day and get to know them, and it goes quicker. The other is to see different patients every day. If you don't see the patients, even though you hear about them in card rounds, when you go and see them it's like starting a whole new service. And if you see the same patients every day, you could be missing the same thing each time (Second-year female resident).

The shared responsibility continues throughout the day, and which patient a resident sees during morning rounds does not affect his or her daily responsibilities. In general, treatment duties are divided between "patient work" (putting in or pulling out I.V. lines, pulling tubes, checking drainage in tubes, monitoring vital signs, doing admission interviews) and "laboratory work" (checking pathology reports, reading films, and checking blood work). Such lab work occurs each day, as do admission interviews. One resident checks all lab values, another consults with radiology, a third and fourth will begin the day's interviews. The remaining "patient work" also occurs daily, but is done on an as-needed basis by whomever a nurse calls with the problem or whom a more-senior resident assigns to the work.

Thus, on a given day, a patient's case will typically be handled by as many as five residents and no fewer than three. The following scenario is not unusual: Resident A sees a patient during morning rounds; Resident B operates on the patient; Resident C checks laboratory and pathology reports; Resident D rounds with an attending in the late afternoon; and Resident E does post-op rounds and is on call during the night. Who does what changes daily.

By conducting work in this way, and by rationalizing and medicalizing treatment, residents participate in a task structure that subordinates the subjective aspects of both illness and healing to that of surgical efficacy and management efficiency. Teamwork relies on maintaining impersonality between residents and patients, offers residents little continuity with patients, and structures residents' responsibilities according to discrete medical tasks rather than ongoing relationships. Patients feel the revolving door that this structure suggests; often they cannot remember a resident's name, are confused about who is responsible for their treatment, and cannot find the continuous contact they may look for or expect:

> A male second-year resident was finishing an admission interview with a 45-year-old female admitted for a lumpectomy and axillary dissection for breast cancer. The interview took 30 minutes as the patient explained the progression of her disease and the treatment proposed by the attending. The resident explained more about the procedure, did a physical exam, and asked her to sign the consent form.

When the interview ended and we were leaving the room, the patient asked the resident, "Are you going to come back here tomorrow [after the surgery]?" The resident said: "It's someone's job to check you after surgery. Me or someone else will be back." The patient said, "Oh," as we walked out.

A first-year female intern explains how this ordering of work affects patients but also its implications for the quality of physicians' work:

You can be a better doctor when you relate to patients and their needs. [Patients need] to have someone talk to them, rather than the doctor rushing in and out and not getting to know them. It makes them feel calm, more relaxed, more in control.

An obstetrics/gynecology resident reveals her frustrations about this ordering of work:

My biggest disappointment with the surgical service is that you don't get to follow particular patients. I went home and told my husband I was so bummed out because I can't get to know the patients. I pop in and out of different patients' rooms every day . . . . It even prevents the patients from telling us all their aches and pains. Sometimes a patient might pull me aside and tell me that the other doctor they saw seemed so busy that they didn't want to bother them, and tell me about something bothering them.

And yet a fifth-year female resident reveals the personal costs of attempting to maintain continuity:

I try to see every patient every day. It's important. But I go home and cry every night. I can't do it all.

Residents who try to integrate both medical and humanistic concerns in their work are often doomed to failure, not only because they can jeopardize attendings' approval or risk high personal toll, but also because of the norms of collegiality operating in the resident team. Because residents routinely interact with and rely on one another, directly observe one another's work, and have a personal stake in their teammates' performance, they are stringently pressured by their peers to pace their work according to team standards, even when compliance includes suspending the humanistic aspects of care.

Team Allegiance and Patient Care

The interdependence of teamwork forges loyalty and commitment among residents on two levels. First, the success of an individual resident depends ultimately on the success of the team and hence on the working relationships that he or she develops with teammates. Second, the efficacy of the team as a corporate body demands a routine control over the work patterns, actions, and priorities of team members. This team self-monitoring is an agent of residents' socialization in that the group teaches technical and moral responsibility, specifies what constitutes blameworthy error, defines and reinforces the strength of residents' relationships with one another, and constructs the views of patient care that residents adopt. We will discuss two dimensions of team self-control, regulating the flow of information and setting and meeting work standards.

Regulating Information

Given the organization of residents' work and their collective responsibility, successful teamwork requires a thorough sharing of information. Not surprisingly, communicating information about patients consumes much of residents' informal discussions during meals, in hallways, and in the operating room. Residents also convey patient information more formally during "card rounds," where each patient's case is reviewed. Participating in these rounds is a crucial duty of all residents because they are the primary arena where medical information about patients is shared, treatment decisions are discussed and proposed, and patient care is organized.

Card rounds not only aid in technical decision making and clinical monitoring; they also serve as a mechanism of social control. Senior residents use rounds to test junior teammates on how well they interpret findings, to evaluate their surgical-management skills, and to catch them making surgical-management errors.

One test of junior residents is whether they can discern which information needs to be exchanged and which withheld. The first and most concrete way residents learn to make these distinctions is to eliminate "social histories" and irrelevant medical histories:

> Edwards, a male intern, described the new chief, Goldstein, whom we had first met that morning in rounds: "[She] is to the point. She doesn't even want past medical history. She wants age, attending, complaint, procedure, labs and results. That's it."

Facility at weeding out "extraneous" information is an important sign of having mastered the understanding of what is surgically relevant. By learning to regulate information and define legitimate arenas of surgical concern, residents also see that surgical management can proceed on the basis of numeric values and need not rely on direct contact with patients. The technological and biomedical priorities that make up the dominant medical perspective not only obscure the personal dimensions of healing but also relegate patients' perspectives on their illnesses to a subordinate place. Residents, then, spend inordinately more time discussing patients in card rounds than they spend with patients themselves.

Another series of information norms requires the transmission of information. Although residents lack the punitive standards available to attendings, similar standards of responsibility about information exchange appear in residents' obligations to one another. Joint responsibility dictates that residents alert one another to patients' medical conditions and potential complications, own up to uncertainties and mistakes, and, most important, communicate all medical information to team members. As expected, given residents' shared responsibility for patients, failure to communicate information constitutes a serious normative mistake:

> Farmer, Bernstein, and Tolbert were discussing a problem with the new intern, John. A patient had been placed on a medication that was contraindicated, and John had not notified the team members. Tolbert: "Is the patient still in this world?" Bernstein: "[John] says everything's fine when it isn't." Farmer [chief resident]: "That's not a good thing for him to do, especially for his first day on a new service."

By not reporting the change, the intern compromised the patient's health and violated his fiduciary responsibility to discover and transmit vital information. These moral lapses are particularly serious, moreover, when the efficacy of teammates is threatened:

> According to the chief resident, Guttentag: "Last night everyone bolted without telling me. I was in the O.R. on a late case and everyone left, leaving Aaron [the intern who was on call], who didn't know what was going on. I talked to them and told them they couldn't bolt like that. It was mostly Tolbert [fourth-year resident]. She was the most senior person out. I told her if everyone was done, she could let people go home. But she should have come to the O.R. and let me know what was going on. You can't bolt on a big service like this."

In this instance, "bolting" left the service virtually uncovered; it compromised the on-call residents' ability to cover patients because the most current information on each patient was not transmitted. Deviating from standards of information exchange violated allegiance not only to patient care but also to teammates' needs. It jeopardized the credibility of the entire team, since attendings hold residents collectively culpable when mistakes occur (see also Bosk 1979).[11]

Exchanging information is not the only function of card rounds; they also serve as the place where work assignments are made, team tasks are coordinated, and conscientiousness in performing work is assessed. We shall see that the system of contolling productivity has critical implications for humanistic approaches to healing.

Setting and Meeting Work Standards

Accomplishing team responsibility and teamwork require a stringent coordination of the work activities among all residents. As we might expect, a dominant concern of residents and a primary topic of discussion involves what work has to be done, who has to do it, who should have done it and did not, and so forth. Residents continually monitor one another's work patterns and activities and, as with their control over information exchange, test one another's suitability and trustworthiness as colleagues.

Often in card rounds (but also during informal discussions), residents monitor whether their teammates have done their day's work assignments:

> Tolbert asked at card rounds: "Did anyone order the x-ray on Terny?" Farmer and Aaron, in unison: "No." Tolbert [agitated] to Aaron: "I thought you were going to do it." Aaron: "Honest to God, we didn't discuss it, Mary." Tolbert: "We were standing right here and you said you would do it." Aaron: "Honest to God, I wasn't here."

Residents feel this team pressure to fulfill their work quota. In fact, peer pressure often structures the level of activity:

> Tolbert and Oran [male intern] were waiting for two other residents to get out of the O.R. They cannot leave for the day until they "card out" and report on patients. Tolbert: "I don't want to put the central line in . . . . It's a complicated one. He [the patient] had one already." Oran: "I just assume we leave it for Bernstein [fourth-year resident who was on call that night]." Tolbert: "I would too but he'd beat my face in." Oran: "We did all the scut work and admissions, so we could card [sign out]." Tolbert: "We'll tell him we didn't want to do anything that radical [laughs]. I like [the patient] anyway. I don't feel like brutalizing him." After a couple of minutes, Tolbert stood up and said, "I've got to do things or I'll feel guilty for not doing anything."[12]

Residents make a wise investment by performing their share of work and doing so expeditiously; it facilitates the work process and satisfies teammates' expectations. Indeed, cooperating with colleagues is an important interpersonal strategy that a resident can use to gain a teammate's favor:

> Flannigan [second-year female resident] and Farmer [third-year male resident]) were in the ICU one evening when Farmer asked, "Who are you on call with?" Flannigan: "Bernstein [fourth-year resident]." Farmer said, "Sorry to hear that," and he walked away. Flannigan explained to me: "Bernstein has a reputation for saying, 'Take care of everything. If there's a problem, take care of it yourself.' I tell him, you're ultimately responsible for what goes on. I let him know the rules. But I smile and use sarcasm and charm. He'll be chief next year. I want him to drop cases my way, and not to brutalize me, so I say yes."

Sometimes the pressures of team responsibility can take extreme forms:

> All week Tolbert was talking about her upcoming vacation, which began on Saturday. That Saturday morning she showed up and rounded as the other residents did. Halfway through sign-out rounds later in the day, the chief said: "Mary, aren't you on vacation? What are you doing here? I didn't remember that when I spoke to you last night [about work that needed to be done in the morning]." Tolbert: "That's o.k. If I didn't come in, you guys would have to round by yourselves."

A serious deviation from both the normative standards and the task structure of teamwork occurs when a resident spends time with a patient at the cost of completing work responsibilities. Such a violation of team obligations does not go unnoticed:

> Guttentag and Farmer ran into each other in the recovery room. As usual, they discussed work schedules for the afternoon. Farmer was annoyed at Bernstein, who "only saw five of the six patients on nine [ninth floor] during [morning] rounds and then went off to the dogs [dog surgery]. He spent an hour with [one patient]. I asked him what the hell he was doing."

Spending more time with a patient than peers consider medically necessary is one of the most serious breaches of a resident's responsibilities. This is not because surgical residents believe patients' concerns are unimportant (although some do believe that), but because spending that amount of time with a patient creates problems in maintaining work schedules. Thus, attempts to integrate humanistic approaches to healing are negatively sanctioned, primarily because they can create additional work for an already overloaded colleague:

> I know the patients here need more support than we give them. But there is peer pressure. Everybody [every patient] has got to be seen [in morning rounds] before we go to the O.R. We have obligations to do that work . . . . The family-practice interns [who occasionally rotate on the surgical service] spend more time with the patients. But then we have to make the work up (Second-year female resident).

The pressures residents feel to demonstrate collegial responsibility shape their commitment to completing their share of the work load. By enacting this allegiance, however, residents must sacrifice relationships with patients:

> A fifth-year male resident said that he considers it part of his responsibility to explain to patients the nature of their operation when he gets consent forms signed. He said that he doesn't like to spend five minutes, like many of his colleagues. I asked him if he ever found that hard to do. "Sure. There are so many patients to see. If the chief resident says you gotta finish this floor in an

hour, you're torn between what you need to do, and you end up pushing to get ends to meet. And if you had an hour to see the floor, you had to see the floor in an hour. So you really don't have the time. That's the business here. It isn't necessarily the way you want to do it. You get hurt a little bit and go on."

Violating colleagues' expectations signals a resident's failure to properly distinguish between essential and peripheral surgical responsibilities. This distinction is embedded in the task structure, since the work system can be reproduced only by relegating patients' emotional needs as marginal to the essential task of healing. Given this, residents have little structural opportunity to integrate patients' concerns into their routine responsibility, and they are forcefully discouraged from doing so.

CONCLUSION

According to Hughes (1971), the source of tension between lay and medical cultures lies primarily in conflicting expectations of physicians' social responsibilities. While laypersons share with professionals many assumptions about the nature of disease and treatment, they experience disappointment and uncertainty in their interpersonal encounters with physicians. Yet how physicians manage their role relations to patients has consequences for their inclusion into collegial circles. In Hughes' formulation, professionals define the quack as one who champions the client's interest and perspective over those of the professional community. Becoming an insider depends largely on maintaining the proper balance between allegiance to patients and allegiance to colleagues.

In this study, we have seen that the work structure influences how residents establish rules of appropriate patient-resident relationships. The medical task system is situated in and around collegial interdependence and cooperation, which requires residents to prioritize their institutional, team responsibilities and to marginalize patients' needs that threaten work protocols. Constructing norms of patient care on the basis of medical rather than human complexity is a strategy that residents develop to manage the contingencies created by teamwork. The source of this strategy lies in work arrangements; deviations are managed on the shop floor, and the collectively constructed standards of effort becomes guides for everyday action. For surgery residents, it is not patient satisfaction and comfort but allegiance to teamwork relations that defines the proper focus of social role performance.

Whether a resident follows these norms of performance is a test of their professional allegiance and a measure of their community loyalty. Because of the order of work, trustworthiness is assessed largely by how residents mediate between their social responsibilities to patients and to teammates. Going it alone, or failing to honor team codes of productivity, violates the moral codes of collegial obligation. It is not surprising, then, that we see little deviation from this standard of patient care. The ethic of collegial allegiance virtually eliminates a resident's willingness to disregard team standards and instead pursue patients' needs. The medicalization of responsibility and objectification and dehumanization of patients represents an expression of ethical commitment and is a prerequisite for insider status.

This report indicates that the organization of the treatment context mediates rationales and activities of medical responsibility. The nature of patient care derives not from a practitioner's assumptions about healing but from the everyday work arrangements in which treatment occurs. Further research should be directed toward (1) explicating how structural conditions of physicians' work shapes medical culture and (2) identifying the structural conditions under which humanized care can and cannot occur. This approach is especially important today, as medical care increasingly takes place in large-scale institutional settings and group practices, where pressures of bureaucratization and rationalization may be especially great. It is not until we take account of organizational conditions of work that we can hope to create a medical system that delivers humane care.

ACKNOWLEDGMENTS

The author would like to thank Maureen McNeil, Charles Bosk, and especially Judith Levy for their helpful comments on an earlier draft of this paper. A Woodrow Wilson Foundation Fellowship in Women's Studies supported portions of this research.

NOTES

1. Portions of this paper were presented at the annual meetings of the American Sociological Association, August 1987. This study is drawn from my dissertation, *Expressive Work and Teamwork: Conflicting Responsibilities in Surgical and Psychiatric Residencies* (University of Pennsylvania 1988).

2. I define humanism as an expansion of the prevailing biomedical model of physician responsibility to one that integrates compassion, support, and sensitivity in the construction of the healing role.

3. My normal procedure was to follow one resident for as much of the day as possible. This meant that I met the team of residents in the Surgical Intensive Care Unit each morning at about 6:15 and chose one to stay with until about 8:30 p.m., when the residents signed out for the day. Thus, I went through the workday with a resident: morning rounds, (sometimes) a gulped-down breakfast; the operating room; collecting laboratory, pathology, and x-ray results; doing admission interviews; attending to special needs of patients (medication changes, new I.V. lines, talking to families); dinner (again, sometimes) and sign-out or card rounds. On some days, I was more interested in watching interactions outside the operating room and would stagger my time with the residents on the wards.

4.   For notable examples, see Fox (1957), Merton et al. (1957), Becker et al. (1961), Fox and Lief (1963), Mumford (1970), Knafl and Burkett (1975), Bucher and Stelling (1977), Bosk (1979), Coser (1979), Light (1980), Broadhead (1983), and Mizrahi (1986).

5.   Although they do so from varying perspectives, most sociologists view attending physicians as a primary agent in medical socialization. Students model their values and behaviors on those of their teachers (Fox and Lief 1963; Mumford 1970; Light 1980), or they pick and choose from multiple and sometimes conflicting models (Shuval and Adler 1980), or they are less interested in finding and following role models than in trying to impress them (Becker et al. 1961; Scully 1980; Mizrahi 1986). Yet each study also implies, if not states, that it is in the context of student culture that the level and the direction of trainee commitment are forged.

6.   Most of these studies focus on residents' development of clinical judgment, skill, and perceptions of mastery. They tell us strikingly little, however, about how specialty training shapes residents' relationships with patients (Mumford 1970; Burkett and Knafl 1974; Knafl and Burkett 1975; Bosk 1979; Coser 1979; Light 1980; Scully 1980; Mizrahi 1986).

7.   Seeman and Evans's (1961) study of surgery training suggests that the scope of expressive responsibility that interns take is rooted in the ideologies of their superordinates, who control the treatment environment. On wards where attendings keep decision making highly stratified, interns spend less time collecting information from patients, less time explaining problems and treatment plans, and less time explaining postdischarge care to patients and their families than interns on surgery wards that have low stratification. In their emphasis on the determining role that ideology plays, however, they fail to examine how the structural features of the work context itself—including the hierarchical basis of decision making—may affect residents' relationships with patients.

8.   See Light (1988) for a discussion of the psychologizing implicit in the sociology of medical education.

9.   One formal arena for this testing occurs during attending rounds. These rounds take place at the discretion of attendings, in the late afternoon between 3:00 and 6:00. The attending calls a resident, beginning with the most senior in rank, until he finds one who is not in the operating room, which is the only legitimate reason to be excused from rounding. A second formal arena are the weekly Mortality and Morbidity Rounds, during which the most senior resident on each service presents the week's complications and deaths, and fields questions from the assembled group of attendings, residents, and students. When senior residents are occupied in the operating room, a junior colleague can be called on to present the cases. The unpredictable way that residents are selected for rounding requires them to be prepared with the relevant medical information at all times during the day.

10.   Sometimes, attendings are not careful to meet these responsibilities to patients. Residents, then, are drawn into this work when families and patients feel antagonistic and angry about the lack of information and attention.

11.   This collective culpability, in fact, is reinforced by the norm of privacy that operates among the residents. What Bosk does not deal with, and what has fateful consequences for the structuring of social control, is that both normative and technical errors are more apparent to team members than to attendings and are discussed and resolved privately as a corporate group. While residents attempt to protect patients by their sustained scrutiny of the actions of fellow residents, they are willing to sacrifice the patients' well-being for the sake of maintaining their own corporate integrity. Incompetence comes to constitute a private, and often secret, matter. From this private regulation, team relationships and team cooperation assume special salience for residents and therefore create significant pressures of social control; this insularity institutionalizes the rigid distinction between insider and outsider, and, in a work structure that relies on interdependence, requires severe forms of social control.

12.   Tolbert may feel special pressures to conform, or hyperconform, to team standards in part because she had committed the normative error of "bolting" temporally prior to this incident and

may feel the need to demonstrate reliability more acutely than normal. Moreover, as a woman and thus an outsider in a male-dominated setting, her cooperation as a teammate may be subjected to particular scrutiny.

REFERENCES

Abbott, A. 1981. "Status and Status Strain in the Professions." *American Journal of Sociology* 86:819-35.

Becker, H., B. Geer, E. Hughes, and A. Strauss. 1961. *Boys in White: Student Culture in Medical School.* Chicago: University of Chicago Press.

Bosk, C. 1979. *Forgive and Remember: Managing Medical Failure.* Chicago: University of Chicago Press.

Bosk, C., and J. Frader. 1980. "The Impact of Place of Decision-Making on Medical Decisions." *Proceedings of the Fourth Annual Symposium on Computer Applications in Medical Care* (November):1326-1329.

Broadhead, R. 1983. *The Private Lives and Professional Identity of Medical Students.* New Brunswick, NJ: Transaction Press.

Bucher, R., and J. Stelling. 1977. *Becoming Professional.* Beverly Hills, CA: Sage.

Burkett, G., and K. Knafl. 1974. "Judgment and Decision-Making in a Medical Specialty." *Sociology of Work and Occupations* 1:82-109.

Coser, R.L. 1979. *Training in Ambiguity: Learning Through Doing in a Mental Hospital.* New York: Free Press.

Fox, R.C. 1957. "Training for Uncertainty." Pp. 207-241 in *The Student-Physician*, edited by R. Merton, G. Reader, and P. Kendall. Cambridge: Harvard University Press.

————. 1980. "The Human Condition of Health Professionals." Distinguished Lecture Series, School of Health Studies, University of New Hampshire, Durham.

————. 1989. *The Sociology of Medicine: A Participant Observer's View.* Englewood Cliffs, NJ: Prentice Hall.

Fox, R.C., and H. Lief. 1963. "Training for 'Detached Concern' in Medical Students." Pp. 12-35 in *The Psychological Basis of Medical Practice,* edited by H. Lief, V. Lief, and N. Lief. New York: Harper & Row.

Haas, J., and W. Shaffir. 1984. "The 'Fate of Idealism' Revisited." *Urban Life* 13:63-81.

Hughes, E.C. 1971. *The Sociological Eye: Selected Papers on Work, Self and Society.* Chicago: Aldine-Atherton.

Knafl, K., and G. Burkett. 1975. "Professional Socialization in a Surgical Sub-Specialty: Acquiring Medical Judgment." *Social Science and Medicine* 9:397-404.

Light, D. 1979. "Surface Data and Deep Structure: Observing the Organization of Professional Training." *Administrative Science Quarterly* 24:310-22.

————. 1980. *Becoming Psychiatrists: The Professional Transformation of Self.* New York: W.W. Norton.

————. 1988. "Toward a New Sociology of Medical Education." *Journal of Health and Social Behavior* 29:307-22.

Merton, R., G. Reader and P. Kendall. 1957. *The Student Physician.* Cambridge: Harvard University Press.

Miller, S. 1966. "Exchange and Negotiated Learning in Graduate Medical Education." *Sociological Quarterly* 7:469-79.

Mizrahi, T. 1986. *Getting Rid of Patients: Contradictions in the Socialization of Internists to the Doctor-Patient Relationship.* New Brunswick, NJ: Rutgers University Press.

Mumford, E. 1970. *Interns: From Students to Physicians.* Cambridge: Harvard University Press.

Scully, D. 1980. *Men Who Control Women's Health: The Miseducation of Obstetrician-Gynecologists.* Boston: Houghton-Mifflin.

Seeman, M., and J.W. Evans. 1961. "Stratification and Hospital Care: I. The Performance of the Medical Intern." *American Sociological Review* 26:67-80.

Shuval, J., and I. Adler. 1980. "The Role and Models in Professional Socialization." *Social Science and Medicine* 14:5-14.

MORE THAN A JOB:
WOMEN AND STRESS IN
CAREGIVING OCCUPATIONS

Nancy L. Marshall, Rosalind C. Barnett,

Grace K. Baruch, and Joseph H. Pleck

ABSTRACT

The authors examine the relationship between job characteristics and mental and physical health, using data from a random sample of 403 women employed as social workers or licensed practical nurses. These caregiving jobs often offer limited opportunities for advancement, and involve heavy workloads and overtime hours. Women in direct care jobs with a combination of heavy job demands and low decision authority or challenge, were more likely to report greater psychological distress. In addition, women in jobs with a combination of heavy demands and little supervisor support or few rewards from helping others, were more likely to report poorer physical health and greater psychological distress. The authors discuss the implications of this study for theory and practice.

Current Research on Occupations and Professions, Volume 6, pages 61-81.
ISBN: 1-55938-236-8

INTRODUCTION

While women made up only 44% of the labor force in 1985, fully 61% of the employees in the services industries were women.[1] In 1985, 43% of employed women were employed in the services industries, the majority as nurses, teachers, social workers, housekeepers, and in other caregiving occupations.[2] Caregiving occupations are generally recognized as highly stressful (Karasek, Triantis and Chaudry 1982; Cherniss 1980; Jayaratne and Chess 1984; Jayaratne, Chess and Kunkel 1986). This paper focuses on women who are employed in caregiving occupations, and on the impact of their working conditions on their psychological and physical health.

We take as background for this work research indicating that employment per se does not negatively affect the health of women (LaCroix and Haynes 1987). However, for both women and men, particular characteristics of jobs may be stressful and may lead to psychological distress, reduced well-being and poorer physical health.

Job stress research is part of a larger stream of research on life stress which posits that "stressors" give rise to feelings of "stress" which, in turn, contribute to psychological strain or distress and physical illness. Prior research on job stress has taken many forms and has measured different aspects of the workplace. One major line of research attempts to identify those job conditions that are associated with stress-related health problems. Some researchers within this tradition have examined the relationship between illness and job conditions, such as heavy workloads, time pressure or tensions at work (Theorell 1976; Caplan, Cobb, French, Van Harrison, and Pinneau 1975). Others have focused on the relationship of job satisfaction to autonomy, control, and decision latitude (Turner and Lawrence 1965; Walker and Guest 1952; Hackman and Lawler 1971).

Over time, our understanding of job conditions and job stress has become more complex. Karasek, Baker, Marxer, Ahlbom, and Theorell (1981) proposed that "job strain" results when individuals are in jobs with heavy demands and little opportunity to moderate the resultant stress. Their work originally examined the combined effects of job demands and decision latitude (defined as control over time allocation, control over organizational decisions, and control over the use of skills or the extent to which work is repetitive or monotonous). This Job Strain model has been expanded to include job insecurity, exposure to physical hazards, physical exertion, and social support at work (Landsbergis 1986).

Several studies lend support to the relevance of the Job Strain model for caregiving occupations. Cherniss (1980) found that one of the major strains faced by nurses, social workers, teachers, and poverty lawyers in their first jobs after training was the burden of being responsible for others, and of feeling inadequate to the task because of inadequate or irrelevant training, and lack of resources with which to address the problem. Bates and Moore (1975) report that heavy workloads, inadequate staffing, and feeling unable to influence administrative decisions are sources of stress for nurses.

In this chapter we explore and refine the Job Strain model for women in caregiving occupations. We argue that the model must be expanded to include the importance of the rewards from helping others to women in caregiving occupations. This paper is divided into three sections. In the first section, we describe those job conditions most characteristic of social workers and LPNs. In the second section, we focus specifically on the impact of concerns about those job conditions on the emotional and physical health of social workers and LPNs who are involved in direct care for patients and clients. Women not in direct care positions were excluded from this section because their jobs are different from the jobs of other social workers and LPNs with respect to caregiving responsibilities. In the third section, we discuss the implications of our findings.

METHODS

The data to be presented in this chapter come from a study of occupational stress and health among 403 women, ages 25 to 55, who were currently employed at least half time as social workers or licensed practical nurses (LPNs) and were living within a 25-mile radius of Boston. The sample was randomly drawn from the registries of those two occupations and was stratified within occupation by race, by whether or not the respondent had children and by whether the respondent was single or partnered (married or living with a partner). Fifteen percent of the sample were black, 85% were white. Approximately half had children and half did not, half were partnered and half were single. The mean age of the respondents was 39.5 years. It is important to note that, in Massachusetts, individuals with the job title of social worker are not required to be registered. By limiting our sample to *registered* social workers, our sample overrepresents social workers with bachelor's and master's level training in social work. In addition, social workers and LPNs who worked nights (starting after 8 p.m.) or rotating shifts, who were self-employed, or who had been at their current job for less than 3 months or in the field for less than a year, were excluded from the sample. On average, the respondents had been working in their respective fields for 11 years (ranging from 2 to 35 years) and at their current jobs for 6 years. The respondents were interviewed face-to-face for about two hours, about various aspects of their work and family lives. (For a full description of the sample, see Barnett [1988]).

CHARACTERISTICS OF CAREGIVING OCCUPATIONS

Social workers and LPNs describe their jobs as often offering limited opportunities for advancement, and involving heavy workloads and overtime hours. They also describe their jobs as sometimes providing limited resources, restricted decision authority, unsupportive supervisors, and involving discrimination, and exposure to illness or injury. Most of this section is based on the social workers' and LPNs' responses to a checklist of 30 job conditions. They were asked to indicate, on a 4-point scale from 1 = Almost Never/Never to 4 = Almost Always/Always, how frequently each item was *true* for their job. The items were written to encourage reports of objective job conditions, rather than the respondent's subjective feelings about job conditions. However, these are self-reports of job conditions, not objective measures. The following section describes the frequency of these job characteristics among social workers and LPNs.[3] Most LPNs worked in hospitals or nursing homes. Social workers were employed in various subareas of social work practice, including child protective services, psychiatric social work, medical social work, and work in the schools, community mental health centers, the courts or with the elderly. Job conditions vary from workplace to workplace and, when relevant, these differences are specified.

Salaries and Benefits

The LPNs in our sample who are employed at least 30 hours a week were paid an average of $1455 per month, or $17,460 a year in 1985; the social workers who are employed 30 hours a week or more were paid an average of $25,068 a year in 1985. Certain fringe benefits appear to be standard for full-time employees; most of the respondents working 30 hours or more a week report that they receive paid sick leave, paid vacation and paid or partially paid health insurance. However, only 75% of LPNs employed by nursing homes receive health insurance benefits. In addition, over one-third of part-time workers in both occupations do not receive health insurance benefits; 30% do not have paid sick leave and 18% do not have paid vacation.[4]

Advancement Opportunity

As a group, these caregiving jobs are characterized by little advancement opportunity—89% of social workers and LPNs report that only occasionally, if at all, are people with similar jobs at their place of employment able to advance. Lack of advancement opportunity is more often reported by social workers employed in the schools, the courts or in work with the elderly, and by LPNs employed in hospitals. Over one-quarter of psychiatric social workers and social workers working with the elderly report that people in their field often have periods of unemployment.

Workload

The jobs of social workers and LPNs are characterized by heavy workloads— 87% of the women report that often, or almost always, their jobs require working very hard; 76% report that their jobs often make heavy emotional demands on them. Many social workers have to deal on a regular basis with families in crisis, incidents of child abuse, individuals with severe emotional problems, suicidal clients, or families responding to the illnesses or deaths of loved ones. Licensed practical nurses are involved in physical caretaking of individuals in hospitals and nursing homes. They often have to deal with issues of death and dying, and with the emotional needs of their patients and of their families. For almost a third of the respondents, their jobs require working outside the usual work day, or working more than 40 hours a week.

Many of the respondents have to work under time pressure. Over two-thirds of protective social workers (responsible for child abuse and neglect cases) report that the amount of work they must do often or always interferes with the quality of their performance and that they rarely, if ever, have enough time to finish their work. Almost half of social workers working in the schools or with psychiatric patients, as well as LPNs employed in hospitals, also report that they work under time pressure.

Decision Authority

LPNs and social workers working with the elderly or in protective services report limited decision authority—one-third to over half report that they often have to do what other people tell them to do.

Limited Resources

One-third of the respondents often must meet the demands of their jobs with inadequate resources—especially protective social workers, social workers working in the courts or with psychiatric patients, and LPNs employed in nursing homes.

Supervision

Almost half (45%) of the women in both occupations have supervisors whom they consider to be poorly qualified as managers and 29% have supervisors whom they feel are not qualified for their own jobs. Almost two-thirds of the respondents feel that their supervisor is only occasionally, if at all, helpful to them in getting their jobs done. A similar proportion reported that their supervisors only occasionally, if ever, praise them when they have done a good job. Supervisors are most likely to receive poor ratings among protective social workers, social workers working in the courts or with psychiatric patients, and social workers who are teaching at the college level.

Hazard Exposure

Over three-quarters of LPNs working in hospitals, and about half of LPNs working in nursing homes and social workers employed in hospitals, report that their jobs expose them to illness or injury. Over three-quarters of LPNs working in hospitals, and about half of LPNs employed in nursing homes report that their jobs are often physically strenuous.

Monotony

The jobs of almost all LPNs and of about half of the protective social workers, adoption workers, and social workers working with the elderly are often monotonous, requiring them to do the same tasks over and over.

Discrimination

About one in five social workers and LPNs report that people doing their kind of job are only occasionally, if ever, treated with respect by other professionals at their workplace—this is especially true for protective workers and social workers working with the elderly. Eight percent of the respondents report that they often or almost always experience sex discrimination or sexual harassment on the job; another 18% report that they occasionally do. Twelve percent of Black respondents report that they often or almost always experience race discrimination on the job; another 44% report that they sometimes do.

THE IMPACT OF JOB CONDITIONS

We turn now to an examination of the impact of concerns about these job conditions, as well as the rewards of these jobs, on psychological and physical health.[5] In this section, we focus on the 326 social workers and LPNs in direct care.[6] We begin by describing the measures we used, and the types of concerns and rewards caregivers experience on the job. We then look at the relationship between these concerns and rewards and the respondents' health.

Measuring the Concerns and Rewards of Caregiving

To assess the concerns and rewards in caregiving occupations, we asked respondents to complete a scale that asked how much concern or reward they experienced from a series of job conditions. This measure paralleled the job conditions checklist described above, but differed in wording and response options since it was designed to elicit the respondent's *subjective* sense of concern or reward related to job conditions.

The Concerns of Caregiving

To assess the concerns of caregiving occupations, we asked each respondent how *concerned* she was, on a 4-point scale from not at all to extremely concerned, about a series of job conditions. The five factors that comprise this scale, their composite items, the mean score for each factor, and the Cronbach alphas, are shown in Table 1. The five factors are: Overload, Dead-End Job, Hazard Exposure, Poor Supervision, and Discrimination. (The factor structure of this and the following scale was confirmed using LISREL for confirmatory factor analysis. For details, see Marshall and Barnett [1990]). On average, the respondents were most concerned about the sense of overload on their jobs— "having too much to do, the job's taking too much out of you, and having to deal with emotionally difficult situations."

The Rewards of Caregiving

To assess the benefits of caregiving occupations, we asked each respondent how *rewarding* a part of her job she found each of a series of job conditions. The six factors that comprise this scale, their composite items, the mean score for each factor, and the Cronbach alphas, are shown in Table 2. The six factors are: Helping Others, Decision Authority,[7] Challenge, Supervisor Support, Recognition, and Satisfaction with Salary.

Relationship of Job Concerns and Job Rewards to Health

The concerns and rewards that women experience in caregiving occupations are directly related to their mental and physical health. We assessed two aspects of mental health—psychological distress and psychological well-being—and used one measure of physical health.

Psychological Distress

Psychological distress was assessed by the depression and anxiety subscales of the SCL-90-R (Derogatis 1975). We combined the depression and anxiety subscales because they were correlated .80 with each other, and showed similar patterns of relationship to other variables of interest. The SCL-90-R has high levels of both internal consistency and test-retest reliability. In this sample, Cronbach's alpha was .88 for depression and .89 for anxiety.

Table 1.   Job Concern Factors

Factor	Cronbach's Alpha	Average Score*
Overload	.72	2.3
1. Having too much to do		
2. The job's taking too much out of you		
3. Having to deal with emotionally difficult situations		
Dead-End Job	.82	2.0
1. Having little chance for the advancement you want or deserve		
2. The job's not using your skills		
3. The job's dullness, monotony, lack of variety		
4. Limited opportunity for professional or career development		
Hazard Exposure	.66	1.8
1. Being exposed to illness or injury		
2. The physical conditions on your job (noise, crowding, temperature, etc.)		
3. The job's being physically strenuous		
Poor Supervision	.85	1.6
1. Lack of support from your supervisor for what you need to do your job		
2. Your supervisor's lack of competence		
3. Your supervisor's lack of appreciation for your work		
4. Your supervisor's having unrealistic expectations for your work		
Discrimination	.48	1.2
1. Facing discrimination or harassment because of your race/ethnic background		
2. Facing discrimination or harassment because you're a woman		

Note: *Scores ranged from 1 = not at all concerned to 4 = extremely concerned.

Table 2. Job Reward Factors

Factor	Cronbach's Alpha	Average Score*
Helping Others	.69	3.2
1. Helping others		
2. Being needed by others		
3. Having an impact on other people's lives		
Decision Authority	.82	3.1
1. Being able to make decisions on your own		
2. Being able to work on your own		
3. Having the authority you need to get your job done without having to go to someone else for permission		
4. The freedom to decide how you do your work		
Challenge	.78	3.1
1. Challenging or stimulating work		
2. Having a variety of tasks		
3. The sense of accomplishment and competence you get from doing your job		
4. The job's fitting your interests and skills		
5. The opportunity for learning new things		
Supervisor Support	.87	2.8
1. Your immediate supervisor's respect for your abilities		
2. Your supervisor's concern about the welfare of those under him/her		
3. Your supervisor's encouragement of your professional development		
4. Liking your immediate supervisor		
Recognition	.68	2.6
1. The recognition you get		
2. The appreciation you get		
Satisfaction with Salary	.72	2.4
1. The income		
2. Making good money compared to other people in your field		

Note: *Scores ranged from 1 = not at all rewarding to 4 = extremely rewarding.

Psychological Well-being

Psychological well-being was assessed using a modified version of a 14-item scale developed by the Rand Corporation (Davies, Sherbourne, Peterson, and Ware 1985). This scale measures positive affect. Subjects are asked to respond on a 6-point scale (1 = not at all to 6 = extremely) to such items as: How often in the past month did you feel relaxed and free of tension? How often in the past month did you expect in the morning to have an interesting day?

This scale has high internal consistency and test-retest reliability. In this sample, Cronbach alpha was .94, which is essentially identical with the .96 figure given by Veit and Ware (1983), who also report a one-year test-retest correlation of $r = .64$.

Physical Symptoms

We measured physical health using a 29-item symptom checklist derived from measures developed by the Mind-Body Program at the Beth Israel Hospital. This scale assessed the frequency and associated discomfort of each of 29 symptoms (e.g., dizziness or feeling faint, chest pain, and respiratory congestion).

The Costs of Caregiving

To assess the relationship of the five concern factors listed in Table 1 to these three health measures, we estimated a series of regression models. Each model controlled for age, race, per capita household income, and SES,[8] since these variables have each been related to health measures. The R^2s and unstandardized regression coefficients for separate regressions of each of the factors listed in Table 1 are shown in Table 3.

Table 3.   Direct Costs of Caregiving

R^2 and Unstandardized Regression Coefficients of Job Concern Factors
Controlling for SES, Per Capita Household Income, Race, and Age

Factor	Psychological Distress	Well-being	Physical Health
Controls Only: R^2	0.04*	0.03	0.02
Overload: R^2	0.23***	0.12***	0.06**
B	7.20***	−4.85***	4.72***
Dead-End Job: R^2	0.07**	0.06**	0.02
B	2.89**	−3.05**	0.82
Hazard Exposure: R^2	0.15***	0.06**	0.06**
B	6.29***	−3.27**	5.13***
Poor Supervision: R^2	0.09***	0.07***	0.02
B	4.38***	−3.75***	1.77
Discrimination: R^2	0.04*	0.04*	0.02
B	0.74	−3.06	1.44

Notes: * $p < 0.05$.
          ** $p < 0.01$.
          *** $p < 0.001$.

Almost all job-concern factors are significantly related to psychological distress and to well-being, after controlling for age, race, income and SES. Overload makes the greatest contribution to the R^2 for psychological distress and well-being—an increase of 19% and 9% respectively, over the contribution of the control variables alone.[9] Overload and Hazard Exposure are both significantly related to physical health. Interestingly, concern about discrimination was not significantly related to any of the health measures. We examined whether discrimination might be related to health only for black women by including the interaction term: race × discrimination. There was no significant relationship between this term and the health measures, indicating that, even when considering the possibility of race differences, our measure of concern about discrimination was not related to the health measures.

When we included all five job-concern factors in a single regression, on each of the health measures, we found the same pattern of results as when we examined the factors separately. As Table 4 shows, Overload and Hazard Exposure are both important predictors of psychological distress and physical health, even after controlling for the impact of the other job concern factors. Overload is the only job concern factor, after controlling for the other factors, that significantly predicts well-being.

In sum, while four of the five job-concern factors are each related to the health measures, when we estimate a model with all of the job concern factors, only Overload and Hazard Exposure have a direct effect on psychological distress and physical health, and only Overload has a direct effect on well-

Table 4. Comparing the Costs of Caregiving

	R^2 and Unstandardized Regression Coefficients of Job Concern Factors Controlling for SES, Per Capita Household Income, Race, and Age		
Factor	*Psychological Distress*	*Well-being*	*Physical Health*
Overload	5.70***	−3.89***	3.74**
Dead-End Job	−0.10	−1.53	−1.36
Hazard Exposure	3.61**	−0.44	4.38**
Poor Supervision	1.95	−1.72	0.42
Discrimination	−1.97	−1.09	−2.93
R^2	0.26***	0.14***	0.09**

Notes: * $p < 0.05$.
       ** $p < 0.01$.
       *** $p < 0.001$.

being. While the other factors—Dead-end Job, Poor Supervision and Discrimination—may be related to the overall quality of the job and to job satisfaction, they are not related to psychological distress, well-being or physical health, after considering the impact of Overload and Hazard Exposure.

The Benefits of Caregiving

The rewards women experience in caregiving occupations are also directly related to their mental and physical health. To assess the relationship of the five reward factors listed in Table 2 to the three health measures, we estimated a series of regressions. The R^2 and unstandardized regression coefficients for separate regressions of each of the reward factors are shown in Table 5. Each regression controlled for age, race, per capita household income, and SES.

Table 5. Direct Benefits of Caregiving

R^2 and Unstandardized Regression Coefficients of Rewards
Controlling for SES, Per Capita Household Income, Race, and Age

Rewards	Psychological Distress	Well-being	Physical Health
Helping Others: R^2	0.11***	0.11***	0.05**
B	−6.53***	6.50***	−5.96**
Decision Authority: R^2	0.15***	0.07***	0.02
B	−7.15***	4.23***	−1.53
Challenge: R^2	0.10***	0.09***	0.02
B	−5.51***	5.53***	−2.00
Supervisor Support: R^2	0.06*	0.06*	0.04*
B	−2.31*	2.52**	−3.18**
Recognition: R^2	0.09***	0.10***	0.02
B	−4.01***	4.58***	−0.37
Satisfaction with Salary: R^2	0.05*	0.03	0.04
B	−1.45	0.75	−2.97*

Notes: * $p < 0.05$.
      ** $p < 0.01$.
      *** $p < 0.001$.

Almost all the job-reward factors are significantly related to psychological distress and well-being. Unlike job concerns, no one factor stands out as the most important predictor. Only Helping Others, Supervisor Support and Satisfaction with Salary are significantly related to physical health.

When we include all six job-reward factors in a single regression, we find three different patterns for the three different health measures. As Table 6 shows, Decision Authority and Helping Others are both important predictors of psychological distress, even after controlling for the impact of the other job reward factors. Helping Others and Recognition are important predictors of well-being, after controlling for the other factors. Helping Others, Satisfaction with Salary, and Supervisor Support are all significant predictors of physical health. The other job-reward factors are not significantly related to health after considering the importance of the factors noted above.

Additive Effects of Job Concerns and Job Rewards

Table 7 provides a summary of the significant main effects that we have found so far. We have demonstrated strong direct effects of Overload, Hazard Exposure, Helping Others, and Decision Authority on psychological distress. Similarly we have found strong effects of Overload, Helping Others, and Recognition from Others on well-being. For physical health, significant direct effects are found for Overload, Hazard Exposure, Helping Others, Satisfaction with Salary, and Supervisor Support.

Table 6. Comparing the Rewards of Caregiving

R^2 and Unstandardized Regression Coefficients of Job Reward Factors
Controlling for SES, Per Capita Household Income, Race, and Age

Factors	Psychological Distress	Well-being	Physical Health
Helping Others	−4.50***	4.41**	−6.97***
Decision Authority	−5.71***	1.30	0.31
Challenge	−0.12	0.91	1.71
Supervisor Support	0.14	0.52	−3.17*
Recognition	−0.68	2.43*	2.79
Satisfaction with Salary	−0.38	−0.20	−3.27**
R^2	0.19***	0.14***	0.10***

Notes: * $p < 0.05$.
     ** $p < 0.01$.
     *** $p < 0.001$.

Table 7.   Summary of Main Effects

	Psychological Distress	*Well-being*	*Physical Health*
Concerns	Overload	Overload	Overload
	Hazard Exposure		Hazard Exposure
Rewards	Helping Others	Helping Others	Helping Others
	Decision Authority	Recognition	Supervisor Support
			Satisfaction
			with Salary

Table 8.   Overload and Decision Latitude

	Psychological Distress	*Well-being*	*Physical Health*
Overload	6.03***	−3.92***	4.69***
Decision Authority	−4.68***	1.44	0.28
Challenge	−0.98	3.40*	−0.48
R^2	0.28***	0.15***	0.06***

Notes: Each regression equation controlled for SES, per capita household income, race and age.
  * $p < 0.05$.
  ** $p < 0.01$.
  *** $p < 0.001$.

The next step in our analyses is to simultaneously include job-concern factors and job-reward factors in our models. As noted earlier, the Job Strain model posits that jobs with high demands and low decision latitude have negative effects on health. Two of our job-reward factors—Challenge and Decision Authority—are two components of what Karasek et al. (1981) call decision latitude in the Job Strain model. Based on the Job Strain model we would expect, therefore, that respondents in our sample whose jobs are high on Overload (our measure of demand), and low on Challenge and Decision Authority would have the poorest health.

Table 8 contains the results of regressions of the control variables, Overload, Decision Authority and Challenge on each of the health measures. The applicability of Karasek's Job Strain model varies with the health measure being considered for women in caregiving occupations. Overload and Decision Authority have an additive impact on psychological distress, but not on well-being or physical health. Overload and Challenge have an additive impact on well-being, but not on psychological distress or physical health.

Alternative Models

In fact, when we estimate regression equations with the significant factors from Table 8, plus the other significant factors from Table 7, we find that psychological distress is related to Overload, Hazard Exposure, Decision Authority and Helping Others (see Table 9). That is, Overload, Hazard Exposure, Helping Others and Decision Authority have an additive effect on psychological distress.

The model is different for well-being—Overload, Helping Others and Recognition have an additive effect on well-being. As Table 9 shows, Overload and Helping Others are significantly related to well-being. Challenge is not significantly related to well-being once we consider the rewards of Helping Others. Recognition approaches significance ($p < 0.10$). If we remove the nonsignificant Challenge from the equation, Recognition reaches significance at $p < 0.05$ (not shown).

A third model predicts physical health—Overload, Helping Others, and Satisfaction with Salary have an additive effect on physical health. As Table 9 shows, Overload and Helping Others are significantly related to physical health. Hazard Exposure and Satisfaction with Salary approach significance at $p < 0.10$. Supervisor Support is not related to physical health. If we remove Supervisor Support from the equation, Satisfaction with Salary reaches significance at $p < 0.05$; Hazard Exposure remains marginally significant at $p < 0.10$ (not shown).

Table 9.   Overload and Job Reward Factors

	Psychological Distress	*Well-being*	*Physical Health*
Overload	5.05***	−3.63**	2.87**
Hazard Exposure	2.52*	—	2.58+
Decision Authority	−3.88***	—	—
Challenge	—	0.85	—
Helping Others	−3.59**	4.35**	−4.14*
Recognition	—	1.92+	—
Satisfaction with Salary	—	—	−2.26+
Supervisor Support	—	—	−1.46
R^2	0.32***	0.18***	0.12***

Notes: Each regression equation controlled for SES, per capita household income, race and age. A minus sign [−] indicates that the factor was not included in the equation because it was not significant at an earlier stage of analysis.
   * $p < 0.05$.
  ** $p < 0.01$.
 *** $p < 0.001$.
   + $p < 0.10$.

It is important to note that Helping Others is significantly related to each of the health measures. We will return to this in the next section.

Interactions Between Job Concerns and Job Rewards

While some of the prior work on the Job Strain model has considered only the additive effects of demand and decision latitude, if we include interaction terms in our models we can test whether individuals whose jobs are characterized *both* by high demand *and* low decision latitude are worse off than those whose jobs are characterized by high demand but not by low decision latitude. Put another way, we can test whether the rewarding aspects of jobs, such as decision latitude, can protect individuals from the negative effects of high demand.

Based on the Job Strain model we would expect that respondents in our sample whose jobs are high on Overload, and *low* on Challenge and Decision Authority would have the poorest health. In other words, the interactions between Overload and Challenge, and Overload and Decision Authority should be significantly related to the health measures. To test this, we estimated a series of regression models on the three health measures. Each model contained the control variables, the significant main effects for that health variable and one interaction term of the form: Overload $\times$ reward factor. Again, as Table 10 indicates, for women in caregiving occupations, Karasek's Job Strain model is only applicable to psychological distress. As Table 10 shows, the interaction between Overload and Decision Authority, and the interaction between Overload and Challenge, are significant predictors of psychological distress, as would be expected from Karasek's Job Strain model. That is, women in caregiving occupations whose jobs are characterized by high Overload *and* low Challenge or low Decision Authority experience greater psychological distress than women with high Overload and high Challenge or high Decision Authority or women with low Overload. However, the interactions of Decision Authority and Challenge with Overload are not significant predictors of psychological well-being or physical health. While Overload has a direct effect on well-being and physical health, decision latitude has no additive effect and no interactive effect on either health measure.

Other Factors

As with the additive model, other factors must be considered. The results shown in Table 10 indicate that we need to add two new variables to our model of job strain for caregivers—Helping Others and Supervisor Support. Respondents with high Overload *and* low rewards from Helping Others are more likely to experience psychological distress or poor health than are other

Table 10.   Interactions Between Job Rewards and Overload

R^2 and Unstandardized Regression Coefficients
of the Interactions between Rewards and Overload

Interaction of Overload and:	Psychological Distress	Well-being	Physical Health
Decision Authority: R^2	0.33***	0.19***	0.08***
B	−3.53**	1.10	0.36
Challenge: R^2	0.33***	0.19***	0.09***
B	−3.39*	1.25	−3.23
Helping Others: R^2	0.33***	0.19***	0.11***
B	−3.62**	1.86	−6.09**
Supervisor Support: R^2	0.33***	0.19***	0.11***
B	−2.11*	0.03	−4.06**
Recognition: R^2	0.33***	0.18***	0.09***
B	−1.33	0.33	−2.24
Satisfaction with Salary: R^2	0.32***	0.19***	0.09***
B	0.10	1.82	−1.13

Notes: Each regression equation controlled for SES, per capita household income, race and age, and included all significant main effects for that health measure, the interaction term of the form: Overload × reward factor, and the direct effect of Overload and of the relevant reward term.
    * $p < 0.05$.
    ** $p < 0.01$.
    *** $p < 0.001$.

respondents with high Overload and high rewards from Helping Others or with low Overload. Put another way, the rewards of Helping Others buffer the negative impact of Overload on psychological distress or physical health. That is, women with high Overload who experience greater rewards from Helping Others are better off than women with high Overload and low rewards from Helping Others. Similarly, Supervisor Support can buffer the impact of Overload on psychological distress and physical health.

Summary

When we put together all of the results reported in this chapter (see Table 11), we find that our model of the relationship between job rewards and concerns and psychological and physical health varies depending on the particular health measure. For psychological distress, the rewards of Decision

Authority have a significant direct effect, and individuals with high Overload *and* low Decision Authority or low Challenge are in poorer health than other women, thus confirming Karasek's Job Strain Model. However, we also found that Helping Others has an important direct effect on psychological distress and that women with low rewards from Helping Others *and* high Overload suffer greater psychological distress. Women in caregiving occupations are at least partially motivated to enter those occupations because of their desire to help others. It appears that, when their jobs are structured in such a way that they are actually able to be effective helpers, this directly reduces psychological distress and helps to reduce the consequences of heavy workloads and emotional demands. When their jobs are demanding and they experience little reward from helping others, they experience greater distress. A supportive supervisor is also an important buffer of the impact of heavy workloads and emotional demands on psychological distress among women in caregiving occupations.

Table 11.   Summary

	Psychological Distress	Well-being	Physical Health
Main Effects			
Concerns	Overload	Overload	Overload
	Hazard Exposure		Hazard Exposure
Rewards	Helping Others	Helping Others	Helping Others
	Decision Authority	Recognition	Satisfaction with Salary
Buffers of			
Overload	Helping Others		Helping Others
	Supervisor Support		Supervisor Support
	Decision Authority		
	Challenge		

When we consider the results concerning well-being, we get a somewhat different picture. The rewards of Decision Authority and Challenge are not at all important to psychological well-being, once we consider the importance of the rewards of Helping Others. Psychological well-being is associated with greater rewards of Helping Others and greater Recognition and appreciation from others. Well-being seems to be more strongly tied to the rewards found in relationships with patients, clients and colleagues than to decision latitude. In addition, job rewards do not moderate or buffer the negative impact of Overload on well-being.

Finally, Supervisor Support and Helping Others play an important role in predicting physical health. Helping Others has a significant direct effect on physical health. In addition, women with high Overload *and* low Supervisor Support or low rewards from Helping Others report poorer physical health than do women with high Overload *and* high Supervisor Support or high rewards from Helping Others.

IMPLICATIONS

The results of this research have implications for both theory and practice. Our theory must be expanded to incorporate the importance of helping others as a moderator of job demands. Additional research is needed to clarify whether this model applies only to caregiving occupations or only to women, or whether it is applicable to all workers.

Our practice can also be informed by this study. Caregiving occupations bring with them heavy workloads and emotional demands as caregivers respond to crises and assist individuals and families facing emotionally difficult times. Caregiving can also be physically strenuous and involve exposure to illness or injury, particularly when caring for the sick. Concern about these job characteristics contributes to greater psychological distress, poorer physical health and reduced well-being. To the extent that workloads and exposure to hazards can be reduced and caregivers can receive assistance in managing emotional demands, the negative impact of these job conditions can be reduced for women in caregiving occupations.

However, caregiving, by its nature, requires responding to individuals in crisis or in poor health. A certain level of demand is built into the work. It therefore becomes particularly important to note under what conditions such job characteristics become destructive, and to identify other aspects of the job that can be strengthened to improve caregivers' health. Consistent with Karasek's research, opportunities for workers to make decisions about their work and to be engaged in work that is stimulating and permits them to use their skills can reduce psychological distress. This study has also shown that, for women employed as caregivers, the opportunity to help others and the availability of a supportive supervisor is equally important, if not more so. It is as if the heavy demands of caregiving occupations are tolerable as long as the worker finds the demands of the job challenging, has the decision authority she needs to do the best she can, feels that her supervisor is doing all that can be done to make the job a better job, and finds reward in helping others.

ACKNOWLEDGMENT

This research was supported by a grant from the National Institute of Occupational Safety and Health No. 1 - R01 - OHO1968 - 01.

NOTES

1.   The services industries include professional and related services, personal services, business and repair services, and entertainment and recreation services.

2.   Based on information provided by the Bureau of Labor Statistics. All figures are for 1985.

3.   The frequencies of job characteristics, and mean salaries, reported in this section are based on weighted data. The sample was stratified by race, parental status and partnership status. Because these factors are related to the types of jobs respondents held, this stratification could alter the relative incidence of various job characteristics. Therefore, information gathered during screening calls to a full random sample of the two occupations was used to weight this sample back to represent the population of social workers and LPNs who were employed 20 hours or more at the time of the screening call, were not self-employed, and had been employed at least one year at the time of the call.

4.   Twenty-five percent of LPNs and 15% of social workers are employed part-time, that is, between 20 and 30 hours each week (weighted data).

5.   Because there is no consensus on the *operationalization* of the terms "stressors" and "stress" (Barnett, Biener, and Baruch 1987), we will avoid the use of these terms in the discussion of the *results* of our research.

6.   "Direct care" jobs are defined as jobs that respondents characterize as often or always involving responsibility for the physical or emotional well-being of others. We did not initially limit our sample to social workers and LPNs in direct caregiving positions. We defined social workers as anyone registered in their field and working in social work or a related field. Similarly, LPNs were defined as registered LPNs working in their field, who had not earned an RN as well. As a result, our sample included 63 social workers who report that their jobs only occasionally, if ever, require them to be responsible for others' well-being—many of them are administrators or planners in government or social service agencies. Similarly, 14 LPNs report that their jobs rarely require them to be responsible for others' wellbeing—many of them are working in doctors' offices or in student health.

7.   We purposely chose to use the label "decision authority" for this scale because its component items are similar to those in the scale that Karasek et al. (1981) call Decision Authority.

8.   Our SES measure is the sum of occupation (1 = LPN, 2 = social worker) and number of years of education, based on a principle components analysis that indicated that they contributed equally to the first component.

9.   Because the job concern factors are all scored so that each represents the average per item score for that factor, the unstandardized regression coefficients can be compared to each other across the regressions, within each outcome measure. Because the outcome measures use different metrics, the unstandardized regression coefficients cannot be compared across outcome measures.

REFERENCES

Bates, E.M. and B.N. Moore. 1975. "Stress in Hospital Personnel." *Medical Journal of Australia* 2: 765-767.

Barnett, R.C. 1988. "Rewards and Concerns in the Employee Role and Their Relationship to Health Outcomes." Working Paper No. 185, Wellesley Center for Research on Women, Wellesley, MA.

Barnett, R.C., L. Biener and G.K. Baruch, eds. 1987. *Gender & Stress.* New York: The Free Press.

Caplan, R.D., S. Cobb, J.R.P. French, Jr., R. Van Harrison, and S.R. Pinneau, Jr. 1975. *Job Demands and Worker Health* (Publication No. 75-168). Cincinnati, OH: National Institute for Occupational Safety and Health.

Cherniss, C. 1980. *Professional Burnout in Human Service Organizations.* New York: Praeger Publishers.

Davies, A.R., C.D. Sherbourne, J.R. Peterson, and J.E. Ware, Jr. 1985. *Scoring Manual: Adult Health Status and Patient Satisfaction Measures Used in Rand's Health Insurance Experiment. WD-2742-HHS.* Washington, D.C.: Department of Health and Human Services.

Derogatis, L.R. 1975. *The SCL-90-R.* Baltimore, MD: Clinical Psychometrics.

Hackman, J.R., and E.E. Lawler. 1971. "Employee Reactions to Job Characteristics." *Journal of Applied Psychology Monographs* 55: 259-286.

Jayaratne, S., W.A. Chess, and D.A. Kunkel. 1986. "Burnout: Its Impact on Child Welfare Workers and Their Spouses." *Social Work* 31: 53-58.

Jayaratne, S., and W.A. Chess. 1984. "Job Satisfaction, Burnout, and Turnover: A National Study." *Social Work* 29: 448-453.

Karasek, R.A., K.P. Triantis, and S.S. Chaudry. 1982. "Coworker and Supervisor Support as Moderators of Associations Between Task Characteristics and Mental Strain." *Journal of Occupational Behavior* 3: 181-200.

Karasek, R.A., D. Baker, F. Marxer, A. Ahlbom, and T. Theorell. 1981. "Job Decision Latitude, Job Demands, and Cardiovascular Disease: A Prospective Study of Swedish Men." *American Journal of Public Health* 71: 694-705.

LaCroix, A.Z., and S.G. Haynes. 1987. "Gender Differences in the Health Effects of Workplace Roles." Pages 96-121 in *Gender & Stress,* edited by R. Barnett, L. Biener, and G. Baruch. New York: The Free Press.

Landsbergis, P.A. 1986. "Occupational Stress Among Health Care Workers: A Test of the Job Strain Model." Paper presented at the Second National Conference on Social Stress Research, University of New Hampshire, Durham.

Marshall, N.L., and R.C. Barnett. 1990. "Development of the Job-role Quality Scale." Working Paper No. 195. Wellesley Center for Research on Women, Wellesley, MA.

Theorell, T. 1976. "Selected Illness and Somatic Factors in Relation to Two Psychological Stress Indices: A Prospective Study on Middle-aged Construction Building Workers." *Journal of Psychosomatic Research* 20:7-20.

Turner, A.N., and P.R. Lawrence. 1965. *Industrial Jobs and the Worker.* Cambridge, MA: Harvard University Press.

Veit, C.T., and J.E. Ware. 1983. "The Structure of Psychological Distress and Well-being in General Populations." *Journal of Consulting and Clinical Psychology* 51: 730-742.

Walker, C., and R. Guest. 1952. *The Man on the Assembly.* Cambridge, MA: Harvard University Press.

EMERGENCIES AND ROUTINES

Howard Robboy and Bernard Goldstein

ABSTRACT

This paper examines the panic behavior of long-term, continuous-use, ventilator-dependent patients and the resulting disruptions in hospital routines and procedures. These patients are generally cared for in acute-care environments, creating a mismatch between institutions and persons. The term "continuous medical emergencies" has been created to describe these panic reactions. Hughes' concept of emergency and routine in work is extended to include emergencies of continuous duration and the concerns and actions of the patients' significant others. Ogburn's concept of cultural lag is applied to interpret the gap between health statuses created by the new medical technology and the norms guiding medical caretakers, patients and their significant others.

> [O]ne man's routine of work is made up of the emergencies of other people.
> —Hughes (1971a, p. 316)

Current Research on Occupations and Professions, Volume 6, pages 83-98.
Copyright © 1991 by JAI Press Inc.
All rights of reproduction in any form reserved.
ISBN: 1-55938-236-8

INTRODUCTION

Emergencies are defined as significant social events which are normally unexpected and short-lived, are disruptive of both normal routines and may be life threatening. Emergencies last just minutes, hours or at most, a few days and cause us to reorder our daily routines and priorities. Appropriate caretakers are expected to make effective response.

Hughes, in his analysis of practitioner-client relationships, writes:

> In many occupations, the workers or practitioners (to use both a lower and a higher status term) deal routinely with what are emergencies to the people who receive the services. This is a chronic source of tension between the two. For the person with the crisis feels that the other is trying to belittle his trouble; he does not take it seriously enough. His very competence comes from having dealt with a thousand cases of what I like to consider my unique trouble. The worker thinks he knows from long experience that people exaggerate their troubles. He therefore builds up devices to protect himself to stall people off (Hughes, 1971b, p. 346).

Hughes' discussion of emergencies emphasizes crises of short duration, the perspectives of clients, caretakers and caretaker institutions and the behavioral consequences which follow. Examples of such emergencies and the occupations affected are: plumbers who routinely respond to emergency calls of homeowners with flooding basements, fire-fighters who rescue apartment dwellers in blazing buildings, and tow-truck drivers who regularly jump-start cars on excessively cold winter mornings.

This paper examines the implications of Hughes' notion of emergency and routine by focusing on repeated crises of extended duration. The case of long-term, continuous-use, ventilator-dependent patients is used to introduce the concept of "continuous emergencies" which refers to patient-defined events of extended duration, which do not fit the typical "emergency" time frame and some of the social consequences that follow. We argue that because of their unique nature, continuous emergencies present special problems in normalization and routinization for the patients as well as their caretakers. To this end, we: (1) explore and expand the implications of Hughes' concept of emergency and routine for medical emergencies of prolonged duration (continuous medical emergencies) encompassing the perspectives of all relevant role players: (2) use Ogburn's concept of cultural lag to examine the consequences of the slow adaptation of norms to innovations in medical technology: and, (3) examine the behavioral manifestations of definitional conflicts for medical caretakers which may arise as a result of variations in the rates at which the declarations of patients' continuous medical emergencies are normalized.

Continuous emergencies represent a largely unexplored but reoccurring social phenomena. While long-term macro-level social emergencies such as the

Crusades, the Black Plague and the Holocaust have been studied extensively by historians, they have not been analyzed from a micro-level sociological perspective, focusing on occupations and their relationship to emergencies and routines. More particularly, in the health-care context, as a result of developments in therapeutic regimens, surgery and technological innovation, the frequency of continuous emergencies is likely to increase. The medical emergencies experienced by ventilator-dependent patients are therefore both intrinsically informative and an entree into the study of this social process.

THE NORMALIZATION OF EMERGENCIES

In response to emergencies, social systems seek to solve the problem, minimize disruption, re-establish equilibrium and declare an end to the crisis and related behavior (normalization). As Cantrill (1940) and Erickson (1976) illustrate with reference to panics and disasters, it is in the nature of emergencies that events perceived as life-threatening, suddenly and drastically disrupt and reorder daily routines, priorities and status relationships (Metz 1981, pp. 7-17), creating a state of "collective excitement" (Blumer 1969, p. 170). The normalization of emergencies leads to the re-establishment, where possible, of pre-existing social relationships, meanings and priorities. Conflict is likely to emerge among the forces which produce emergencies and those which maintain the social order. The pressure from social systems is to normalize emergencies as soon as possible, to contain the additional costs and to incorporate the necessary coping mechanisms into ongoing systems of social control.

Some of the dilemmas in emergencies include: Which norms are to be suspended, for how long and by whom, who has the authority to declare and terminate these events, and who should specify the criteria to be used in this process? Due to the social and economic costs associated with emergencies, there may be a delay in their declaration. Furthermore, social control agents need to determine the frequencies with which similar types of emergencies may be declared, the sanctions which may follow when normal limits have been surpassed, and to establish the mechanisms with which to protect the public from exploitation.

During medical emergencies, physicians have the authority to declare and legitimate the emergency claims of others which "authorizes" the assignment of patients to the sick role (Parsons 1951; Goffman 1963; Mechanic 1968; Freidson 1970; Zola 1972; Twaddle 1973; Clark 1983; Schneider and Conrad 1983, p. 5). Patients are expected to cooperate with medical caretakers to stabilize their medical conditions, to normalize medical emergencies, to routinize behavior and, as quickly as possible, to resume normal role responsibilities. Clearly, such expectations are rarely appropriate, as Parsons (1975) later acknowledged, for severely chronically-ill patients, such as those who are ventilator dependent.

The declaration of emergencies can be used as disclaimers before the fact (Hewitt and Stokes 1975), or as accounts after the fact (Scott and Lyman 1968) for justifying unmet role responsibilities. Norms of reciprocity obligate others to assume the role responsibilities of those involved in the emergencies (Gouldner 1960). Few keep score of the emergencies declared by others. However, social margins exist which grant individuals the credibility to call on others when they are in severe need (Wiseman 1979, p. 223). Emergencies declared "too frequently" by some may raise questions as to their validity, the declarers' competence or the readiness of the caretakers to respond (Roth 1972). These "suspicious" individuals are likely then to acquire a label equivalent to that of hypochondriacs.

Individuals, institutions or societies anticipate the possibilities of emergencies and seek to minimize their impact by hedging, or by making side bets (Becker 1960), a major component of the routinization process (Hughes 1971a, p. 316). People purchase insurance to circumvent negative consequences if the unlikely occurs. Hospitals and fire departments plan on a community-wide basis to manage large-scale emergencies and insurance companies spread their risks to avoid disastrous losses. Societies search for buffers against destructive surprises such as the evolution of new strains of influenza or other public health hazards.

People who work in occupations that regularly confront life-threatening situations are trained in techniques and routines with which to handle them. At low levels of emergency, what may be involved is simple first aid, mouth to mouth resuscitation or the Heimlich maneuver. At another level, police officers (Rubinstein 1973) and fire fighters must learn to cope with a broader range of hazards to themselves and potential victims. At a still greater level of hazard, persons such as high iron workers (Haas 1972, 1977) and coal miners (Fitzpatrick 1980) are likely to develop complex cultural norms for ordering their behavior vis-à-vis their hazardous working conditions.

Physicians and nurses, having been formally trained and mandated to respond to medical emergencies, are likely to anticipate such events, and treat them as routine. The same training and experience that serve to routinize (to make habitual) the reactions of medical caretakers to events defined by patients as emergencies, may undercut the patients' sense that a consensus exists as to the state of their medical condition. This in turn generates patient resentment, as medical caretakers, in establishing and maintaining their professional competence, are likely to take a distant attitude towards patients. Any emotionality expressed while treating patients would only act to unnerve the patients even further (Hughes 1971b, pp. 346-347).

In the world of work, the routines of practitioners can create emergencies for clients. For example, building subcontractors and craftspersons routinely maximize their own interests by overbooking to hedge against cancellations or slow periods (Glaser 1972). Likewise, airlines and hotels indulge in the same practice to protect against "no-shows," knowing full well that on occasion this will create emergencies for clients. And of course, physicians routinely "squeeze in" more clients per time slot than can possibly be seen.

The demands of new technologies create emergency situations as they cause old rules to be suspended. Ogburn's (1964) theory of cultural lag is used to help explain the disruptions in normal hospital routines and procedures caused by ventilator-dependent patients. The introduction of new technology often results in the development of new social problems because social norms, slower to change, lag behind in their adaptation to the social conditions generated by the use of the technology. In this regard, hospitals become the institutional setting in which new social problems emerge, generated by the lack of fit between the emerging technology and the pre-existing norms.

THE SOURCES OF DATA

The research is based on a snowball sample or a sample of opportunity with: medical caretakers—physicians (6), nurses (13), respiratory therapists (10), ancillaries (2) and administrators (2); and seven family members and friends of ventilator-dependent patients. Forty interviews were conducted in hospitals or in patients' homes, primarily on the Eastern Seaboard of the United States. (The amount of care and skill level required precludes the admission of such patients into most nursing homes.) The interviews were semi-structured around a set of topics that were adapted to the particular circumstances and lasted from thirty minutes to several hours. Nearly all ventilator-dependent patients were unable to speak because of tracheotomies. Others were basically brain dead or comatose.

We also observed behavior and conducted interviews in hospital intensive-care and step-down units in North America and Great Britain. In addition, we attended medical conferences, interviewed leading physicians and government bureaucrats and participated in the design of United States Government sponsored research on the ventilator-dependent elderly (Goldberg 1985). We also contacted administrators of hospitals and home-care organizations, manufacturers of mechanical ventilators and representatives of companies providing home care for ventilator-dependent patients.

VENTILATOR TECHNOLOGY AND THE PROBLEMS OF CONTINUOUS EMERGENCIES

The American Association of Respiratory Therapists (1984) estimates that over six thousand people in the United States are being kept alive on mechanical ventilators at an annual cost of $275,000 per hospitalized patient. Patients with lung cancer, amyotrophic lateral sclerosis (Lou Gehrig's Disease), muscular dystrophy, emphysema, severe heart conditions, the final stages of AIDS and accident victims with upper spinal-cord injuries or severely damaged lungs are candidates for long-term, continuous-use, ventilator dependence. While keeping people alive is the function of the health-care system, the peculiar nature of this technology generates a set of work relationships and ethical problems which have roots and consequences far beyond the boundaries of hospital intensive-care or step-down units. An assistant vice president of a large general hospital provides an overview of the situation:

> Ventilator patients are the bastards of the hospital. We don't know what to do with them. They take up valuable and expensive beds for long periods of time and cause problems in staff morale.... [They] produce high frustration rates for physicians. They make them feel like failures. Nurses burn out quickly too. Families fight with the physicians and nurses. They [the family members] hear what they want to hear.   (*Interview 6*)

Previously, many of these patients would have died during the onset of their medical crises. Now their medical conditions can be stabilized and their lives saved and prolonged with the use of mechanical ventilation. However, the patients' chronic pulmonary disorders and continuous machine dependency frequently result in panic reactions as they see themselves as living on the verge of death by suffocation. These panic reactions become the precipitating source for disruptions in normal hospital routines and procedures and frequently lead to patients being labeled as "demanding" by the medical caretakers. As an ICU nurse comments:

> These patients are always frightened. They are frightened on the ventilator, and they are frightened to be alone. So you give them a bell and they push it one hundred and eighty to two hundred times per shift. They ring a bell or they hit their hands on their ring on the side rail. You can hear it all over the unit. They would like someone to sit there and hold their hands all of the time. You would like to be able to do that, but it is not realistic. They are so afraid, so fearful. They are fearful that they cannot breathe, that the machine will stop and they will stop breathing.   (*Interview 30*)

As suggested above, Hughes recognition of the caretakers' need to use their time efficiently and effectively might well be interpreted by others as examples of callousness and indifference. Frightened and distraught, ventilator-dependent patients repeatedly seek emotional support, reassurance and sympathetic human contact, for which medical caretakers are neither professionally trained nor temporally able to provide.

Ventilators are highly reliable and contain built-in alarms to signal in the rare event of malfunction. Why then are ventilator-dependent patients so frightened? Numerous explanations have been offered for the panic experienced and exhibited by these patients. First, prior to ventilator use, pulmonary patients are likely to have experienced severe anxieties generated by a fear of death by suffocation. People who cannot breathe do not die in their sleep. Rather, suffocation is a slow and torturous experience; the process itself is often defined by its victims as synonymous with death. Therefore, becoming ventilator dependent objectively solves the patients' breathing problems, but often perpetuates their sense of being on the verge of death by suffocation.

Second, despite social change in the form of the technological revolution, these patients are reluctant to trust their lives to machines, let alone unfamiliar high-tech equipment. This implausibility often results in a tendency to initially resist ventilator dependence. Thus the onset, imagined or real, of additional episodes of breathing difficulties with only machines to save their lives can easily terrorize patients. An ICU nurse provides the following graphic account:

> We had one man who died last year. He was not that old. He was maybe fifty-five years old. And the man literally was frightened to death and died frightened to death. He was the worst, the very worst. We tried all sorts of things. We paralyzed him with medications. We gave him all the narcotics we could just to let him sleep because even in the middle of the night, three o'clock in the morning, he would never relax. (*Interview 30*)

A third source of panic is the patients' perceived lack of emotional and social support which cannot be met by the machines and/or professional medical caretakers. They respond routinely to stabilizing and normalizing the medical conditions of their patients. Pulmonary and other physicians monitor their overall health; respiratory therapists check their machines and nurses suction their tubes and care for their basic bodily needs. For these patients, life seems to hang by threads—tubes connected to ventilators.

A fourth source of panic for these patients is their communication difficulties. Being mostly nonambulatory, they have few opportunities to discuss and analyze their life situations with each other, their significant others and medical caretakers. Most have undergone tracheotomies (incisions in the throat) which interfere with the normal speech process.

Some patients are able to communicate nonverbally through lip movements, others by writing on small blackboards, or by employing voice enhancers. One patient in our sample who is paralyzed, except for her eye lids, communicates with the aid of a computer and specially designed software. By blinking her eye lids, she is able to move the sensor and construct sentences. She can direct the computer to either print her message or activate a voice synthesizer to speak for her. Nevertheless, even with the employment of modern technology, communication between patients, significant others and medical caretakers is difficult, frustrating, and time consuming. Being in such isolated and disabled states generates insecurity and panic reactions which cannot be ameliorated by scrupulous attention to the technical care of their bodies. Their medical conditions result in a greater emotional deficit than usual; these same conditions deny them opportunities to experience and benefit from primary group interaction. This imbalance both perpetuates their sense of living in states of continuous medical emergencies and delays the normalization of their medical conditions.

The significant others' normalization of patients' continuous medical emergencies is accompanied by the normalization of their own emotional reactions, social relationships and routines, weakening the social bonds between themselves and patients. Patients are left lonely, out of touch and not likely to perceive a regular schedule of family visits as adequate (Strauss 1975, pp. 55-57). The longer patients remain hospitalized, the greater their felt needs for attention. Ironically, the more patients demand hospital visitations and attention, the more likely that significant others will gradually withdraw their attention as their emotional reserves become depleted to the point of bankruptcy (Strauss 1975, pp. 55-57).

Patients' felt needs are further frustrated by increased pressures on significant others to attend to their other daily concerns. As time goes on, significant others pay an increased social price for maintaining patients' definition of their health status. Postponed social obligations may need to be met, chores attended to and they may need a break from the stress of frequent hospital visitations. Furthermore, business associates and significant others of the significant others may be less willing to accept these social consequences. An observer, a friend of one patient and his wife comments as follows:

> The most depressing thing to me when I used to visit at Island Hospital was how few visitors there were at any given time.... I came during the day and maybe other visitors came later in the evening. Even as infrequent as our visits became, we would go in there and there would be this echoing. We were the only people speaking in the whole ward. I felt guilty about curtailing my visits and I rationalized it relatively easily by saying that he had not been the closer friend. It had been she (the patient's wife) who had been closer. If it had been she who had been in there, it would have been a tougher rationalization.... The other fact was, golly, if his own family wasn't coming to see him, didn't that make it easier? How could we spend four days a week at the hospital when his own family wasn't visiting. (*Interview 21*)

The withdrawal from patients by their friends and family members throws the entire load of physical care and emotional support onto the health care staff.

As a result of varying stakes in the emergency/normalization process, significant others are likely to normalize continuous medical emergencies at a faster rate than patients, generating conflict with patients and a coalition with medical caretakers.

CONTINUOUS EMERGENCIES AND THE NORMALIZATION OF HEALTH CRISES

Employing high-tech medicine hastens the medical staffs' normalization of medical emergencies. Medical procedures such as laser technology are viewed as short-term, crisis-intervention mechanisms wherein successful outcomes result in patients recuperating without further use of the technology. Likewise, the anxieties and concerns of significant others have a short trajectory when such technology is employed. However, with the use of mechanical ventilators or dialysis equipment, treatment trajectories become continuous (although intermittent for dialysis patients) and extend the span of panic, anxiety and concern for both patients and their significant others. As predicted by cultural lag theory, the social and psychological consequences of this new, extended-use technology have yet to be satisfactorily incorporated into patient care. Thus definitions of their medical conditions as continuous emergencies are perpetuated and simultaneously, normalization is delayed in the minds of patients and their significant others.

From the perspective of medical caretakers, the employment of such technology eases their work as it reduces the time patients spend under crisis treatment, stabilizes their medical conditions and accelerates normalization of their medical emergencies. According to medical caretakers, normalization involves four steps. First, patients must be socialized to accept machine dependency. Second, medical caretakers must establish trusting relationships with patients in order for their competence to be accepted. If these steps are achieved, then third, these patients may become candidates for weaning in which they gradually are helped to withdraw from the machines. Fourth, with successful training, a small proportion of the candidates will be weaned, removed from ventilator dependence. This outcome is preferred by almost everyone, because weaned patients can return to living near-normal lives.

Successful weaning is dependent on both physiological and psychological factors. First, the medical staff must conclude that patients' lungs have recovered to the point that these organs are able to function with partial or no mechanical aid. Second, patients must be able to free themselves from psychological machine dependency. For this to occur, patients must give up the perceptions that they are living in states of continuous medical emergencies. Weaning is a gradual and difficult procedure, proving successful for only a minority of patients who attempt it and any setback returns them to the starting point of the process. An even smaller number may go on to lead almost normal lives or even live as role models, ventilator-dependent patients who have "made it." While seen as heroes by some, and sources of frustration by others, this numerical minority is overwhelmed statistically by those who never leave their beds or ventilators. Said in other terms, the majority of long-term, continuous use, ventilator-dependent patients, unweanable, not candidates for either home-care or rehabilitation, have much in common with inmates on death row. Both are housed in total institutions awaiting their final destiny.

Unsuccessful weaning is a very frustrating process for all. It leads the medical caretakers to view these patients as being medically stable but permanently machine dependent, a view which may not be accepted by patients or their significant others. It is likely to result in a lack of consensus on the patients' medical condition among the three sets of role players, perpetuating the patients' sense of being in a continuous medical emergency, making the care of these patients more difficult. An ICU nurse provides the following example:

> I remember another patient we had that we would go in and say, "Betty we are going to put you on oxygen [take her off the ventilator] for fifteen minutes." Each patient room has a clock that they can face which is on the opposite wall. She would just stare at the clock and it got to the point where even after five minutes or so, she would start getting all worked up and saying she couldn't breathe. Yet, physically it appeared that she could breathe. Like her blood gases, her oxygen levels were fine. Finally we had to cover the clock because she would just sit there and watch the seconds tick by. So there is a big psychological effect on patients. (*Interview 32*)

For stability to be restored in the hospital, patients who cannot or who successfully refuse to be weaned must give up their identities as acute-care patients, and accept new chronic-care, seriously-disabled identities with little if any hope for full or even partial recovery (Charmaz 1987; Schneider and Conrad 1983). For this to occur, they must be taught to gain confidence in the dependability of mechanical ventilators and their medical caretakers. Ironically, although the health status "chronically ill" has both social and medical legitimacy, the social system has largely eliminated facilities for this category of patient so that it is difficult to locate them in an environment that will reinforce the normalization process. Some hospitals have attempted to ameliorate this problem through the creation of "step-down" units, that is, units with less equipment and fewer staff than ICUs.

Although functional from the standpoint of hospital routine, being defined as chronically rather than acutely ill has important social implications for patients. Seen as chronically ill but housed in an acute care setting, tending to be in stable though poor health, requiring and demanding regular but more frequent care than most other categories of patients, remaining hospitalized for prolonged periods of time, and for technical reasons, in intensive-care units, ventilator-dependent patients are structurally least likely to develop the attributes of the "good patients" which acute-care oriented medical caretakers prefer to treat (Hughes 1971c, p. 403; Lorber 1975; Papper 1970).

The medical caretakers interviewed frequently claim that ventilator-dependents are among their least favored patients even though they do their utmost to save their lives and treat other medical conditions which may arise. Nurses report feeling unappreciated by these patients no matter how much medical care and attention they provide. In addition, as O'Brien (1983, pp. 89-91) notes for dialysis patients, it is more difficult for medical caretakers to maintain professional distance from those who are chronically ill. An ICU nurse comments:

> I would have to say that I enjoy a surgical patient more so versus a medical patient. I used to work on a general surgical floor before coming to the recovery unit. I think I found a lot more satisfaction out of seeing someone come in that was acutely ill, caring for their problem for a week, say, and eventually within two or three weeks, seeing them discharged. With a lot of our patients now on the recovery unit, it is not the case at all. Most of them are more chronic. One year we did a study on the survival rate of the recovery unit, and it was twenty-five to thirty percent survival rate because they are just treating system units that have failed and when they get to this point, these people can't be weaned off their ventilators. (*Interview 32*)

From the perspective of hospital administrators, acute-care institutions are bureaucratically and technically equipped to stabilize the medical conditions and normalize the continuous medical emergencies of these patients. However, the dilemma for all concerned is that such patients want assurances that not only will they live, but that they will recover. Such assurances would encourage and hasten the rates at which they normalize their continuous medical emergencies. To date, medical science cannot provide these assurances. However, medical caretakers do try to minimize panic reactions by building trust. An ICU nurse comments:

> This particular lady, she will put her bell on and you walk out of the room she will put it on again. She will do it over and over again. Sometimes it involves retraining them as you have to do with any person. Retraining them means to say, 'I will be back in a certain amount of time. You're going to have to rest and not put your bell on.' You have to develop that trust and get them to relax a little bit. (*Interview 30*)

With acute-care patients, the routine assurances by medical caretakers become more credible with signs of recovery. Chronically-ill patients however, must deal with the discrepancy between similar routine assurances in the absence of recovery. No matter how well medical caretakers do their work, patients deny them psychic rewards. Emergency personnel in other areas, for example, forest fire fighters or members of the National Guard during a flood, can soon expect to be relieved from these emergency situations. But medical caretakers contending with patients with continuous emergencies are rarely accorded such relief. Hence, burnout and high turnover are occupational hazards.

NORMALIZATION AND WITHDRAWAL: MEDICAL CARETAKERS AND SIGNIFICANT OTHERS

The process of establishing consensus with regard to the patients' health status is complicated for medical caretakers by their need to contend with both patients and significant others. Such consensus is important for several reasons. It helps to establish the primacy of the medical caretakers in the situation thereby confirming professional status and legitimating the course of treatment. Consensus reduces conflict in the hospital unit and smoothes the work process for the medical staff. As significant others gradually reject patients' claims to be living in states of continuous emergencies and instead, accept the medical caretakers' view of patients as stabilized and normalized, they redefine them as chronically rather than acutely ill. This involves accepting the fact that medical caretakers cannot offer their loved ones any further return to normalcy. They also transform their hope for substantial recovery into a more realistic hope for continued though severely disabled lives.

CONTINUOUS EMERGENCIES IN HOME CARE

With home care, the nature of responsibility shifts as significant others of ventilator-dependent patients assume the duties of medical caretakers. Unless personal finances or insurance permit the hiring of round-the-clock staff, family members and close friends must place themselves in social debt, seeking others to share the burden of care and social support. Consequently, significant others frequently declare continuous medical emergencies of their own as home-care responsibilities begin to dominate their lives. For example, the husband of an A.L.S. patient laments:

> To them it's a job. They do it for eight hours and then go home and forget all about Clara. They go out with their husbands or their whomever and go for dinner, go to a baseball game or wherever and then come back the next day.... To be there twenty-four hours a day is not a job. It really gets to be a hassle after a while. And I really feel for the people who have to go through this life. (*Interview 31*).

The declarations of continuous medical emergencies add to the work burdens placed on available home-care nursing staffs. They are asked to respond to domestic needs peripheral to their professional domain, undermining their ability to control the treatment setting. Clearly, home-care settings are not as conducive as hospitals to the establishment of professional emergency/routine relationships premised by Hughes. Rather, significant others are present and more likely to participate in shaping the basic interaction.

Any around-the-clock work situation carries with it special problems (Robboy 1976). However, employing nurses for such duty on a daily basis presents its own set of dilemmas for family members who are dependent on prompt and scheduled arrivals of twenty-one shift changes of nurses per week. Inevitably there will be disappointments—some nurses will fail to report, a portion of whom will not have even given adequate notice to find replacements. These "no shows" create both medical and social emergencies for family members as they scramble to make arrangements to take unexpected time off from work and/or to orient persons unfamiliar with the equipment.

The worry that something unexpected will go wrong, thereby creating an emergency, hangs uppermost in family members and patients' minds. For example, there is a constant concern over power failures even though rechargeable batteries are provided which can run continuously for twenty-four hours. On the East Coast, where much of the data were collected, it is rare for homes to lose power for more than a few hours. Furthermore, utility companies maintain lists of homes where life-saving equipment are in regular use. Nevertheless, the onset of a storm generates panic about "What do we do if the power goes out?"

Such fears culminate in atmospheres of continuous medical emergencies which frequently permeate the homes and lives of significant others and ventilator-dependent patients, delaying the routinization of care. Hospital bound ventilator-dependent patients are likely to be the last segment of the triad to normalize their medical emergencies because they have the least to gain by accepting their caretakers definition of them as chronically ill.

By contrast, the home care experience is likely to hasten the patient's definition of medical normalization because: (1) there is a self-selection process whereby only the most physiologically and psychologically able patients are permitted to leave the hospital; (2) they are removed from an acute-care medical setting; and (3) at the same time they are placed in the "going home from the hospital" category, usually associated with "getting better." Paradoxically, home care is likely to prolong or re-arouse the sense of continuous medical emergencies for significant others as they try to cope with the overwhelming responsibilities connected with caring for these patients.

SUMMARY AND CONCLUSIONS

Hughes' shrewd insight into an underlying feature of the interaction between practitioners and clients, that is, the tension generated by the fact that one person's emergency is anothers' routine, has contributed significantly to our analysis and understanding of this processual relationship. Hughes analysis however, is limited to the interacting pair and the relatively short period of time encompassed by an "emergency" in the traditional use of the term. In this paper, we examined the benefits of including a broader range of role players in a situation of a prolonged emergency context as a contribution to the further understanding of work and occupations.

Emergencies are significant events because they disrupt the normal flow of interaction. In response to emergencies, social systems seek to minimize disruption and to re-establish as much as possible, the previously existing social order through the processes of normalization and routinization at the individual and group levels. Appropriate caretakers are expected to respond to and meet the emergency needs of society. As Hughes indicates, the caretakers' responses to the emergency needs of others become routines in themselves.

While the successful employment of high-tech medicine is viewed as another contribution of science to human welfare, the long-term use of this innovation creates havoc in the lives of many patients, their significant others and medical caretakers. More specifically, the disruptions in normal medical work routines and procedures caused by chronically-ill, lung diseased and impaired patients on mechanical ventilation are the focus of this paper.

The panic behavior characteristic of these patients can be explained, in part, by Ogburn's theory of cultural lag. The social system and within it, the health-care system, have created new medical technologies that have outstripped traditional definitions of health and illness and the social role of patient. Consequently, the traditional health care occupations are at a serious disadvantage in establishing their dominance. They have as yet not evolved new conceptions within which to place patients with new kinds of trajectories. Inevitably, this creates a work situation fraught with frustration, dissatisfaction and anomie.

With an increasingly larger older population and continuous technological medical innovations, the consequences of chronic illness are bound to become much more salient as social problems. For decades it has appeared that modern industrial society had moved beyond the need to deal with long-term illness. But clearly, this problem has re-evolved, necessitating the re-creation of appropriate health-care occupations and facilities.

ACKNOWLEDGMENTS

This is revised version of "Continuous Emergencies," presented at the Annual Meetings of the Society for the Study of Social Problems, New York, August 1986. The authors wish to thank the following people who made important comments and suggestions on various drafts of this paper: Sally Bould, Harry C. Bredemeier, Algonquin J. Calhoon, Candace Clark, Debra David, Coralie Farlee, Eugene Gallagher, Judith Gerson, Regina Kenen, C. Eddie Palmer, Carol Reichman, Julius A. Roth, and Eugenia Shanklin.

REFERENCES

American Association of Respiratory Therapists. 1984. *Chronic Ventilator Dependent Individuals: Results of Survey*. Dallas, TX: The Association.

Becker, H.S. 1960. "Notes on the Concept of Commitment." *American Journal of Sociology* 66:32-40.

Blumer, H. 1953. "Elementary Collective Behavior." Pp. 168-208 in *Principles of Sociology*, edited by A. McClung Lee. New York: Barnes and Noble.

Cantrill, H. 1940. *The Invasion From Mars*. New York: Harper & Row.

Charmaz, K. 1987. "Struggling for a Self: Identity Levels of the Chronically Ill." Pp. 283-321 in *The Experience and Management of Chronic Illness: The Sociology of Health Care*, Vol. 6, edited by J.A. Roth and P. Conrad. Greenwich, CT: JAI Press.

Clark, C. 1983. "Sickness and Social Control." Pp. 346-365 in *Social Interaction: Readings in Sociology*, 2nd ed., edited by H. Robboy and C. Clark. New York: St. Martins.

Erickson, K.T. 1976. *Everything in Its Path: Destruction of Community in the Buffalo Creek Flood*. New York: Simon and Schuster.

Fitzpatrick, J. 1980. "Adapting to Danger: A Participant Observation Study of an Underground Mine." *Sociology of Work and Occupations* 7:131-158.

Friedson, E. 1970. *Profession of Medicine*. New York: Dodd, Mead.

Glaser, B. 1972. *The Patsy and The Subcontractor*. Mill Valley, CA: Sociology Press.

Goffman, E. 1963. *Stigma: Notes on the Management of a Spoiled Identity*. Englewood Cliffs, NJ: Prentice-Hall.

Goldberg, A. 1985. *Life Sustaining Technology and the Elderly: Prolonged Mechanical Ventilation*. Contract Number 533-4935.0. Washington, D.C.: Office of Technological Assessment, United States Congress.

Gouldner, A. 1960. "The Norms of Reciprocity: A Preliminary Statement." *American Sociological Review* 25:161-178.

Haas, J. 1972. "Binging: Educational Control Among High Steel Ironworkers." *American Behavioral Scientist* 16:27-34.

_____. 1977. "Learning Real Feelings: A Study of High Steel Ironworkers Reactions to Fear and Danger." *Sociology of Work and Occupations* 4:147-170.

Hewitt, J., and R. Stokes. 1975. "Disclaimers." *American Sociological Review* 40:1-11.

Hughes, E.C. 1971a. "Mistakes at Work." Pp. 316-325 in *The Sociological Eye*, edited by E.C. Hughes. Chicago: Aldine-Atherton.

_____. 1971b. "Work and Self." Pp. 338-347 in *The Sociological Eye*, edited by E.C. Hughes. Chicago: Aldine-Atherton.

_____. 1971c. "The Making of a Physician: General Statement of Ideas and Problems." Pp. 397-407 in *The Sociological Eye*, edited by E.C. Hughes. Chicago: Aldine-Atherton.

Lorber, J. 1975. "Good Patients and Problem Patients: Conformity and Deviance in a General Hospital." *Journal of Health and Social Behavior* 16:213-225.

Mechanic, D. 1968. *Medical Sociology: A Selective View*. New York: The Free Press.

Metz, D. 1981. *Running Hot: Structure and Stress in Ambulance Work*. Cambridge, MA: Abt Books.

O'Brien, M.E. 1983. *The Courage to Survive: The Life Career of the Chronic Dialysis Patient*. New York: Grune & Stratton.

Ogburn, W. 1964. *Social Change*. Gloucester, MA: Peter Smith.

Papper, S. 1970. "The Undesirable Patient." *Journal of Chronic Disability* 22:777-779.

Parsons, T. 1951. *The Social System*. Glencoe, IL: The Free Press.

_____. 1975. "The Sick Role and the Role of the Physician Reconsidered." *Milbank Memorial Fund Quarterly* 53:257-278.

Robboy, H. 1976. *They Work by Night: Temporal Adaptations in a Technological Society.* Unpublished Doctoral Dissertation, Department of Sociology, Rutgers University.

Roth, J.A. 1972. "Some Contingencies of the Moral Evaluation and Control of Clientele: The Case of the Hospital Emergency Service." *American Journal of Sociology* 77:836-839.

Rubinstein, J. 1973. *City Police.* New York: Farrar, Straus and Giroux.

Schneider, J. and P. Conrad. 1983. *Having Epilepsy.* Philadelphia, PA: Temple University Press.

Scott, M. and S. Lyman. 1968. "Accounts." *American Sociological Review* 33:46-61.

Strauss, A. 1975. *Chronic Illness and the Quality of Life.* St. Louis, MO: Mosby.

Twaddle, A. 1973. "Illness and Deviance." *Social Science and Medicine* 7:751-762.

Wiseman, J. 1979. *Stations of the Lost.* Chicago: The University of Chicago Press.

Zola, I. 1972. "Medicine as an Institution of Social Control." *Sociological Review* 20:487-504.

AT AN IMPASSE:

INSIDE AN ABORTION CLINIC

Wendy Simonds

ABSTRACT

In this paper, I reflect on two-and-a-half years spent working part-time as a counselor in an abortion clinic in New York City. The opposing ideologies of medical workers and counselors are contrasted, as are clinic workers' complex moral standpoints on the issue of abortion. The medical perspective depicts abortion as an event in pregnant women's lives to be managed by medical workers, whereas the nondirective tenets of social work cast abortion as an event through which women can—with the facilitating assistance of counselors— achieve a certain amount of control over their actions. Neither perspective is clearly or purely articulated through clinic workers' behavior on the job. Tensions resulting from divergent visions of clinic work, and the ultimate dominance of the medical perspective are discussed. Finally, suggestions for overcoming such an impasse in health care are explored.

Current Research on Occupations and Professions, Volume 6, pages 99-115.
Copyright © 1991 by JAI Press Inc.
All rights of reproduction in any form reserved.
ISBN: 1-55938-236-8

INTRODUCTION

During my first winter as a graduate student, I began working as a counselor in a gynecology and abortion clinic in New York City. I had wanted to do counseling in women's health issues for a long time, and the isolation and unreality of graduate student life—reading all day every day—finally gave me the impetus to act. In retrospect, I see that it was not wholly laziness that had kept me from doing this kind of work sooner; something about the desire, itself, made me uncomfortable. It had to do with the guilt behind my middle-class "altruistic" urge that is, I suppose, common. The same sort of idealistic and possibly self-centered motivations that impelled upper-middle-class Victorian women (real, and fictional) to visit the poor—I imagine Dickensian characters bearing Bibles more often than food—was what I felt, edged with feminist anger and conviction. I knew women in college who had counseled battered women, battered children and rape victims, and hearing them talk about their work intimidated me. I was afraid of confronting violence over and over, afraid it would be too depressing and make me too angry. Yet I felt ridiculous as I pondered over choosing between *other* women's unpleasant realities. Abortion seemed like a positive issue, especially when compared to rape and abuse—and it held obvious political significance for me.

My own discomfort with my motives was strengthened by my first meeting with the social worker who supervised all the counselors. She said, "you know, most of the women who come here are different from you." I am white, have never been poor, and have never, in fact, had an abortion. She was afraid I would not be able to relate well to clinic clients. I was afraid I would be seen as one more person in a position of authority, whose job it was to reprimand mildly and give orders for the future.

I worked between 4 and 15 hours a week at the clinic from February 1985 through August 1987. Counseling was a frustrating yet often rewarding experience—as I expected it would be. I was, however, unprepared for the tension, even hostility at times, between the people working at the clinic. I had thought that the other women who worked in the clinic would be there at least partly because of their feminist commitments, and that the clinic would be run accordingly. What I found was that although the work being carried out had feminist implications, the patriarchal and paternalistic principles embodied in the practice of traditional medicine dominated all clinic activities. The longer I worked at the clinic, the clearer it became that the medical and counseling groups operated on completely different premises, based on often diametrically opposed sets of values. No one was immune from the tension resulting from this ideological split, or from the dominance of medical ideology.

Since the clinic was not the feminist mecca I rather naively expected, my original goals gradually were amended. I became a "smoother of the way." I concentrated on being benevolent and benign in my interaction with clients to make up for the abruptness and authoritarianism I perceived that they experienced in their encounters with medical workers. I offered disparaging excuses about the cold, bureaucratic process which governed women's experiences at the clinic. I made faces about the waiting, about the paper shoes, the stirrups, the informal but enforced policy that did not allow a woman's friend/mother/lover/child to accompany her past the main waiting room. I was both anti-medical and a medical apologist: resisting and priming at the same time.

THE RUNNING OF THE CLINIC

Most of the counseling at the clinic where I worked centered on abortion: pre-abortion counseling and contraceptive counseling (which can be—though it is not necessarily—preventive of abortion).[1] There was usually no post-abortion counseling, unless a client requested it. Most of the clients were teenagers; many had children. Most were on Medicaid. Most were Black or Latina. Many of the women who had abortions at the clinic would be back several times in the future for abortions. Women could make appointments for pregnancy tests and abortions to take place on the same day, or could come two separate times. Between 5 and 25 abortions were performed under local anesthesia each morning, five mornings a week.

The clinic staff was composed, on average, of five counselors (including a social worker), three nurse practitioners, and five administrators. Several part-time doctors divided up the mornings when abortions were performed, and worked solely performing abortions. Two nonmedically trained women worked as assistants to these doctors. Though the staff, like its clientele, was racially diverse, the clinic director, manager, and social workers were all white women. The doctors performing abortions were all men (two were white and one was Asian).

When I first began working, I was taught how to move clients—a job called "trafficking" which has since been made unnecessary by painted signs giving directions throughout the clinic. When a woman seeking an abortion first entered the clinic, she would approach the reception desk, where she would pay, or show her medicaid I.D. card and another form of identification. (A woman who arrived without the proper identification usually had her appointment rescheduled). A women who called in advance for an appointment was always told how much the services she requested would cost, and what forms of payment were acceptable. After paying, she would be sent to sit in a large waiting room, where she would fill out several lengthy forms. Eventually, she would be taken to the lab, where blood and urine would be analyzed. Outside the lab was another waiting room, where the woman would sit until called by a counselor. After a 20- to 30-minute session with a counselor, she would be escorted (by the counselor) to a separate waiting room for abortion patients only. Here, she would be told to change into a paper gown and paper slippers, which she wore while she waited—often for prolonged periods of time—to see the doctor. If she had to go to the bathroom during this period of time, she would walk through a room where fully-clothed patients were waiting.

There was a television in the abortion patients' waiting room, with a sign attached informing patients that they were not to adjust the set in any way, but rather, that they should ask a staff member to do so. A similar sign adorned the door of the staff's bathroom, which informed patients that (in case a staff member had been so lax as to leave this door unlocked!) they were not to enter. The woman would sit in the waiting room until the doctor's assistant called her name. This assistant would then weigh her, measure her height, and tell her to "empty her bladder." She would be instructed to climb onto the examining table and to put her feet in the stirrups, often before the doctor came into the room.

In his essay "Commonsense Knowledge of Social Structures: The Documentary Method of Interpretation in Lay and Professional Fact Finding," Garfinkel (1967) describes commonsense knowledge as: "socially-sanctioned-facts-of-life-in-society-that-any-bona-fide-member-of-the-society-knows" (p. 76). Women who came to the clinic were usually well-versed in the "commonsense" knowledge of what being a patient meant; that is, they were well aware of the type of behavior expected of them, and seldom challenged the dynamics of traditional doctor-patient relationships. Many were intimidated by doctors, whether they felt sick or not. They rarely questioned a doctor's authority and power over them, and often expected that counselors would behave similarly to the doctors they had encountered in the past.

The standard treatment of patients helped to confirm, for clinic workers, the women's nameless, faceless status in the medical exchange. Women were spoken of by the staff in terms of the color of their charts. That is, a staff member would say, "she is a yellow," when wishing to convey to another staff member that a woman had come for a pregnancy test; or "I saw two reds and a blue," when one had counseled two women who were having abortions and one who was seeking contraceptive counseling. The folder color was determined by the interaction between the woman and the phone operator who answered her call for an appointment. Phone operators filled out appointment cards which designated when and for what particular procedure each woman was coming, and how she would be paying for the services rendered. An appointment card was then paper-clipped to the outside of each woman's folder. Women who came to the clinic for abortions were scheduled in a certain order, and each was assigned a number which was written in red ink across her appointment card. This allowed counselors and medical staff to know the order in which the women should be "taken." A roster hung outside the abortion rooms. After the completion of each abortion, DONE was written in red crayon across each woman's name on the list. Though these practices may have gone unnoticed by clients, they were not carried out covertly. Clinic procedures attested to the lack of personhood attributed to people within medical establishments. "[T]he triumph of the technocratic consciousness, as embodied in the dominant voice of medicine, had as its consequence the dehumanization of clinical practice" (Mishler 1984, p. 139). The usual dehumanization inherent in becoming a patient is exacerbated for women in paternalistic medical settings, which operate within a culture where women's procreative freedom has a long history of being controlled by doctors (Fee 1983; Gordon 1974; Ruzek 1978).

THE MEDICAL PERSPECTIVE

The medical group's behavior centered around the dichotomy of sickness and health, and presumed that the answers to problems (and each patient is seen as having a problem) came from medical workers, not from the people they served. Medical workers referred to their customers as patients.[2] Though people did come to the clinic when things were physically "wrong" with them (infections, diseases, and so forth), most clients came for routine gynecological care, pregnancy tests, or abortions. So the women who were served by the clinic may have been pregnant, and they may have been distressed about being pregnant, but they were usually not sick. In this regard, Conrad and Schneider (1980) describe how the medical profession has increasingly framed its judgments in terms of deviance, thereby gradually shaping itself into an agent of social control. "As illnesses are social judgments, they are negative judgments....Common sense also tells us that an entity labeled an illness or disease is considered undesirable" (p. 31). Since abortion clients experienced their pregnancies as personally undesirable, a framing of their "condition" in terms of deviance was not contested.

This definition of abortion as deviant is reinforced by medicine's focus on male physiology as the "healthy" norm. Thus, pregnancy—wanted or unwanted—can only be considered a deviation. "While medical science no longer defines pregnancy and birth as pathological events, as it did at the turn of the century...the contemporary 'solutions' to these problems still assume a disease orientation" (Riessman and Nathanson 1986, p. 264). Doctors do not, of course, attempt to cure pregnancy. Rather, pregnancy becomes a dangerous condition to be monitored and managed (Rothman 1982, 1986). So, regardless of a woman's physical or mental state upon arrival at the clinic, medical workers examined her within a system which centers on pathology. For instance, clients were asked routinely whether they had been "feeling sick," or had any "symptoms"—indications of a diseased state—of pregnancy. Doctors and nurse practitioners saw themselves as dispensers of solutions to the pathological condition of pregnancy. There were two methods by which pregnancy could be solved by medical workers: by abortion or by referral of patients to other clinics for prenatal care.

Medical workers at the clinic saw their judgments as objective observations of facts, which at rare times required the verification of two technicians. There may be, however, discrepancies in medical opinions. Unless women have come up against a situation in which doctors' views clash, they generally accept the doctor's word as a factual assessment of their condition. For instance, one woman came to the clinic a few days after her own doctor had examined her and told her she was ten weeks pregnant, only to be told by our medical staff that she was fourteen weeks pregnant, and would have to seek a second trimester (a more difficult and more costly) abortion elsewhere. Even in such a case, where the client was sufficiently displeased to express her anger to a counselor, she had no authority with which she could alter the medical decision that she has received. As Freidson (1986, p. 174) observes:

> In the vast majority of cases ... clients are neither sophisticated nor powerful, so that the professional's position as gatekeeper of desired resources combines with a monopoly of organizationally relevant knowledge about how the system works to create a position of interpersonal power that few are in a position to challenge.

Clients' lack of authority is reinforced by medical professionals' view of them as unreliable and errant. In the eyes of the physicians and nurse practitioners at the clinic, unwanted pregnancy resulted from contraceptive ignorance, contraceptive failure (reported fairly often and viewed suspiciously by the staff) or a psychological problem: inability to foresee the consequences of one's actions—failure to face the grave physiological reality of sperm and egg meeting, and so forth. Contracepting was also seen as each individual woman's problem, and once the solution (contraceptive drug or device) had been prescribed by medical workers, the problem need no longer exist, as they saw it. For instance, once a woman had learned how to insert her diaphragm, it was presumed she would use it every time she had sexual intercourse. Within this framework, anyone who did not contracept successfully after being given a method was classified by the medical group as careless, irresponsible, immature, or just plain stupid.

Medical workers treated clients' procreative dilemmas as the result of a lack of restraint or responsibility. As Conrad and Schneider (1980) note, seeing problems as self-inflicted—and, therefore, avoidable with the exertion of personal self-control—is central to, though not confined by, medical ideology. Rather, this notion holds a great deal of salience in our culture as a whole:

> The medicalization of deviance is part of a larger phenomenon that is prevalent in our society: the individuation of social problems .... Rather than seeing certain deviant behaviors as

symptomatic of social conditions, the medical perspective focuses on the individual, diagnosing
and treating the illness itself and generally ignoring the social situation (p. 250).

Unwanted pregnancy was seen by medical workers as a social problem only
because numerous individuals shared it. Clients' perceptions were outweighed
and often completely dismissed by medical reasoning. In his linguistic analysis
of physicians' conversations with their clients, Mishler (1984) shows that "the
discourse of medicine" rarely allows clients' reality—or the "voice of the
lifeworld"—any legitimacy.

Women who came to the clinic too late for a first-trimester abortion were
harshly judged, and often harshly treated by the staff, especially by medical
workers. I heard doctors ask women, "when did you say your last period was?"
with thinly-veiled suspicion, many times. One doctor, while examining a
woman who had reported a much more recent date of menstruation than was
suggested by his manual assessment, asked her, "feel that? ...Baby moving."
Staff members assumed women were aware of the division of pregnancy into
trimesters, and aware of the clinic's performance of first-trimester abortions
only. When women naively lied about their periods, medical workers seemed
to feel a sense triumph when they showed women how pregnant they really
were. They resented what they saw as women's attempts to fool them, rather
than recognizing these lies for what they were: desperate and certainly
depersonalized attempts to obtain abortions.

Members of the medical group were much freer with their criticism of
patients than those in the counseling group, who generally griped only to each
other. Medical workers were aware, however, that accusational comments were
not in keeping with enlightened counseling behavior (which they were supposed
to practice also), but they also tended to doubt the effectiveness of "just talk,"
which is what they saw counselors as providing. One nurse practitioner told
me: "Some of these women get me so annoyed when they don't want to use
any of the available methods. I finally tell them, and I know I shouldn't say
this, 'Look, you have to take responsibility for your actions. If you're adult
enough to be sexually active, you have to protect yourself, or you'll be back
here for an abortion.'" Medical workers believed that the *right* kind of talk—
directive and authoritative—would produce better results than the carefully
neutral conversations counselors had with clients. In their discussion of
interviews with health department nurses. Riessman and Nathanson (1986, p.
263) describe similar ideas about the responsibility and failure of clients as
central to nurses' conceptions of the problem of teenage pregnancy.

Perhaps of most importance, an exclusive focus on the "willful" ("immature,"
"irresponsible") teenager as the obstacle to effective intervention acts to deflect attention
from other possible loci of responsibility for continued high rates of teenage pregnancy
and birth: the organizational structure of contraceptive services; the inadequacies of

available contraceptive methods; the ambivalence of adult society ... toward teenage sex,
... contraception, and abortion; the circumstances under which teenagers have sex and
use contraception; and the complex agendas of teenagers themselves.

The belief that it is more difficult to achieve demonstrable physical results
than to interact with people comes from what appears to be the medical
profession's general inability to value interaction with people who can most
efficiently be served when they are quiet and immobile. During abortions, if
a woman cried out, or tried to close her legs, she was told by the doctor's
assistant, "He can't finish unless you keep still." If she continued to move, she
was asked whether she wanted to go to another clinic where "they put you
out" so "you won't feel anything" during the abortion. The doctor rarely told
women what he was doing during the abortion procedure. This was something
a counselor had discussed already. Theirs was the realm of action, not
conversation.

THE COUNSELING PERSPECTIVE

Like medical ideology, counseling ideology portrays short-term counseling as
a situation involving a "problem" or "crisis." However, counselors didn't see
themselves as rectifiers of crises, but as facilitators of discussions that would
lead clients to evaluate and improve their situations themselves (though not
to completely eliminate their problems). But because the medical group's
influence insidiously found its way into all work carried out at the clinic, many
counselors did view counseling as a solution or cure to perceived problematical
attitudes or dysfunctional emotional behavior of clients.

Each counselor was given a copy of the clinic's counseling manual when
she began working. According to this manual, a counselor "needs" to have
the following qualities or personality traits: "accurate empathy" (which implies
that there is some level of empathy which is inaccurate); "nonpossessive
warmth" (read: there is such a thing as too much warmth); and "genuineness"
(which either means counseling cannot be faked, or counselors must be able
to cover when they are faking—which is what seems to happen). The counseling
manual repeatedly insists on objectivity; counselors "do not give advice," they
"do not tell clients what to do," "they do not interpret behavior and feeling,"
and their questions "should be neutral, nonloaded, and nonleading." This
prescription basically negates the personality of the counselor.

The manual states that the most effective way to counsel is to "reflect" off
the client "without comments." So, for instance, when asked how she feels
about being pregnant, a client might say, "I feel terrible," clueing the counselor
to respond, "You feel terrible?" in the hopes that the client will then elaborate
upon her terrible feeling. ("Yes, I am so worried that my parents will find out."

"You're worried that your parents will find out?" *ad infinitum*.) This method may work in drawing people out at times, but cannot sustain itself if the client is not willing.

During the many counseling sessions which I observed, I never saw a counselor sustain the reflective method, perhaps in part because, typically, it was not difficult to start clients talking. Also, this method contradicted the view most counselors held of themselves as workers. Most saw themselves not as mere sounding boards, but as active agents in helping others. They felt that rewarding work involved more than repetition and echoing. Most counselors found the least attractive aspect of their jobs to be the inevitable repetition involved when conveying standardized clinic-mandated information to every client, or, as one counselor put it, "feeling like a tape recorder." Several told me they dispelled this feeling by trying to treat each new client as a "different experience."

Despite the counseling manual's repeated insistence on a nondirective and value-free approach, the clinic staff had definite opinions about abortion, and definite goals which it hoped to accomplish with each woman seen. Neither the guidebook nor the staff questioned the attitude that abortion is or should be something a woman keeps secret, or something about which she would feel embarrassed or ashamed. When staff members talked about abortion patients among themselves, they often whispered the word "abortion," or called it "the procedure." They referred to women who were having abortions as "ABs" or "reds" or "greens" (red and green are the chart colors issued to women having abortions). Such examples of depersonalizing clients may be ways in which abortion workers attempt to distance themselves from the emotional demands and moral ambivalence involved in abortion counseling. In her ethnographic study of family planning workers at a clinic in Philadelphia, Joffe (1986) describes "coping strategies" she observed counselors undertaking, such as passive resistance to or subversion of specified job activities, and "anticlient humor" (pp. 123-140).

In a section of suggested questions counselors might use to get a conversation rolling with a client, the guidebook includes the following series of questions: "Does anybody else who is close to you know you are pregnant?" "Does he/ she know you are here today?" "What was his/her reaction to your decision?" "Do you think your relationship will be changed by this?" Though many women did keep their pregnancies and/or abortions secret, this line of questioning perhaps needlessly reaffirms the treatment of pregnancy and abortion as private, clandestine events in women's lives, and reinforces the implications that it is women who must be held responsible for and bear the burdens of unwanted pregnancies and their terminations.

When "writing up charts," counselors were required to include a woman's reason for having an abortion. We were also supposed to discuss options to abortion, and write that we had done so in our notes, allegedly to protect the clinic against potential future legal action. The counseling manual treats abortion as an option (to be considered against continuing the pregnancy and keeping the child, or giving the child up for adoption). In keeping with social work's vision of its goal as helping people to empower themselves, the counseling process was supposed to make women feel "positive" about their decisions, in part because they were experienced during the session *as* decisions. Most of the women I counseled said they did not feel as though they had alternatives to abortion—that is, none of the so-called alternatives were in any way feasible for them. The most common answer women gave when I asked them how they made their decisions to abort, was to say that they "had no other choice." Clearly, an "only choice" is no choice at all. This "reason," then, is all-encompassing, not simply a course of events, or a particular argument acting as an impetus to action. But one cannot really write, "Ms. X is firm in her decision to have an abortion because of her life." Within the prescribed constraints governing counselor-client interaction and medical records, the reason for aborting comes from the woman, and is not seen as influenced or caused by outside sources. Having had experience with medical workers before, and daily interaction with a society which holds the poor responsible for their poverty, these women accept that the burden of proof is upon them. They fully expect that they will be asked to justify their actions: "I can't take care of another now." "I can't afford to have a baby now." "My boyfriend left me." "I'm just starting high school." "My father would throw me out of the house if he knew."

Counselors believed strongly that each abortion patient should leave with some form of contraceptive. One counselor told me that she felt that assisting a woman in this decision was the most important task she could accomplish during a session. After observing one of my counseling sessions, she said, "I don't say, 'Have you thought about what type of contraceptive you want to use after the abortion?' I say: 'What type of contraceptive are you *planning* to use after the abortion'" She said that she did her best not to offer women the opportunity to say they didn't know, or would think about it and decide when they came for their "post-op" checkup two weeks later, because "most of them don't come back, anyway." There was a general feeling on the part of employees in both the medical and the counseling groups that abortion should not be used as a method of birth control. Repeat abortions were a cause of dismay and even astonishment for counselors. Joffe (1986) found that counselors in the clinic she observed often felt angry at repeat aborters. Along with "rais[ing] questions about counselors' competence," repeat aborters "were a confirmation of counselors' suspicion that there is an emergent group of women who are content to use abortion as their sole means of birth control" (p. 117). Most counselors in the clinic where I worked preferred to deal with a woman who had never had an abortion than with a woman who had had several, despite the fact that it was easier to prepare a woman for an experience she had undergone in the past. Someone who returned again and again served as evidence of the failure of counseling, or, at least, of the ineffectiveness of counseling as a remedy for the problem of unwanted pregnancies.

Over time, counselors seemed to become either cynical and non-empathetic toward women who Had many abortions, or to become overwhelmed by their own redefinition of the problem from one of getting individual women to act responsibly to one involving a much more complex—and not individually soluble—societal problem. One social worker told me that she felt it was important to let every woman know she had options, even if she felt she did not. To her, the counseling session could empower a woman by making her feel she *had* a decision to make. I came to feel that the most empowerment I could offer in a counseling session was to make a woman feel comfortable with her "decision," and possibly even positive about its impact on her life.

Very few counselors located the problems of aborting women in a larger context, perhaps because that would have simply proven once and for all that the type of counseling they were doing was, in many ways, irrelevant. Besides serving as an indication of the ineffectiveness of counseling, women returning for their fifth abortions could not be processed by the usual counseling route prescribed by the guidebook. Many counselors were judgmental, at least in private conversations with other staff members; they felt such women had something "wrong" with them, especially if they did not expose their own grief and/or guilt over the abortion to the counselor. One social worker told me that in cases of repeat abortions, she made it her policy to ask women "how do you feel about being here again?" in a "nonthreatening tone." Whatever the tone, all questions have theoretical implications behind them. The implications behind this question are that a woman *must* feel something—and presumably something negative—about returning for yet another abortion, and that she must be willing to expose her feelings to a professional. Counselors often expressed their inability to understand why women who didn't want to continue to get pregnant. It was difficult for them, as women who felt, for the most part, a good deal of control over their lives—as well as women who saw themselves as very conscientious contraceptors—to imagine the experiences of other women who lacked what they saw as such easy-to-possess control. Talking with as many as six such clients a day could, and did, dull counselors' disbelief into mild resentment.

Because most counselors viewed the abortion procedure with distaste, and avoided being present during it, they could not comprehend the motives of women who would "put themselves through" abortions repeatedly. One counselor told me that she had begun to feel "sort of anti-abortion" sentiments. She said she found it depressing to see people coming over and over again for abortions, and that at the rare time when a woman decided to continue her pregnancy, she was really glad. A social worker told me she thought it was important that counselors attend abortion procedures on a regular basis, "so we can remind ourselves what it is we're doing here." Both women were quick to assert that they were, of course, "pro-choice," but that they had come to feel that the choice of abortion should involve careful decision making— more careful decision making than they felt they were observing. Joffe (1986) cites similar sentiments among the counseling staff she observed: one counselor said, "I wouldn't say we're committing murder, but there is the death of *potential* life" (p. 115). Another spoke of the ease with which women have abortions, saying, "It makes me uncomfortable to be part of that conveniencing" (p. 115). Counselors in the clinic where I worked also resented abortion decisions they regarded as "easy outs." Counselors generally shared the belief that repeated "use" of abortion signalled either distress through a recognizably self-destructive or self-punitive act, or a failure to treat abortion with the seriousness counselors felt it merited. They sought the confirmation of these beliefs in their counseling.

Luker (1975) describes what she calls a "cost-benefit approach" to decision-making that women utilize—often unconsciously—in negotiating procreative or non-procreative choices. She writes that abortion workers' treatment of clients as irrational and indecisive is certainly an ineffective tactic in dealing with repeat aborters:

> Lacking an understanding of why she is doing what she is doing and forced to accept the prevailing view that she is acting "irrationally," a woman is often condemned to repeat that process over and over again. The high rate of repeaters ... underscores the fact that the decision processes leading to risk-taking can remain obscure even to the women themselves. Unless women with unwanted pregnancies, and the professionals who deal with them, can reach an understanding of how those pregnancies come about, such pregnancies will continue to occur (p. 110).

By focusing on the decision-making process that brings a woman to the clinic and ignoring the decision-making process that led her to become pregnant, counselors do not confront the problem as Luker describes it.

Counselors did not seem to consider the possibility that there might be reasons why abortion seemed a more serious experience to them than it did to many clients. In "Abortion Counseling: A Description of the Current Status of The Occupation Reported by Seventeen Abortion Counselors in Metropolitan New York," Detlefs (1984) found that counselors felt abortion was such a serious issue because they remembered clearly the fight to legalize it, whereas many of their clients didn't share these memories. Such memories enhanced counselors' commitment to the right to abortion, but also their commitment to the general import of the decision to abort. Many younger women—such as those coming to the clinic for abortions—did not think of abortion as a hard-won legal right or a difficult moral issue, but as simply a way to terminate unwanted pregnancies.

INTERACTION BETWEEN THE MEDICAL
AND COUNSELING PERSPECTIVES

Of course, the two models are not completely clear cut, nor are they mutually exclusive. There were, for instance, nurses who adopted certain aspects of the counseling model. One part-time nurse attempted to improve the atmosphere of the recovery room by turning off the lights, so that clients could rest without fluorescent brightness. She also had more informal conversations with women than other more medically "professional" nurses, who stuck to the basic speeches about post-abortion care, and birth control pill-taking.

Counselors also engaged in many purely medical activities. Most wore lab coats, and many wore name pins with initials after their names (SSC for Social Services Counselor) like doctors. Counselors also did light medical chores to save the time of the medical examiners; we took the temperature, pulse, and blood pressure of each client we saw, and often weighed her as well. Job requirements enforce counselors' investment in the medical way of measuring people.

There were several counselors who identified more strongly with the medical than the counseling ethic. These women had been working at the clinic for at least fifteen years, beginning when abortion was not performed there; thus, they did not come to their work because of any political or feminist motivation. These women saw themselves as medical assistants, and deferred to the judgment of doctors or nurses at all times. They were averse to any counseling staff meeting discussions of stress, counseling problems, and so forth. They resented being observed by the social worker supervising all counselors, and were highly critical of newcomers to the staff.

Similarly, the doctors who worked at the clinic had not sought employment there because of any commitment they felt toward women's rights to obtain abortions. They seemed to be working at the clinic because alternative employment was difficult to find. From my past experience with doctors, these did not seem out of the ordinary; they were generally non-communicative, though usually friendly in a superficial way toward other members of the staff and the patients they treated. They were always addressed by their titles, whereas the women working in the clinic—from the clinic director on down— were always identified by their first names, by both other workers and by clients.

The medical staff viewed counseling cynically; after all, it did not serve a concrete purpose, and often did not appear to remedy the problem as they saw it. Women came back again and again for abortions in spite of their discussions about contraceptive methods with counselors. Medical workers saw their jobs as much more difficult, because they had to do more than "just talk" to women in order to finish all the tasks for which they were held responsible. They detected infections, did pap smears, gonorrhea cultures, breast exams, fitted diaphragms, and so forth. A nurse practitioner told me candidly: "If your job is twice as hard as a normal job, ours is twice as bad as that."

Medical workers' authority was constantly reinforced by the very procedures under which counselors operated. When discussing oral contraception, it was recommended that we explain to clients that "the final decision as to whether you can use The Pill lies with the nurse-practitioner who examines you." In preparing women for the abortion experience, we were supposed to tell them that the very performance of the abortion was left to the doctor's discretion. Thus, we were not advised to explain that certain physical factors—such as high blood pressure in the case of prescribing contraceptive pills, or pregnancy beyond the first trimester in the case of abortion—would result in denial of specific services. We were told not to reveal the results of pregnancy tests to clients, although we knew the results before counseling sessions. This somewhat unofficial "policy" was instituted for fear that women who had scheduled abortions and whose pregnancy tests were negative would leave the clinic without being examined. Again, we were not advised to explain that every test of urine carries a probability of error and that an examination can confirm or refute pregnancy test findings, but were told that only medical workers were "authorized" to reveal the results of the tests to patients. These counseling practices operated on the assumption that it was sometimes easiest not to be straightforward, not to bother explaining exactly what was going on, but simply to keep women waiting until a professional medical worker told them what to do.

On the rare occasion when counselors would accompany women through the abortion procedure, they would encounter strong resistance, even hostility, from medical workers. Medical workers' resentment can be explained, in part, because a counselor's presence in the abortion room was a deviation from standard clinic procedures. A change in standard practice was looked at as an inconvenience, simply because it was a change. It was assumed that counselors would attend an abortion only with a woman who seemed especially apprehensive or who was especially young, and that we would ask for permission to attend from the doctor and his assistant beforehand. Very few counselors would offer to go with clients in the first place. (Personally, I found this part of counseling to be the most rewarding, as I felt most strongly during these times that I had really helped women through difficult experiences.)

The first time I stayed with a client during her abortion, I could tell that the doctor's assistant resented my being there. She told me: "You stand *there*" and pointed to the other side of the examining table from where I was standing. This let me, and the woman having the abortion, know that I was dispensible; my job was to "just stand there," and I was even incapable of standing in the right place on my own. At one point, I asked the woman if she wanted to squeeze my hand, and the doctor's assistant said: "No, she doesn't need to do that now." Throughout the abortion, she issued orders to me and to the client.

The second time I arranged to attend an abortion, this same assistant purposefully neglected to call me before the client went into the abortion room, after assuring me she would remember to come get me beforehand. She decided that it was unnecessary for me to attend the abortion, and simply glared at me when I confronted her about it. Later, she insisted she would not assist in abortions which I would attend.[3] She clearly felt that my presence was a commentary on her job performance. The fact remained that, with no counselor present, a woman would have two people stationed at her crotch—and no one at her side—neither of whom considered it their job to offer comfort or reassurance. Doctors seemed wary of my presence, because it meant they would have to spend longer with a nervous patient. When a woman was very apprehensive, doctors commonly sent her back out to see a counselor who would make her an appointment at another clinic, where abortions were performed under general anesthesia.

Beginning as an experiment, an attempt was made to reconcile the two groups by having one member of each work together in a "team." Counselors were assigned to nurses, and moved (usually leaving their own offices) to sit in rooms adjacent to the nurses' examining rooms. What resulted varied very little from the way things worked before, when counselors and nurses did their respective jobs independently. Several counselors were quite dissatisfied with the new procedure when it was first implemented, because they felt their work was being interfered with by nurses who didn't understand why they would take longer with some clients than others. Several nurses would interrupt counseling sessions to inform counselors that they were ready for "their" patients. Nurses would often consider themselves the managers of processing the patient; one nurse told me how difficult her job was when she didn't have an "assistant," and another often asked me to run errands in other parts of the clinic for her.

Despite the clinic management's knowledge of conflict between medical and counseling perspectives, few changes were implemented with success during my time at the clinic. I had many conversations with social workers and with the clinic manager, in which I talked of the rift between the medical and counseling staff, and protested what I saw as unreasonable instances of medical control over clients and counselors. In general, clinic administrators seemed to feel that the clinic worked remarkably well considering its problems with underfunding and understaffing. A doctor's "bedside manner" mattered little in light of his low complication rate during abortions. Qualitative changes in care were seen by management as the most elusive to articulate and the hardest to accomplish.

In order to last in a "street-level bureaucracy," Lipsky (1980, pp. xii-xiii) writes that workers must eventually adopt the agency's point of view regarding the service of its clients. Workers' adjustments to the job's demands "permit acceptance of the view that clients receive the best that can be provided under prevailing circumstances" and that such adjustments are considered, within the bureaucracy, to be mature decisions backed by realism. Improvement can come to seem not only unnecessary, but impossible.

Is the impasse insurmountable? Writing about my experiences has forced me to question not only my original perceptions, but also my growing conviction (while I remained at the clinic) that there was very little hope of change. In retrospect, I believe I remember most clearly what I liked least about the clinic. I have thought long and hard about why a group of generally well-intentioned people comes to seem, at times, quite the opposite. Like other jobs in the service sector, working in an abortion clinic is not a job with many "perks" (outside of the benefits of free contraceptives and gynecological care), nor is it an experience rife with new challenges or positive feedback. In short, such jobs are demanding, draining, and repetitive, and it is unsurprising that workers conserve or exhaust their energy and compassion. It is, however, a pity. Hughes (1971) wrote, "perhaps it is well to recall that the opposite of service is disservice, and that the line between them is thin, obscure, and shifting" (p. 305). This, indeed, becomes the case when workers feel they are overworked.

There are distinct steps which can be taken to empower those engaged in street-level work. Lipsky (1980) recommends monetary reward, peer review and other forms of evaluation which lead to rewarding jobs well-done, client involvement in establishing service procedures, and a spirit of self-critique within the bureaucratic organization as measures to improve service (pp. 196-211). Self-conscious measures such as these were occasionally attempted during staff meetings at the clinic, with varying levels of success and resistance on the part of staff members. But without a basic and genuine confrontation of the dilemmas involved in—and definitions of—abortion work, no changes can emerge.

Work conditions are, as I have demonstrated, complicated by moral ramifications. Though the work involved in providing abortion is not now a deviation from the law, it still falls within Hughes' (1971) category of "dirty work." Ball (1967) wrote about illegal abortionists' attempts to neutralize the then ultra-deviant act of performing abortions; they legitimated their activities by utilizing standard medical practices, adopting both medicine's verbal rhetoric and physical accessories. Clinic workers in both the medical and counseling groups at the clinic where I worked relied on the legitimization provided by medical costumes, equipment and routines. Medical workers' most profound effort at distancing themselves from the "dirty work" of abortion consisted in delegating all but the basic performance of the abortion to assistants or counselors, while counselors rarely set foot in the room where abortions were performed. Ultimately, as long as abortion providers share a view of abortion as stigmatized and morally reprehensible, clients will be serviced, but not well-served. I feel certain that appropriate solutions to the rift between the medical and counseling groups' opposing definitions of the clinical situation will come about only with the reconceptualization of the goal of abortion work to be woman-centered assistance, not medical judgment and control.

NOTES

1. During pre-abortion counseling, counselors would ascertain that the client was sure that she wanted to have an abortion, would describe the abortion procedure, risks, and post-abortion care, and would discuss contraceptives for future use.

2. Incidentally, the word "patient" derives from the Latin *pati,* meaning "to suffer," and doctor from the Latin *docere,* meaning "to teach."

3. The one other assistant was more amenable to—though certainly not pleased by—my presence in the abortion room.

REFERENCES

Ball, D.W. 1967. "An Abortion Clinic Ethnography." *Social Problems* 14(Winter):293-301.

Conrad, P., and J.W. Schneider. 1980. *Deviance and Medicalization: From Badness to Sickness.* Columbus, OH: Merrill.

Detlefs, M. 1984. *Abortion Counseling: A Description of the Current Status of the Occupation Reported by Seventeen Abortion Counselors in Metropolitan New York.* Unpublished Master's Thesis. Graduate Center, City University of New York.

Fee, E., ed. 1983. *Women and Health: The Politics of Sex in Medicine.* Farmingdale, NY: Baywood.

Freidson, E. 1986. *Professional Powers.* Chicago, IL: University of Chicago Press.

Garfinkel, H. 1967. *Studies in Ethnomethodology.* New York: Polity Press.

Gordon, L. 1974. *Woman's Body, Woman's Right: A Social History of Birth Control in America.* New York: Penguin.

Hughes, E.C. 1971. *The Sociological Eye. Selected Papers.* Chicago: Aldine.

Joffe, C. 1986. *The Regulation of Sexuality: Experiences of Family Planning Workers.* Philadelphia, PA: Temple University Press.

Lipsky, M. 1980. *Street-Level Bureaucracy: Dilemmas of the Individual in Public Services.* New York: Russell Sage Foundation.

Luker, K. 1975. *Taking Chances: Abortion and the Decision Not to Contracept.* Berkeley: University of California Press.

Mishler, E.G. 1984. *The Discourse of Medicine: Dialectics of Medical Interviews.* Norwood, NJ: Ablex.

Riessman, C.K., and C.A. Nathanson. 1986. "The Management of Reproduction: Social Construction of Risk and Responsibility." Pp. 251-281 in *Applications of Social Science to Clinical Medicine and Health Policy,"* edited by L.H. Aiken and D. Mechanic. New Brunswick, NJ: Rutgers University Press.

Rothman, B.K. 1982. *Giving Birth: Alternatives in Childbirth.* New York: Penguin.

———. 1986. *The Tentative Pregnancy: Prenatal Diagnosis and the Future of Motherhood.* New York: W.W. Norton.

Ruzek, S.B. 1978. *The Women's Health Movement: Feminist Alternatives to Medical Control.* New York: Praeger.

TEXT, SOCIAL CONTEXT, AND THE STRUCTURE OF MEDICAL DISCOURSE

Howard Waitzkin

ABSTRACT

Focusing on how patients and doctors deal with contextual problems, this paper asks if medical discourse can be read as a text and whether it conveys a typical underlying structure. Prior studies in conversation analysis and sociolinguistics have found that medical encounters contain common structural elements but have not emphasized enough the exclusion of social context from critical attention as a fundamental feature of medical language. Structuralist theories suggest that the surface meanings of signs in medical discourse are less important than their structural relationships. By effacing the boundary between literature and nonliterary texts, theoretical work in post-structuralism, deconstruction, and Marxist literary criticism also becomes useful in building a theory of medical discourse. The marginal, absent, or excluded elements of a text help clarify problems in the social context of discourse. While ideology and social control may appear at the margins of discourse, contextual features

Current Research on Occupations and Professions, Volume 6, pages 117-146.
Copyright © 1991 by JAI Press Inc.
ISBN: 1-55938-236-8

that shape a text include social class, sex, age, and race. Expressed marginally or conveyed by absence of criticism about contextual issues, ideology and social control in medical discourse remain largely unintentional mechanisms of achieving consent.

INTRODUCTION

The personal troubles that clients bring to health professionals often derive from social issues beyond medicine. In approaching a physician for help, a patient brings not only a physical problem but also a social context. This context includes relationships at work, in the family, and in the wider community. A patient's experience of physical problems is interconnected with the context within which physical problems occur. Pain and pathology are not pure experiences that trouble a person only at the somatic level. Instead, somatic processes are troublesome also as they affect and are affected by a person's general life experience. When patients and doctors talk with each other, their words have much to do with the social context in which they find themselves.

I have examined the linkages between medical discourse, on the "micro" level of interaction, and "macro"-level issues in the social context of professional-client communication (see Waitzkin 1989). Medical discourse frequently conveys ideologic messages supportive of the current social order, communication in medical encounters contributes to social control, and medical language tends to exclude criticism of the social context. Further, similar patterns may arise more generally as clients and the members of other "helping" professions—such as law, psychology, and social work—communicate with one another.

Can medical discourse be read as a text? Does it convey a typical underlying structure? How patients and doctors deal with contextual problems is a focus of this analysis. The first section presents a critical account of prior attempts in conversation analysis and sociolinguistics to study medical discourse. The second section offers a new theoretical approach to medical discourse, influenced by certain aspects of structuralist and post-structuralist literary criticism. In this effort, I search out a deeper structure in discourse that may have little to do with patients' and professionals' conscious thoughts about what they are saying and doing.

THE LANGUAGE OF MEDICAL ENCOUNTERS

Several studies of communication in medicine have suggested that medical encounters contain common structural features. For instance, in a sociolinguistic analysis of doctor-patient conversations, West (1984) has found typical "troubles" that arise in encounters. When patients express concerns about events in their lives that are not amenable to doctors' technical intervention, West argues, questions and interruptions are mechanisms by which doctors steer patients' concerns back to a technical track. As West notes, other studies also have observed that doctors interrupt patients frequently and initiate more questions than patients do (Beckman and Frankel 1984; Frankel 1986). In West's tape-recorded sample of medical interactions, male doctors tended to interrupt patients more often than did female doctors. West interprets interruptions and frequent questioning as gestures of dominance, by which doctors control the flow of conversation. She also postulates a connection between social power and sexual differences in language use, in conversations generally and more specifically in professional-client encounters.

By questioning, interrupting, and otherwise shifting the direction of conversation from nontechnical problems to technical ones, doctors *exclude* certain topics from talk and *include* others. Of particular interest here are the verbal techniques that divert attention from sources of personal distress in the social context. Such techniques may cut off the possibility of considering the context critically, let alone changing it. How medical encounters convey ideologic messages, and how they invoke social control, sometimes may involve doctors' explicit pronouncements about what patients should or should not do. It is also likely that ideology and social control emerge from what doctors and patients exclude from their talk, and how it comes to be excluded.

In another study of medical encounters, Mishler (1984) demonstrates how medical discourse cuts off contextual issues and redirects the focus to technical concerns. Mishler presents detailed transcripts from recordings of doctor-patient communication (Waitzkin 1985) and describes two "voices" that compete with each other. The "voice of medicine" involves the technical topics (of physiology, pathology, pharmacology, and so forth) which concern doctors in their professional work. Alternatively, the "voice of the lifeworld" comprises the everyday, largely nontechnical problems that patients carry with them into the medical encounter. For instance, Mishler analyzes an encounter in which the patient raises lifeworld concerns about marriage, work and unemployment, and drinking, while the doctor continues to return the conversation to technical aspects of the patient's gastrointestinal symptoms.

According to Mishler's analysis of transcripts, patients often try to raise contextual issues through the voice of the lifeworld. Doctors, however, are ill-equipped to deal with such issues and therefore repeatedly return to the voice of medicine. For instance, patients may raise personal troubles that do not pertain to technical problems. Or, although related to technical problems, these personal troubles may not seem amenable to technical solutions. Or, the raising of personal troubles may lead to discomfort for the professional, the client, or both. Under these circumstances, doctors typically introject questions, interrupt, or otherwise change the topic, to return to the voice of medicine.

While Mishler's approach conveys how medical language encourages the saying of some things and the leaving unsaid of others, the "lifeworld" remains rather general. Mishler implies that patients' concerns about contextual issues in the lifeworld are very important to them and that cutting off these concerns is undesirable. When the voice of medicine gains sway, however, this achievement also has much to do with ideology and social control. That is, in diverting critical attention away from the lifeworld, doctors may subtly reinforce ideologies that pattern the lifeworld and may help win acquiescence to those features of the lifeworld that patients find most disconcerting. In short, a re-reading of Mishler's materials might emphasize that the voice of medicine not only tends to suppress the voice of the lifeworld but also reinforces the orderliness of the lifeworld in its present form.

Class differences in language use help pattern the ways that professionals and clients deal with, or exclude from verbal consideration, the social roots of personal troubles. Predictably, within the medical encounter, the linguistic performance of working-class patients may not lend itself to developing verbally such linkages between individual distress and social issues. Because of class-based sociolinguistic differences, working-class patients tend to take little verbal initiative in questioning and directing doctors' attention to sources of suffering in the social context. Working-class patients also are less likely than middle-class clients to raise verbal disagreement with physicians who hold a higher class position (Waitzkin 1985; Waitzkin and Stoeckle 1972). From a sociolinguistic perspective, then, the patterning of medical discourse varies, depending partly on the class positions of the participants.

What is left silent, unsaid, or hidden in medical encounters has fascinated other researchers, who have interpreted rich textual materials but with little or no contextual theory. For instance, Katz (1984) provides an extensive account of the "silent world" of the doctor-patient relationship. He shows how medical language overlooks or downplays some important features of doctors' and patients' experience. Thus, Katz argues, doctors tend to gloss over their patients' concerns, and patients tend to leave these concerns unsaid. In Katz's account, doctors and patients remain silent about many topics, but especially those that would require patients' informed consent. Similarly, Cassell (1985) interprets the confusions, misunderstandings, insensitivities, and communication lapses in transcripts of doctor-patient interaction. He reiterates a viewpoint frequently expressed, that doctors in training should learn better communication skills to avoid such gaffes in practice.

Commenting on the unsaid socioemotional content of medical encounters, Cassell urges that health practitioners pay more attention to what is excluded from conversation, as well as the reasons why.

These accounts of the unsaid in medical language do not emphasize enough the pertinence of the unsaid for the context of professional encounters. Doctors do not simply overlook or downplay or suppress patients' contextual concerns. The exclusion of social context from critical attention is a fundamental feature of medical language. Inattention to social issues, especially when these issues lie behind patients' personal troubles, can never be just a matter of professional inadequacy, or the inadequacy of professional training. Instead, this *lack* is a basic part of what medicine *is* in our society.

APPROACHES TO MEDICAL DISCOURSE FROM STRUCTURALISM

Structuralist theories can help in any search for deeper structures that lie within the more obvious meanings of discourse. Whereas a structural approach will be adapted to help explain how medical discourse deals with social issues, I also want to clarify at the outset two points about my selective use of structuralism.

First, by seeking an underlying structure in medical discourse, I am arguing that this structure manifests itself in a substantial number of doctor-patient encounters at a specific place and time in history: the United States and probably certain other advanced capitalist countries during the late twentieth century. I am not arguing, as some structuralists might, that a similar structure arises as a universal feature of medical discourse at all times and places. In other social contexts, different structures of medical discourse predictably become apparent, and the current structure might well change in the future. Because the structure of medical discourse is viewed as an historically specific pattern, I want to avoid a quest for universal, invariant, or essential structures— a quest for which structuralism has received wide criticism. By acknowledging the possibility of, and in fact hoping for, change in the structure that I describe, I accept the common post-structuralist argument that no deep structure continues to exist (or to remain, as it were, "ontologically grounded") in all historical circumstances. On the other hand, I try to show how a characteristic structure does emerge in the medical discourse that confronts many of us during the current period of history.

Second, the structure of medical discourse does not emerge in the abstractions of language alone, but rather within the concrete interactions of individuals who deal with specific material conditions in the here and now. From this view, medical discourse does not occur as an isolated phenomenon of language, as it might be seen by at least some traditional structuralists, but rather within a social context. As a micro-level process, doctor-patient communication reflects macro-level patterns in a given society and also cumulatively helps reproduce those patterns. While other research on medical discourse (for instance, in conversation analysis and sociolinguistics) has looked for structures in interpersonal speech, the links between micro-level speech and macro-level patterns of society often have remained ambiguous. Further, in seeking these structures, such studies generally have not tried to apply structuralist theories to doctor-patient communication. By adapting some features of structuralism to medical discourse, my arguments are based on concrete instances of interpersonal interaction, involving patients and doctors who face the material conditions of everyday life.

Among the rich and controversial contributions of structuralism, the most important involve a search for underlying structure beneath the diverse surface details of interpersonal discourse. In structuralist thought, this quest for underlying structure began with linguistic research concerning the nature of language itself but later extended to studies of literature and eventually to nonliterary discourse. As background for my own later attempt to locate a structure that links medical discourse with its social context, certain structuralist accounts of language, literature, and nonliterary elements of culture become pertinent.

Structural linguistics treats language as a system of signs in structural relationship among each other. From this viewpoint, a sign contains two components: a signifier, which is its sound or graphic equivalent in writing, and a signified, which is its meaning in structural relation to other signs. Saussure ([1915] 1986), the founder of structural linguistics, argued that *langue,* the underlying structure of signs that makes speech possible, is much more important for an understanding of language than is *parole,* which consists of actual speech. From a Saussurian perspective, medical discourse involves a system of signs whose surface meanings prove less important than their structural relationships among one another. For instance, it is revealing to look behind such signs in the clinical history, physical examination, and so forth to locate an underlying structure that goes beyond the words exchanged by a particular doctor and a particular patient.

A similar search for structure emerges in literary criticism influenced by structuralism. The structural analysis of literature seeks constancy of structure amid a great diversity of texts. Among structuralist critics like Jakobson (1985), for instance, the surface meanings of particular poems, stories, novels, and folktales hold interest—no matter how intriguing in their separateness—mostly insofar as they manifest common structural elements. Further, these underlying structures are usually unconscious, intuitive, or "subliminal." Thus, a writer or artist rarely recognizes on a conscious level the structure that a creative product manifests. From this viewpoint, a writer or artist expresses these structures through a creative process whose rules, though socially learned, usually remain below the level of conscious intentionality.

Seen in this theoretical perspective, the verbal elements of medical encounters predictably reveal common structural elements that appear within a diversity of surface meanings. That is, while doctors and patients converse about many topics and express a wide spectrum of concerns, a structuralist critic would see a smaller number of structures that cut across many superficial differences among encounters. Further, from Jakobson's viewpoint, participants in medical encounters most likely would not perceive these structures consciously. Instead, commonalities of structure would emerge for the most part unintentionally in discourse, without doctors' or patients' conscious awareness.

Beyond linguistics and literary criticism, structuralist analysis also has extended to nonliterary elements of culture; this line of work, I will argue, also pertains to medical discourse. In anthropology, for example, Lévi-Strauss (1967) looks at the structural relationships among elements of culture, including language, magic, religion, art, kinship, and myth. By grouping these elements into structural units, Lévi-Strauss uncovers commonalities that appear within many different types of cultural expression. In his reading of myth, Lévi-Strauss (1967) uses a two-dimensional scheme of categorizing binary oppositions. The surface elements of the myths appear on the horizontal axis; the structural "features" then emerge through interpretive grouping on the vertical axis (pp. 209-212). Lévi-Strauss (1961, 1969) applies this approach to explain different versions of the Oedipus myth, the Zuni origin and emergence myths (which themselves strikingly resemble the Oedipus myth), the Ash-Boy and Cinderella tales, and eventually other forms of cultural expression such as science, art, dress, and food preferences. By recognizing both the similarities and differences among the versions, and by allowing some "simplifications," Lévi-Strauss claims that the reader then can clarify a unifying structure despite wide surface variations.

While medical discourse is not exactly mythic, or even literary, it does comprise a series of surface elements whose underlying structure might become apparent through a similar kind of reading. Lévi-Strauss (1967, pp. 181-201) confronts medical discourse as he interprets a South American song that a shaman sings to facilitate a woman's difficult childbirth. The song's therapeutic impact, to which Lévi-Strauss refers as "the effectiveness of symbols," arises from the verbalization and bringing to consciousness of previously unconscious conflicts and resistances. In this sense, he claims, the shamanistic cure compares favorably with psychoanalytic technique. Although Lévi-Strauss' structural analysis of ethnomedical discourse explores a confluence between primitive and psychoanalytic "myth," he does not try to navigate the more humdrum texts of modern medicine.

That is the next destination. To get there, we need to look more closely at the flow of medical talk. While a structuralist compass might help to see what is present in medical discourse, other theoretical scopes are useful to find what is absent and why what is absent might have import.

APPROACHES TO MEDICAL DISCOURSE FROM POST-STRUCTURALISM, DECONSTRUCTION, AND MARXIST LITERARY THEORY

Reading Nonliterary Texts

I will contend that both structuralist techniques and techniques of "deconstruction"—perhaps the hallmark of the post-structuralist period—can help in understanding medical discourse. As already noted, such an approach takes into account the much discussed weaknesses of structuralism by looking for underlying structures as historically specific parts of current medical discourse, rather than as universal or invariant structures. The approach also addresses the weaknesses of sociolinguistics, conversation analysis, and discourse analysis in the social sciences, by emphasizing elements of social context and how they come to be excluded or marginalized.

Literary theory of the past two decades has effaced the boundary between literature and nonliterary discourse as targets for critical interpretation. That the tools of literary criticism can and should be brought to nonliterary texts has become a frequent call among critical theorists. Derrida (1987a, 1987b), for instance, has deconstructed texts like love letters and art reviews, which bear little resemblance to what traditionally has been labeled literature even though they still involve mainly written materials. Barthes (1977, 1982) has attended critically to photography, film, sports, and theater, in addition to more traditional written texts. These efforts begin to move beyond literature in the traditional sense as a focus of critical theory.

Influenced by deconstruction, post-structuralist thought, and Marxist analysis, some literary critics and sociologists also have argued that nonliterary texts are quite appropriate for critical reading. From this view, television programs, popular romances, films, advertisements, and public policy statements in such areas as law, housing, and health care all merit attention, especially as they reinforce current patterns of political-economic power. (For statements of this perspective in literary criticism, see Eagleton [1983]; Frow [1986]; Jameson [1981]; Ohmann [1987]; Ryan [1982]; and Sumner [1979]. A similar argument for applying literary theory to sociologic phenomena appears in Giddens [1986].) Unfortunately, such calls for critical work on nonliterary texts—like those of medical encounters—to illuminate social problems often appear toward the end of critical studies of literary texts, with little indication of how such efforts might proceed.

In the pages that follow, then, I will use an expansive definition of a text. Specifically, a text is a written or spoken unit of language that is available for appraisal by one or more observers. This definition assumes that a critical analysis of nonliterary, spoken texts is both acceptable and desirable. The texts to be considered are those of spoken medical discourse in actual encounters between doctors and patients.

Margin, Context, and Ideology

Deconstruction, among its goals, tries to clarify what is *marginal, absent,* or *excluded* from a text. While deconstruction has mainly studied the margins of philosophy and literature, this approach also can help bring into focus what does and does not happen in the spoken discourse of medical encounters.

In emphasizing what is strategically excluded from or marginalized within a text, deconstruction holds that the absence or deemphasis of one or more elements is key in trying to interpret a text critically. According to Derrida (1982), for instance, such elements often appear at the margin of a text, within passages that superficially seem tangential, extraneous, unessential, or otherwise unimportant. Yet these same elements, Derrida argues, tend to break down the explicit principles by which the text is organized. Studying the margin then becomes a way, perhaps the best way, to study a text. Where is the appropriate margin to study for a given text? Derrida refers to elements of history, politics, economy, sexuality, and so forth, as constituents of a text's margin. In short, a critical reading of a text may find many marginal elements, and these elements are likely to reflect the text's *social context.* Derrida's readings through a wide range of philosophical, literary, and anthropologic texts have shed light on contextual concerns that appear at the margins, expressed by de-emphasis, by absence, or by exclusion.

A text, then, tends to break down at its margins, facing tensions, incompatibilities, and contradictions between itself and its social context. While Derrida—ever mindful that his own texts are subject to deconstruction—is reluctant for theoretical reasons to voice calls to action, Marxist critics influenced by him have argued that the search for elements of social context in the margins should be an essential task for critical theory. Jameson (1981), for instance, has suggested that criticism properly should elucidate the social contradictions which are "absent causes" underlying a given text. This search involves a close reading of the inconsistencies, the breaks in logic, the interruptions, the overlooked, the ignored, and the otherwise absent though pertinent components that a text either expresses or might express. Accordingly, it is at the margin between text and social context that criticism finds its most fertile ground. This productive space presumably exists no less in nonliterary, spoken discourse than it does in more traditional literary or philosophic texts.

Ideology predictably appears at the margins of discourse, including nonliterary discourse like that of medicine. While difficult to define simply, ideology is an interlocking set of ideas and doctrines that form the distinctive perspective of a social group. Through such ideas and doctrines, ideology represents—on an imaginary level—individuals' relationship to the real conditions of their existence (Waitzkin 1989; cf. Althusser 1971, pp. 162-165). How and to what extent is ideology transmitted in medical discourse? It is likely that ideologic notions about work, the family, and other parts of the social context arise subtly if they are voiced at all. Further, ideology may manifest itself by lack of explicit discussion of alternatives to the present, or by a deemphasis of contextual problems, or by absence of critical attention to such problems.

The apparent absence of explicit ideologic statements in discourse becomes an important mechanism by which ideology is reproduced. Eagleton (1978), a Marxist critic influenced by deconstruction, states this point, as applied to literary texts:

> Ideology, rather, so produces and constructs the real as to cast the shadow of its absence over the perception of its presence . . . . These absences—the *'not-said'* of the work—are precisely what bind it to its ideological problematic: ideology is present in the text in the form of its eloquent silences (pp. 69, 89, emphasis in original).

Eagleton applies this perspective to interpret the underlying ideologies of literary texts by examining what alternatives remain unsaid. Further, he argues that the illumination of textual absence is one of literary criticism's most challenging tasks. There is ample reason to extend this perspective to nonliterary texts as well. In doing so, it is reasonable to expect—for instance, in medical discourse—that ideology presents itself explicitly at certain times, but more often through the absence of key themes that are unspoken or referred to in a marginal way.

To understand the ideologic components of discourse, however, depends on seeing the relationships between discourse and its social context; as Bakhtin (1973, 1981), Jameson (1971, 1981), and other Marxist literary critics have argued, social class is a key contextual element that shapes the ideologic content of discourse. To state what probably is already obvious: relationships of social class are crucial parts of the context in which discourse arises and in which ideology is transmitted. From this contextual viewpoint, a dominant ideology conveyed through discourse tends to legitimate the position of whatever class holds power during a given historical period. Discourse, according to Jameson (1981), frequently is the scene of a subtle struggle between this dominant ideology and an oppositional ideology that "will, often in covert and disguised strategies, seek to contest and to undermine the dominant 'value system'" (pp. 84-85).

In the nonliterary discourse of face-to-face speech, social class also becomes a critical contextual element that shapes the transmission of ideology. Returning to the problematic of medical discourse: To the extent that doctors and patients occupy different class positions, class predictably helps pattern the ideologic content of their discourse. Doctors, for instance, may explicitly voice ideologic messages that legitimate the current class structure of society; or the transmission of ideology may occur more subtly, conveyed by the absence of criticism about class structure and its various injuries. In medical encounters, marginalization may affect an oppositional voice, perhaps that of a patient in distress, through interruption, cut-off, or deemphasis. This way of looking at medical discourse provides a slightly different theoretical prism to see the same problems uncovered by sociolinguists who observe a "diffidence" of working-class patients in medical encounters, or who note contention between the "voice of medicine" and the "voice of the life-world" (Waitzkin 1989; Mishler 1984). Such observations find that social class relations, as an element of context, pattern ideology within discourse.

But social class is not the only contextual element that affects discourse; other crucial elements include gender, age, and race. All these contextual elements can become the basis of dominance and subordination, and they are closely linked to social class. Ideologies of gender pertain in large part to the roles men and women occupy in the family and at work. Through ideologies of gender, expectations about what men and women appropriately should and should not do enter everyday language. Arising in the context of discourse, these ideologies profoundly affect what is or can be said, what appears at the center of discourse, and what slips in at the margins. Similarly, as people age, they encounter a changing set of expectations and demands, which vary a great deal among societies. In the United States, for instance, ideologies of aging can convey the image of a trash heap, where elderly people actually or symbolically move when their productivity, or reproductivity, is used up. Other societies tend to be more lenient, or even respectful, in ideologies of aging. Ideologies of race have entered discourse, whenever societies have encountered the contrast between majority and minority groups. Expressions of racial ideologies have ranged from the master-slave vernacular to the only slightly more subtle versions of modernity.

Why highlight these contextual elements here? Class, gender, age, and race are some of the contextual elements that pattern ideologic language in face-to-face discourse, like that of medicine. It is not enough to acknowledge that ideology may be reproduced in medical discourse; the question is how this happens. That is, in concrete examples of discourse, the critical reader needs to seek specific places where ideologic reproduction occurs, and where context impinges on discourse. From structuralism, one expects that these places may become apparent as part of an underlying structure, that is not obvious or consciously appreciated in surface meanings. From post-structuralism and deconstruction, one expects that such a structure is an historically specific one, contingent on a certain social context and changeable in other contexts; and also that ideology and context make themselves felt, at least partly, in the margins of discourse—in what is left unsaid, interrupted, cut off, or deemphasized.

Unintentionality, Consent, and Social Control

As noted already, the transmission of ideology is a subtle process, rarely reaching the consciousness of the participants in medical discourse, but their unintentionality goes beyond the level of individuals engaged in discourse. Jameson (1981) argues that a *political unconscious,* embedded in language, patterns the discourse of everyday life. The political unconscious, according to Jameson, shapes discourse particularly through "strategies of containment," which subtly express only a narrow range of possibilities for action, while repressing others. Specifically, these strategies within discourse repress the possibility of alternatives, such as collective action, that would fundamentally change present social organization. By leaving such alternatives unsaid, Jameson claims, strategies of containment also help make these alternatives unthinkable. That is, while ideology is conveyed by an absence of criticism, possibilities for change become drastically constricted, to the extent that they remain unexpressed in discourse. By mechanisms such as leaving alternatives unsaid and thus marginalized, Jameson argues, the most profound historical, social, and political impulses can be "managed."

The management of social issues in medical discourse also contributes to social control, which refers to the mechanisms that achieve people's adherence to norms of appropriate behavior. In medicine, ideology and social control are closely related. To the extent that doctors transmit ideologic messages which reinforce current social patterns—at work, in the family, and in other areas of life—they help control behavior in ways that are defined as socially appropriate (Waitzkin 1989). Social control in medicine also involves unconscious strategies of containment, in Jameson's terms, that express a narrow range of possibilities for change while repressing alternatives such as collective action.

Dealing with problems outside the limited realm of technical medicine tends to "medicalize" a wide range of psychological, social, economic, and political problems. Historically, numerous areas gradually have fallen under medical control. Examples include sexuality and family life, work dissatisfaction, problems of the life cycle (including birth, adolescence, aging, dying, and death), difficulties in the educational system (learning disabilities, maladjustment, and students' psychological distress), criminality, and many other fields. By participating in these areas, practitioners may believe that they are extending the caring function of the medical role. However, medicalization has emerged as the object of a critique that focuses on health professionals' expanding role in social control. As medical management of social problems has increased, the societal roots of personal troubles have become less apparent. That is, by responding in limited ways to some of patients' nontechnical problems, medical practitioners tend to shift the focus of attention from societal issues to the troubles of individuals (Conrad and Schneider 1980; Fox 1977; Zola 1983, pp. 243-296). Crucial features of medicalization include inattention to societal causes of individuals troubles and the exclusion of alternatives that involve broader social change.

The largely unconscious ways that social control and the transmission of ideology occur in medicine again point to the subtlety of these processes. Within medical discourse, ideology may appear implicitly more than explicitly— through structural relations within language and through absence rather than direct ideologic manipulation. Similarly, social control achieves its impact mainly through absence of key alternatives and through marginalization of certain concerns, rather than through specific controlling statements. Such subtle mechanisms in discourse may help achieve consent to current ways of organizing society.

On the other hand, the participants in medical discourse also gain substantial gratifications that can overshadow in consciousness whatever ideologic reproduction and social control occurs. All that doctors have to offer contributes to the gratification that patients experience in medical encounters. These offerings include technical intervention, advice, emotional support expressed through words, emotional support expressed nonverbally through the laying on of hands, and so forth. Further, doctors obtain innumerable sources of gratification from interacting with patients. Among other things, these rewards include experience of technical mastery, money, prestige, gratitude, and the pleasing though complex sensations of helping those in need. It would be a great mistake to underestimate such gratifications, since they comprise so much of the conscious experience of medical encounters. Yet these undeniable gratifications of medical discourse also tend to obscure its less pleasurable and much less obvious characteristics. (For an analysis of similar gratifications in the "lived experience" of the labor process that help achieve consent, see Burawoy [1979].)

That medical discourse becomes consciously pleasing to its participants while it helps achieve consent through ideologic language should come as no surprise, since much of modern culture operates in similar ways. During recent decades, such dubious cultural achievements have disconcerted many commentators, who have noted the ideologic and controlling effects of the mass media, art, film, music, literature, and science. Meanwhile, all these cultural forms have achieved wide popular enthusiasm (Jameson 1981; see also Horkheimer and Adorno 1982; Marcuse 1964). Similarly, professional-client discourse provides keenly felt gratifications, which mask elements of ideology and social control that are present on a deeper level.

The subtle yet powerful ways that the political unconscious operates in discourse lead to what seems a discouraging view. If problems of context present themselves marginally or through absence, and if the participants in discourse are mainly unaware of elements that reproduce ideology and achieve social control, the potentialities of language become rather drab and unappealing. Even the task of bringing these matters to awareness takes on an aura of futility. As Eagleton (1983, pp. 186-187) has written, such a perspective leaves us "in the grip of ideology, conforming to social reality as 'natural' rather than critically questioning how it, and ourselves, came to be constructed, and so could possibly be transformed." For instance, is the clarification of ideologic reproduction and social control in actually spoken medical texts worthwhile? Are such problems and processes pervasive enough that they cannot be modified or improved upon?

Critical theorists vary widely in their opinion of their work's social import. Practically oriented theorists—usually influenced by characteristically Marxist concerns—do hope to help bring about change in society, especially to the extent that current forms of social organization cause or maintain human suffering. This approach to politically engaged criticism links the analysis of discourse to collective political action. From this viewpoint, the critical theorist's "praxis"—his or her attempt to unite theory with concrete practice—aims toward basic change in the contradictory social context in which discourse occurs (Jameson 1981; Eagleton 1983). The critic therefore analyzes discourse and points out the troubling vicissitudes in the relation between discourse and social context. But one goal of this analytic effort usually involves making a contribution to change in the social context itself.

TWO MEDICAL ENCOUNTERS

Now let me turn to two actual doctor-patient encounters. Transcripts of these encounters were prepared as part of a large study of doctor-patient communication that involved random sampling from private practices and hospital outpatient departments; methodologic details about the sampling procedures and transcript preparation are reported elsewhere (Waitzkin 1985, 1989). These encounters illustrate typical patterns in the sampled interactions, as doctors and patients deal with personal troubles that derive largely from broader contextual issues (cf. Mills 1959, pp. 3-24). For each encounter, a brief summary appears first. Some information about the participants' personal backgrounds then follows; data about the doctors and patients derive from questionnaires that they answered after their interactions were recorded. Next, I interpret the encounter, using excerpts from the transcript for substantiation. (Full transcripts are available on request.) As a heuristic tool, a schematic figure is presented for each encounter that gives a visual picture of the proposed structure.

Returning to Work After a Heart Attack

A man comes to his doctor several months after a heart attack. He is depressed. His period of disability payments will expire soon, and his union is about to go on strike. In response, the doctor tells him that he is physically able to return to work and that working will be good for his mental health. The doctor also prescribes an antidepressant and a tranquilizer.

Here is some information about the participants in this encounter. The patient is a 55-year-old white male high school graduate who works as a radial drill operator. He is Protestant, Irish, married, and the father of an 18-year-old child. There is no information available about the patient's wife, who accompanies him during part of the encounter. The doctor is a 38-year-old white male specializing in internal medicine and gastroenterology. He is Protestant and states that his ethnic background is English. The doctor has known the patient for five and one-half years and believes that the primary diagnoses are "coronary artery disease" and "severe recurrent depression." The encounter takes place in a private practice near Boston.

The patient's role in economic production becomes a focus of this encounter. Asking about the patient's work situation early in the interaction, the doctor needs to be reminded that the patient has not returned to work after his heart attack (lines 74-100):

74	Doctor:	How are things coming at work?
75	Wife:	He hasn't been to work yet.
76	Patient:	Well they, you know, they prolonged it, they've
77		extended the contract for 10 days.
78	D:	Yeah.
79	P:	Which is a good sign.
80	D:	Yeah.
81	P:	From what I heard that's a good sign.
82	D:	So when would you be able to, when would they be
83		ready to go if they approve a contract?
84	P:	Oh, it'd probably be, well the contract runs out
85		the 26th.
86	D:	Of this month, that's this Saturday.
87	P:	That's this Saturday.
88	D:	And it's prolonged . . .
89	P:	It'll be a week and a half.
90	D:	Yeah, so if they arrange something, they'll know if
91		by mid-June.
92	P:	They should.
93	D:	Is that bugging you? The idea of going back to work?

94   P: Well . . . actually I think I want to go back.
95   D: Yeah, I think you should go back.
96   P: Actually I think I want to go back, but then go back
97   and go on strike? That seems to bother me.
98   D: Yeah. But if you go back mid-June it won't,
99   won't bother you.
100   P: No . . . .

After this long pause, several interrelated issues then arise. First, although details are incomplete, it is clear that the patient is receiving disability payments, apparently because of his heart disease. The doctor previously has certified that this disability would end by a specific date (lines 118-126):

116   D: Just strip down to your waist, Mr. ____.
117   ((door opens and closes))
118   D: ((to wife)) What did I say on that form last time,
119   I don't remember. Did I say first of June? For
120   returning to work.
121   W: On one of the forms you did, you said the first
122   of June . . .
123   D: I thought that's what we decided on, the first
124   of June . . .
125   W: We thought perhaps he could go back, yeah,
126   around the first.

A second problem is an impending strike that the patient anticipates may begin shortly after the disability period ends (lines 96-97). The patient worries about a potential scenario in which his disability payments stop, he goes back to work, but then he must go out on strike, thus losing income. Perhaps because the patient does not elaborate, the doctor does not acknowledge this issue explicitly. Instead, he focuses on a third concern, the postulated association between the client's emotional distress and unemployment. According to the doctor, the patient's depression will become worse if he does not return to work (lines 127-131):

127   D: I think he's gotta go back.
128   W: He is, I told him
                                    [
129   D: I tell you if this guy stays
130   home, he's going to curl up in a ball, you know, he's gonna
131   be unreachable.

Later the physician reiterates his view that getting back to work will prove beneficial (lines 173-179):

173 D: I'll check the cardiogram. I would think that
174   maybe we would plan on getting you back, say
175   mid-June, you know, to work, which I think is
176   the *best* thing in the world for you, to get
177   back to work. Your heart's strong enough, your
178   blood pressure's good, there's no reason why we
179   can't get you back in the middle of things.

Whether the doctor is oblivious to the financial problems that may arise if the patient returns before the strike, or whether he consciously chooses to ignore the issue, remains unclear. The overall implication is that working is good for this patient specifically and perhaps for workers in general. In this sense, health is subtly defined as the capacity to work.

This passage illustrates social control over labor, and the transmission of ideologic messages about work, at the level of the doctor-patient relationship. The doctor controls this working-class patient's role in economic production by withholding the continued certification of illness. Despite some attempts to communicate concern about the timing of his return to work, the patient does not participate actively in this decision. With benevolence, the doctor expropriates the decision-making process regarding both health and work. The patient explicitly states that returning to work in the face of an impending strike "seems to bother me." The doctor invalidates this concern and implies that the strike will be settled by "mid-June," although he could not know this with any certainty. If the patient returns by mid-June, the doctor argues, "it . . . won't bother you." The patient feebly replies, "No," after which a long pause occurs in the dialogue (lines 96-100).

Beyond the decertification of illness and loss of decision-making power, the patient receives a strong ideologic message that work is beneficial for his health. In many people's lives, work contributes to emotional stability and feelings of personal worth, even if work is alienating and conflictual. The point here, however, is that a professional assumes directive control over a worker's role in production. Despite the pressures of work and contract negotiations, the doctor argues, the patient will feel better, mentally and physically, if he is working than if he is idle.

While the patient remains quite concerned about the contextual issue of work and its discontents, the doctor marginalizes the social context by focusing on the patient's emotional disturbance, which then becomes amenable to technical intervention through drugs. The marginalization of social context by invoking psychiatric technology becomes apparent as the doctor abruptly shifts attention from the forthcoming strike to the need for psychotropic medication (lines 96-105):

96	P:	Actually I think I want to go back, but then go back
97		and go on strike? That seems to bother me.
98	D:	Yeah. But if you go back mid-June it won't,
99		won't bother you.
100	P:	No . . . .
101	D:	I think if you're going to take anything,
102		you ought to take the Mellaril. We ought to
103		maybe add some Elavil. 'Cause I think most of
104		your symptoms are depression and frustration
105		right now.

Mellaril is a medication for psychosis; Elavil is an antidepressant. The doctor shows these actors to the stage immediately after the patient voices concern about a script that dictates returning to work in the face of an impending strike.

In his verbal behavior, the patient gives no evidence of psychosis; his statements seem appropriate, grounded in reality, and without bizarre or incomprehensible features. On the other hand, the patient is clearly upset and perhaps suicidal, although he expresses his feelings laconically. One revelation is the patient's terse statement of suicidal thoughts:

48	D:	Uh, uh what are you taking for medication now?
49	P:	Well I don't know. I take Mellaril. Some days I take 4, I
50		take 6, I'm right at a point now I don't know if I should
51		take Mellaril, Librax
		[
52	W:	Librium
53	P:	um, Librium . . . or poison.
54	D:	You're just all wound up now . . . . You want to take poison?
55	P:	Jeepers I don't know what, I don't know what to take. I'm right
56		at a point now, I don't know what would do any good.

This danger signal about poison leads to two brief questions by the doctor, apparently intended to assess the patient's suicide potential. Quickly, however, the issue of suicide disappears from the conversation, as the doctor refocuses attention on medications.

The doctor does not attempt to explore the patient's distress in depth. Instead, two professional interventions occur, neither of which encourages the patient to seek the roots of his depression in psychodynamics or in the social environment. First, the doctor offers technologic assistance in the form of drugs. To manage the patient's emotional problems, the doctor uses polypharmacy—a variety of medications without clearcut pharmacologic rationale. Prescriptions include: (a) Mellaril, a major tranquilizer whose indication is schizophrenia or other serious psychosis; (b) Librium, a minor tranquilizer intended for relief of anxiety and/or neurosis; (c) Librax, a combination of Librium and an antispasmotic for emotion-related gastrointestinal disturbances; and (d) Elavil, an antidepressant (lines 48-68, 101-111, 165-172, 194-199). The literature of psychopharmacology sheds doubt on the usefulness of any of these agents for this patient, whose distress seems to derive in large part from the social situation, especially work, and from concern about heart disease. Moreover, when suicide is a possibility, the danger of overdose from these drugs, especially in combination, is severe (Baldessarini 1985). Despite these quibbles, the point here is not to criticize the doctor's medical judgment but instead is to see how this judgment communicates an ideologic message. Specifically, polypharmacy converts a socioemotional problem to a technical one. Drug treatment objectifies a complex series of psychologic and social questions. Symbolically, scientific medicine shifts the focus to the physical realm, depoliticizes the social structural issues involved, and mutes the potential for action by the patient to change the conditions that trouble him.

A second intervention concerning emotional distress involves the medicalization of work. A rosy picture of work's psychic benefits diverts attention from its physical, socioemotional, and economic hazards. The patient voices concern (though not too articulately) about these hazards, but the doctor portrays idleness as a root of psychic disaster and re-employment as a mode of adjustment if not cure. Voiced with the authority of medical science, this ideologic message reproduces the worker's place in the relations of production. The professional's words convey the promise of happiness, or at least relative happiness, in work as currently organized.

Throughout the interaction, technical knowledge occupies a minor place, in comparison to the ideology and symbolism of scientific medicine. The doctor asks a few questions from the standpoint of cardiology (regarding chest pain, lines 27-32), inquires about the use of a cardiac medication (nitroglycerine, lines 62-66), discusses gauze and nail care (lines 140-155), performs a brief physical exam, and orders an electrocardiogram. Otherwise, it is difficult to find evidence in this encounter of scientific medicine per se. On the other hand, the doctor offers a series of pronouncements about work, leisure, and emotional difficulties. These utterances contain little or no scientific rationale, yet their impact derives from the symbolism of scientific knowledge and technique. In this sense, the professional assumes control over major areas of life inside and outside the medical realm.

What are the underlying structural elements of this encounter? (See Figure 1.) The contextual issue of greatest concern involves the patient's work (A). Depression is a personal trouble that the patient experiences, partly in anticipation of a return to uncertain employment (B). In the medical encounter (C), the patient expresses concern about returning to work while his union intends to go out on strike (D). The doctor, however, interrupts him or otherwise deemphasizes the patient's worries about what will face him when he returns to work (E). Instead of pursuing the contextual problem, the doctor reassures the patient and the patient's wife that work will affect his mental health in a beneficial direction. Moreover, the doctor uses the technical resources at his disposal to prescribe a tranquilizer and an antidepressant medication (F). After the patient leaves the encounter, he presumably continues to prepare himself for a return to work.

This discourse offers little technical information but many ideologic messages. Much of the communication mystifies the social roots of distress with the symbolism of scientific medicine, as the professional assumes decision-making control over wide areas of the patient's existence. In all this, the patient acquiesces. The doctor truly cares for the patient, the patient appreciates the doctor's concern, and for all the participants' conscious intents and purposes, this is probably an excellent doctor-patient relationship. That the encounter may reinforce social sources of discontent in the workplace escapes notice entirely. Such are the puzzling anomalies of a caring relationship between doctor and patient in this society.

Physical Difficulties in Housework

A woman visits her doctor because of irregularities in her heart rhythm. She complains that palpitations and shortness of breath are interfering with her

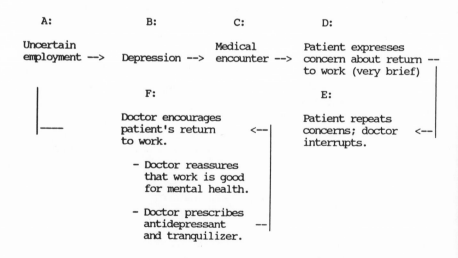

Figure 1. Structural Elements of Medical Encounter
With a Man Anticipating Return to Work After a Heart Attack

ability to do housework. The doctor checks an electrocardiogram while she exercises, changes her cardiac medications, and encourages her efforts to maintain a tidy household.

Some characteristics of the participants, known from the questionnaires that they filled out, are as follows. The patient is age 50, white, married, Roman Catholic, and "English-Irish-French" in ethnic background. She attended some college, has four children, and reports her occupation as "wife." The doctor is a 39-year-old man who practices general internal medicine. The encounter takes place in a Boston suburb. According to the doctor, the patient, whom he has known for five years, has "rheumatic heart disease with mitral insufficiency" and "menopausal syndrome."

A highly technical orientation distinguishes this encounter from the relatively nontechnical orientation of the last one. The patient suffers from rheumatic heart disease that affects principally the mitral valve. In the past she has endured episodes of congestive heart failure and irregularities of heart rhythm. She takes at least two cardiac medications: hydrochlorothiazide (Hydrodiuril) to reduce fluid accumulation and propranolol (Inderal) to control rhythm disturbances. Although the patient has been able to manage fairly well with limited physical exertion, her heart disease is serious enough that the doctor is contemplating heart surgery with valve replacement.

Much of the interaction deals with technical issues of diagnosis and treatment (lines 1-170, 235-467). The doctor asks questions about exercise tolerance, compliance with medication schedule, symptoms of heart failure (pain, shortness of breath, ankle swelling), menstrual symptoms, and ear symptoms. He does a partial physical exam and an electrocardiogram. He then spends considerable time explaining his notion about the relation between the patient's symptoms and her irregular heart rhythm. Since he apparently believes that her rhythm abnormality may have returned because she decided on her own to reduce her medication, he requests that she use the prescribed dose and check with him before making further changes.

The patient takes an active role in the technical discussion. When confused about the doctor's explanation or instruction, she asks frequent questions. The doctor confirms her competence, when she describes her reaction to digoxin, a cardiac medication (lines 340-347):

```
340   D:      The digoxin slowed you too much
                                              [
341   P:                                       Yeah. Except that
342           not that extreme. But it would just get very very
343           feathery and very very tired.
344   D:      Yeah, well I know you're sensitive and a good
345           observer, I
                      [
```

346   P: And when I cut it back to one, every-
347   thing seemed to be so much better

Despite this compliment, he suggests that she not modify her medications independently. That the patient does understand is clear from her response to a question in the interview after the medical encounter. The questionnaire asks: "Did Dr. __ say that anything was wrong with you? What did he say?" She replies: "Bigeminy [coupled extra heart beats] has returned with exercise. We will attempt to control it with increased medication." Regarding the technical basis of the encounter, the doctor seems eager to share full information with the patient and to encourage her autonomous participation. Although the doctor's professional knowledge remains a basis of asymmetry in the relationship, he communicates this knowledge in a straightforward way. He thus reduces the inherent inequality of the relationship and avoids domination in the encounter. Interestingly, these positive features of the interaction seem to stem in part from its focus on predominantly technical issues relating to the patient's physical illness.

Against this background, the messages of ideology and social control that the physician does convey are noteworthy. Although the interaction in this encounter appears very egalitarian, the overriding goal is still the client's adequate functioning in work: in this case, the occupation of "wife." The patient's physical symptoms are problematic mainly insofar as they interfere with this occupation. Exertion in housework triggers the patient's symptoms of irregular heart rhythm. This experience makes her unhappy and even guilty (lines 65-77):

65   P: But if you really feel my pulse, it's not uh,
66   it just seems like a normal pattern.
67   D: Is it fairly regular? Or does it seem to be skipping?
68   P: Well, if I'm doing anything at all, it gets irregular.
69   D: Mmm hmm.
70   P: I can cook the dinner and wash the clothes, but you
71   know, any sweeping, cleaning that I do, that kind of
72   sounds like an excuse, but it really isn't.
73   D: (laughs) Yeah. No, I . . .
74   P: It's just when I used to do it, like in 15 or 20 minute
75   intervals, and then sit and relax for five or 10 minutes,
76   then I could carry on. Now I can't do that. It's sort
77   of maddening,

The patient hopes for a way to improve her physical capacity to perform the labor that her household chores require.

At this point, the doctor has several options. He could try to explore and to ease the patient's guilty feelings about her physical limitations. Also, he could suggest alternative social arrangements, including greater division of labor in housework. Instead, he opts for a pharmacologic solution, increasing the dose and frequency of a medication to suppress irregularities in heart rhythm. He views this technical intervention as a desirable alternative in dealing with physical or emotional demands (lines 357-375):

```
357  D:      Yeah, well it seems that the irregularity is when
358          you place, you know, when there is either increased
359          tension or increased stimulation to your heart or
360          more demands on it because you're starting to work
361          more. And that
                         [
362  P:                     What worries me is that the demand
363          is such a little thing
                         [
364  D:                     Yes.
365  P:      That I, I cut out so many things, that you have to do.
366  D:      Oh, absolutely. And you see what we wanted you to do
367          is allow you to do those things without, without having
368          the tendency to the irregularities or the poundings,
369          and if we can suppress, you know, the intent of the
370          Inderal, uh, or propranolol, is to, it blocks, if you
371          will, some of the extra, you know, some of the extra
372          beats. So that when your heart is being pushed by
373          any sort of external or internal influence, this can
374          slow that down.
```

An extraordinary expression of this attitude is the doctor's encouraging comment as he instructs the patient to exercise more strenuously during the electrocardiogram (lines 271-279):

```
270  D:      ... I guess that showed it as being absolutely regular,
271          and what we'll do is, I'm just going to have you
272          exercise a little bit and let's just run the uh,
273          run the machine. OK. Could you do some sit-ups
274          for me? Just put it on, you're on lead two.
275  Nurse:  Yes.
276  D:      Just, do them a little bit faster. You can stop it
277          now and then. And, uh, OK. Just do about, uh,
278          try to get yourself a little bit short of breath . . .
279          Try it again . . . . Just scrub one more room.
```

Through this possibly humorous instruction, the doctor indicates that he is trying to replicate the physical demands of housework, so that the electrocardiogram can record any resulting rhythm abnormality. Presumably, the purpose here is to make technical adjustments, informed by scientific observations, so that the patient can keep on scrubbing.

The implicit ideologic message is that the woman's role in housework is worthwhile, desirable, and necessary. Again, alternatives remain ambiguous. It is hard to fault the doctor for seeing as his main task the optimization of the patient's physical capacity. Struggling against sexism perhaps would be too much to expect in such an encounter. Questioning or challenging the patient's work at home might upset her deeply; on some level, the doctor may be aware of this dilemma. Yet the doctor reinforces this woman's household activities, and even her troubled feelings about them. Such work by women is crucial in reproducing the relations of economic production. Here a well-intentioned doctor contributes to this socioeconomic arrangement. There is no critical appraisal of any aspect of the woman's role, even those physical demands that exacerbate symptoms of heart disease.

In this encounter, a number of structural elements emerge (see Figure 2). Women's gender role in the family comprises a problematic contextual issue (A). The patient tries to perform her household work—an important activity in reproducing her husband's economic role. Physical symptoms and emotional distress arise because her cardiac symptoms interfere with housework (B). In the medical encounter (C), the patient expresses this concern (D). The doctor responds supportively and tries to address the problem through technical means. Specifically, he performs an electrocardiogram during exercise, to replicate the physical demands of housework. Through this maneuver, more basic questions pertaining to the woman's role expectations and possible alternatives move to the margin of the conversation, as both participants attend to scientific observations (E). In managing the contextual problem, the doctor intervenes technically by changing the patient's cardiac medications. By this adjustment, he encourages her efforts to maintain a tidy household. The ideologic assumption that a woman should maintain her reproductive work in the home therefore goes unquestioned, even though such activities entail a certain physical risk (F). After a largely technical dialogue, the patient continues consenting to the challenge of housework despite serious illness.

Again, the communication seems admirable. Both patient and doctor maintain a strong orientation to the technical details of the patient's physical illness. The doctor shares information openly. The patient participates actively. They convey an impression of mutual respect and cooperation. Nonetheless, themes of ideology and social control arise, albeit to a lesser degree than in the first encounter. A primary goal of the encounter is the client's ability to function in household work. By not examining the

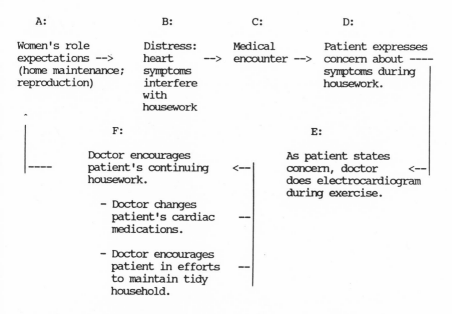

Figure 2. Structural Elements of Medical Encounter With a Woman
Whose Heart Symptoms Interfere With Her Housework

problematic features of women's role, the discourse implicitly supports it. Aside
from the positive communication that occurs, the encounter still reinforces
things as they are.

CONCLUSION: A CRITICAL THEORY
OF MEDICAL DISCOURSE

In this section, I map some islands around which medical discourse seems to
flow (Figure 3). From these and other encounters, I interpret these islands as
underlying structures in medical discourse, rarely discerned consciously by the
doctors and patients who travel there.

A. Social issue as context: The economic, social, and political context of
society contains difficult conditions. These "social issues" often lie behind and
help create some of the "personal troubles" that clients experience in their
everyday lives (Mills 1959, pp. 3-24). (In the two encounters above, the pertinent
social issues are uncertain employment and gender role expectations.)

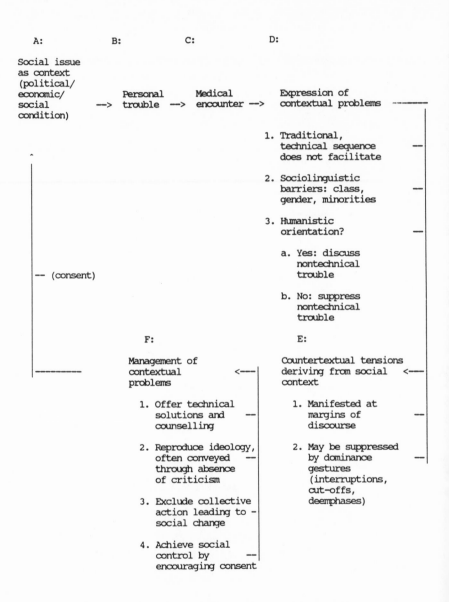

Figure 3.   The Micropolitical Structure of Medical Discourse

B.   Personal trouble: Clients tend to experience these troubles privately, as their own individual problems. They are unlikely to recognize consciously the social issues that lie behind their personal troubles. (In the same two encounters, personal troubles include depression centering partly on work, and emotional distress that heart symptoms interfere with housework.)

C. *The medical encounter:* Clients come to medical professionals with complaints that very often (though not always) have economic, social, and political roots. Such contextual sources of personal troubles include class structure and the organization of work; family life, gender roles, and sexuality; aging and the social role of the elderly; the patterning of leisure and "substance use"; and limited resources for dealing with emotional distress.

D. *Expression of contextual problems in medical discourse:* The traditional and technical sequence of the medical encounter does not facilitate the expression of contextual concerns. Regarding patients' own characteristics, the relations between language and social structure may make the expression of contextual concerns more difficult for working-class people, women, and racial minorities (Waitzkin 1989). Certain "humanistic" or "progressive" doctors may encourage patients to talk about the nontechnical components of their problems that pertain to the social context. These patients can express concerns and vent emotions about such personal troubles. Less "humanistic" or "progressive" doctors tend to discourage patients from expressing such concerns or to ignore them when expressed.

E. *Countertextual tensions deriving from social context:* However, the social context creates tensions in medical discourse. Periodically, such tensions that derive from troubling social issues erupt into the discourse, or appear at its margins, and create a countertextual reality that cannot be resolved in the framework of a medical encounter. Doctors tend to suppress such tensions by dominance gestures like interruptions, cut-offs, and deemphases, that get the discourse back on a technical track. The inherent hierarchy and asymmetry of the doctor-patient relationship reinforce this pattern of dominance in discourse.

F. *Management of contextual problems:* Whether such tensions are expressed or suppressed, the language of medicine leaves few options for action. Limited options for action apply to both "humanistic" encounters, when doctors encourage patients to talk about nontechnical components of their personal troubles, and to less humanistic encounters, where such concerns are discouraged. Generally, doctors respond with technical solutions and counsel patients how best to adjust to their previous roles. The language of medical science can convey ideologic content, especially when it converts social problems into technical ones. Ideologic language also may arise at the margins of medical discourse or may have its impact through absence. That is, by a lack of criticism directed against sources of distress in the social context, medical discourse ideologically reinforces the status quo. The discourse of medicine thus tends to exclude basic social change as a meaningful alternative. In accepting the present social context as given, and in remaining silent about collective political action, medical discourse encourages consent by rendering social change "unthinkable." This achievement of medical discourse may be its main contribution to social control.

Future reports from this research will show how this structure helps us understand what is happening as doctors and patients deal with contextual problems of work; the family and gender roles; aging; sexuality, leisure, substance use, and other "vices"; and emotional problems. In addition, medical discourse in which this structure is not apparent will be a matter of particular interest.

To whatever extent this theory is persuasive, other questions immediately suggest themselves: Can the structure of medical discourse be reformed? Can medical discourse include a criticism of the sources of personal distress in the social context of the professional encounter? A reformed medical discourse would encompass self-criticism of its own micropolitical structure and no longer would encourage consent to contextual sources of personal troubles. By suggesting collective action as a meaningful option, medical professionals perhaps might begin to overcome the impact that its exclusion exerts. Can this be done without further medicalizing social problems? If so, critical discourse in medicine also would recognize the limits of medicine's role and the importance of building links to other forms of praxis that seek to change the social context of medical encounters. Moving beyond the current structure of medical discourse thus becomes one goal of the attempt to analyze it. The reform of medical discourse is a problem to which it is well worth returning.

ACKNOWLEDGMENTS

This paper is one of a series of papers from an ongoing research project on medical discourse. The research has been supported in part by grants from the National Center for Health Services Research (HS-02100), the Robert Wood Johnson Foundation (through the Clinical Scholars Program), the National Institute on Aging (1-F32-AG05438), the Fulbright Program, and the Academic Senate of the University of California, Irvine (Honorary Faculty Research Fellowship). During a span of many years, John Stoeckle, Elliot Mishler, Sam Bloom, members of the primary care research discussion group at the University of California, Irvine, and participants in the Society of General Internal Medicine have given me constructive suggestions about the project. Stephany Borges, Theron Britt, J. Hillis Miller, Mark Poster, Leslie Rabine, and John Carlos Rowe have helped in my attempts to negotiate the terrain of critical theory in the humanities. My errors are no fault of theirs. The themes presented in this paper are developed further in Waitzkin (1991).

REFERENCES

Althusser, L. 1971. "Ideology and Ideologic State Apparatuses." Pp. 127-186 in *Lenin and Philosophy and Other Essays.* New York: Monthly Review Press.

Bakhtin, M.M. 1973. *The Dialogic Imagination.* Austin: University of Texas Press.

_____. 1981. *Marxism and the Philosophy of Language.* New York: Seminar Press.

Baldessarini, R.J. 1985. "Drugs and the Treatment of Psychiatric Disorders." Pp. 387-445 in *The Pharmacological Basis of Therapeutics,* edited by A. G. Gilman, L.S. Goodman, T.W. Rall, and F. Murad. New York: Macmillan.

Barthes, R. 1977. *Image-Music-Text.* New York: Hill and Wang.

_____. 1982. *A Barthes Reader,* edited by Susan Sontag. New York: Hill and Wang.

Beckman, H.B., and R.M. Frankel. 1984. "The Effect of Physician Behavior on the Collection of Data." *Annals of Internal Medicine* 101:692-696.

Burawoy, M. 1979. *Manufacturing Consent.* Chicago: University of Chicago Press.

Cassell, E.J. 1985. *Talking With Patients,* 2 vols. Cambridge, MA: MIT Press.

Conrad, P. and J.W. Schneider. 1980. *Deviance and Medicalization: From Badness to Sickness.* St. Louis, MO: Mosby.

Derrida, J. 1976. *Of Grammatology.* Baltimore, MD: Johns Hopkins University Press.

_____. 1982. *Margins of Philosophy.* Chicago: University of Chicago Press.

_____. 1987a. *The Post Card: From Socrates to Freud and Beyond.* Chicago: University of Chicago Press.

_____. 1987b. *The Truth in Painting.* Chicago: University of Chicago Press.

Eagleton, T. 1978. *Criticism and Ideology.* London: Verso.

_____. 1983. *Literary Theory: An Introduction.* Minneapolis: University of Minnesota Press.

Fox, R.C. 1977. "The Medicalization and Demedicalization of American Society." *Daedalus* 106:9-22.

Frankel, R.M. 1986. "Talking in Interviews: A Dispreference for Patient-Initiated Questions in Physician-Patient Encounters." In *Interaction Competence,* edited by G. Psathas. Norwood, NJ: Ablex.

Frow, J. 1986. *Marxism and Literary History.* Cambridge, MA: Harvard University Press.

Giddens, A. 1986. "Action, Subjectivity, and the Constitution of Meaning." *Social Research* 53:529-545.

Good, B.J. and M.-J. D. Good. 1981. "The Meaning of Symptoms: A Cultural Hermeneutic Model for Clinical Practice." Pp. 165-196 in *The Relevance of Social Science for Medicine,* edited by L. Eisenberg and A. Kleinman. Boston: Reidel.

Horkheimer, M., and T.W. Adorno. 1982. "The Culture Industry: Enlightenment as Mass Deception." Pp. 120-167 in *Dialectic of Enlightenment.* New York: Continuum.

Jakobson, R. 1985. *Verbal Art, Verbal Sign, Verbal Time.* Minneapolis: University of Minnesota Press.

Jameson, F. 1971. *Marxism and Form.* Princeton, NJ: Princeton University Press.

_____. 1981. *The Political Unconscious: Narrative as a Socially Symbolic Act.* Ithaca, NY: Cornell University Press.

Katz, J. 1984. *The Silent World of Doctor and Patient.* New York: Free Press.

Lévi-Strauss, C. 1961. *Tristes Tropiques.* New York: Criterion.

_____. 1967. *Structural Anthropology.* Garden City, NY: Anchor.

_____. 1969. *The Raw and the Cooked.* New York: Harper & Row.

Marcuse, H. 1964. *One-Dimensional Man.* Boston, MA: Beacon.

McKeown, T. 1979. *The Role of Medicine: Dream, Mirage, or Nemesis?* Princeton, NJ: Princeton University Press.

Mills, C. W. 1959. *The Sociological Imagination.* New York: Oxford University Press.

Mishler, E.G. 1984. *The Discourse of Medicine: Dialectics of Medical Interviews.* Norwood, NJ: Ablex.

Ohmann, R. 1987. *Politics of Letters.* Wesleyan, CT: Wesleyan University Press.

Ryan, M. 1982. *Marxism and Deconstruction: A Critical Articulation.* Baltimore, MD: Johns Hopkins University Press.

Saussure, F. de. (1915) 1986. *Course in General Linguistics.* La Salle, IL: Open Court.

Sumner, C. 1979. *Reading Ideologies.* London: Academic Press.

Waitzkin, H. 1983. *The Second Sickness: Contradictions of Capitalist Health Care.* New York: Free Press.

_____. 1984. "Doctor-Patient Communication: Clinical Implications of Social Scientific Research." *Journal of the American Medical Association* 252:2441-2446.

_____. 1985. "Information Giving in Medical Care." *Journal of Health and Social Behavior* 26:81-101.

_____. 1989. "A Critical Theory of Medical Discourse: Ideology, Social Control, and the Processing of Social Context in Medical Encounters." *Journal of Health and Social Behavior.*

_____. 1991. *The Politics of Medical Encounters: How Patients and Doctors Deal with Social Problems.* New Haven: Yale University Press.

Waitzkin, H., and J.D. Stoeckle. 1972. "The Communication of Information About Illness: Clinical, Sociological, and Methodological Considerations." *Advances in Psychosomatic Medicine* 8:180-215.

West, C. 1984. *Routine Complications: Troubles With Talk Between Doctors and Patients.* Bloomington: Indiana University Press.

Zola, I.K. 1983. "The Medicalizing of Society." Pages 243-296 in *Socio-Medical Inquiries.* Philadelphia, PA: Temple University Press.

PART III

PROFESSIONAL IDEOLOGY AND SOCIAL CONTROL

COMPETING OCCUPATIONAL IDEOLOGIES, IDENTITIES, AND THE PRACTICE OF NURSE-MIDWIFERY

Phyllis Ann Langton

ABSTRACT

Interactions between occupational ideology and occupational identity and the practice of work are examined in this paper using the "hybrid" occupation, nurse-midwifery. This occupation combines two disciplines: nursing and midwifery. Using a social history approach, I trace the evolution of occupational ideologies and identities. Occupational and social changes which shape occupational ideology and identity are analyzed. The relationships among occupational ideology, identity, and the practice of work are examined using three models of nurse-midwifery practice: dependent, interdependent, and independent.

INTRODUCTION

This paper examines the interaction between occupational ideology and identity and the relationship that interaction has to the practice of work in

Current Research on Occupations and Professions, Volume 6, pages 149-177.
Copyright © 1991 by JAI Press Inc.
All rights of reproduction in any form reserved.
ISBN: 1-55938-236-8

149

the occupation of nurse-midwifery.[1] Occupational ideology and identity are two aspects of occupational culture. Occupational ideology represents the system of beliefs, ideas, language, and attitudes that forms the distinctive perspective of an occupation and justifies its existence. Occupational ideology provides members a basis for interpreting social situations. Occupational identity is the view that members have of their occupation that makes it distinct from other occupations or groups. It is also the view that members present to others, often times as an occupational title.

Occupational ideology and identity are significant in the practice of work. They are useful in helping members handle the problems they encounter both in their work lives (Ritzer and Walczak 1986) and beyond (Pavalko 1988). To this degree, they act as agents of social control (Pavalko 1988). In addition, ideology and identity are significant influences on how occupations structure their relationships with other occupations to gain legitimacy and power (Krause 1971; Larkin 1983). If we understand the interaction between occupational ideology and identity, we can determine what goals an occupation is trying to reach. Extending this relationship to include the practice of work may tell us more about how occupational ideology shapes the practice of work.

Sociologists have studied occupational ideology and identity in traditional and deviant occupations, but no systematic theory of how these concepts are linked, or how they relate to the practice of work, has been developed. Some sociologists who have studied either occupational ideology and/or identity presume socialization or training in an occupation will prepare recruits to adopt shared identities, values, and beliefs (Merton, Reader, and Kendall 1957). Others question the assumption of "homogenization" of recruits into an occupational identity (Becker, Greer, Hughes, and Strauss 1961; Lovell 1964). For example, sociologists who have studied deviant occupations have not found that occupational ideology establishes occupational identity or legitimacy in the community (Bryan 1966; Dressel and Peterson 1982; Langer 1977). However, that function probably exists in traditional occupations. In this paper, I show the relationship between occupational ideology and identity in the occupation of nurse-midwifery, and how the effects of that relationship change the practice of work.

THEORETICAL APPROACH

Occupational ideologies and identities develop as occupational and social changes interact with them. Occupations are active in shaping their identities by engaging in control strategies (Larkin 1983), such as: (1) establishing formal institutions to transmit knowledge of the occupation and to develop standardized training programs (Caplow 1954; Denzin 1972); (2) developing social organizations such as occupational associations to ensure perpetuation of the occupation through time (Denzin 1972); and (3) establishing lobbying mechanisms at federal, state, and local levels. Occupations also act to defend their own interests when other groups act to impose constraints on them (Larkin 1983).

Social, economic, and political events, both internal and external to the occupation, also shape its ideology and identity (Begun and Lippincott 1987; Hughes 1958, 1959; Larkin 1983; Pavalko 1988; Strauss 1972). Many of these changes occur simultaneously, for example: (1) the emergence of social movements; (2) changes in social demographics; and (3) changes in technology. Interaction among these events and the occupation may take the form of deliberate bargaining, negotiation, and accommodation, or sometimes may involve more subtle manipulation or social control (Albrecht and Levy 1982; Rothman 1979, 1987).

In the following section, I will review historical and recent occupational and social changes and analyze how these have interacted with the occupational ideologies and identities of nurse-midwifery. The history will be organized primarily to highlight the theoretical issues, rather than the chronology of events.

OCCUPATIONAL CHANGES

An occupation engages in many activities as it seeks to establish its boundaries and tasks. In the area of health occupations, there has been considerable activity as many occupations seek to expand their bases of power and legitimacy (Arney 1982; DeVries 1986a; Larkin 1983). This analysis of the impact of occupational changes on the development of ideology and identity will draw on a review of the sociology and nurse-midwifery literatures. Major occupational changes and events will be considered that are part of the activities that nurse-midwifery participates in to gain power and establish its boundaries of competence.

In 1925, Mary Breckenridge, a public health nurse, started the Frontier Nursing Service (FNS) in Hyden, Kentucky. It was the first nurse-midwifery service in the United States, designed for impoverished "remotely rural areas" without physicians (Dye 1984; Rooks and Fischman 1980). Between 1931 and 1933, the Maternity Center Association (MCA), in collaboration with Dr. Lobenstine, established the first school of nurse-midwifery in New York City: The Lobenstine Midwifery Clinic and School (Hogan 1975; Litoff 1978). It covered the needs of urban poor populations (Hogan 1975). A new idea in maternity care had emerged, combining nursing and midwifery into a new occupation (Radosh 1986, p. 137). In the sixty-five years since the occupation of nurse-midwifery began, many changes have occurred in the occupation that have influenced the interactions between occupational ideology and identity.

Table 1.   Social History in the Evolution of Nurse-Midwifery: 1925-1986

Occupational Changes

1925	Frontier Nursing Service started in Kentucky
1928	Kentucky State Association of Nurse-Midwives
1932	Lobenstine Midwifery Clinic and School, New York City
	First Nurse-Midwifery Training Program in America
1944	First university affiliated nurse-midwifery program
	Catholic Maternity Institute, New Mexico
1945	Nurse-midwifery Section of the National Organization for Public Health Nursing (NOPHN)
1952	NOPHN Disbanded
1955	American College of Nurse-Midwifery (ACNM) founded
1969	Merger of ACNM with the American Association of Nurse-Midwifery in Kentucky
1969	Nurses Association of the American College of Obstetricians and Gynecologists (NAACOG) established
1971	Certification of Nurse-Midwives by ACNM
1971	Joint Statement on Maternity Care- American College of Obstetricians and Gynecologists and ACNM
1975	Supplementary Statement
1982	Joint Statement of Practice Relationships Between
	Obstetrician/Gynecologists and Certified Nurse-Midwives
1984	ACNM Division of Accreditation Recognized by the United States Department of Education
1985	Nurse-Midwifery in America Report
1986	National Conference on Nurse-Midwifery in America

Social Changes

1930s-	Infant mortality rates
1946-1964	Baby boom
1950	Almost all births take place in hospitals
1950s-	Physician shortage
1950s	Natural Childbirth Movement
1960s	American Civil Rights Movement
1965	Medicaid legislation
1960s	Self Help Movement
1960s	Consumer Movement
1960s	Home Birth Movement
1960s	Women's Health Movement
1970s	In-Hospital Reform Movement
1970s	Rise of the Free Standing Birthing Center

During the period when FNS and MCA were developing, several events reduced the importance and influence of nurse-midwifery: (1) births moved from women's homes to hospitals and (2) obstetrics took over the management of birth,[2] defining it as a pathological condition (Dye 1984, p. 339). Furthermore, a basic ideological disagreement ensued between FNS and MCA. FNS wanted to further the autonomy of nurse-midwives, establishing them as independent health care providers. On the other hand, MCA argued that nurse-midwives were, at best assistants to physicians. In addition, MCA saw the title of midwife to be more a handicap than a help (Dye 1984, p. 338). And so, from its inception, nurse-midwifery claimed more than one occupational identity: midwife and medical assistant. This division may explain, in part, why the occupation has been slow to develop and to be recognized as a legitimate occupation.

Establishing an Occupational Association

Sociologists have documented the importance of an occupational association in shaping an occupation's identity and its relationships with other groups (Caplow 1954; Hughes 1958; Larkin 1983; Pavalko 1971; Strauss 1972). Hughes (1958, p. 40) states that an occupation develops its own association for control of the occupation and for the practice of its prerogatives. Strauss (1972, p. 250) argues that occupational associations promote professionalism. Pavalko (1971, p. 105) argues that occupational associations function as a source of identity and continue the socialization begun during training. National occupational associations having representative and inclusive memberships politically empower occupations, enabling them to lobby more effectively for the group's collective interests. Occupational associations reinforce identity for members, especially today as work becomes increasingly bureaucratized and organizations become collections of specialists (Pavalko 1971, p. 107).

The First State Association

In 1928, the FNS staff established the first state association, Kentucky State Association of Midwives (Dye 1984, p. 338).[3] Mary Breckenridge worked to gain professional recognition and certification, hoping to create conditions that were similar to those in England (Dye 1984, p. 338). She wanted nurse-midwives to be autonomous midwifery practitioners.

The National Organization for Public Health Nursing

The first national association that nurse-midwives joined was founded in 1945. It was a special section of the National Organization for Public Health Nursing (NOPHN). This group formulated a philosophy, planned curricula, developed a roster of nurse-midwives, and formulated plans to meet the need for better maternity care (Hogan 1975, p. 10).

In 1952, during a general re-organization of the Nursing Organization, NOPHN disbanded. "When completed there was the ANA [American Nurses Association] and the NLN [National League of Nursing]. . . . NOPHN had been absorbed, and there was no place for the nurse-midwife" (Hogan 1975, p. 10).

Nurse-midwives attempted to work within several professional associations: NLN and ANA, and the American Public Health Association (APHA). For a brief time, nurse-midwives joined MCH-NLN [Maternal Child Health-National League of Nursing] Interdivisional Council (Hogan 1975). None of these efforts was successful in helping nurse-midwives establish themselves as a self-regulating occupation (Ernst 1984). Nurse-midwives formed a committee on organization to organize a separate occupational association (Hogan 1975). In 1955, Articles of Incorporation were filed and the first ACNM Executive Board was elected, 30 years after the inception of the occupation (Hogan 1975).

The American College of Nurse-Midwifery

In 1955, the American College of Nurse-Midwifery (ACNM) emerged as an independent association for nurse-midwives. The first tasks faced by this group were: (1) locating and unifying memberships (Hogan 1975); (2) obtaining international recognition; (3) developing legal definitions (Barrett 1979, p. 15); and (4) obtaining licensure (Hogan 1975, p. 11). The Bulletin for Nurse-Midwives became the official publication.[4] Membership in ACNM was slow to grow: by 1968 ACNM had fewer than 400 members (Teasley 1983, p. 95). This may have been a factor in the decision to merge, in 1969, with the Kentucky-based American Association of Nurse-Midwifery. It eventually changed its name to the American College of Nurse-Midwives (Hogan 1975). This merger marked a return to the occupation's roots with the Frontier Nursing Service and with public health nursing, and as such, can be interpreted as a justification for returning to the roots of nursing, rather than reinforcing nurse-midwifery's ties with medicine.

Nurses Association of the American College of Obstetricians-Gynecologists (NAACOG)

Concomitantly, the American College of Obstetricians and Gynecologists (ACOG) formed NAACOG to provide a forum for all obstetric nurse practitioners (including nurse-midwives), maternity care specialists, and neonatal specialists. These practitioners share information and problems associated with obstetric and well-women care. As a political organization, NAACOG collaborates with ACOG to lobby for effective legislative reform. As an educational organization, it disseminates information and research through a newsletter and the *Journal of Obstetric , Gynecologic and Neonatal Nursing.*

ACOG's move to establish NAACOG can be seen as their attempt to reinforce its influence over nurse-midwifery. NAACOG is part of an occupational association governed by medicine. However, fewer than 250 nurse-midwives have joined although there are approximately 21,000 members of NAACOG (personal communication, December 1988).

Midwives Alliance of North America (MANA)

Another occupational association that includes nurse-midwives is the Midwives Alliance of North America (MANA). Midwives with diverse educational backgrounds started this association in 1982. MANA wants to unify the occupation of midwifery ("Midwives Alliance" 1985). The purpose of MANA is to foster cooperation among all types of midwives and to promote *midwifery* as a means of improving well women's maternity care and health. Today, MANA has approximately 600 members; only a few nurse-midwives are members (personal communication, December 1988).

In 1983, the President of ACNM urged good relationships with MANA; however, she argued against merging with them (Rooks 1983). "To be "lay" specifically means to be not part of a profession. It is the exact opposite of what we have worked for" (Rooks 1983, p. 6). Because lay-midwives have not established standards and other credentials that are characteristic of a profession, it is difficult for the public to be clear on what services lay midwives provide (Rooks 1983). This argument can be interpreted as ideological support for an occupational identity of nurse-midwife, rather than an identity of midwife.

Maintaining ACNM

Besides division in the occupation, ACNM faces several problems in maintaining its organization: (1) the decline in student enrollments; (2) the problem of who to admit to the association; and (3) the problem of obtaining physician back-up services.

Decline In Enrollments

One sociologist, in reading the 1985 conference report on the profession, identified the problem of uncertainty about professional identity in nurse-midwifery (DeVries 1986b). Resolution of this uncertainty is important because it will affect the policies that ACNM pursues. If the nurse-midwifery profession defines success in terms of protecting and improving the health of mothers and their babies, it will take different actions than if the primary goal is survival of the occupation. ACNM is struggling with a decline in student enrollments.

Carrington (1983) observed that the public is increasing its demand for nurse-midwifery services. This is so in a time when student population may be on the decline.

By the end of the 1970s and the early 1980s, student enrollments in nurse-midwifery programs had begun to decline. The continuation and expansion of educational programs for nurse-midwives depends on the ability of these programs to recruit applicants from nursing. Raisler (1987) reports a mean decline in applicants for nurse-midwifery programs of 42% in 17 programs from 1984-1986. Her explanations include: malpractice insurance problems, increasing cost of education, and alternative careers for women (Raisler 1987, p. 2).

Who To Admit to ACNM

In 1983, ACNM considered the question of whether to admit non nurse-midwives to ACNM. Although two regions of the country supported this move (Rooks 1983), nurse-midwives, on the whole, did not approve the measure. Even so, the association still suffers from multiple occupational identities: (1) nurse-midwives who see themselves primarily as nurses or junior physicians, rather than nurse-midwives; (2) nurse-midwives who see themselves primarily as nurse-midwives; and (3) nurse-midwives who see themselves more as midwives than nurses.

The first group of nurse-midwives want to maintain ties with medicine. The second group wants to retain the tie to nursing that has been so carefully developed to this point by ACNM (Ernst 1984; Rooks 1983; Sharp 1983). The third group argues for a move away from the occupation's roots in nursing and medicine.

Physician Back-up Requirement

Dye (1984) argues that the requirement for back-up service and supervision by the obstetrician has tended to devalue nurse-midwifery's initiative and importance. The back-up requirement discourages women from entering the profession, which ultimately weakens ACNM's power and legitimacy as an occupational association. Cass (1988) argues that nurse-midwives must act politically to obtain legislation that frees them from the requirement of a back-up physician. Until this occurs, she argues that nurse-midwifery will remain dependent upon obstetrics to delegate tasks to nurse-midwifery.

Developing and Accrediting Educational Training Programs

From its beginnings, medicine has been actively involved in shaping nurse-midwifery's education, practice, and ideology (Teasley 1983, p. 90). For example, obstetricians were part of the group who started the first school of midwifery in New York City in 1931: The Lobenstine Midwifery Clinic and School (Hogan 1975; Litoff 1978). In 1939, FNS established the Frontier Graduate School of Nurse-Midwifery in Hyden, Kentucky (Litoff 1978).

During the early 1940s, two new schools were started as training programs for Black nurses who provided nurse-midwifery care to rural Alabama. In 1944, the Catholic Maternity Institute in New Mexico opened the first university affiliated degree program (Radosh 1986).

The demand for nurse-midwifery programs increased significantly during the middle 1950s. Columbia admitted its first class in 1955, followed by Johns Hopkins and Yale, as the demand for health providers with nurse-midwifery began to rise. In 1957, ACNM formed a Committee on Curriculum and Accreditation. In 1962, the National League of Nursing (NLN) voted not to accredit nurse-midwifery programs that nurses did not administer in their graduate schools (Conway-Welch 1986). ACNM decided to develop its own accreditation program.

By 1960, 7 nurse-midwifery educational programs were in operation (Rooks and Fischman 1980, p. 992). Nurse-midwifery education had entered the mainstream of nursing and medical educational facilities (Teasley 1983, p. 94).

In 1984, the United States Office of Education recognized the Division of Accreditation of ACNM, thus meeting Department of Education criteria that they are reliable authorities on the quality of training offered (Conway-Welch 1986). Such recognition is necessary for programs to be eligible for federal financial assistance.

In 1985, ACNM revised the statement of core competencies for which each nurse-midwifery program was responsible. These include an emphasis on nursing theory and research, especially for the master's program. Two types of educational programs are available today: (1) basic certificate programs (9) and (2) basic graduate programs (16). The former does not grant an academic degree (Conway-Welch 1986, p. 12). The latter leads to an academic degree at the master's or doctoral level. Together, these programs prepare about 250 nurse-midwives each year.

Achieving National Certification

Credentialing is a generic term that refers to several procedures designed to legitimize the roles of occupations (Gaumer 1984, p. 382). The most common forms used are: registration, certification, and licensure. These credentialling forms differ on: (1) the source of legitimation; (2) the rigor of entry screening; and (3) the mechanisms for securing compliance (Gaumer 1984, p. 382).

Registration

Registration is the weakest credential and form of regulation. Upon completion of an accredited program in nursing, nurses take an examination to qualify to be licensed as a registered nurse. A nurse who enters a nurse-midwifery program must be registered as a nurse in any of the 50 states or the District of Columbia. Currently, ANA is considering a policy that would reserve the title "registered nurse" for nurses trained in baccalaureate programs (DeVries 1986a).

Certification

This type of regulation varies by state and occupation. In the late 1960s, a testing committee developed and validated a national certification examination for nurse-midwives. Official testing began in 1971. The ACNM Division of Examiners, an administratively independent part of ACNM, administers the examination. They certify nurse-midwives who: (1)are licensed as registered nurses in the United States; (2) are graduates from an accredited nurse-midwifery program; and (3) who pass the national certification examination (Foster 1986, p. 14). Only these nurse-midwives are eligible to use the initials "CNM" after their names, and to join ACNM.

Licensure

This form of state regulation is the strongest of the three. There is great variation among the states on how they regulate health occupations. Because the number of allied health occupations continues to grow, the division of labor is likely to shift as negotiating and bargaining take place among the various occupations. Under these conditions, the state may play a crucial role in the establishment of legitimacy of the competing occupations through the mechanism of licensure (Begun and Lippincott 1987; DeVries 1986a). And so, for an occupation to gain power and legitimacy, it needs to make alliances with the state. This is especially the case when one occupation tries to encroach on another occupation or to negotiate another division of labor (Begun and Lippincott 1987).

As of 1978, ACNM recognized the importance of making stronger alliances with the political system at the state and federal levels. Alliances are necessary to obtain more power in its negotiations with medicine and other groups. The ACNM Board of Directors met and reviewed its current committee structure to determine how to develop a more effective political organization. Thus, ACNM employed a political lobbyist to work predominately at the federal level. It established voluntary lobbying groups at the state level.

Negotiating Relationships with Obstetrics[5]

Besides negotiating recognition and accreditation from the state, occupations form relationships with other occupations. These interrelationships are important in tracing the evolution of an occupation (Bucher 1988, p. 133). Because the occupation of obstetrics is responsible for maternity care in the United States, obstetricians set the rules for nurse-midwifery.

After ACNM had achieved certification in 1971, ACOG officially recognized nurse-midwifery. It negotiated a practice agreement with ACOG and NAACOG, which was essential for nurse-midwifery practice. ACOG, NAACOG, and ACNM negotiated a Joint Statement on Maternity Care in 1971, which established the division of labor and political relationships among these groups. Maternity care would be provided by a team of health professionals, directed by the obstetrician-gynecologist. Nurse-midwives would manage normal labor and delivery under the supervision of qualified obstetricians.

In 1975, ACOG, NAACOG, and ACNM negotiated a Supplementary Statement that attempted to clarify further the team concept. Because obstetricians were facing changes in their work demands, they were unable to be physically present to direct the health team. They developed mechanisms for team interaction: (1) there would be written agreements among team members specifying consultation and referral policies, and standing orders and (2) the obstetrician-gynecologist would accept full responsibility for direction of medical care provided by the team.

In 1982, ACNM and ACOG negotiated a new agreement. This agreement emphasized again that the maternity team was to be directed by a qualified obstetrician-gynecologist, but added several new features: (1) clients would be informed and consent to the relationship between the nurse-midwife and the obstetrician; (2) the collaborating obstetrician would periodically review women's charts; and (3) ACOG would support the granting of hospital privileges for those nurse-midwives in practice relationships with obstetricians (Rooks and Haas 1986, p. 97). This agreement strengthened the tie between nurse-midwifery and medicine and a medical definition of birthing care that defines pregnancy as a pathological condition.

These statements can be interpreted as political efforts by ACOG to influence the occupational ideologies and practice of nurse-midwifery. On the other hand, nurse-midwives gained in this negotiation because ACOG agreed to support strongly the provision permitting nurse-midwives hospital privileges. This appears to be a concession on their part because if nurse-midwives have hospital privileges, they can establish themselves as independent practitioners. However, the process of obtaining hospital privileges requires further negotiation between nurse-midwifery and the state.

SOCIAL CHANGES

Hughes (1959) observed that in times of social unrest, a demand may arise for more conformity and attention to lay ideas and influence. The social turbulence of the 1960s created many challenges to professional and bureaucratic authorities resulting in new relationships among occupations, clients, and other groups. Dramatic social changes occurring in the United States during the last several decades have interacted with the occupation of nurse-midwifery. These include: (1) the emergence of social movements; (2) changes in social demographics; and (3) changes in birthing technology.

Social Movements

Social movements serve many purposes in a society, one of which is to alter basic elements of the social structure and to redistribute the rewards in society (Jenkins 1983). Challenges to institutional dominance posed in the 1960s and 1970s altered consumer attitudes and demands. Several major social movements that affected the occupation of nurse-midwifery are: American Civil Rights, Self-Help, Consumer, Women's Health, Home Birth, In-Hospital Reform, and Birthing Center movements. Many of these movements developed simultaneously as consumers began to seek alternative practitioners for health and birthing care.

American Civil Rights Movement

The American Civil Rights Movement included health care issues. Federally-funded neighborhood health centers, which began to emerge in the 1960s, are an example. One of the consequences of the Civil Rights Movement was to open the doors of southern hospitals to blacks, resulting in the disappearance of the 'granny midwife' (Yankauer 1983). Poor women were able to choose their birth sites and birth practitioners because of the provisions of Medicaid legislation.

Self-Help Movement

The Self-Help movement in health care that emerged in the late 1960s was a response to the counter-cultural movement. Some people saw this as a return to "nature" and one way to overcome alienation. Ivan Illich (1975) was one of the main advocates for self help in health care who argued for a move away from dependence upon medicine. Also, movements for 'community control' urged people to return to simple and informal life-styles. Some people distrusted experts and institutions, including doctors, nurses, and hospitals (Yankauer 1983).

The Consumer Movement

The Consumer Movement in health care is part of a larger movement by consumers aimed at creating changes that give consumers more choice as they become aware of their environments and purchasing power. In maternity care, this includes giving women more choice in birth sites and birth practitioners.

The Women's Health Movement[6]

In the late 1960s and early 1970s, the Women's Health Movement emerged as part of the general feminist movement (Ruzek 1979). Well-informed middle-class women began to assert themselves to gain control over their health and reproductive activities (Rooks 1986, p. 19). These women advocated lay control over health services, an action consistent with Hughes' (1959) observation that in times of social unrest, lay control may emerge. Some women chose to have their friends and lay midwives help them with their births at home. Others chose to have nurse-midwives help them with their births in hospitals, and eventually birthing centers. Rooks (1986, p. 19) observes that these women were influential in creating a private sector nurse-midwifery clientele. Women found nurse-midwives, rather than nurse-midwives seeking a role in private practice (Rooks 1986, p. 11).

The Home Birth Movement

The Home Birth Movement, the Women's Health Movement, and the Self-Help Movement are closely related (Rosengren and Sartell 1986, p. 137). Rothman (1984, p. 95) analyzes the home birth movement by examining the schism between two groups of women who support home birth: (1) traditionalists and (2) feminists. Both groups of women are challenging the medical model and the profession of medicine. The traditionalists define the childbirth issue to include family involvement and control over birth, which are not present in hospital births. They see birthing as part of a family system with rights and obligations. Feminists, however, move beyond this position by challenging the patriarchal family structure (Rothman 1984, p. 95). They see childbirth as just one of the areas in which women are struggling for control over their lives.

The home birth movement can be viewed as an example of how public ideology interacted with the occupation of nurse-midwifery. Nurse-midwifery became more involved with home birth in the late 1960s and 1970s after women began requesting their services. These women wanted help with home births. The number of nurse-midwives practicing home births increased.

In 1975, Suzanne Arms wrote an important critique of American birthing practices. She describes the American nurse-midwife as another deception in the process of hospital birth (p. 197). According to Arms, the occupations of nursing and midwifery are not complementary and thus, not easy to combine.

> The midwife has a deep faith, upheld by experience, that nature has designed a complex and perfect process she could not hope to improve. She knows that birth is seldom in need of assistance .... A nurse-midwife, on the other hand, is a person preselected by her interest in helping others through illness and disease. It is a rare nurse who leaves her training unscarred by that emphasis and expectation of disease or disorder (p. 199).

The core of her criticism against nurse-midwives is that they act more like physicians, than like guardians of normal birth (p. 199).

Her criticism pushed the nurse-midwifery community to re-examine its position on home births. In 1976, the *Journal of Nurse-Midwifery* asked nurse-midwives to rethink the practice of home births. The editorial concluded by asking members to support all types of practice that met the standards of safe care. In 1977, the president of ACNM argued for diversity in nurse-midwifery that is reflective of the history of the occupation (Burst 1977).

> Historically, our beginnings, at a time when the majority of all births in the United States were in the home, was in the conduct of home births. . . . Today, nurse-midwives continue to conduct satisfying and safe home births. . . . Our history also finds us in the hospitals serving our common goal . . . to serve those who chose to deliver in the hospitals (Burst 1977, pp. 10-11).

However, the official position of ACNM does not support home birth. In 1976 ACNM formally stated that it considers the hospital or maternity home as the preferred site for childbirth. Concern for the safety of childbearing families included the ready availability of obstetrical resources.

In-Hospital Birth Reform Movement

In-hospital birth reform was one response to demands by birth reformers for alternatives in childbirth. The presence of the father as coach in labor and delivery rooms, and the family-oriented Caesarian section, are examples of changes that occurred in the 1970s. Many hospitals set up "birthing rooms" to resemble a home birth. In this arrangement, labor and delivery take place in the same room, eliminating the need to move the mother during the birthing experience. The ideology behind this is to reduce the bureaucratic influence of most hospitals.

The Birthing Center Movement

The birthing center movement emerged as an alternative to home and hospital births.[7] Most birthing centers are independent of hospitals. The short history of these centers suggests that growth may be slow, if at all. Only 140 were operating in 1987, although 300 had been planned. Lutz (1987, p. 44) includes the following reasons for the slow development of this alternative: (1) malpractice insurance problems and (2) stiff competition from hospitals, as a result of in-hospital reform efforts.

Social Demographics

Since the beginning of American history, the population has grown steadily. While many demographic changes have occurred, I discuss three demographic events as they indirectly and directly interact with the occupation of nurse-midwifery: (1) the "baby boom"; (2) changes in the birth rate; and (3) the projected decline in annual births in 1988.[8]

The "Baby Boom"

The "baby boom," rapid growth in the birth rate following World War II, lasted until about 1964. Although the peak year was 1957, the birth rate continued with a rate of over 20 live births per 1000 population until 1964. These births resulted in a demand for more maternity services, including nurse-midwifery services.

Nurse-midwifery expanded during the 1960s because of the perceived critical shortage of physicians, and to meet the demands of the baby boom (Sullivan and Weitz 1988, p. 203). Since these potential mothers would give birth in hospitals, where 88% of births took place in 1950 (Dye 1984, p. 339), and since many poor women would choose hospitals for birthing because of changes in government insurance, Medicaid (Barrett 1979, p. 16), nurse-midwives increasingly worked in hospitals.

Changes in Birth Rate

Changes in the number of babies being born as well as who is having these babies interacts with the occupational ideology of nurse-midwifery. As birth rates increase, it is likely that the demand for nurse-midwives will increase, especially if socially deprived women are experiencing the greatest increase in birth rate.

Birth rates interact with the types of health care occupations that provide maternity care. When the birth rate was increasing rapidly, accompanied by a perceived shortage of obstetricians, nurse-midwifery grew as an occupation. As the birth rate stabilized, and then decreased, nurse-midwives were in less demand, especially since there was a perceived oversupply of obstetricians. In addition, as women reduce the number of babies they are having, they increase their expectations that those babies that are born will be "perfect." This desire for a "perfect" child keeps most births in the hospital. As long as birth occurs primarily in hospitals, a medical definition of birth will prevail (Mundy 1988, p. 65).

Furthermore, the occupation of nurse-midwifery is also affected by which segment of the population is experiencing the greatest increase in the birth rate. While there was a decline in the general birth rate, the number of births among socially deprived and unmarried women increased. The obstetrical and nurse-midwifery literatures report that these women require more complicated and expensive care. Nurse-midwifery has a long history of providing this care effectively and safely. Hence the widespread misperception that nurse-midwives "only take care of the poor" (Rooks and Haas 1986).

Projected Decline in 1988

Women are having fewer babies and having them at later ages (Willson 1989, p. 125). In 1965, 24% of married women age 20-24, and 12% of those age 25-29, were childless (Willson 1989, p. 125). In 1983, these figures were 39.7% and 26.8% respectively (Willson 1989).

The Census Bureau projection that annual births will begin to decline in 1988 is likely to influence nurse-midwifery goals. For example, the present median age of the population is 30.3 years. It is expected to rise to 36.3 by the year 2000 (Rose 1983, p. 1). The number of women of childbearing age will decrease while the number of women beyond the childbearing age will increase, including an increase in the number of elderly women. In 1970, 9.8% of women in the United States were over 65 which increased to 14% in 1985 (Willson 1989). Rose (1983, p. 2) suggests that nurse-midwifery needs to rethink its goals to include nurse-midwifery care to women of all ages. This may be another issue that will divide nurse-midwifery. Because it is a small occupation, too much diversity can weaken a small occupation that is having difficulty in recruiting new students.

Changes in Birthing Technology

Technology is a major social force influencing the development of health occupations. At least one new health occupation in maternity care arose as a direct response to rapid changes in technology: Perinatology. Perinatologists work almost exclusively with a form of ultrasound technology, the sonogram.

Rosengren and Sartell (1986, p. 93) observe that there is a sharp division in the medical literature on two technology models: high and low. High technologies, amniocentesis and internal fetal monitoring,[9] are most often found in large, urban hospitals to reduce infant mortality. Low technologies are those that support a view of the birth process as dictated by the mother's own physiological timing and ability (Rosengren and Sartell 1986, p. 94).

The application of technology in maternity care has sometimes resulted in nurse-midwives and pregnant women having little choice of whether technology will be used. At least one hospital requires the use of internal monitoring, which monitors fetal blood, with clinic patients regardless of the nurse-midwife's judgment (Rothman 1984, p. 71). Ernst (1984, p. 299) argues that forced technology has created extreme confusion and frustration for nurse-midwives.

OCCUPATIONAL IDEOLOGIES AND IDENTITIES IN NURSE-MIDWIFERY

Nurse-midwives have developed at least three occupational identities in response to occupational and social changes: nurse, nurse-midwife, and midwife. Also, they have developed three occupational ideologies respectively: medicine, nursing, and midwifery.

Nurse

A nurse-midwife whose occupational identity approximates that of a nurse, justifies her identity in the ideology of medicine that defines birth as a pathological state. This justifies to clients and the public the necessity for hospital birth to ensure a safe outcome. The language used is medical language, based in science and technology: they "deliver" babies.

Nurse-Midwife

A nurse-midwife whose occupational identity approximates that of nurse-midwife, justifies her identity in the ideology of nursing that defines birth as normal, although complications can occur. This justifies to the public the necessity for a "back up" collaborative relationship with obstetrics, if "something goes wrong" (Rothman 1984). The language used is scientific language. They "manage" births; they do not "deliver" babies.

Midwife

A nurse-midwife whose occupational identity approximates that of a midwife, justifies her identity in the ideology of midwifery in which birth is viewed as a normal, family-centered event. This justifies to the public the necessity for alternative birthing sites, such as the birthing center or the woman's home. The language used is nonmedical language: they "catch" babies instead of "delivering" or "managing" births.

Table 2. Occupational Ideologies and Identities in Nurse-Midwifery

Ideology	Identity
Medicine	Nurse
Nursing	Nurse-Midwife
Midwifery	Midwife

The nurse-midwifery identity is dominant now. ACNM, as the leading nurse-midwifery association, is politically active in promoting this identity, although it calls for tolerance of diversity in the occupation. ACNM, however, is not likely to confront directly the profession of obstetrics by actively supporting home births.

MODELS OF NURSE-MIDWIFERY PRACTICE

There is great variation in where and how nurse-midwives practice their occupation. One sociologist observed, "Exactly what a nurse-midwife is and what she does seem to vary with the eye of the beholder" (Rothman 1984, p. 64). I develop three models of nurse-midwifery practice—dependent, interdependent, and independent—as a heuristic device to understand this variation. These models fall on a continuum based on the degree of nurse-midwifery dependence on obstetrics. Types of dependence include: (1) the requirement that obstetricians supervise nurse-midwives when they manage births in hospitals; and (2) the requirement that nurse-midwives have back-up service arrangements with obstetricians.

Components of the Models

These models build upon the sociological literature on work and occupations by using some of the criteria found to be important in understanding the practice of work: occupational goals, work setting, division of labor, reimbursement, social control, and state regulation.

Occupational Goals

While some occupations may claim one activity or goal, most occupations have multiple goals (Hughes 1959). Political, social, and economic values inform the choices that occupations make in choosing their goals, which change over time. Occupations vary in the degree to which they are able to determine and control their goals and activities. Hughes (1959) suggests that an occupation that is strongly "historic" will resist efforts by other occupations and groups to determine the occupation's goals and work practice.

Nurse-midwifery is a specialty that is part of a "historic" occupation, nursing. The general goal of both occupations is to provide "care" to people when they need it, but nurse-midwifery is further limited to providing maternity and well women care. For some nurse-midwives, the main goal of nurse-midwifery is to provide alternative safe *and humane* birthing options for women. Others see the goal of nurse-midwifery to be primarily safety as obstetricians define this in a medical model. For these nurse-midwives, a goal is to intervene and "deliver" the baby as quickly as possible. There are multiple goals in this occupation that are reflective of its history as a "hybrid" occupation. These goals change as social values change.

Work Settings

The settings in which workers practice interact with how an occupation is controlled (Hughes 1958; Krause 1971; Ritzer and Walczak 1986). Today, most work in the United States takes place in large organizations with elaborate control systems. Workers, as part of an occupational group, learn how to negotiate and bargain within these systems to obtain resources to move them toward the occupation's goals. Negotiation is a constantly changing activity as both the organization and the workers seek to gain control over work.

Nurse-midwives work in a variety of settings and hold a range of control in these settings: hospitals, clinics, health maintenance organizations (HMOs) that are prepaid health plans, public health departments, practitioners' offices, birthing centers, and women's homes. Most nurse-midwives work in large scale organizations, a pattern that is increasing as the benefits of employment improve (Cass 1988; Goings 1986).

The Division of Labor

Work as social interaction is the central theme of sociological study of work (Hughes 1958), and the division of labor implies interaction (Hughes 1958, p. 68). Occupations are constantly negotiating the boundaries of their competence, their occupational tasks, and their relationships with other groups and occupations.

The number and variety of new health care occupations continue to grow (DeVries 1986a). The division of labor in the health care system has changed with continual expansion of health occupations. On the other hand, the health care system supports a division of labor notorious for its rigid hierarchy. Rules are developed that classify people by defining the limits of their tasks and thus assigning them subordinate roles in the hierarchy (Hughes 1958, p. 47).

Reimbursement

Nurses receive payment for their services from two general sources: (1) organizations pay them a salary, such as a hospital or birthing center and (2) clients pay them a fee-for service that may come from private monies or some form of third party insurance or Medicaid.

Social Control

The four most common types of social control of the practice of nurse-midwifery are: state, organizational, collegial, and client. The type of control varies with the work setting. For example, state control predominates with entrepreneurial practice of nurse-midwifery; client control, when birth occurs in women's homes.

State Regulation

Registration, certification, and licensing are three means by which the state can regulate occupations (Gaumer 1984; Pavalko 1988). Sociologists have argued that these serve the purpose of assuaging the fears of potential clients more than to control the behavior of the practitioners of an occupation (Pavalko 1988, p. 102). It also is a mechanism for excluding members from an occupation (Gaumer 1984).

The state enacts licensure laws and accreditation requirements to achieve hegemony over health occupations. Variation among state laws and regulations is great.

Models of Nurse-Midwifery Practice

Dependent Model

Nurse-midwives in this model support the goal of providing safe, quality care to women who are under served and who are in prepaid health care programs. Most of these nurse-midwives work in large scale organizations such as hospitals, medical clinics, public health agencies, and health maintenance organizations (Cass 1988; Flanagan 1986).

Table 3.   Dependent Model of Nurse-midwifery Practice

Goals	To provide safe, quality care to underserved and prepaying clients
Work Settings	Hospitals
	Health Maintenance Organizations (HMOs)
	Public Health Departments
	Obstetricians' Offices
Division of Labor	Hierarchical
Reimbursement	Salaried employee
Social Control	Organizational
State Regulation	Secondary to organizational control

Obstetricians delegate occupational tasks to nurse-midwives in this model, through the structure of the employing organization. These tasks vary from providing prenatal care, counselling, and education in clinics and public health agencies, and managing births in hospitals, to providing post-natal care in a variety of organizational settings. Obstetricians determine the division of labor and make the rules for nurse-midwives, while the organization is the final authority in setting work standards. The state grants this authority to the organization.

Nurse-midwives in this model receive a salary and the occupational benefits associated with employment in large scale organizations. These include: malpractice insurance coverage, fringe benefits, and freedom from the problems of managing a practice, such as being 'on call' and finding a physician back-up (Goings 1986).

On the other hand, nurse-midwives experience multiple contextual pressures and conflicts. For example, to be cost-effective for the employing organization, nurse-midwives provide care for several women simultaneously (Goings 1986). They often manage the labor of women they have never seen before. Under these circumstances, the nurse-midwife is not able to 'labor sit' or to provide the one-on-one care that is inherent in midwifery ideology. Thus, the relationship between the nurse-midwife and the birthing woman is somewhat less personal than in other models.

Interdependent Model

Nurse-midwives in this model support the goals of: (1) providing safe, quality care to private clients and (2) providing well-women's care of all ages through education and counselling. Most of these nurse-midwives manage births in hospitals and provide well-women's care in their offices.

Table 4.   Interdependent Model of Nurse-Midwifery Practice

Goals	To provide safe, quality care to both public and private clients
	To provide well women's care and to promote women's knowledge through education
Work Settings	Hospitals, Nurse-midwives' Offices
	Obstetricians' Offices
Division of Labor	Integrated hierarchy
Reimbursement	Fee for service
Social Control	Mixed: organizational and client
State Regulation	May defer to organizational control

In this model, the division of labor is integrated because obstetricians and nurse-midwives work together as a team. Even though they collaborate, it is not an egalitarian relationship. Nurse-midwives are required to have a written agreement with the obstetricians, who will provide backup support to the nurse-midwife if 'anything goes wrong' (Rothman 1984).

These self-employed nurse-midwives receive payment from their clients through a variety of methods: Medicaid, private insurance, or cash. Similar to obstetricians, nurse-midwives are "on call" for all their clients. On the other hand, there are benefits to this type of practice. Organizational control over these workers is likely to be less than for others, because they are not employees of an organization.

State control in this model is more dominant than in the dependent model. Nurse-midwives, in some states, write and file written protocol agreements with the state licensing agency. Thus, there are additional procedural requirements and legal technicalities that nurse-midwives must meet in order to practice independently.

Independent Model

Nurse-midwives in this model support several goals: (1) to provide safe, quality care to private clients; (2) to provide continuity of care to families; (3) to minimize cost of birthing care to clients; and (4) to educate families about personal responsibility for health.

Table 5.   Independent Model of Nurse-Midwifery Practice

Goals	To provide safe, quality care to private clients
	To provide continuity of care to families
	To minimize cost of birthing care to clients
Work Settings	Birthing Centers, Homes
Division of Labor	Egalitarian, complete management by nurse-midwives
	Consultation with obstetricians when indicated
Social Control	Client
Reimbursement	Salaried employee of birthing center
	Fee-for service
State Regulation	Only a few states regulate birthing centers and home deliveries

In this model, the division of labor is egalitarian. Obstetricians do not supervise nurse-midwives. Instead, the relationship is a consultative one where the nurse-midwife calls the obstetrician only when the nurse-midwife determines the need for assistance. For a home birth, the nurse-midwife usually has an agreement with a hospital or a physician on where to refer a woman who may develop complications beyond the nurse-midwife's competence to manage.

Nurse-midwives in this model work in a birthing center, or they "catch" babies at home. In the latter location, the nurse-midwife does have the problem of managing a practice.

There are advantages for both clients and practitioners in this model. Interventionist techniques are used at a minimum and families are encouraged to manage the births. In the home birth, the danger of infection is reduced from that of a hospital or birthing center birth. The economic costs to the family are reduced considerably from hospital births. Nurse-midwives are able to practice midwifery without intervention from those who wish to practice obstetrics.

Client control in this model is dominant although women using a birthing center are to some degree constrained by the established rules. This is not the case with home births where the client is in direct control.

State control in this model is minimal because only 15 states regulate birthing centers, and fewer regulate home births. ACNM's practice standards require that all nurse-midwives have available to them referral services when indicated. This is not a problem for nurse-midwifery employees in the birthing center. It is a major problem for nurse-midwives who help at home births, because very few obstetricians are willing to take the risks that are, in their view, present.

DISCUSSION AND CONCLUSION

One way to understand the political and social activities of an occupation is to examine the interaction between occupational ideology and identity, and the relationship of that interaction to the practice of work. In the occupation of nurse-midwifery, members have developed conflicting ideologies that have been useful in determining the directions of the occupation. The social value of defining childbirth as a pathological condition reinforces the ideology of health professionals who want to retain the control of pregnancy within the system of medicine. The social value of defining childbirth as healthy and normal reinforces the ideology of health professionals who want to return the control of pregnancy and birth to women. Where nurse-midwifery fits into this controversy can be understood by analyzing the interaction between occupational ideology and identity and the relationship that interaction has to the practice of work.

Table 6.   Relationships Between Occupational
Ideology, Identity, and Practice

Ideology	Identity	Practice
Medicine	Nurse	Dependent
Nursing	Nurse-Midwife	Interdependent
Midwifery	Midwife	Independent

Nurse-midwives who support a medical ideology of childbirth and pregnancy are likely to identify themselves as nurses and to practice as employees in large organizations. Underlying this ideology is a commitment to intervention during the birthing process with the use of multiple obstetrical technologies. Hospitals have formal procedures and policies for the use of these technologies, which nurse-midwives must follow.

Nurse-midwives who support a nursing ideology are likely to identify themselves as nurse-midwives and to be self-employed practitioners. While they may define pregnancy as normal, they adopt the use of some obstetrical technologies for the safety of the mother and the unborn infant. These nurse-midwives manage their deliveries in hospitals, where technology is available. They are in the position of mediating between the hospital and their clients who want non-interventionist birthing care but for whatever reasons choose to be in a hospital during birth.

Nurse-midwives who support the midwifery ideology are likely to identify themselves as midwives and to practice in birthing centers and women's homes. They believe that women should control the birthing process. Nurse-midwives are there to support women in this natural process.

What are the consequences of such diversity for a small occupation as it continues to negotiate its position with other groups and occupations? One way to approach this question is to examine the occupational goals of each group and to determine how these are shaped by occupational ideology. The goals are important in shaping the practice of work.

A nurse-midwife whose occupational identity is nurse (or "junior" physician) and who works in a large organization is primarily committed to having a job. There is no career structure for a nurse-midwife who works in a subordinate position in a large organization. She has adopted, not adapted, the medical model of birthing care. The nurse-midwife has little opportunity for using her judgment, if it is contrary to hospital policy. It is unlikely that these nurse-midwives are going to work politically to bring about social changes that will alter their chances to work as nurse-midwives in hospitals.

A nurse-midwife whose occupational identity is nurse-midwife and who is a self-employed practitioner is primarily committed to a career in nurse-midwifery. She is committed to advancing the profession of nurse-midwifery, as a clinical specialty in nursing. The career route for nurse-midwives is in education, research, and clinical practice. Some nurse-midwives combine all these activities, especially those with a doctoral level degree. Career advancement includes a commitment to obtain more credentials and to "upgrade" the profession of nurse-midwifery. One nurse-midwife stated it simply, "All that we lack is a clear, strategic vision upon which to develop a long-range plan . . . a vision that becomes our life—not our job" (Ernst 1984, p. 298).

For these nurse-midwives, the survival of the occupation of nurse-midwifery is paramount. If this means accepting a subordinate position in the medical division of labor, then they will adjust their ideology to support this status. On the other hand, while in this position, they continue to work effectively to bring about change at a slow pace by negotiating with medicine the delegation of additional tasks. Also, these nurse-midwives have worked effectively in making alliances with some states to obtain more enabling legislation that often permits them to increase the boundaries of their competence.

A nurse-midwife whose occupational identity is midwife, and who is helping women in birth either at home or in the birthing center, is committed to providing women *humane* birthing care. This includes letting women choose alternative birthing sites and approaches to care. This nurse-midwife is committed to advancing the profession of midwifery to a level where all types of midwives provide humane maternity and well-women care that is family-centered. It is a career that is grounded in giving all women the opportunity to define pregnancy and birth for themselves.

Larkin (1983, p. 198), in his study of occupational monopoly in modern medicine, identified two forces that are significant in an occupation's ability to negotiate the boundaries of its competence: (1) a historically more powerful profession [external force] and (2) acceptance by an occupation of the benefits derived from accepting the subordinate position [internal force]. Nurse-midwifery has acted and reacted to the many forces and events using different strategies with different groups, and at different times in history.

The basic strategy used by ACNM is to accept its subordinate position to obstetrics, a historically more powerful profession. In Rooks' view, nurse-midwifery practice involves a collaborative view with obstetrics. "Nurse-midwifery would not have survived in this country without the essential support of numerous outstanding physicians. In fact, every nurse-midwife practicing today is doing so in collaboration with one or more physicians" (Rooks 1983, p. 3).[10] This strategy has worked successfully for nurse-midwifery as it grows in public esteem and social status. Changes resulting in benefits to nurse-midwifery, however, have been slow. Today, in many states, nurse-midwives have the authority to write prescriptions, the right to apply for hospital privileges, the right to admit patients to the hospital in their own names, and the right to bill clients directly and to receive direct reimbursement from Medicaid and third-party insurance.

There are tradeoffs, however, in accepting a subordinate position in the division of labor. The ideology of the dominant occupation becomes the ideology of the subordinate occupation. This is part of the controversy in nurse-midwifery today.

In conclusion, nurse-midwifery has negotiated its boundaries of competence with obstetrics and other groups. On the one hand, these boundaries are slowly growing as more tasks are delegated to nurse-midwives. The basic strategy used by ACNM is to accept its subordinate position to obstetrics, while at the same time negotiating for change. On the other hand, obstetrics reinforces its control over nurse-midwifery by requiring obstetric supervision of nurse-midwifery care, and the requirement for a back up arrangement with a physician. This dialectical process has resulted in multiple occupational ideologies and identities in the occupation of nurse-midwifery which have shaped the practice of work.

ACKNOWLEDGMENTS

The author wishes to thank Dianne Kammerer, Donna Carter, and two anonymous reviewers, for their generous comments on this paper. This paper was written while the author was on sabbatical leave from the George Washington University, Washington, D.C.

NOTES

1.   Nurse-midwifery is a "hybrid" occupation. It combines two complementary occupations where one is not the out-growth or extension of the other. The possession of credentials in one occupation, however, is a prerequisite for entry into the other.

"A certified nurse-midwife is an individual educated in the two disciplines of nursing and midwifery, who possesses evidence of certification according to the requirements of the American College of Nurse-Midwives" (ACNM) (Rooks and Haas 1986, p. 9). There are approximately 3000 certified nurse-midwives.

2.   For a thorough and critical review of the rise of obstetrics in the United States, see Arney (1982).

3.   The Kentucky State Association changed its name to the American Association of Nurse-Midwives. It merged with the American College of Nurse-Midwifery in 1969. The new organization became the American College of Nurse-Midwives (ACNM) in 1955.

4.   This was changed in 1973 to the *Journal of Nurse-Midwifery*.

5.   It is not possible in this paper to include the history of the relationships between nurse-midwives and lay midwives who were and continue to be important actors in the struggle of nurse-midwifery as an occupation. There are many excellent sources (Arms 1975; DeVries 1985; Eakins 1986; Litoff 1978; Radosh 1986; Sullivan and Weitz 1988; Wertz and Wertz 1977).

6.   Women's perception of childbirth and how these have changed over time can be found in Leavitt and Walton (1984).

7. A free standing birthing center is a short-stay, ambulatory, health care facility with access to in-hospital obstetrical and newborn services. They operate independently from hospitals (Eakins 1984, p. 49).

8. Other demographic measures not included in this paper are infant mortality and morbidity. Nurse-midwives have been very effective in the reduction of infant mortality among poor women.

9. Electronic fetal monitoring (EFM) is equipment that may be placed on the fetus/scalp (internal) or placed on the mother's abdomen (external). The purpose is to monitor the heartbeat of the unborn infant. Amniocentesis, a procedure done on "high risk" women, is used to determine the probability of genetic defects in the unborn infant.

10. Even a nurse-midwife who assists at a home birth must have a physician or hospital to call if she feels that a laboring woman needs medical assistance.

REFERENCES

Albrecht, G.L., and J.A. Levy. 1982. "The Professionalization of Osteopathy: Adaptation In The Medical Marketplace." Pp. 161-206 in *Research In The Sociology Of Health Care,* edited by J.A. Roth. Greenwich, CT: JAI Press.

Arms, S. 1975. *Immaculate Deception: A New Look at Women and Childbirth in America.* New York: Bantam Books.

Arney, W.R. 1982. *Power and the Profession of Obstetrics.* Chicago: University of Chicago Press.

Barrett, P.C. 1979. *The Legitimation of an Occupational Role: The Case of the Nurse-Midwife.* Unpublished doctoral dissertation, University of Florida.

Becker, H.S., B. Greer, E.C. Hughes, and A.L. Strauss. 1961. *Boys in White: Student Culture in Medical School.* Chicago: University of Chicago Press.

Begun, J.W., and R.C. Lippincott. 1987. "The Origins And Resolutions Of Interoccupational Conflict." *Work and Occupations* 14: 368-386.

Bryan, J.H. 1966. "Occupational Ideologies And Individual Attitudes Of Call Girls." *Social Problems* 13: 441-450.

Bucher, R. 1988. "On the Natural History of Health Care Occupations." *Work and Occupations* 15:131-147.

Burst, H.V. 1977. "Harmonious Unity." *Journal of Nurse-Midwifery* 22: 10-11.

Caplow, T. 1954. *The Sociology of Work.* Minneapolis: University of Minnesota Press.

Carrington, B. 1983. "Projected Student Declines: Seeking Solutions." *Journal of Nurse-Midwifery* 28:1-2.

Cass, P.S. 1988. *National Survey of Certified Nurse-Midwives: Perceived Position in the Health Care System and Potential for Mobilization.* Unpublished doctoral dissertation, University of Michigan.

Conway-Welch, C. 1986. "Assuring the Quality of Nurse-Midwifery Education: The ACNM Division of Accreditation." Pp. 10-13 in *Nurse-Midwifery in America,* edited by J. Rooks and J.E. Haas. Washington, D.C.: The American College of Nurse-Midwives Foundation.

Denzin, N.K. 1972. "Incomplete Professionalization: The Case of Pharmacy." Pp. 55-64 in *Medical Men and Their Work,* edited by E. Freidson and J. Lorber. Chicago: Aldine Atherton.

DeVries, R.G. 1985. *Regulating Birth.* Philadelphia, PA: Temple University Press.

_____. 1986a. "The Contest for Control: Regulating New and Expanding Health Occupations." *American Journal of Public Health* 76: 1147-1150.

_____. 1986b. "Barriers to Nurse-Midwifery: Is the Enemy Us?" *Journal of Nurse-Midwifery* 31:277-278.

Dressel, P.L., and D.M. Peterson. 1982. "Becoming a Male Stripper: Recruitment, Socialization, and Ideological Development." *Work and Occupations* 9: 387-406.

Dye, N.S. 1984. "Mary Breckinridge, The Frontier Nursing Service, and the Introduction of Nurse-Midwifery Service in the United States." Pp. 327-344 in *Women and Health in America,* edited by J.W. Leavitt. Madison: The University of Wisconsin Press.

Eakins, P.S. 1984. "The Rise of the Free Standing Birth Center: Principles and Practice." *Women and Health* 9: 49-64.

————. 1986. *The American Way of Birth.* Philadelphia, PA: Temple University Press.

Ernst, E.K. 1984. "Pioneering Interdependence in a System of Care for Childbearing Families." *Journal of Nurse-Midwifery* 29: 296-299.

Flanagan, J.A. 1986. "Childbirth in the Eighties: What Next?" *Journal of Nurse-Midwifery* 31: 194-199.

Foster, J.C. (1986) "Ensuring Competence of Nurse-Midwives at Entrance into the Profession: The National Certification Examination." Pp. 14-16 in *Nurse-Midwifery in America,* edited by J. Rooks and J.E. Haas. Washington, D.C.: The American College of Nurse-Midwives Foundation.

Gaumer, G.L. 1984. "Regulating Health Professionals: A Review of the Empirical Literature." *Health and Society* 62: 380-416.

Goings, J.R. 1986. "Success in a Health Maintenance Organization: Kaiser Permanente of Anaheim, California." Pp. 36-37 in *Nurse-Midwifery in America,* edited by J. Rooks and J.E. Haas. Washington, D.C.: The American College of Nurse-Midwives Foundation.

Hogan, A. 1975. "A Tribute to the Pioneers." *Journal of Nurse-Midwifery* (Summer): 6-11.

Hughes, E. 1958. *Men and Their Work.* Glencoe, IL: The Free Press.

————. 1959. "The Study of Occupations." Pp. 442-460 in *Sociology Today: Problems and Prospects,* edited by R.K. Merton and L. Broom, and L.S. Cottrell, Jr. New York: Basic Books.

Illich, I. 1975. *Medical Nemesis.* London: Calder and Boyars, LTD.

Jenkins, J. 1983. "Resource Mobilization Theory and the Study of Social Movements." Pages 527-553 in *Annual Review of Sociology,* edited by R.J. Turner and J. Short. Palo Alto, CA: Annual Reviews.

Krause, E.A. 1971. *The Sociology of Occupations.* Boston: Little, Brown.

Langer, J. 1977. "Drug Entrepreneurs and Dealing Culture." *Social Problems* 24: 377-386.

Larkin, G.V. 1983. *Occupational Monopoly and Modern Medicine.* London: Tavistock.

Leavitt, J.W. and W. Walton. 1984. "'Down to Death's Door': Women's Perceptions of Childbirth in America." Pages 155-165 in *Women and Health In America,* edited by J.W. Leavitt. Madison: The University of Wisconsin Press.

Litoff, J.B. 1978. *American Midwives: 1860 to the Present.* Westport, CT: Greenwood Press.

Lovell, J.P. 1964. "The Professional Socialization of the West Point Cadet." Pages 119-158 in *The New Military,* edited by M. Janowitz. New York: Russell Sage Foundation.

Lutz, S. 1987. "Some Freestanding Birthing Centers Falter." *Modern Healthcare,* p. 44.

Merton, R.K., G. Reader, and P.L. Kendall. 1957. *The Student-Physician.* Cambridge, MA: Harvard University Press.

"Midwives Alliance of North America." 1985. *Mana Times* (July).

Mundy, K.C. 1988. "Illusions of Place: The Social Effects of New In-Hospital Birthplaces." Pp. 39-70 in *Research In The Sociology Of Health Care,* edited by D.C. Wertz. Greenwich, CT: JAI Press.

Pavalko, R. 1971. *Sociology of Occupations and Professions.* Itasca, IL: F.E. Peacock Publishers.

————. 1988. *Sociology of Occupations and Professions.* Itasca, IL: F.E. Peacock Publishers.

Radosh, P.F. 1986. "Midwives in the United States: Past and Present." *Population Research and Policy Review* 5: 129-145.

Raisler, J. 1987. "Nurse-Midwifery Education: Issues for Survival and Growth." *Journal of Nurse-Midwifery* 32, 1-3.

Ritzer, G., and D. Walczak. 1986. *Working: Conflict and Change.* Englewood Cliffs, NJ: Prentice-Hall.

Rooks, J. 1983. "The Context of Nurse-Midwifery in the 1980s: Our Relationships with Medicine, Nursing, Lay-Midwives, Consumers and Health Care Economist." *Journal of Nurse-Midwifery* 28: 3-8.

————. 1986. "History and Evolution of Nurse-Midwifery in the United States." Pp. 17-20 in *Nurse-Midwifery in America,* edited by J. Rooks and J.E. Haas. Washington, D.C.: The American College of Nurse-Midwives Foundation.

Rooks, J., and S.H. Fischman. 1980. "American Nurse-Midwifery Practice in 1976-1977: Reflections of 50 Years of Growth and Development." *American Journal of Public Health* 70: 990-996.

Rooks, J., and J. E. Haas, eds. 1986. "Appendix E." Pp. 97-98 in *Nurse-Midwifery in America.* Washington, D.C.: The American College of Nurse-Midwives Foundation.

Rose, P. 1983. "Nurse-Midwifery Practice: Implications for the Future." *Journal of Nurse-Midwifery* 28:1-2.

Rosengren, W.R., and K.L. Sartell. 1986. "Current Obstetrical Technologies: A Clash of Values." Pp. 93-146 in *Research in The Sociology of Health Care,* edited by J.A. Roth and S.B. Ruzek. Greenwich CT: JAI Press.

Rothman, B.K. 1984. *Giving Birth: Alternatives in Childbirth.* New York: Penguin Books.

Rothman, R. A. 1979. "Occupational Roles: Power and Negotiation in the Division of Labor." *The Sociological Quarterly* 20: 495-515.

————. 1987. *Working: Sociological Perspectives.* Englewood Cliffs, NJ: Prentice Hall.

Ruzek, S.R. 1979. *The Women's Health Movement: Feminist Alternative to Medical Control.* New York: Praeger.

Sharp, E.S. 1983. "Nurse-Midwifery Education: Its Successes, Failures, and Future." *Journal of Nurse-Midwifery* 28: 17-23.

Strauss, G. 1972. "Professionalism and Occupational Associations." Pp. 236-253 in *The Social Dimensions of Work,* edited by C.D. Bryant. Englewood Cliffs, NJ: Prentice-Hall.

Sullivan, D.A., and R. Weitz. 1988. *Labor Pains: Modern Midwives and Home Birth.* New Haven, CT: Yale University Press.

Teasley, R. 1983. *Birth and the Division of Labor: The Movement to Professionalize Nurse-Midwifery, and its Relationship to the Movement for Home Birth and Lay Midwifery, A Case Study of Vermont.* Unpublished dissertation. Michigan State University.

Wertz, R.W., and D.C. Wertz. 1977. *Lying-In: A History of Childbirth in America.* New York: Schocken Books.

Willson, J. R. 1989. "Educating the Obstetrician-Gynecologist for the Future." *Obstetrics and Gynecology* 73: 125-129.

Yankauer, A. 1983. "The Valley of the Shadow of Birth." *American Journal of Public Health* 73: 635-638.

THE TRANSFORMATION AND FATE OF FORMAL KNOWLEDGE:

THE CASE OF SENSORY INTEGRATION

Arnold Arluke

ABSTRACT

The goal of this study was to examine the application of a single body of formal knowledge, that of sensory integration, and the implications of its use for the professional power of occupational therapy. If the diffusion and institutional-ization of knowledge are signs of professional power, then sensory integration has furthered occupational therapy's influence. A number of different occupational groups now authorize its use or actually apply it in a variety of settings. Yet with its diffusion, formal knowledge about sensory integration has been diluted and compromised as each occupation interprets and applies it. Several types of knowledge were found to result from the use of sensory integration, including orthodox, counterpointal, borrowed, revelatory, rationalized, and pragmatic knowledge. If professional power is construed as a monopoly of knowledge and technique by a single group, then occupational therapy has not furthered its power through sensory integration.

Current Research on Occupations and Professions, Volume 6, pages 179-199.
ISBN: 1-55938-236-8

INTRODUCTION

A major component of professional power is the ability to produce and maintain a body of esoteric knowledge which requires substantial interpretation in its application. Arguments for deprofessionalization contend that some groups may be unable to control their knowledge base either in terms of how it is used or who applies it (e.g., Haug 1973; McKinlay 1982; Oppenheimer 1973; Toren 1975). It is argued that the knowledge gap between practitioners and clients has generally narrowed, and that competing or subordinate occupations may also claim expertise to apply and to interpret the same knowledge.

Freidson (1986), however, reminds us that professions continue to produce knowledge or elaborate former knowledge, such that a knowledge lag may always exist between practitioners and clients. More importantly, he points out that it may be shortchanging the power of professions to see encroachment of their knowledge, whether in substance or form, as a sign of impotence. Once institutionalized, knowledge can influence human affairs, justify expansion into new professional markets, and foster increased demand for services. Simultaneously, of course, the very success some groups have in institutionalizing their knowledge may lead to its dilution and compromise.

Although Freidson offers a more balanced view of professional power than those who maintain that such power is waning, his work on this subject is more hypothesis than test. Patently, there is a need for a sustained empirical analysis of a single body of knowledge and its diffusion and transformation over time. Such analysis could test and refine Freidson's work in at least two ways. First, Freidson argues that formal knowledge may be recast by each separate group that uses it. He notes that practitioners coin a working version of formal knowledge, while administrators create a more formalized version of such knowledge. Yet entirely other kinds of transformations may occur and need to be identified. Second, Freidson suggests that such transformations have implications for the professional power of the group that first authored the knowledge. But it is unclear how different types of transformations compromise professional power.

This paper examines the application and use of a single body of formal knowledge, that of sensory integration, and the implications of its use for the professional power of occupational therapy. In the mid-1960s, Jean Ayres, an occupational therapist and educational psychologist, formulated what is now known as sensory integration theory and technique. Ayres observed that children sometimes had an over or under sensitivity to touch, movement, sights or sounds, an unusually low or high activity level, coordination problems, or delays in speech, motor skills and academic achievement. She believed that these problems were often due to the brain's inability to automatically and unconsciously process and link information coming into the senses. Lacking efficient sensory integration, children might manifest signs of sensory integrative disorder in their development, behavior, or learning.

Originally developed as a treatment for children with cerebral palsy (Clark and Shuer 1978), sensory integrative procedures were soon applied to children with learning disabilities, thus enabling practitioners to take advantage of new laws, particularly PL 94-142, which provided reimbursement for treating learning disabled school children. So-called "normal" children in schools who suffered from "invisible disabilities," such as clumsiness, were also thought to benefit from sensory integrative treatment. More recently, other clinical populations, including the aged, have been advanced as potential clients for this approach.

Ayres maintained that improving the entire neurophysiological system was a more effective way to treat learning disabilities than to take the symptomatic approach of western medicine or the cognitive strategy of education. She argued that it was necessary to create a situation where the brain itself could learn (Dellman 1977). To do this, the therapist had to provide the impaired child with various physical experiences and challenges centering on the importance of motion and coordination, such as balancing on a large ball or swinging on a rope.

Ayres also encouraged practitioners to modify their treatments and equipment to meet the unique needs of each child. Practitioners were to develop interesting activities which challenged each child at an appropriate level of difficulty. This one-to-one "child-directed therapy" now includes a large number of devices and activities, some of which are unstandardized and improvisational. If successful, these experiences are believed to alter the brain's general ability to process and to use certain sensory information.

To explain and elaborate her approach, Ayres and others have created a body of formal knowledge about sensory integration. This literature describes the neurophysiological theory of learning, provides diagnostic labels for sensory integrative problems (e.g., "tactile defensiveness"), suggests various sensory integrative therapies, offers a test battery to make such diagnoses, and attempts to confirm this approach through anecdotal and quasi-experimental means. The application of this knowledge, however, has departed from the manner in which it is described by Ayres and her followers. Why and how this formal knowledge has been transformed, and the implications of such transformation for the professional power of occupational therapy, are the subjects of this paper.

The research reported here is based on 45 interviews with occupational therapists, physical therapists, special education directors, adapted physical educators, psychologists, physicians, occupational therapy administrators, and parents of learning disabled children. Respondents were obtained nonrandomly through a snowballing technique of referrals from prior respondents. The interviews followed an open-ended, semistructured schedule which allowed respondents to elaborate their responses and to redirect the line of questioning when so desired. With few exceptions, an exceedingly high level of cooperation was obtained; some respondents wanted an opportunity to get thoughts and feelings "off their chests" about sensory integration, while others were deeply committed to sensory integration and welcomed the opportunity to talk about a topic of high priority to them. Additional information was obtained by reviewing the major journals and newsletters in the respondents' fields.

ORTHODOX KNOWLEDGE

Those who create formal knowledge, especially when that knowledge is directed to understanding and reducing human problems, may campaign for the acceptance and use of their ideas and techniques. It may be particularly important for knowledge producers to campaign outside their profession when they do not have the administrative authority to apply their thinking, or when they do not have the moral and scientific authority to convince others that their thinking is worthy. Of higher priority, however, is to get their own discipline to accept the knowledge—a task which by no means is assured, especially when that knowledge is seen as controversial.

Some form of enclaving may be necessary for innovative knowledge to become codified and institutionalized. Enclaving allows for the discovery of colleagueship (Bucher 1988) and the formation of proponent roles, while garrisoning and protecting an innovative approach which might otherwise be threatened by those negative or hostile to it within a profession. After a process of intellectual gestation and strategizing in such enclaves, there may be subsequent spillover beyond the enclave but within that occupational group. Publishing and more informal evangelizing help the knowledge to "catch on."

Proponents of new knowledge may insist that there is only one right way to learn and to apply this knowledge, despite critics who often advocate a simpler version of the knowledge and who advance less stringent requirements for its mastery. Yet orthodox knowledge is not static; its content will change as proponents refine, modify and extend it. Long after the initial creators and proponents disappear, there still may be different opinions as to the proper make-up of knowledge—whether in its orthodox form or some other version. These opinions not only shape the content of knowledge, but their sheer presence often perpetuates the idea of an orthodoxy of knowledge since one set of opinions typically seeks to defend the original form of that knowledge against those who seek to change it.

To develop sensory integration, its proponents separated themselves organizationally and professionally from mainstream occupational therapy. In the 1960s and 1970s, Ayres was aware of the fragile state of sensory integration within her field. Initially ostracized by occupational therapy, Ayres organized a structure outside of the discipline that could provide a supportive context and a power base for her innovative thinking to survive and to mature. An inner circle of occupational therapists was created, later to become the "faculty," with whom Ayres could develop her novel approach. Ayres also strove for an association with the University of Southern California to give sensory integration some academic legitimacy. Courses offered at Ayres' sensory integration clinic and the faculty who taught them became university courses and faculty.

During the late 1960s and early 1970s, Ayres defined her approach to a wider collegial group by publishing key works in the *American Journal of Occupational Therapy (AJOT)*. Although there was some reference to the concept of "integration" before this period (Ayres 1958), it was not until 1964 (Ayres 1964) that she postulated causal attachments between, for example, hyperactivity and tactile functions, and in 1965 (Ayres 1965) she isolated "five syndromes" purportedly reflecting sensory-motor dysfunctions. By the late 1960s, Ayres began to consider an expanded list of objectives for her therapy, with terms such as "learning disability" appearing more frequently in her writings (e.g., Ayres 1968). Also during these years, the importance of vestibular and tactile stimulation emerged more clearly in her articles. The use of remedial techniques, as well as the need to have children actively participate in one-to-one therapy, were soon discussed in a text (Ayres 1972).

Not until the decade of the 1970s did Ayres and her followers achieve some degree of recognition within occupational therapy and some formalization of their approach. Textbooks and required courses in occupational therapy programs began to note and to teach sensory integration, although major learning disabilities texts outside the field of occupational therapy still made no mention of it (e.g., Gearheart 1973). As early as 1971, the American Occupational Therapy Foundation recognized sensory integration as part of occupational therapy when the Foundation decided to focus on the child with minimal brain dysfunction. In 1972, the Center for the Study of Sensory Integrative Dysfunction was organized (AOTA 1979). By the late 1970s, some occupational therapists pushed for official recognition of sensory integration by the American Occupational Therapy Associaiton (AOTA). One "sensory integration therapist," writing in *AJOT,* called on AOTA to "endorse and support the movement toward recognition of sensory integration as an integral element of occupational therapy" (Price 1977, p. 287). A sensory integration specialty section was formed in 1978 "to nurture sensory integration theory" and because it had "a unique body of knowledge" (AOTA 1978, p. 2). More informally, some AOTA members began to refer to themselves as "sensory integration specialists," although this has been discouraged by both the AOTA and Sensory Integration International.

Proponents of sensory integration found that younger occupational therapists were particularly interested in such knowledge. Perpetually plagued with a nebulous professional identity (AOTA 1988), sensory integration could empower novice therapists in search of a clear and exclusive identity for occupational therapy. One therapist (Price 1977, p. 288) observes that sensory integration can have a "revitalizing" and "energizing" effect on occupational therapists by helping to retain those "discouraged with the limitations of conventional methods." This therapist also notes that sensory integration's medical and scientific appearance can accord recognition and respect to the practitioner and lay to rest the "play lady stereotype" of the occupational therapist. Another therapist adds that "many don't want to keep doing ADL [activities of daily living] things—they want to be more like experts than people who do very concrete skills without any theoretical base, and which are easily understandable and borrowable by other professionals."

As her following grew, Ayres' supporters began to advocate the use of sensory integration for groups other than learning disabled children and to publish studies in journals outside of occupational therapy on the use and effectiveness of sensory integration. In addition, proponents of this knowledge actively campaigned to win support from a small number of pediatricians and neurologists who could refer patients to therapists in private practice and endorse recommendations by school therapists for sensory integrative treatments.

By the early 1980s, the AOTA was pressed to issue formal proclamations on the state of sensory integration. Initial statements sought to clarify who should receive sensory integrative treatment (Hightower-Vandamm 1980), questioning its application to adults while affirming its use with children (Posthuma 1983). The AOTA also moved to set practice standards, recommending "certification" for those using the sensory integration test battery and "advanced training" for those who apply sensory integrative treatments. Sensory Integration International faculty were to conduct certification and to teach intensive courses on sensory integrative theory.

These steps by the AOTA served to institutionalize sensory integrative knowledge and technique within the field. The AOTA's official backing of sensory integration, however, does not mean that it has been enthusiastically embraced by most occupational therapists. While there is no organized opposition, criticisms of sensory integration, in the form of research articles, editorials, and letters to editors, continue to appear in official occupational therapy publications and elsewhere.

Some critics have focused on the cultish use of sensory integration. For instance, one discussion (Werder and Bruininks 1982) describes sensory integration as "important but mysterious....Sensory integration is characterized by neurological terminology which is viewed as complex, and even intimidating by many educators. Because of its lack of guidelines, its complexity, and exclusive jargon, sensory integration is rarely questioned and widely accepted in schools throughout the country." Others (e.g., Posthuma 1983, p. 343) oppose the "widespread use" of sensory integration, suggesting that the approach is "taking on 'fad' characteristics, everyone is using it to treat everything!" While still others call attention to the methodological flaws of studies claiming to demonstrate the efficacy of sensory integrative treatments (e.g., Ottenbacher 1982).

More than simple differences of professional opinion or alternative theories, the consequence of sensory integration's promotion and dissent within occupational therapy has been to create an orthodoxy regarding what practitioners should know. Its proponents have become defenders of this orthodoxy and have acquired some degree of intellectual if not moral authority over the content and teaching of sensory integration. They have also taken on the responsibility of confronting in the literature those outside the profession who are seen as making "politicized" and "unfounded" attacks against sensory integration. Its detractors within occupational therapy further define this orthodoxy by accepting the general idea of sensory integration, but having qualms over particular aspects of it. Thus, the question facing most occupational therapists today is not whether sensory integration is legitimate knowledge, but how people should become certified in it and what people should master to do it.

COUNTERPOINTAL KNOWLEDGE

When one field frames the formal knowledge of another field such that its legitimacy is questioned, then counterpointal knowledge is created. Counterpointal transformations principally stem from the paradigmatic clashes of different fields, although they can result from competition over the control of specific techniques or the right to treat certain groups of patients. Under such circumstances, the filtering, reinterpreting, and distorting of formal knowledge will transform its content and make it possible to categorize and understand it with like approaches also deemed questionable. With such a transformation, formal knowledge becomes a type of institutionalized deviance.

For the most part, the medical profession's reaction to sensory integration has been to transform it into counterpointal knowledge. This transformation has occurred as certain medical specialties have expanded their practices to include problems formerly managed by sensory integration therapists. Pediatricians, for example, have expanded their claims to treat childhood problems, including learning disabilities, due to decreased demand for their services (Blim and Matlin 1987) and opportunities presented by PL 94-142 (American Academy of Pediatrics 1985a). Neurologists, too, have also moved into the learning disabilities arena in recent years.

This expansion has been supported and guided by the creation of new medical concepts. The "difficult child" (Thomas, Chess, and Birch 1968) has been the essential notion behind pediatrics' expansion. At first, this disorder was found in children between the ages of two and ten who demonstrated arrhythmic behaviors, poor adaptability, distractibility, and slow or excessive activity. Over time, additional symptoms were added to the diagnosis of "difficult child" that clearly overlapped the learning disabled population treated by allied health workers in schools. By the late 1980s, the "difficult child" also suffered from "poor scholastic performance" and "developmental problems," as well as from "reactive problems in behavior in areas such as social competence, task performance or self-relations" (Chess 1986, p. 43).

For neurologists, the concept of the "soft sign" has made it possible to expand their domain to include treatment of learning disabilities. The "soft sign" has been used in two different ways by neurologists (Levine, Brooks, and Shonkoff 1980). For some, it refers to a subtle manifestation of mild brain deficit. For others, soft signs are considered to be positive but normal findings in an examination. This latter definition of soft signs has been associated with neuromaturational delay or "lag" (Kinsbourne 1973).

Both pediatricians and neurologists have incorporated their notions of the "difficult child" and the "soft sign" into a "developmental" view of motor disabilities in children (Kruckey and Gubbay 1983). This perspective maintains that most sensory integrative dysfunctions are usually outgrown, adapted to quite easily, and can be found by proponents of this approach in almost any child, including honor students (e.g., American Academy of Pediatrics 1985b: Chamberlin 1985; Lerer 1981; Levine personal correspondence with R. Chamberlin April 22, 1985). Thus, when filtered through the developmental approach, much of what is treated by the sensory integration therapist is not seen as a legitimate medical problem because it will go away and because the child seems to cope well with it.

Sensory integration is discredited further because it has been categorized by medicine as one more "process-oriented approach" to treating children with learning disabilities and handicaps (Clark personal communication with T. Lombard December 9, 1985). Articles that list "controversial," "unproven," and "unorthodox" therapies for children typically include sensory integration with therapies such as megavitamin therapy, special diets, patterning, perceptual motor training, and optometric exercises (e.g., Ferry 1985; Silver 1975). Pediatricians and neurologists warn their colleagues "to resist the temptation to follow each new treatment fad willy-nilly" (Sieben 1977, p. 133). The result of such lumping is that much of the uniqueness of sensory integration is lost by equating it with entirely different approaches and by reducing its complexity to make such lumping possible.

Neither is such lumping of formal knowledge limited to medicine. Special educators are also skeptical of sensory integration. On the whole, they see sensory integration as an abstract, theoretical understanding of why a child has a functional problem, but do not see it as helpful for treatment. Instead, learning disabilities are thought to be best addressed at the academic level, in a direct and practical way. Their "cognitive" perspective sees the work of both perceptual motor theorists and sensory integration therapists as of "questionable usefulness and as simply part of the legacy of the field of learning disabilities" (Reid and Hresko 1981). Such treatments are seen as "ineffective" ways to increase academic achievement. Reid and Hresko (1981, p. 85), for example, conclude that "the only recommendation that can be made to teachers who work with children who exhibit such deficits is that they concentrate on teaching the curriculum."

The filtering of sensory integration, through the developmental approach and the medical model, has reconstituted its content, while the lumping of sensory integration has simplified it. One notable example of such transformation is a recent review (Arendt, MacLean, and Baumeister 1988) of research on the efficacy of sensory integration. According to Clark and Primeau (1988), this article simplifies and distorts Ayres' theory on a number of counts. For instance, it maintains that Ayres' model sees sensory integration as the sole cause of, and indistinguishable from, adaptive responding, when in fact the model contends that sensory integration is only one contributor to adaptive responding, and that the two can be distinguished; that Ayres' model sees every kind of maladaptive behavior as indicative of sensory integrative dysfunction, when in fact the model distinguishes those children with maladaptive behaviors who have sensory integrative dysfunction from those who do not; that Ayres' model sees incoordination problems as categorically sensory integrative problems, when in fact the model maintains that poor motor coordination can be caused by many different factors, some having little to do with sensory integration; that Ayres' model embraces full-fledged recapitulation theory, when in fact the model does not; that Ayres' model is a grab bag of sensory stimulation techniques, when in fact the model requires adherence to certain theoretical principles; and that Ayres' model can be fixed and given to a passive child, when in fact the model insists that it be adapted to the child, and that the child be an active participant in treatment.

If sensory integration is framed as counterpointal knowledge, its use may be restricted or prevented in organizational settings. For example, to the extent that physicians have been able to carve out a professionally dominant role in schools and to distinguish their knowledge base from that of other practitioners, their rulings on the use of sensory integration are weighty. Pediatricians who become the "liaison" between the family, the educator, and the psychologist in schools, may be granted authority to rule on treatments provided to children, including sensory integrative therapies. As one physician notes: "It is not sufficient to say that trampoline, balance board, dominance, and visual training are matters that are esoteric but the physician should recognize their lack of credibility and direct the child to proper educational resources" (Goldberg 1983, p. 1200). Physicians may also be given organizational control over other occupations and can use their authority to influence what people do as well as how they do it, including the provision of sensory integration. Many school districts require a physician's order for occupational therapy, even though such a prescription is not officially required by the state (Okamoto, McEwen, Marlowe, and Hammons 1983). In addition, school physicians often assume a managerial role during team meetings where evaluations and educational plans are discussed.

Yet, physicians in school systems have not always been able to impose a definition of sensory integration as counterpointal knowledge. In recent decades, occupational therapists have succeeded in establishing the legitimacy of their services and a niche for their presence in schools. Garnering important allies, such as the parents of special needs children, has also helped to keep in check physicians opposed to the use of sensory integration. Nevertheless, in other settings, such as hospitals, physicians have more successfully sustained a definition of sensory integration as a form of counterpointal knowledge because they exercise substantial authority over the work of allied health professionals.

BORROWED KNOWLEDGE

Formal knowledge developed within a particular discipline may be borrowed by other fields when paradigms are compatible and authorship of knowledge is not contested. Such borrowing does not entail an equivalent repayment for the knowledge taken with other knowledge. But there is a return for what is taken in that borrowing does further the institutionalization and legitimacy of knowledge. It is likely, however, that some shaping of this knowledge will occur as it is incorporated into other fields.

For example, the physical education specialty that designs and adapts exercise for exceptional children has borrowed and transformed sensory integration. Adapted physical education textbooks typically discuss sensory integration as an adjunct to perceptual-motor approaches. This grouping does not stigmatize sensory integration, since perceptual motor approaches are seen as legitimate by adapted physical education. But the grouping does categorize sensory integration with treatments that are often quite different from it and, in the process, its meaning is changed.

More direct and substantial change in the meaning of sensory integration has resulted from its selective absorption by adapted physical education. While ignoring sensory integration's theoretical side, many of its treatments and its test battery have been accepted. Not surprisingly, texts in the field (e.g., Sherrill 1986) limit their discussion of sensory integration to problems faced by the adapted physical educator, such as inhibiting abnormal reflexes and stimulating normal postural reactions. The possibility that sensory integrative treatment can help learning disabled students with academic problems is ignored in these textbooks; defined as a "nonacademic" discipline, no claims are made that adapted physical education can effect classroom performance.

Of course, borrowing knowledge may not only transform its content; the right to apply it may also be claimed. The adapted physical education literature is not consistent about this question regarding sensory integration. Sherrill (1986, p. 35), for instance, notes that since "many occupational therapists are now using equipment previously thought to belong in gymnasiums: scooter boards, therapy balls, and balancing apparatus," an occupational therapist should be contacted if sensory integrative treatment is needed. Another author (Pyfer 1988), however, is not as willing to delegate sensory integrative evaluations and treatments to occupational therapists; she maintains that adapted physical educators, as well as physical therapists, can do such evaluation and treatment.

REVELATORY KNOWLEDGE

When the formal knowledge of professions is explained in a way that the laity can understand, it may become revelatory knowledge. But revelatory knowledge is more than demystification; it is also a striking disclosure because of its impact on those who receive it. It can suddenly clarify confusion, confirm suspicion, reassure anxiety, and reverse despair. As a consequence, it can rally strong support for such knowledge, but the knowledge may undergo simplification and personalization.

When Ayres started her private clinic, she found it difficult to explain sensory integration to parents, and her earlier text (Ayres 1972) was too technical for them. She soon published a book to "help parents recognize sensory integrative problems in their children, understand what is going on, do something to help the child, and then understand what the sensory integration therapist is doing for the child" (Ayres 1979, p. 10). Nearly two-hundred pages long, this work does not describe every aspect of sensory integrative theory and practice to parents, but it does attempt to share an enormous amount of its formal knowledge. Three chapters are devoted to a theoretical and scientific discussion of the nervous system and brain, six chapters detail different diagnostic categories of sensory integrative dysfunction, and two chapters show parents what they can do at home to treat their children. Also, many occupational therapists have taken it upon themselves to educate parents about the nature, cause, and treatment of sensory integrative dysfunction.

Despite attempts to educate parents, their understanding of sensory integration falls short of the orthodox conception of this knowledge. What parents do know is often restricted to the specific problems of their children. For example, one parent believes that her child's awkwardness is the only problem that sensory integration can treat, and that her child's treatments constitute the entire approach. In some cases, parents may also include activities in their definition of sensory integration which, although fun and perhaps even useful for their children, are not sensory integrative treatments per se. For one parent, taking her child to Gymboree—a national franchise featuring music, games, sights, and sounds to stimulate young children—is sensory integration. Nor are these personal conceptions of sensory integration restricted to the parents of children in sensory integrative therapy; they are sometimes shared with other parents as well as school administrators and teachers.

However they may interpret sensory integration, learning about it is a relief for many parents who have found that since the birth of their children "things aren't quite right" with them. For some reason unknown to parents, even things such as giving their children baths or getting them dressed become "complete disasters." These problems puzzle parents even more when their children have normal if not high intelligence. Not knowing what causes the problems, they may even blame themselves. As one parent notes: "I didn't know what was going on—I started to doubt myself." Although general practitioners, pediatricians and neurologists may be consulted by parents, physicians often deny that problems exist or, more likely, brush the problems off as minor and temporary. Parents are left feeling disappointed, confused, and frustrated.

Many of these concerns are eased for parents when they discover sensory integration. Most importantly, it provides a label for what they have struggled with as an anonymous entity, and it validates that the problem is worthy of professional help. More than clarification and validation, the discovery of sensory integration means less guilt for parents. They learn that such problems are "internal" to the child and not the result of "something I have or haven't done." Once armed with new knowledge about the nature, cause, and treatment of their children's problems, including how to do some treatments themselves, parents may no longer feel powerless in their contacts with health-care professionals; they can now challenge professionals unsympathetic to the problems of their children.

Possession of this knowledge encourages a strong entrepreneurial and litigious attitude in many parents, as it does among other parents in similar situations (Darling 1988). Parents have mounted considerable "heat" on school administrators in order to obtain desired services, such as sensory integration. In Cambridge, Massachusetts, for example, a "Parents Advisory Committee" was organized to pressure the special education director to reinstate cutbacks in occupational therapy. Beyond informal and spontaneous groups that emerge among concerned parents, more formal advocacy groups to aid parents have been formed to advance special services in schools. For instance, in 1987, the

Minnesota branch of the Association for Retarded Citizens created a task force to help parents win desired physical and occupational therapy services and to mobilize parental support as a group (ARC 1987). Among other things, the task force warned that because school districts were facing shortages of funds and therapists, administrators might pressure therapists to provide minimal service, establish overly restrictive criteria for services, use auxiliary personnel instead of therapists, and encourage inappropriate assessments of children. The Association has produced a pamphlet listing those occupational and physical therapy services, including sensory integration, to which parents are entitled. Also, groups such as the Federation for Children with Special Needs in Massachusetts, have acquired funding to teach social change strategies to professionals and parents.

RATIONALIZED KNOWLEDGE

When formal knowledge is applied in the human services, administrators must take responsibility for its costs. They monitor, assess, define, and allocate knowledge according to the demands its use places on organizational employees and other resources. As a result, formal knowledge becomes shaped by "protocols," "plans," "priorities," and "criteria" which detail, in as much specificity as possible, the content and use of applied knowledge. The effect of rationalizing knowledge is to increase its formality, even though there is a certain amount of ambiguity inherent in formal knowledge—a feature which permits professionals to tailor it to the unique situations they face.

Schools have been one setting in which sensory integration has undergone rationalization. The administrative authority granted to special education directors makes it possible for them to influence how knowledge is applied in schools. Dominating the special education director's perspective is the need to "exercise control" over services for children. In the face of burgeoning numbers of requests for services, special education directors see themselves as "gatekeepers" of all requests for special services and adopt various "managerial strategies" to contain costs. "The institutional response," says one administrator, is to "throw the kitchen sink at a problem; I need to make it difficult for people to do that." Another administrator agrees: "once the kid is blessed with the label 'child with special education needs,' the kid is entitled to virtually anything if you want to pursue it through the courts....I mean individual computers....[T]he sky is the limit...after-school programs, individual tutorials, adaptive equipment."

Many special education administrators seek to restrict the use of sensory integration because they question its educational value and fear its endless demand by parents. One administrator claims that parents will "battle" for sensory integration because they "want their kid to be normal in other [noneducational] ways. It should not be the school's responsibility to teach kids to ride bikes and tie shoes." They often see parents as overly protective of their children: "instead of letting the child stumble and fall... they want a perfect environment, a bubble" which exceeds the educational goals of schools. "Once it [sensory integration] is started," soberly notes another special education director, "they say it is beneficial and has to be continued." Another bemoans the fact that there are "no guidelines for exactly when this procedure should be used with what sort of child and vice versa," thus leading to the mushrooming of services and costs.

Whether sensory integration is seen as a form of "voodoo," or as a service of value, administrators inevitably exercise some control over its provision and, as a consequence, restructure its meaning. One way this is done is to specify when sensory integration can be used. The effect of such restrictions on sensory integration is to transform what it is. In some school systems, for instance, it is informally understood that requests for sensory integrative treatment are never questioned if it is for preschoolers, but that administrators will exercise "judgment" if such requests are for children over the age of five. In these schools, sensory integration is defined as a technique for preschoolers, despite the fact that Ayres and her proponents see sensory integration as a rather open-ended technique, perhaps taking years to work, and as useful for older children and adults.

Sometimes restrictions on the use of sensory integration are specified in formal criteria. The effect of rationalizing the allocation of services through formal criteria is not only to define sensory integration as appropriate for only a narrow population of recipients by age, but also to define sensory integrative problems more narrowly than construed in the occupational therapy literature. In one public school system (Bisbicos 1987), criteria were constructed to cap the delivery of occupational therapy services and, in particular, sensory integration. Of first "priority" were children under eight years of age who demonstrated serious sensory-motor deficits. Sensory integrative problems, specified in these guidelines as "fine motor, muscle tone, and perceptual problems leading to marked tool-use awkwardness or weakness in bilateral coordination," were defined as second priority and were restricted to only children in kindergarten and first grade.

Special education directors can also restrict the provision of sensory integration and shape its content by deciding who can provide it through hiring, transferring, and firing personnel. Since there is a considerable difference in the quantity and type of knowledge that occupational therapists have about sensory integration, let alone those outside occupational therapy (Tickle-Degnen 1988), deciding who can deliver it will influence the content of sensory integration. Occupational therapists with sensory integration certification will generally provide a more orthodox version of it than will therapists without such certification, whose version of sensory integration will generally be less diluted than that done by most adapted physical educators, for instance. Depending on the form of sensory integration which is performed, teachers, parents, and administrators will come to understand the meaning of sensory integration accordingly. Administrators may also "struggle" to distinguish the competencies of professionals in their schools and, in so doing, redefine the population of recipients. In one case, the special education director sought to distinguish adapted physical education from occupational therapy and finally "carved out the lower end of the spectrum developmentally as being OT," thus effectively stopping older children from receiving sensory integration.

Another way administrators can shape sensory integration is to formalize its delivery. In order to be "cost effective," one administrator required the delivery of sensory integration to groups of children rather than to individual children, a feature clearly stipulated in Ayres' writing. In other cases, administrators may specify in official school policies that sensory integration is to be used only for purposes other than those for which it was originally devised, as was done in one school system where occupational therapists can provide such therapy merely for "exercise and training activity." Special education directors also control the allocation of school resources for the purchase of equipment and the availability of rooms for therapy. Restricting resources will limit the range of sensory integrative therapies which can be given, thereby constricting the content of treatment itself and what people come to know as sensory integration.

Attempts by special education directors to control sensory integration are often buttressed by the authority of the state. Pressure on state governments to reduce the cost of special education has resulted in the reduction, modification, and streamlining of occupational therapy services in many public schools (Royeen 1986). In one case, the state legislature mandated a fiscal analysis of occupational therapy in public schools and posed a specific "challenge" to sensory integration (Lombard 1985), questioning its effectiveness and its mushrooming demand.

More specifically, the state focused on the ability of sensory integration to improve learning disorders and the appropriateness of providing such care under PL 92-142. The state chose to define narrowly the meaning of "related service" in PL 94-142, only allowing the use of public funds for students with "overt physical or motor ramifications to their handicaps" (Lombard 1985, p. 15). This definition dealt a severe blow to sensory integrative services by opposing occupational therapy's broader conception of "related services" which allowed the use of public funds for students with mild learning problems and developmental delays. Recently, some local school districts have had to defend their use of sensory integration when it was being used "for something motorically funny," according to state officials. A further blow to sensory integration came when this state labeled it an "experimental procedure." This recommendation officially excluded PL 94-142 support for sensory integration since state board of education rules required school districts to fund experimental programs only through Chapter 3525.1320. It is also likely that such labeling has set back progress made by occupational therapists to establish the legitimacy of sensory integration in this state.

PRAGMATIC KNOWLEDGE

Practitioners who apply formal knowledge in organizational settings will be yet another source for its theoretical and practical transformation. Application of knowledge requires its interpretation so that it can meet the organizational constraints influencing its use and fit the exigencies of the concrete situations faced by practitioners, given their professional training and judgments about the knowledge. Dilution is especially likely when knowledge appears rather simple to reproduce and use by those untrained or unfamiliar with its mechanics and rationalization. Although dilution expedites the diffusion of knowledge by making it part of a common vocabulary of professional work, in so doing, it becomes unrestricted in its application and interpretation.

Some dilution, in terms of the labeling of sensory integration, has occurred as a deliberate strategy to use this knowledge in settings where it is strongly opposed. By calling it something other than sensory integration, practitioners can mask and conceal its use from those who object to it. One school-based occupational therapist calls it "sensory motor program" so that her supervising physician, who prohibits its use, would not know what she is doing. In another case, an occupational therapist in a hospital was told by her supervisor, who in turn was told by "someone above her," "never" to write in her evaluations that a patient has "sensory integrative dysfunction." Despite this warning, she still is able to get other hospital therapists who read her evaluations to provide sensory integrative treatments by using "code words" in her reports, such as "motor planning" or "tactile defensiveness," which give her intentions away to knowledgeable staff members. Another hospital-based occupational therapist says that when she runs in-service sessions for special educators, pediatricians, and psychologists, she talks about sensory integration and its test battery without specifically mentioning them because "it is like waving a red flag." She claims to "package" sensory integration in a way that does not get people angry and critical; merely saying "SI" at these sessions, she fears, "might start an emotional battle." In fact, one AOTA (1986) publication shows practitioners how to describe sensory integrative problems in educational plans and obtain such services without explicitly requesting sensory integration.

Part-time or "itinerant" occupational therapists in school systems are partly responsible for the dilution of sensory integration. In many cases, they think they are doing sensory integrative treatments in the hallways of schools for fifteen minutes, twice a week, even though they may have limited or no formal training in sensory integration theory or test interpretation. Some therapists do such a highly modified version of sensory integration, the only thing in common with the original is the equipment. One occupational therapist works in a mental health center where patients receive "sensory stimulation," a "form" of sensory integration in her opinion. "I don't back it up with theory...and I don't use specific techniques to get a specific result." While she uses sensory integrative techniques, such as the scooter board, she does it "more as a stimulatory thing rather than thinking that I would get better muscular coordination or improved reading abilities." Sometimes there may be nothing in common with the original knowledge, theoretically or practically. One itinerant therapist, for example, believes that exposing her patients to different smells is a form of sensory integration because it stimulates their olfactory nerves. Another such therapist "experimented with sign language as an offshoot of SI kinds of things—that motoric learning facilitates other kinds of learning."

Practitioners other than occupational therapists sometimes use what they call sensory integration, but substantially modify its orthodox form. In schools, for example, adapted physical educators tend to dismiss the theoretical side of sensory integration. They say that neuropsychological explanations of behavior are not easily understood by fellow staff members or parents and do not fit into the educational models used in schools. Nor does the theory, in their opinion, have direct implications for school work. For these practitioners, sensory integration is but a collection of clinical techniques.

In addition to dropping the theory behind sensory integration, some practitioners also transform its application. There may be rejection of much of the equipment associated with the traditional application of sensory integration. For example, equipment for vestibular treatment is large, bulky, and strange-looking, requiring special structural adaptations which tend to alienate physical education teachers. So some practitioners may treat vestibular problems with the "wrong" apparatus, but still call such treatments sensory integration. Many practitioners have also curtailed the open-ended length of time which occupational therapists tend to provide sensory integrative treatment. One educator notes that "there comes a point when you really need to understand that this person is not going to get this abstractness—I mean, we've been spinning and leaping and doing the scooter forever. Well, we've got to get on with life here." Some suggest that if a child is not writing well by age twelve, then "they need to be put on the computer...and rote learn skills."

Adapted physical educators look for "concrete examples" of sensory integrative therapy which seem to provide children with "survival" and "functional" skills. These examples define "sensory integration" for them and, in turn, for the students, parents, administrators, and teachers with whom they come into contact. One such educator, for instance, feels that sensory integration involves the application of procedures to address "tactile defensiveness," since this is the only aspect of the approach which "really seems to help" and is "really a problem in the child I can see." Another respondent says that "the part that helps kids is the vestibular training that they do, that we as adapted physical educators need to do as well." Yet another educator points to the "motor planning issues" which she thinks help the child.

Severe bastardization of sensory integration often happens when it is taught to or copied by educators and therapists from other fields. Regular physical education teachers, for example, may do their own version of sensory integration, especially if an occupational therapist is not on the school's staff (Sherrill 1986). This may include a copied or modified version of sensory integrative treatments as part of what they informally call "special gym." Sensory integrative treatments, which gym teachers or adapted physical educators see performed by occupational therapists, may be converted to their own needs, completely transforming the purpose of the treatment itself. Scooter board therapies, for instance, may be borrowed by physical educators to work on gym skills, but they may say they are doing sensory integrative treatment.

CONCLUSION

Rather than treating formal knowledge as an independent variable, and examining how it influences those who use it, this analysis has treated formal knowledge as a dependent variable. Formal knowledge, in the case of sensory integration, has been shaped not only by those who create it, but also by those who apply it and by those who control its use. The implications of such transformations for professional power are subtle and complex.

If the institutionalization of knowledge can be considered a sign of professional power, then sensory integration has contributed to the influence of occupational therapy. Sensory integration has gained substantial acceptance in many, but not all, settings in which occupational therapists work. It seems to be used mostly in schools and private clinics where it has active proponents, particularly in the form of sensory integration faculty, sympathetic special education directors and physicians, and parent advocate groups. In these cases, sensory integration has attained a status of routine knowledge, and its content has often remained faithful to the orthodox conception of this knowledge. In fields outside of occupational therapy, such as physical therapy, and to a lesser degree adapted physical education and neuropsychology, sensory integration has gained some degree of endorsement and use. Such diffusion of knowledge means, at least to some extent, that sensory integration has left its mark on human affairs in that it has become yet another institutionally endorsed way to look at and intervene in childhood development and behavior.

Moreover, the development of sensory integration has helped to prevent occupational therapy's knowledge base from becoming so technically routine that it can be taught easily to occupational therapy assistants or others lower in the division of labor. Because sensory integration is new and esoteric knowledge, its application and mastery, it can be argued, require substantial training, clinical experience, and professional judgment. Such knowledge keeps occupational therapists from being seen as overqualified to perform relatively standardized tasks, as happened to pharmacists (Eaton and Webb 1979).

Yet if professional power is construed as a monopoly of knowledge and technique by a single group, then the institutionalization of sensory integration has come at a high price for occupational therapy. The limited power of occupational therapy has meant that it has been unable to control the application of sensory integration in many settings where it has been introduced. Although occupational therapists have some power of discretion, they have had little direct power to determine the allocation of resources necessary for sensory integration to be used in organizational settings such as schools or hospitals. Nor have they had the power to restrict who may use sensory integration or in what form it is applied. When they have been unable to rely on allies such as parent groups, friendly competitors, and sympathetic physicians, occupational therapists have found it difficult to provide sensory integrative treatment in a manner consistent with their conception of it.

By not maintaining control over sensory integrative knowledge, its content has been transformed and its use compromised. Physicians have ruled on sensory integration's legitimacy and have reconstituted it; adapted physical educators have taken parts of it into their body of formal knowledge and have abridged it; administrators have detailed and restricted its use and have made it more formal and inflexible; parents have shared it and have simplified it; and practitioners have reinterpreted it and have created an idiosyncratic and at times highly distorted version of sensory integration. Rather than enhancing occupational therapy's image and influence, these transformations may feed into and reaffirm the long-held belief that occupational therapy is an unscientific and murky discipline of questionable value whose skills are easily learned by those outside the field (Gritzer and Arluke 1985). Institutionalization of knowledge, then, may backfire for occupations of limited professional power.

ACKNOWLEDGMENTS

The author is grateful to the many individuals associated with Sensory Integration International for their support and assistance, and to Frederic Hafferty for his critical readings of several drafts. Of course, the opinions contained herein are the private views of the author.

REFERENCES

American Academy of Pediatrics. 1985a. "Provision of Related Services for Children with Chronic Disabilities." *Pediatrics* 75:796-797.

_____. 1985b. "School-Aged Children with Motor Disabilities." *Pediatrics* 76:648-649.

AOTA. 1978. "Why is Sensory Integration a Separate Specialty Section?" *Sensory Integration Specialty Section Newsletter* 1(1), p. 2.

_____. 1979. "Center for the Study of Sensory Integrative Dysfunction." *Sensory Integration Specialty Section Newsletter* 2(2), p. 1.

_____. 1986. *Guidelines for Occupational Therapy Services in School Systems.* Rockville, MD: AOTA.

_____. 1988. "Gilfoyle Urges Promotion of OT During AOTA Conference Ceremony." *OT Week* 2(April 28), pp. 1, 31.

ARC. 1987. "Policy Paper on Physical and Occupational Therapies Provided in Educational Settings." Minneapolis, MN: ARC.

Arendt, R., W. MacLean, Jr., and A. Baumeister. 1988. "Critique of Sensory Integration Therapy and Its Application in Mental Retardation." *American Journal of Mental Retardation* 92:401-411.

Ayres, A.J. 1958. "The Visual-Motor Function." *American Journal of Occupational Therapy* 12:176-182.

_____. 1964. "Tactile Functions: Their Relation to Hyperactive and Perceptual Motor Behavior." *American Journal of Occupational Therapy* 18:6-11.

_____. 1965. "Patterns of Perceptual-Motor Dysfunction in Children: A Factor Analytic Study." *Perceptual and Motor Skills* 20 (monograph supplement I):335-368.

_____. 1968. "Sensory Integrative Processes and Neuropsychological Learning Disabilities." *Learning Disorders* 3:41-58.

_____. 1972. *Sensory Integration and Learning Disorders.* Los Angeles: Western Psychological Services.

_____. 1979. *Sensory Integration and the Child.* Los Angeles: Western Psychological Services.

Bisbicos, M. 1987. "Criteria for Delivery of OT Services." Memorandum to the School Department of Cambridge, MA, November 25.

Blim, D., and N. Matlin. 1987. "Health Care Systems: A Pediatric Perspective." *Pediatrics in Review* 9:5-9.

Bucher, R. 1988. "On the Natural History of Health Care Occupations." *Work and Occupations* 15:131-147.

Chamberlin, R. 1985. "A Review of What is Being Taught about Sensory Integration, Dysfunction, and Therapy." Unpublished manuscript. Bureau for Handicapped Children, Concord, NH.

Chess, S. 1986. "Commentary on the Difficult Child." *Pediatrics in Review* 8:35-38.

Clark, F., and L. Primeau. 1988. "Obfuscation of Sensory Integration: A Matter of Professional Predation." *American Journal of Mental Retardation* 92:415-420.

Clark, F., and J. Shuer. 1978. "A Clarification of Sensory Integrative Therapy and its Application to Programming with Retarded People." *Mental Retardation* 16:227-232.

Darling, R. 1988. "Parental Entrepreneurship: A Consumerist Response to Professional Dominance." *Journal of Social Issues* 44:141-158.

Dellman, R. 1977. "A Visit with Jean Ayres." *Somatics* (August):37-41.

Eaton, G., and B. Webb. 1979. "Boundary Encroachment: Pharmacists in the Clinical Setting." *Sociology of Health and Illness* 1:69-89.

Ferry, P. 1985. "Controversial Therapies for Handicapped Children." Child neurology course, American Academy of Neurology.

Freidson, E. 1986. *Professional Powers.* Chicago: University of Chicago Press.

Gearheart, B. 1973. *Learning Disabilities: Educational Strategies.* St. Louis, MO: Mosby.

Goldberg, H. 1983. "Dyslexia and Learning Disabilities." *Pediatric Clinics of North America.* 30:1195-1200.

Gritzer, G., and A. Arluke. 1985. *The Making of Rehabilitation: A Political Economy of Medical Specialization, 1890-1980.* Berkeley: University of California Press.

Haug, M. 1973. "Deprofessionalization: An Alternative Hypothesis for the Future." *Sociological Review Monograph* 20:195-211.

Hightower-Vandamm, M. 1980. "The Perils of Occupational Therapy in Several Special Arenas of Practice." *American Journal of Occupational Therapy* 34:307-309.

Kinsbourne, M. 1973. "School Problems." *Pediatrics* 52:697.

Kruckey, N., and S. Gubbay. 1983. "Clumsy Children: A Prognostic Study." *Australian Pediatrics Journal* 19:9-13.

Lerer, R. 1981. "An Open Letter to an Occupational Therapist." *Journal of Learning Disabilities* 14:3-4.

Levine, M., R. Brooks, and J. Shonkoff. 1980. *A Pediatric Approach to Learning Disorders.* New York: Wiley.

Lombard, T. 1985. Draft of Legislative Report, memorandum to the Minnesota Department of Education, December 19.

McKinlay, J. 1982. "Toward the Proletarianization of Physicians." Pages 37-62 in *Professionals as Workers: Mental Labor in Advanced Capitalism,* edited by C. Derber. Boston: G.K. Hall.

Okamoto, G., and I. McEwen, K. Marlowe, and G. Hammons. 1983. "Prescriptions for Physical and Occupational Therapy in School." *Archives of Physical Medicine and Rehabilitation* 64:429-431.

Oppenheimer, M. 1973. "The Proletarianization of the Professional." *Sociological Review Monographs* 20:213-227.

Ottenbacher, K. 1982. "Sensory Integration Therapy: Affect or Effect." *American Journal of Occupational Therapy* 36:571-578.

Posthuma, B. 1983. "Sensory Integration: Fact of Fad." *American Journal of Occupational Therapy* 37:343-345.

Price, A. 1977. "Sensory Integration in Occupational Therapy." *American Journal of Occupational Therapy* 31:287-289.

Pyfer, J. 1988. "Teachers, Don't Let Your Students Grow Up to be Clumsy Adults." *Journal of Physical Education, Recreation and Dance* 59:38-42.

Reid, D., and W. Hresko. 1981. *A Cognitive Approach to Learning Disabilities.* New York: McGraw-Hill.

Royeen, C. 1986. "Entry Level Education in Occupational Therapy." *American Journal of Occupational Therapy* 40:425-427.

Sherrill, C. 1986. *Adpated Physical Education and Recreation.* Dubuque, IA: William C. Brown.

Sieben, R. 1977. "Controversial Medical Treatments of Learning Disabilities." *Academic Therapy* 13:133-152.

Silver, L. 1975. "Acceptable and Controversial Approaches to Treating the Child with Learning Disabilities." *Pediatrics* 67:38-41.

Thomas, A., S. Chess, and H. Birch. 1968. *Temperament and Behavior in Children.* New York: New York University Press.

Tickle-Degnen, L. 1988. "Perspectives on the Status of Sensory Integration." *American Journal of Occupational Therapy* 42:427-440.

Toren, N. 1975. "Deprofessionalization and Its Sources." *Sociology of Work and Occupations* 2:323-337.

Werder, J., and R. Bruininks. 1982. "The Effects of Sensory Integration Therapy on Learning Disabled Children." Grant proposal, University of Minnesota. Minneapolis, MN.

A PROFESSION IN CONFLICT:
UNION MILITANCY AMONG
ISRAELI PHYSICIANS

Michael I. Harrison

ABSTRACT

Salaried professionals who use militant union tactics during collective bargaining face a fundamental dilemma: The conflict between withdrawing services as a tactic and the profession's obligation to provide vital public services. This dilemma is explored here through a study of probably the longest and one of the most militant doctors' strikes in history: a 4-month, nation-wide strike by over 8000 Israeli physicians in 1983. After describing the public criticisms of the strike, we examine the efforts by the physicians' union to cope with these criticisms and to resolve their profesional dilemma. These steps included the creation of an entire network of fee-for-service centers. During the strike these centers partially replaced the struck hospital outpatient clinics and the neighborhood clinics, at which patients ordinarily receive unlimited care without direct payments. In the case reported here professionalism was shown to channel and shape union activity, as well as being threatened by it. Moreover, the union's actions were constrained by the structural autonomy and power of subsectors of the profession, as well as by legal restrictions, political pressures, and social and occupational norms.

Current Research on Occupations and Professions, Volume 6, pages 201-221.
ISBN: 1-55938-236-8

INTRODUCTION

The growing complexity and bureaucratization of the organizations employing professionals are challenging traditional forms of professional self-regulation and autonomy (Freidson 1984; Derber 1982, 1984; McKinlay, 1982). Unionization by professionals and the use of militant collective bargaining tactics are among the most dramatic responses to these organizational developments (Antonovsky 1988; Chamot 1976; Harrison and Tabory 1980; Heidenheimer and Johansen 1985; Hoffman 1982; Melosh 1982, pp. 212-217; Raelin 1989; Wolfe 1978; Prandy 1965). The tendencies toward unionization are particularly evident among professionals employed by public and semi-public service organizations. This paper examines one of the main professional dilemmas posed by union militancy: the conflict between withdrawing services as a bargaining tactic and the professionals' obligation to provide vital public services, in this case medical treatment. This dilemma is examined through a case study of probably the longest and one of the most militant doctors' strikes in history: a 4-month, nation-wide strike by over 8000 Israeli physicians in 1983. By examining the doctors' efforts to resolve the dilemma created by this strike, we illuminate possible relationships between unionism and professionalism.

PROFESSIONALISM AND UNIONISM

Following Freidson (1986), we treat *professionalism* as a "folk-concept," upon which there is a degree of agreement (but not total consensus) among the representatives of the various political, legal, and educational institutions that grant professional recognition and privileges to an occupation within a particular society. The defining characteristics of the professions, according to Freidson, are the requirement of higher education as a prerequisite to employment in particular jobs from which others are excluded. Professions are also distinguished by the technical autonomy granted to both self-employed and salaried professionals to decide how best to perform their tasks and by the substantial (but not unrestricted) corporate autonomy granted to the professional body to supervise and regulate the maintenance of professional standards of work (Goode 1957; Freidson 1984). Additional characteristics that professionals often claim for themselves and that are frequently attributed to them by representatives of major social institutions—and by many social scientists—include the following: expertise, allegiance to a body of ethics and standards that require "the socially responsible use" of professional skills (Parsons 1968, p. 536); the members' identification with the profession; and their personal commitment to a professional career (Goode 1957; Greenwood 1957; Parsons 1968; Blau and Scott 1962, pp. 60-66, Raelin 1989).

Professionalism implies both a tendency to organize along the principles just listed and an ideology that uses these traits as the basis for the claim to corporate autonomy and status. The ideal-typical, attribute approach to defining professionalism, on which the above list of professional traits is based, does not explain the market and political processes through which certain occupational groups obtain professional status and power (Freidson 1986; Klegon 1978; Larson 1977). However, the trait approach does capture the features that professions often claim distinguish them from other occupations.

Unionism

Unionism—the adoption of trade union organizational patterns and tactics—may threaten professionalism by introducing bureaucractic and egalitarian forms of organization where collegial, meritocratic forms had prevailed.[1] Among the features of trade unionism that may clash with professionalism are the definition of the individual member as an employee, rather than a professional the membership of the union in a central (nonprofessional) union federation; and the use of militant collective-bargaining tactics (Blackburn and Prandy 1965; Prandy, Steward and Blackburn 1974). On the other hand, professional unions may avoid adopting those characteristics of trade unionism that most strongly clash with professionalism (Blackburn and Prandy 1965; Harrison and Tabory 1983; Prandy 1965). Research on the organization and actions of professional unions may thus help identify conditions under which employment within complex organizations indirectly undermines professionalism or leads to its redefinition and conditions under which professional unions resist such threats to professionalism.

The tension between unionism and professional standards and values is particularly evident when professionals adopt militant collective bargaining tactics (Raelin 1989). Historically, the provision of a vital public service has been a central obligation of the professions (Abbott 1983). Professionals have based their claims to special status and to self-regulation on their commitment to serve their clients even when this obligation conflicts with their personal and group interests. Militant unionism thus creates a dilemma for many professionals: To further their occupational standing they must at least temporarily withold the very services that constitute their raison d' être, and they must call into question their unconditional dedication to service.

How then, do unionized physicians cope with the dilemma posed by the conflict between union militancy and their stated unconditional obligation to treat the sick? The resolution of this dilemma may occur at two levels: that of the profession as a corporate body, organized within one or more professional associations, and that of the individual practitioner. At each of these levels the dilemma may be confronted both *behaviorally* and *rhetorically*—in terms of statements of intent and justifications for action. Because of the complexity of the case to be presented here, we will emphasize the actions of the union leadership and the strike activists. Corporate rhetoric and the behavior of individual physicians will be the subject of separate reports.

RESEARCH METHODS

The major data source for the study is a set of 60 qualitative interviews about the 1983 Israeli physicians' strike. The interviews yielded over 160 hours of material, much of which was taped and transcribed. I conducted the interviews with strike activists, while a group of trained graduate students interviewed clinic and hospital doctors, and head nurses in clinics and hospital departments. Rather than seeking a representative sample of individual participants in the conflict, we looked for people who could serve as informants about developments before and during the strike within a particular organizational arena—the primary care clinics, hospital departments, strike administration, and strike leadership. Since the interviews were conducted during the academic year following the conclusion of the strike, we stressed behavioral information, that is less subject to distortions of recall and reinterpretation. Interviews were conducted in Hebrew, and the quotations from the interviews included below were translated idiomatically by me from the original transcripts or written records. These data were supplemented by documents obtained from strike activists, extensive coverage of the strike in the daily press, transcriptions of radio broadcasts covering the physicians' hunger strike (see the section titled "Chronology of the Conflict"), and two book-length chronicles by key participants (Modan 1986; Yishai 1986). The analysis of the data was inductive, following accepted field-work procedures (Becker 1958; Glaser and Strauss 1967; Schatzman and Strauss 1973; Lofland 1971). Triangulation of data sources was used to validate findings and inferences from the data.

INSTITUTIONAL AND SOCIETAL CONTEXT

The 1983 strike must be viewed within the context of the climate of labor relations within Israel (Blum and Harel 1980) and within the framework of the Israeli medical system (Arian 1981; Ellencweig 1983; Yishai 1982).

Israeli Physicians and Labor Relations

Over 90% of Israeli employees are members of unions that are affiliated with the Histadrut, the General Federation of Labor. The right to strike is legally established for most employees, but the government may take legal measures against strikers in vital public services. In practice, these measures were almost never used during the decade prior to our study (Shirom 1983, p. 235). In fact, public-sector employees have often used strikes and sanctions to promote their wage demands. During the four years preceding the doctors' strike, more than half of the nation's strikes occurred among public and semi-public employees in the services, mass media, and transportation, as opposed to industry or commerce (Bar Tsuri and Batsri 1985). The doctors who went on strike in 1973 and 1976, as well as in 1983, were not alone. Nurses, x-ray technicians, elementary and high school teachers, university professors (Harrison and Tabory 1980), and engineers also struck between 1975 and 1983.

The late seventies and early eighties were a period of rising inflation in Israel in which many occupational groups used militant collective bargaining tactics in an effort to preserve their eroding purchasing power or recoup economic losses. Not surprisingly, Israel had the third highest rate of strike frequency among 16 nations (after Italy and Australia) during 1977 through 1982 and the fourth highest rate of strike intensity (after the United States, Britain and Canada) for that period (Bar Tsuri and Batsri 1985).

The Israeli Health System

Nearly all Israelis are covered by medical insurance.[2] The Kupat Holim (KH) sick fund affiliated with the Histadrut insures around three quarters of the population, while four smaller nonprofit sick funds insure the others. Macabbi, the largest of the other sick funds, insures around 12% of the population, most of whom are concentrated among the middle class in large urban areas. KH operates over 1200 local and regional clinics that provide primary and secondary ambulatory care throughout the country. In addition, KH operates 14 general hospitals, pharmacies, laboratories, and related health facilities. KH provides around 30% of the near 12,000 general hospital beds in the country, while the Ministry of Health provides 37% of these beds in 34 general hospitals. Municipalities, other public, and nonprofit organizations provide most of the rest of the general hospital beds. In addition to receiving unlimited care through the sick funds with little or no direct payment for treatment, many Israelis visit physicians privately. These visits provide for more personal attention or for preferential treatment by hospital physicians through under-the-counter payments known as "grey medicine."

Unionization Among the Physicians

Nearly all Israeli physicians are members of unions that are independent of the Histadrut and are organized within the framework of the Israeli Medical Association (IMA). The IMA serves its members, of whom around 85% are salaried employees, as a professional association and also represents its member unions during nation-wide collective bargaining talks with the Ministry of

Health and the heads of KH. Doctors employed by KH are organized into a Clinic Doctors' Union (3000 members) and a Hospital Doctors' Union (2500 members), while doctors working in state hospitals are organized in a State Doctors' Union (3500 members).[3] The two hospital unions need not be distinguished in the following analysis, but the Clinic Doctors' Union (CDU), played a distinctive role. The Ministry of the Treasury is often a partner to nation-wide collective bargaining between the IMA and the two major employers (the KH and the Ministry of Health), because the Treasury controls the flow of funds to both KH and the Ministry of Health.

CHRONOLOGY OF THE CONFLICT

Here is a brief chronology of the 1983 conflict that provides the background needed for the analysis that will follow.

Pre-strike Period
(December 1981 - March 1, 1983)

For almost a year and a half prior to the outbreak of the strike, the IMA had been unable to renew their wage agreement on more favorable terms than those of the agreement that had expired in April 1982. The IMA leadership faced stonewalling on the part of the Treasury and was unwilling to accept the national, across-the-board wage package that the Treasury ultimately signed with the Histadrut. IMA activists prepared for a strike by establishing a private corporation, known as the Alternative Medical Services, Ltd. (AMS), through which the doctors could provide services on a fee-for-service basis.[4] IMA activists presented their strike plan to union members throughout the country and began preparing public opinion for a strike.

Opening Moves
(March 2, 1983 - March 11, 1983)

At the start of their sanctions, the doctors began charging a 600 shekel (around $16) fee for outpatient and inpatient services within the hospitals, rather than honoring KH insurance. When the government reacted by issuing restraining orders forbidding the collection of fees in public facilities, the doctors (as per plan) walked out of the KH clinics and the hospital outpatient clinics and began establishing a nationwide network of AMS centers at which they offered ambulatory treatment for the 600 shekel fee. The government responded by issuing back-to-work orders to some of the strikers. At a stormy mass meeting attended by 4500 doctors, IMA leaders vowed that the doctors would defy back-to-work orders even if they were punished with jail sentences.

Legalized Sanctions
(March 13, 1983 - May 22, 1983)

A government crisis—or worse—was averted through a compromise in which the government rescinded the back-to-work orders in exchange for the IMA's agreement to provide hospital inpatient services at 30% of their normal level until a wage agreement could be reached. Under this compromise the physicians continued to withold their services from the hospital outpatient and the KH clinics, and the daily administration of the hospitals was placed in the hands of local strike committees—an arrangement that was to endure for the next three months. The fee-for-service AMS centers gradually expanded their operations to include a wide range of ambulatory services. In mid-April thousands of doctors held a demonstration in Jerusalem. Meanwhile the Minister of the Treasury continued to refuse to consider any proposed resolution that would violate the national wage-price package.

During late April the heads of the CDU sought a separate agreement with the head of KH that would have reopened the clinics on an emergency basis. However, the membership failed to support such an agreement, which would have split the IMA. Pressures among rank and file physicians in the clinics and hospitals mounted to intensify the struggle in order to break the stalemate in the bargaining and avoid a split between the hospital and clinic physicians.

Abandonment of the Hospitals
(May 22, 1983 - May 25, 1983)

In response to these pressures, the hospital doctors executed a carefully prepared plan to abandon the hospitals. The national walkout lasted for three days, leaving only minimal emergency staffs. This action again led the government to issue back-to-work orders. These orders were rescinded almost at the moment they were issued in the wake of a second compromise agreement: the KH clinics were opened twice a week for the treatment of the aged and the chronically ill, and hospital staffing was restored to the 30% that had obtained prior to the walkout.

Breakdown and Demoralization
(May 26, 1983 - June 14, 1983)

Despite a renewal of collective bargaining and some genuine progress, the doctors' collective action began to break down as a result of hostile media coverage of the walkout, growing public condemnation, and pressure from both hospital and clinic physicians to reach a settlement. Neither an increase in the fees at the centers nor a work-by-the-book action within the hospitals had any significant impact on the bargaining. As morale among the doctors declined and some hospital and clinic doctors began violating strike discipline, hospital-based militants called for stronger action and immediate results. The need to achieve a quick victory was underlined by growing movement within the CDU toward a separate agreement with KH.

Hunger Strike
(June 14, 1983 - June 27, 1983)

Against this background the doctors in a major KH hospital embarked on a hunger strike that rapidly spread to most other major hospitals and created a governmental and health-system crisis. Faced with a rising public outcry and pressure within the cabinet, the Minister of the Treasury was forced to accept some of the doctors' demands and to submit several outstanding issues to arbitration. Relieved that an agreement had been reached, the doctors closed the AMS centers and returned to their work in the hospitals and the clinics.

PUBLIC ARTICULATION OF
THE PROFESSIONAL DILEMMA

In reaction to the strike, key governmental and institutional representatives, along with the media, clearly articulated the view that the striking doctors were violating their professional obligations and breaking the bond of trust between the public and the medical profession. Certain public figures and groups appear to have favored these views because of their political and social ideologies, and public reactions shifted radically in response to the behavior of the physicians, the government, and the media. Support for the strike ran high at its start and during the hunger strike. During the long stalemate from mid-March to mid-May, the press and the public directed their criticism more at the instransigence of the Treasury, government inaction, and at the doctors' stubbornness, than at the doctors' failure to meet their professional obligations.[5] Nonetheless, the four types of criticism described below did force the doctors to confront the dilemma that their actions raised.

The first focus of attack centered on the physicians' failure to provide vital medical services. The government defined the doctors as failing to provide these services and as abusing their right to collective bargaining when it obtained back-to-work order shortly after the start of the strike and during the May walkout. The nation's president made this view explicit after the May walkout when he stated that, "It's unbelievable that this dedicated body of physicians, whom we all know and admire and who accept the Hypocratic oath, could conceive of using tactics that could endanger Israels' sick" ("Doctors at Centers" 1983).

A second, closely related target of criticism was the doctors' willingness to place material gain before their obligations to treat the sick. Editorial opinion and letters to the editor frequently cited the responsibility of the physicians to set a "good example" for other groups and to put public service before concerns of salary. In like manner, the press gave prominence to statements by dissenting physicians that the strike was unjustified on professional and ethical grounds. The leading morning paper expressed a widely-held view when it noted that the doctors had shown "self-centeredness" and "exploitation of their monopolistic position" when they abandoned the hospitals ("Israel the Beautiful" 1983). Their actions were seen as undermining "the public's view of them as bearing responsibility for the wellbeing of the patient" ("The Doctors" 1983).

Third, the doctors were attacked for undermining the rule of law on the two occasions on which they threatened to deny the back-to-work orders. "You can't bargain with lawbreakers," editorialized the popular afternoon paper in March) "Medical Time Bomb" 1983). During the May walkout, cabinet members were quoted in the press as describing the action as "bordering on rebellion" and as threatening to "undermine the foundations of the rule of law ("Aridor Keeps His Cool" 1983, p. 3).

Fourth, the Histadrut, along with some public figures and members of the press, argued that the doctors' were violating the egalitarian values on which the clinic system was based. These critics noted that patients of limited economic means and those with larger families could less readily afford to visit the treatment centers or to seek private medical care. The deprivations faced by the poor were brought to public attention by occasional reports of verbal and even physical abuse of doctors who sought to collect the fees specified by the IMA. Spokespersons for KH, the Histadrut, and the Labor Party also attacked the strike as an attempt to undermine the entire clinic system in which free and unlimited treatment was supplied to all insured.

In summary, the doctors' failure to provide services and the charge of neglect of the patient in favor of financial gains surfaced periodically throughout the strike but did not become the central focus of public pressure and criticism until after the doctors' walked out of the hospitals in May. Legal pressures to insure the provision of vital medical services prevailed throughout the strike and reached their peak on the two occasions when the doctors' almost totally abandoned the hospitals. Many government members were particularly scandalized by the willingness of the physicians to violate back-to-work orders, which had been respected in similar situations in the past (Modan 1986, p. 34), while the media and the public at large vilified the hospital doctors who could picnic and swim on the shores of the Sea of Galilee while their patients lay neglected in the hospital wards.

RESPONSES TO THE PROFESSIONAL DILEMMA

How then did the IMA and its member unions cope with the conflict between
the militant use of collective bargaining tactics and the need to fulfill their
professional obligations?

Strike Design

The most important response of the union activists to this dilemma lay in
the design of their key weapon: the IMA-controlled AMS Corporation.
Interviews with strike activists, unpublished IMA documents, and public
statements by IMA spokespersons all show that the fee-for-service centers were
designed to shift the financial burden of the sanctions from the patients to the
employers and to transfer the moral burden from the doctors to the employers.[6]
In addition AMS was designed to provide a source of income for striking
doctors. The activists and their legal counsels assumed that they could
withstand legal and moral pressures to end the strike so long as they were
providing medical services in some alternative fashion. Here is a typical
statement of this view taken from a flier dated January 22 that was distributed
to IMA members by the strike organizers and signed by the IMA heads:

> We will insure that the public will be given the essential service of the medical examination
> and *since the strike will not be directed at the public,* but at the employers only, we will
> advise the public to demand the reimbursement of the fees that they pay the doctors from
> their insurer [the sick funds] (Emphasis added)... At [IMA] headquarters we have weighed
> all of the legal responses that the employers may try to use against us . . . The employers
> must understand that any attempt to operate the health services without reaching an
> understanding with us are doomed to failure in advance. Naturally any interference with
> our program of alternative medical services will produce a situation in which there will
> *not be any* medical services at all! (Emphasis in original)[7]

The strike organizers thus regarded their program as providing a perfect
solution to their professional dilemma: The public would receive vital medical
services. Only the employers would suffer because of their obligation to
reimburse the patients for the fees paid to the centers. If the goverment took
legal measures against the doctors, the doctors could not be blamed for the
cessation of vital medical services.

Although the IMA's response to the dilemma created by witholding public
medical services was carefully planned, the union leadership did not anticipate
that the doctors—and not the government—would be blamed for the walkouts
that halted vital hospital services. Moreover, the IMA leaders apparently did
not expect the strike to last so long or expect so many important in-patient
hospital services to be curtailed for over three months. Hence, they did not
prepare any consistent means of coping with the medical and ethical issues

relating to the possible damage to patients that could result from delays in diagnosis or surgery. Nor did they seek to ensure that the quality of care given in their AMS centers would not be significantly diminished by the use of improvised quarters, inadequate medical records, and limited technical facilities.[8] One knowledgeable activist described the situation as follows:

> This whole business—no matter how much it tried to be planned and the centers [were supposed] to be a real alternative medical service, was in the final analysis built . . . like an expanded Magen David Adom [emergency service] . . . Every day we thought that [the strike] would end . . . So they said, wait! don't rent [another place], it looks like it's ending . . . At the start we rented the [facilities for] the centers on a weekly basis...During the second month of the strike, we went over to a monthly basis . . . When you rented a room, they were pretty crummy. For example, in my region there were no well-arranged clinics for rent. There were all sorts of empty, neglected apartments, in which each [doctor in charge] arranged some kind of bed or other that could be used for examining patients.

As the conflict unfolded, the doctors developed several partial solutions to the professional challenges facing them. From the outset of the sanctions, they included high-level hospital doctors among the staffs of the centers, in order to demonstrate to the public—and perhaps to themselves as well—that the centers were offering high-quality medical care. The presence of senior physicians in the centers and at the intake points in the hospital's emergency rooms also helped reduce the likelihood of mistakes in diagnosis that could have resulted in malpractice suits against the IMA as a whole, as well as against the attending physician.

In like manner, the hospital physicians made a concerted effort to uphold professional standards of diagnosis and treatment during the lengthy period in which only urgent surgery was allowed. After a brief period of confusion about how to proceed, the strike committees in each hospital set up an Exceptions Committee—composed of senior physicians, department heads, and strike activists—who had the responsibility of deciding whether requests for surgery from the physicians on the wards were indeed medically justified.

The union leadership also took actions to mitigate the criticism that their fee-for-service system discriminated against the poor and the chronically ill and might discourage those in need of care from seeking it. From the outset, the IMA heads instructed the doctors not to take fees from welfare recipients, army personnel, and emergency cases and to accept signed statements of an obligation to pay the fee from patients who lacked the cash. In addition, physicians staffing the centers were told not to charge for repeat visits. These doctors were instructed to act liberally toward those who refused to pay and to avoid confrontations over the fees.

In contrast to these efforts to retain professional standards, are reports obtained from hospital nurses that union sanctions led doctors in their wards to release patients without a medical summary and with inadequate instructions for further medication and treatment. In addition, there were cases of constraints on the use of diagnostic tests and superficial examinations. Perhaps even more problematic was the practice of referring patients (including cancer patients) to the improvised centers for all ambulatory care that was to follow hospitalization.

The greatest challenge to the profession's ability to provide vital services occured during the two walkouts and the hunger strike. During all three of these episodes, the strike committees in local hospitals assigned a limited number of physicians to provide emergency care. During the highly publicized walkout in May, the strikers created a mobile emergency unit that remained on call in the case of a mass emergency, such as a major accident or a terrorist attack.

Continuing and Expanded Medical Services

The IMA's tolerance of a wide range of medical services during the strike further mitigated public criticism of the profession and allowed striking physicians to assert that the public was not being denied access to medical care. Since some medical services were unaffected by the union's sanctions and other services expanded to fill the gap created by the sanctions, the strike did not weigh heavily on many citizens. Moreover, the strike's impact was felt more by people of limited means, while middle-class Israelis appear to have obtained medical treatment by hook or by crook. As the strike activists put it, despite all their efforts, they only managed to pull off a "strike with luxury conditions."

Ambulatory Services

Throughout the strike the country's emergency services were not significantly altered. The mobile emergency units (Magen David Adom and Shahal) operated on a regular basis, under court order, although the IMA did make some efforts to charge for any nonemergency care provided by the doctors of Magen David Adom. In addition, throughout the strike, the hospital emergency rooms continued to provide free walk-in treatment for minor emergencies, as well as major ones. In some areas the patients' preference for these free services placed additional burdens on the already crowded emergency rooms.

Moreover, physicians who held individual contracts with the smaller Maccabi Sick Fund continued to work as usual. The hospital doctors responsible for outpatient care within Jerusalem's major hospital, which is privately owned, also worked as usual. In like manner, doctors who held independent contracts with the Histadrut's KH provided ambulatory treatment at their private clinics. The IMA made efforts to bring these doctors into the strike and attempted to convince independent contractors to raise their fees and turn over part of the fee to the AMS Corporation. However, most of the independent physicians enjoyed "business as usual" during the strike or even experienced a growth in their patient load. Nor could the IMA curtail the burgeoning private practices that many senior hospital physicians and some clinic-based physicians operated during the strike.[9]

During the last two months of the strike, KH began to exploit the inability of the IMA to control independent contractors by pressing clinic physicians to work for KH as independent practitioners.[10] The IMA vigorously opposed these practices but was unable to halt them. In fact, except for a few well-publicized disciplinary actions against doctors who openly violated the strike, the IMA took no formal action against clinic and hospital physicians who violated union discipline.

Although the sanctions severely curtailed the operations of the KH clinics for most of the strike, the clinics were not shut down totally. Instead, the clinic nurses remained on duty throughout the strike and often delivered services that were ordinarily provided by physicians.[11] Besides their regular duties, the nurses renewed prescriptions for the chronically ill by preparing the renewals for signature by a few KH doctors who were closely tied to the KH administration and refused to cooperate with the strike. The nurses also made referrals to the hospital emergency rooms and the AMS centers, sometimes avoiding referrals to the centers in order to weaken the strike. Some nurses recorded patients visits to the clinic so that medical authorizations for absenteeism from work could be granted after the conclusion of the strike.[12] In some clinics the nurses further expanded their activities to include home visits and follow-up of chronically ill patients who ordinarily received less thorough attention. The cooperation of some of the clinic physicians directly contributed to the nurses' ability to perform these expanded functions (see the section titled "Divisions Within the Profession").

Hospitalization

During most of the conflict, the sanctions in the hospitals restricted admissions and surgery to critical cases, but these sanctions had less impact on the treatment and attention provided to patients who did manage to get admitted to the hospitals. The impact of the sanctions was partially moderated by the initiatives of the hospital nurses, who provided some of the services ordinarily given by the physicians. Some hospital physicians, including some heads of departments, apparently supported this expansion of the nurse's role and worked closely with the nurses to insure adequate patient care. In some instances nurses substituted for the physicians by giving injections and administering infusions, as well as discussing the patients' illness and treatment with their families. During the abandonment of the hospitals in May, the Ministry of Health issued emergency regulations officially granting the nurses the authority to perform medical procedures that some of them had been performing prior to that event. Hospital nurses also became more active in following up the treatment provided to patients, suggesting treatments, and advocating the hospitalization of patients.

For example, the head nurse in an internal medicine ward reported the following episode:

> There's a doctor from the Department of [X] who still isn't speaking to me, because I fixed his wagon. There was an episode where they brought a patient with [a chronic condition ordinarily requiring hospitalization] into our department. They didn't admit him at the Emergency Room [because of the sanctions], but, nonetheless, he was brought up to the ward. He was a miserable old fellow, a survivor of the holocaust without any children. There was no room in our department, even in the hall. So I spoke to the nurse in Department [X] and simply pushed the patient into her department. The doctor approached me and started to shout at me. I told him, "Nothing is going to help you. If you insist, dress the patient and throw him out into the street!" The patient stayed three months in that doctor's department until the condition healed. It was a mitzvah (good deed) [to take care of him].

Although the strike committees within individual hospitals sometimes tried to restrict the nurses' activities and put verbal pressure on them and on the doctors not to undermine the hospital sanctions, the IMA as a body never openly opposed the actions of the nurses in the clinics or in the hospitals. The IMA might conceivably have tried to warn the public that the nurses were overstepping their authority and expertise in the clinics, but to do so would only have further emphasized the physicians' failure to do urgent medical work.

Although the ranks of the hospital physicians were radically reduced during the extended period of legally tolerated sanctions, the thirty percent staffing quota was supplemented from two sources. Some departments had doctors on duty who were performing part of their military service. In addition, a small, but noticeable number of department heads and some of their staff members violated the sanctions during all or part of the strike. These department heads rarely opposed the strike openly but simply continued to come to their department on a regular basis and to oversee the treatment of all of the department's patients. Moreover, our interviews revealed several departments in which the other physicians in the department followed the example of their head. They appear to have understood that they too were to be present, if only to "keep in touch" with what was being done in the department.

The IMA's strike committees put pressure on doctors who arrived at hours to which they were not assigned, and activists from at least one hospital physically blocked their colleagues' entry into the hospital. But the strike committees typically lacked the power to obtain conformity to the sanctions on the part of the powerful and prestigious department heads, who hold their positions for life. On the contrary, the activists, many of whom were young residents or senior physicians without tenure had every reason to avoid confrontations with the department heads and to be satisfied that they did not openly oppose the strike.

Interviews with hospital activists make it clear that professional concerns, as well as pragmatism, constrained the enforcement of the sanctions. One member of the union strike committee in a major hospital put it this way:

> If we discovered anybody [working beyond the assigned hours], it was justified, because we always said one thing: The health of the patients or the need to treat a patient occasionally justifies deviating slightly from the framework [of the agreed-upon sanctions]. If people needed to stay on to complete an operation, you couldn't say no.

Finally, although the evidence is understandably limited, we should note one additional mechanism that undoubtedly provided many well-connected patients with medical services beyond those mandated by the IMA. "Proteksia," the well-established practice of using familial, business, and political networks to obtain special treatment, was rumored to be widespread during the strike. One hospital activist summarized the situation tersely when he noted. "Members of parliament got treated during the strike. They found ways." In like manner, the friends and families of medical personnel sometimes found their ways around the hospital sanctions, although our interviews indicate that they occasionally encountered resistance on the part of militant doctors.

Division within the Profession

Thus far we have presented the IMA's responses to its professional dilemma as if nearly all of the actors within this large, complex body consistently agreed with one another and worked together. In fact, there were major divisions within the alliance of striking doctors, at least one of which was directly related to the ethical and professional dilemmas posed by the strike. Almost from the start of the strike, the heads of the CDU and a substantial proportion of their membership pressed for a speedy settlement and showed much greater willingness to compromise than did the vast majority of the hospital doctors (regardless of their employer). As noted in the chronology above, the CDU conducted separate negotiations with KH and eventually reached an interim agreement with their employer that led to the reopening of the community-based clinics two days per week. Concern for the future of the clinic system and fear of job losses among clinic physicians in the event of a reorganization of the health services were major forces motivating the clinic doctors. In addition, the clinic doctors typically suffered greater financial losses during the strike than did the hospital doctors.

Beyond such material concerns, the clinic physicians were also motivated by genuine concern for the wellbeing of their patients and by their sense of professional responsibility. The conflict between one clinic's physician's professional conscience and his loyalty to the union are vividly described in the following interview. This respondent continued to work as an independent physician under contract to both KH and one of the smaller sick funds during the strike and even expanded his practice.

> I pray that we don't have to strike again. This is a profession that's not suited for strikes. They're in opposition to the physician's oath and to our conscience . . . Someone [like me] who works for years in medicine and comes in contact with people, gradually suffers the same suffering that the patient undergoes. . . . A great physician once said that when one of his patients' dies, part of him dies too . . . I was against breaking the stike. I would never, ever break a strike. So I was relieved [when the union] gave permission to doctors to work as independent physicians. From then on my conscience was clear.

An additional indication of the desire of many clinic doctors to continue treating their patients is the clandestine advice they provided throughout the strike to clinic nurses, who consulted with them about particular patients. For example, the independent practitioner just cited admitted that he violated strike rules by regularly consulting by telephone with the nurses in the local KH clinic. In all three of the geographical areas that we studied intensively, we found that at least one clinic physician was available to the nurses for consultation by telephone and that one or more doctors visited the clinics two or three times a week. In one area the striking clinic doctors decided as a group that one of their members should maintain these contacts. Their decision was known to the strike administration, but it went unchallenged.

The clinic doctors further demonstrated their commitments to their patients in late May when they officially returned to work twice a week. During this period, many treated any patient who came to the clinic, rather than restricting their attention to the chronicly ill and the aged, as per the formal agreement.

Although some hospital doctors expressed similar concerns, as a body they seem to have been less troubled by their actions. How can we account for this difference? First, during most of the strike, the hospital doctors continued to provide what they viewed as the most necessary of their medical services. Only elective surgery was curtailed under the agreement to staff the hospitals at thirty percent of their normal level. In contrast, the clinic doctors struck their clinics altogether and were only able to offer alternative services in exchange for payment. Second, the strike disrupted long-standing personal relationships between some clinic doctors and their patients—relationships of a type that rarely develop in the hospital context. Third, since the clinic doctors knew their patients well and often resided in the communities where they worked, they were exposed daily to their patients' discomforts—or worse. In particular they were acutely aware that some of their patients were failing to obtain necessary medical services because of the cost or physical inaccessability of these alternatives.

Thus, both material and ethical concerns combined to make most clinic physicians anxious to achieve a quick settlement of the wage conflict. This interweaving of pragmatic and professional concerns is evident in the following report by a hospital doctor who worked closely with clinic physicians during the strike:

> They became embittered . . . and came around to tell me so. They also complained about the type of treatment the[ir] patients were getting, that it was inadequate. And they were right [to complain], you can't deny it—especially when the hospital doctors were working 30% of the time and were making more money [than the clinic doctors.]

CONCLUSION

In accordance with a growing body of research, this study showed that salaried professionals may use militant union tactics to promote material goals when they operate within an environment supportive of white-collar and public-sector unionism and when they have sufficient power to employ militant tactics without fear of reprisal. Union militancy of this sort conflicts with several of the defining attributes of professionalism. This conflict is felt and articulated by governmental and institutional representatives, members of the media, the public at large, and members of the profession. Even in a society like Israel, that is inured to union militancy, governmental authorities may take legal action to prevent professionals from witholding vital public services, provided that such actions are likely to produce compliance. Moreover, the members of the profession themselves must struggle with the dilemma posed by withdrawing vital services as a collective bargaining tactic.

In the case of the 1983 doctors' strike, militancy conflicted with professionalism in several ways. First, sanctions that restricted treatment in the hospitals and withdrew the doctors from the hospital and neighborhood clinics posed a threat to the physical wellbeing of the patients and called into question the doctors' commitment to place the welfare of their patients before their personal gain. Second, the threatened violation of the back-to-work orders clashed with the legal recognition and legitimation routinely granted to the profession. Third, toleration of medically problematic procedures, such as restrictions on record keeping, ran counter to the standards of practice that are ordinarily applied within the profession.

The doctors' responses to these conflicts illustrate how professionalism can channel and shape union actions, as well as being threatened by these actions. Rather than proposing the total withdrawal of medical services, the architects of the physicians' struggle, created a set of alternative fee-for-service centers that were designed to shift the financial burden for the sanctions onto the employers without harming the public. In addition, they took steps to insure the quality of care in the hospitals and the ambulatory centers. These measures proved inadequate because of the unanticipated length of the strike. Finally, the IMA was forced to tolerate the persistence and expansion of a wide range of medical services that offered alternatives to those that were withheld under the sanctions.

Although the IMA willingly tolerated the persistence of some forms of practice, such as emergency services, other forms of medical work emerged and flourished because the union lacked the power to impose its discipline on practitioners who enjoyed very high levels of professional autonomy. In particular, the union was unable to control fully the behavior of the heads of hospital departments, private practitioners, and nonsalaried practitioners holding individual contracts with organizations providing primary and secondary care. In addition, when the clinic physicians returned to work on a part-time basis, the IMA was unable to restrict their attentions to the aged and chronically ill, as had been agreed. Finally, as the strike progressed, the union committees faced increasing difficulties in limiting activities of hospital physicians to those hours to which they were assigned under the sanctions.

In summary, the case reported here shows that professionals may indeed use militant union tactics to pursue financial goals or otherwise strengthen their position within a society, but that such actions pose a threat to the legitimacy and professional standards to which the occupation lays claim. Moreover, the actions in which the union may engage are likely to be constrained by the structural autonomy and power of sub-sectors of the profession, as well as by legal restrictions on union activity, political pressures, social and occupational norms.

ACKNOWLEDGMENTS

The fieldwork for this study was partially supported by grants from the Israel Ministry of Health and the Research Authority of Bar Ilan University. Aliyah Koren, Leah Pas, Koti Sadan, Carmelah Smilovitch, and Esther Spector served capably as volunteer interviewers and produced valuable analyses of their findings. Shimon Gal On and Eti Yohai cheerfully helped to organize and summarize the newspaper coverage and the interviews. This study would have been impossible without the cooperation of the many individuals who so generously and frankly responded to our interviews.

NOTES

1. Professionals may resort to unionization in an effort to sustain their professional autonomy and status (Antonovsky 1988; Chamot 1976; Harrison and Tabory 1983; Raelin 1989; Badgley and Wolfe 1967), but there is no evidence that unionization can actually help groups achieve professional status (Raelin 1989).

2. Data from 1983 are used in this section, but the current situation has not changed significantly.

3. The membership figures are from Yishai (1986), who is head of the IMA. Remarkably divergent figures appear in Antonovsky (1988) and Yishai (1982).

4. The AMS was originally established during a wage dispute in 1976, but it was not made fully operational at that time.

5. In examining editorial opinion, I have given special weight to the two major afternoon papers, *Yediot Ahoronot* and *Maariv*. Both of the major morning papers were opposed to the Begin government. Hence their criticism of government inaction on the strike was more predictable. One popular explanation attributed this inaction to the desires of the Minister of Health and the Minister of the Treasury to let the strike drag on so as to irreparably damage the KH clinic system and allow the public to become accustomed to a fee-for-service system of primary care. There is substantial circumstantial evidence in support of these allegations.

6. The strike's architects knew that the insurance agreement between KH and its members required KH to reimburse members for treatments obtained from alternative sources in the event that KH services were not operating. Hence, patients who paid for services in the AMS centers established during the strike were entitled to reimbursement from KH. This interpretation was subsequently upheld by the courts.

7. This public statement closely parallels even more explicit statements in secret IMA materials that I am not at liberty to cite.

8. As the dispute dragged on, some leaders of the strike proposed expanding and improving the services offered by AMS in order to provide the basis for an enduring fee-for-service system that could compete with or even replace the KH clinic system. Other powerful elements within the IMA vigorously opposed this proposal.

9. Patients are also reputed to have made extensive use of traditional and alternative medicine during the strike, but no data are available on this topic (Weingarten and Monnickendam 1985).

10. The physicians who were thus pressed into service were nearing retirement age or just past it. Hence, they were dependent on the good graces of the KH administration for continued employment.

11. The clinic and hospital nurses we interviewed were very careful not to admit to having performed any illegal procedures, but they also hinted that such activities were not rare.

12. The need for this service was reduced by the decision of many employers to permit medical absences without a doctor's certificate (Weingarten and Monnickendam 1985).

REFERENCES

Abbott, A. 1983. "Professional Ethics." *American Journal of Sociology* 88:855-885.
Antonovsky, A. 1988. "The Professional-Proletarian Bind: Doctors' Strikes in Western Societies." In *Cross-National Research in Sociology*, edited by M. Kohn. Beverly Hills, CA: Sage.

Arian, A. 1981. "Health Care in Israel: Political and Administrative Aspects." *International Political Science Review* 2: 43-56.

"Aridor Keeps His Cool as Shostak Hurls Accusations." 1983. *Jerusalem Post* (May 23), pp. 1, 3.

Badgley, R., and S. Wolfe 1967. *Doctors' Strike: Medical Care and Conflict in Saskatchewan.* Toronto: Macmillan.

Bar Tsuri, R., and T. Batsri. 1985. *Strikes in Israel during 1974-1982.* Tel Aviv: General Federation of Workers in Israel. (In Hebrew).

Becker, H. 1958. "Problems of Inference and Proof in Participant Observation." *American Sociological Review* 23:652-660.

Blackburn, R.M., and K. Prandy. 1965. "White Collar Unionization: A Conceptual Framework." *British Journal of Sociology* 16:111-122.

Blau, P., and R. Scott. 1962. *Formal Organizations.* San Francisco: Chandler.

Blum, A. and G. Harel. 1980 . "The Generic Reasons for Strikes: An Interpretation of the Israeli Case." *Relations Industrielles* 35:99-114.

Chamot, D. 1976. "Professional Employees Turn to Unions." *Harvard Business Review* 54:119-127.

Derber, C., ed. 1982. *Professionals as Workers.* Boston: G.K. Hall.

————. 1984. "Physicians and their Sponsors: The New Medical Relations of Production." Pp. 217-254 in *Issues in the Political Economy of Health Care,* edited by J. McKinlay. New York: Tavistock.

"Doctors at Centers Will Receive 50% of Fee." 1983. *Haaretz* (June 9), p. 2. (In Hebrew).

"The Doctors; Pressure: Results and Dangers." 1983. *Haaretz* (May 26), p. 11. (In Hebrew).

Ellencweig, A. 1983. "The New Israeli Health Care Reform: An Analysis of a National Need." *Journal of Health Politics, Policy and Law* 8: 366-386.

Freidson, E. 1984. "The Changing Nature of Professional Control." *Annual Review of Sociology* 10:1-20.

————. 1986. *Professional Powers: A Study of the Institutionalization of Formal Knowledge.* Chicago: The University of Chicago Press.

Glaser, B., and A. Strauss. 1967. *The Discovery of Grounded Theory: Strategies for Qualitative Research.* Chicago: Aldine.

Goode, W. 1957. "Community within a Community: The Professions." *American Sociological Review* 22: 194-200.

Greenwood, E. 1957. "Attributes of a Profession. *Social Forces* 2: 44-55.

Harrison, M., and E. Tabory 1980. "Faculty Unions and the Strike Weapon." *Journal of Higher Education* 51:424-438.

————. 1983. "Professionalism and Unionism: The Case of Faculty Unions in Israeli Universities." *Journal of Collective Negotiations in the Public Sector* 12:57-69.

Heidenheimer, A., and L. Johansen. 1985. "Organized Medicine and Scandinavian Professional Unionism: Hospital Policies and Exit Options in Denmark and Sweden." *Journal of Health Politics, Policy and Law* 10:347-370.

Hoffman, L. 1982. "Housestaff Activism: The Emergence of Patient-Care Demands." *Journal of Health Politics, Policy, and Law* 7:421-439.

"Israel the Beautiful, It Isn't!" 1983. *Haaretz* (May 24), p. 11. (In Hebrew).

Klegon, D. 1978. "The Sociology of Professions." *Sociology of Work and Occupations* 5: 259-283.

Larson, M. 1977. *The Rise of Professionalism.* Berkeley, CA: University of California Press.

Lofland, J. 1971. *Analyzing Social Situations.* Belmont, CA: Wadsworth.

McKinlay, J. 1982. "Towards the Poletarianization of the Physician." Pp. 37-62 in *Professionals as Workers,* edited by C. Derber. Boston: G.K. Hall.

"Medical Time Bomb." 1983. *Maariv* (March 7). (In Hebrew).

Melosh, B. 1982. *The Physician's Hand: Work, Culture and Conflict in American Nursing.* Philadelphia, PA: Temple University Press.

Modan, B. 1986. *Medicine under Siege: The Doctors' Strike and the Crisis of Israeli Medicine.* Tel Aviv: Adam. (In Hebrew)

Parsons, T. 1968. "Professions." Pp. 536-547 in *International Encyclopedia of the Social Sciences,* Vol. 12, edited by D. Sills. New York: Macmillan.

Prandy, K. 1965. *Professional Employees: A Study of Engineers and Scientists.* London: Faber and Faber.

Prandy K., A. Steward, and R.M. Blackburn. 1974. "Concepts and Measures : The Example of Unionateness." *Sociology* 8: 427-446.

Raelin, J. 1989. "Unionization and Deprofessionalization: Which Comes First?" *Journal of Organizational Behavior* 10:1010-115.

Schatzman, L., and A. Strauss. 1973. *Field Methods.* Englewood-Cliffs, NJ: Prentice-Hall.

Shirom, A. 1983. *Introduction to Labor Relations in Israel.* Tel Aviv: Am Oved. (In Hebrew).

Weingarten, M.A., and M.S. Monnickendam. 1985. "The Effect of Direct Charges and Consultations in Family Practice: A Study of a Doctors' Strike." *Family Practice* 2: 35-41.

Woolfe, S., ed. 1978. *Organization of Health Workers and Labor Conflict.* New York: Baywood.

Yishai, R. 1986. *The Doctors' Strike: 2 March 1983 -27 June 1983.* Tel Aviv: Zamora Beitan. (In Hebrew)

Yishai, Y. 1982. "Politics and Medicine: The Case of Israeli National Health Insurance." Social Science and Medicine 16: 285-291.

PART IV

PROFESSIONAL DOMINANCE IN
A CHANGING MEDICAL ENVIRONMENT

CONFLICTING CHARACTERIZATIONS OF PROFESSIONAL DOMINANCE

Frederic W. Hafferty and Fredric D. Wolinsky

ABSTRACT

Recent changes in the structure and organization of the health care industry have profound implications for medicine as a professional organization. Over the past twenty years, three schools of thought (professional dominance, deprofessionalization, and proletarianization) have developed different interpretive strategies for examining medicine's future as a profession. This paper will compare how each of these three perspectives differs in its characterization of professional powers, the indicators they use to structure their respective arguments, and how each handles the issue of change. Areas of contention include the use of different sets of predictors, the employment of different levels of analysis, and the dissimilar treatment of professional powers as a dynamic entity. Suggestions for future research are based on the comparisons made within each of these three areas.

Current Research on Occupations and Professions, Volume 6, pages 225-249.
Copyright © 1991 by JAI Press Inc.
All rights of reproduction in any form reserved.
ISBN: 1-55938-236-8

225

INTRODUCTION

The profession of medicine is changing. An organizational past now nostalgically characterized as medicine's "golden age" has allegedly become tarnished by the presence of corporate and governmental interests. No longer a cottage industry, the image of the solo male practitioner, black bag in hand and housecall-bound, exists today more as an icon to Rockwell's America than as an adequate characterization of medicine's present condition. The recent and forceful *emergence* of corporate interests within our nation's health care system is unmistakable (Relman 1980; Starr 1982; Anderson 1985; Freidson 1989). An adequate understanding of the long-range *impact* of such new institutional arrangements and organizational alliances is, however, more illusive than obvious. Indeed, how the presence of new corporate structures will affect the professional organization of work and the nature of professional identity are of concern to social scientists, health policy planners, and those within the medical profession itself. At root are issues such as the future of medicine's position of control within the health care system and the relationship between corporate priorities and the clinical practice of medicine.

The rise of medicine as a professionally dominant, occupational group has been most systematically chronicled and analyzed by Eliot Freidson. Beginning with his publications[1] *Profession of Medicine* (1970a) and *Professional Dominance* (1970b), he proceeded to advance a highly influential body of propositions, constructs, and observations regarding the nature of profession as a particular form of organizational structure and as a special type of occupation (see Freidson 1971a, 1971b, 1973, 1975, 1976, 1977). Freidson's initial arguments quickly assumed a dominant status within social science circles (Hafferty 1988).

This status notwithstanding, the early 1970s were witness to the rise of several challenges to the professional dominance thesis. Two of the most notable were deprofessionalization, associated with the writings of Marie Haug (1973, 1975, 1976, 1977, 1988; Haug and Lavin 1978, 1981, 1983), and proletarianization, associated with the writings of John McKinlay (1973, 1977, 1978, 1982, 1984, 1986, 1988; McKinlay and Arches 1985, 1986; McKinlay and Stoeckle 1987, 1988). Although each of these two perspectives approach the issue of professional dominance from a somewhat different frame of reference, both conclude that medicine is losing rather than maintaining its professionally dominant status.[2]

The arguments advanced by Haug and McKinlay eventually elicited a series of rebuttals by Freidson (1983, 1984, 1985, 1986a, 1986b, 1987, 1989). Freidson (1986b, Chapter 6; 1989, Chapters 12 and 13) takes sharp exception to what he considers to be the misguided foci, inappropriate data, faulty interpretation of data, and rhetorical arguments advanced by these competing perspectives.[3]

Freidson's work during this period is of particular importance for two reasons. First, these writings were intended to be his review and summation of the professional dominance-deprofessionalization-proletarianization debate. Readers were thus afforded the opportunity to glean not only what Freidson considered to be the core elements in *his* overall model of professional dominance but also the manner and degree to which he considered alternative arguments to deviate from that core. As such, these writings may be viewed as Freidson's own "best evidence" regarding the nature and status of profession as a form of organization in medicine. For example, it is within this body of writings that Freidson most clearly advances his thesis that issues of professional dynamics are most appropriately addressed by viewing medicine as an organized social entity rather than by concentrating on the experiences of clinicians, either as individuals or collectivities.

Second, and perhaps more significantly, these writings contain a brief glimpse into Freidson's thoughts[4] on how medicine might come to lose its dominant status. Although he steadfastly insists that medicine has not lost (nor is losing) its professional prerogatives, it is within this latter body of writings that Freidson briefly suggests how medicine's status as a profession may be undercut.

Collectively, Freidson's early writings, the deprofessionalization and proletarianization alternatives, Freidson's rebuttals and still subsequent counters by Haug (1988) and McKinlay (1988), all represent a fascinating sociological dialogue on the nature and organization of professional work. As might be expected, this exchange raises many more questions than it answers. Indeed, on a number of occasions, the ideals of clarity, cogency, and theoretical completeness take a back seat to the inclinations of advocacy and territorial interests. To redress the resulting impasses, this paper examines how each of the three major perspectives approaches the issue of change, the nature of professional dominance, and the indicators around which each has chosen to structure their respective positions. Given that the deprofessionalization and proletarianization perspectives emphasize the loss of professional dominance while Freidson continues to argue for its maintenance, this paper pays particular attention to Freidson's brief observations on how medicine might come to lose its professional prerogatives. This focus will not only allow us to compare the professional dominance, deprofessionalization, and proletarianization perspectives directly, but will facilitate assessment of the consistency and theoretical completeness with which Freidson himself approaches this issue. We close with suggestions for future research.

THE DEPROFESSIONALIZATION PERSPECTIVE

Haug's early statements (1973, 1975) about deprofessionalization were originally deployed not so much to rebut Freidson's thesis of professional dominance but to counter a then popular argument that all occupations, in post-industrialized societies, were on the verge of becoming professionalized (see Bell 1968, 1973). Drawing support from Wilensky (1964), Haug (1973) challenged this thesis and proposed an alternative process which she labeled "deprofessionalization." In doing so, Haug proposed a leveling process similar to that suggested by the "post industrialists," but in her case, one that moved from the "top down" rather than from the "bottom up."

At its core, Haug's (1988) thesis of deprofessionalization centers around three different yet interrelated themes: the monopolization of esoteric knowledge, autonomy in work performance, and authority over clients. In developing these themes, Haug draws upon two sets of social phenomena: the social organization of consumers (or what she terms the consumer health movement), and the computerization of medical data and related information. Concurrent with the growth of special medical interest groups (e.g., women's health groups or groups focusing on specific disease entities), Haug proposes that patients are becoming better educated and more knowledgeable about health matters. This results in a narrowing of the traditional "knowledge gulf" between physicians and patients, and thus a diminished monopolization of expertise by physicians. As a consequence, Haug sees patients as increasingly able and willing to challenge the central and largely unquestioned role of the physician in clinical decision making. Haug perceives an increase in the public's mistrust of the physician as an "expert" and a revolt against medical authority in general. Physicians, according to Haug, are fast becoming secular experts. The propensity for patients to question physician authority (and physician decision-making) results, for Haug, in a fundamental altering of the traditional physician-patient relationship. Physician autonomy and its traditionally legitimate power over patients is thus undercut. This alleged loss of special status and autonomy is central to Haug's argument that physicians are becoming deprofessionalized.

The rise of technology in medicine and, in particular, the advancement of computer technology and the computerization of medical knowledge is a second and related set of conditions. Haug contends that the physician's traditional monopolization of medical knowledge is undercut as medical information becomes increasingly systematized and formalized. Not only does medical knowledge[5] become more widely accessible to "outsiders," but physicians themselves begin to lose control over how that knowledge is put to use in their own clinical activities (via decision trees and clinical algorithms). In addition, the proliferation of new technologies results in the growth of new occupations populated by workers who have skills physicians are unable to either emulate or control. The traditional jurisdictional monopoly of physicians is weakened.

Finally, Haug is impressed (sociologically speaking) with the trend away from traditional solo fee-for-service to alternative forms of practice. These include health maintenance organizations (HMOs) and proffered provider organizations (PPOs); shifts in reimbursement policies, including the advent of diagnosis-related groups (DRGs); the growth of peer review organizations (PROs); and the general intrusion of bureaucratic constraints within the overall delivery of health care. All are seen by Haug as examples of the increasing rationalization of medical work signifying a loss of professional status by physicians.

At times Haug appears to recognize the importance of distinguishing between activities carried out at the level of the individual practitioner and those of the medical profession as a whole (e.g., see Haug 1988, pp. 49, 50). For the most part, however, her analysis (particularly with respect to issues of autonomy and control) remains rather firmly wedded to social action at the individual practitioner level. Thus, when Haug talks about the narrowing of a knowledge gulf and that point of tension around which issues of autonomy and control are to be decided, she is looking primarily at the interface between physicians and patients. She basically does not address the interface between medicine as a corporate entity and the public as represented by the State or some other organized social body.

THE PROLETARIANIZATION PERSPECTIVE

In comparison with deprofessionalization, the thesis of proletarianization is much more closely identified with a broader theoretical tradition; in this case, Marxist thought. Whereas Haug centers her analysis around the advent of certain political and cultural phenomena most evident during the late 1960s and early to mid-1970s (e.g., the consumer rights movement and the rise of computer technology), McKinlay has chosen to focus more on economic and organizational phenomena associated with the historical forces of capitalism. In particular, McKinlay is concerned with the issues of political economy and, as such, devotes considerable attention to the circumstances of professional work in large organizations. In this respect, proletarianization shares more of an analytical affinity with the professional dominance perspective than it does with deprofessionalization (also see Freidson [1984, p. 6] on this issue).

Building on Marx's theory of history, McKinlay locates his analysis of professions within an evolving struggle between those possessing capital, or serving as the agents of capital (owners or managers), and those who perform the basic productive labor of the economy (the proletariat). McKinlay argues that in the face of a growing corporate and bureaucratic presence in medical care, physicians find themselves swept along by the broader historical forces of capitalism. Physicians, like other workers before them, find themselves stripped of control over their own work. Thus, according to McKinlay, physicians are becoming proletarianized.

McKinlay's analysis of the changing nature of medical work and the future of medicine as a profession focuses on physician employment and employment status. He argues that there is a distinct trend away from self-employment and towards the employment of physicians by large (often multinational) organizations. As physicians become salaried employees, they lose their control of medical work. This includes their ability to set the economic terms of work as well as their discretion over what work is to be done, how it is to be done, and what the goals or aims of that work are to be. McKinlay argues that the growing corporatization of medicine has significantly curtailed the autonomy of physicians. Physicians are becoming subject to routines and organization of work not of their own making. The cornerstone of McKinlay's thesis is the inevitable expansion of capitalist exploitation. Like Haug, McKinlay notes the increasing segmentation and specialization of medical work. Unlike Haug, McKinlay focuses on the control of work and the ownership of the tools of production rather than on physician-client relations.

In many respects, McKinlay's approach to the study of professions shares much in common with that taken by Freidson. Both focus on the role and the relation of professionals to other occupational groups, to capital, and to the State. Like Freidson, McKinlay is concerned with the structural relations between physicians, workers, and owners of corporations, and in the increasing dependence of professionals on sources of outside capital for supplies and equipment. Unlike Freidson, however, McKinlay concludes that medicine is losing its professional status.

THE PROFESSIONAL DOMINANCE PERSPECTIVE

For Freidson (1985), the status of profession as a special type of occupation rests on three different but interdependent factors: (1) relative public trust (imputed or actual), (2) exclusive command over a body of specialized knowledge and skill, and (3) dominance in the division of labor. In some instances Freidson reduces these three factors to those of cultural authority and legal authority, but the dimensions of trust, knowledge, and dominance remain the core elements. Although this is not the place to detail Freidson's overall theory of profession, it is important to note that he centers his analysis around medicine's privileged position as a legally supported, economic monopoly. Freidson notes that this position could not have been established had not medicine first been able to convince the public at large, particularly the power elite, of its special skills, knowledge, trustworthiness, and altruism. The core of medicine's professional status ultimately comes to rest on the conferral of autonomy (represented as occupational dominance) and not on characteristics such as knowledge or trustworthiness. Although the dimensions of cultural versus legal authority have become increasingly intertwined (and thus difficult to clearly separate), the profession continues to evolve and the distinctions remain important for both conceptual and analytical reasons. In summary, buttressed by a tradition of public trust, and secured in part by medicine's command of a body of specialized knowledge and skills, medicine has come to acquire a variety of supportive legal and quasi-legal apparatuses. These latter structures establish medicine's dominance in the division of labor.

Although Freidson's (1989, p. 183) overall model of professional dominance rests on the conjoint factors of cultural/ideological dominance and economic/ legal authority, his claim that medicine continues to *retain* its professional prerogatives rests more on the element of authority than on dominance. In his later writings, Freidson (1985) insists that his theory of professional dominance does not speak to the issues of cultural hegemony but only to medicine's relationship to other health care occupations and its position in that division of labor. Clear, concise, and verifiable data are important to Freidson, and it is from this stance that he considers evidence of cultural hegemony to be unacceptably amorphous and elusive. Instead, he prefers to argue his case on what he considers to be a more empirically demonstrable foundation. This includes the elaborate system of licensing laws, structures designed to establish quality controls, and the accreditation practices of health programs which support medicine's claim to ultimate authority in things medical. Freidson perceives medicine as enjoying a special status in American labor law with a legally protected ability to exercise a meaningful discretion on the job, particularly around the right to admit, treat, and discharge patients. As such, Freidson (1985) argues that answers to questions about medicine's professional status are best found in the study of state licensing laws or in the evolution of federal antitrust law as it pertains to medicine. Freidson similarly advocates examining the representation (and/or the controlling position) of physicians on the governing boards of hospitals. In sum, Freidson (1988, p. 187) centers his study of professional dominance around the issues of occupational authority and legally established monopoly. What is unique and central to the notion of profession is its license and mandate to control its work, a license and mandate granted by society. Based on his analysis of such things as antitrust court decisions, Freidson concludes that there is little evidence that medicine's legally sustained dominance in the division of labor has been significantly diminished.

What indicators does Freidson bring to bear (directly or indirectly) on his analysis of professional dominance? In countering McKinlay's claim that physicians are increasingly likely to be salaried employees, Freidson argues that it is neither employment status in general nor employment in bureaucracies that constitutes the critical element in the maintenance of professional dominance.

Owning property or the means of production is not important in and of itself in assuring control over one's economic fate and autonomy in one's work (Friedson 1984, p. 9).

Instead, Freidson argues, it depends on the value (e.g., the perceived importance or consequentialness) attached to these goods and services in the broader market place: The more valued one's goods or services, the more control one can exercise over the terms, conditions, content, and goals of one's work. For Freidson, "value" can be influenced by a number of additional factors, including medicine's ability to control its own numbers (the issue of a physician surplus) and the occupational identities and structural place of other individuals providing similar or "like" services. Freidson perceives that medicine continues to have an extremely high value placed on its work by society at large as well as by capitalist employers.

Unfortunately, Freidson is not fully clear about how these aspects of "value" are to be operationalized or otherwise determined. On the one hand, it is plausible to argue that the value of one's goods or services is at least partially determined within the public arena, and thus it is appropriate to draw upon indicators such as "public esteem" or "trust." But as we have just noted, Freidson and Haug consider such entities to be empirically elusive and therefore inappropriate.[6] Similarly, Freidson does not provide details on what would unambiguously establish a state of "physician surplus," or what would constitute an unacceptable or "fatal" loss of control over the boundaries of its work. For example, Freidson argues in his 1980 writings that the infringement of other occupations such as midwifery or chiropractic on medicine's traditional jurisdictions remains contained at the fringes of medicine's domain, and thus has a negligible negative effect on the future of medicine as a profession. Freidson, however, does not detail what a non-negligible effect might be. Light and Hafferty (1989) believe that such encroachments are more frequent, extensive, and consequential than Freidson has thus far acknowledged. To date, however, neither Freidson nor Light and Hafferty have provided a yardstick to externally evaluate the presence or absence of "significant change."

These observations aside, it is important to note that Freidson's treatment of profession is more analytically complex than that of either McKinlay or Haug. For instance, Freidson does not treat profession as a singular or undifferentiated entity. The distinctions he draws between consulting and scientific professions (with medicine belonging in the former category) have important implications for understanding medicine's strategic ability to protect its professional prerogatives. Freidson also differentiates between types of physicians. Although Freidson (1970a) has traditionally considered rank-and-file physicians to be the hub of medicine's professional identity, his later writings highlight the emergence of a technical and administrative elite within an increasingly segmentalized medicine. Whereas both proletarianization and deprofessionalization take medicine's professional dominance as a given and focus almost exclusively on its dissolution, Freidson's overall body of writings embraces both the rise of professional dominance and its maintenance (as well as hinting at its potential decline). Even the issue of autonomy is not treated as a unidimensional entity by Freidson. In contrasting medicine in the United States with that in the Soviet Union, for example, he notes that while Soviet medicine lacks *political* or *economic* autonomy, it still maintains *technical* autonomy, allowing it, via legal sanctions, the exclusive right to "perform medical work, to control the selection and training of its members, and to formulate the standards used in evaluating their own" (Friedson 1988, p. 384). Hence we come to find that Freidson considers certain types of autonomy to be more critical than others in the maintenance of professional dominance. In summary, although Freidson's treatment of professional dominance remains theoretically incomplete (Hafferty and Light 1989), it does represent a more comprehensive treatment of the nature of profession and professional dominance than is offered by its critics. Whether it represents the more accurate or even the more useful approach to the study of professional change, however, is open to debate.

Perhaps most critical to understanding Freidson's position that medicine has not lost its status as a profession is his insistence that, regardless of changes in the nature of physician work, physicians are still in charge of establishing standards, reviewing performances, and exercising supervision and control. Constraints of work and judgment, Freidson (1985) maintains, continue to be exercised by a "collective collegial practice" and not by "outsiders" (p. 28). Although we will speak more directly to this issue in a later section, it is within this position that Freidson highlights the two key sets of explanatory variables central to his analysis of profession: (1) the issue of physician identity (or identification), and (2) medicine's legally sanctioned and protected dominance in the medical division of labor.

WHO'S ON FIRST

As noted earlier, the conceptualization of medicine as a "corporate" entity is a major theme embedded in Freidson's later writings on professions. Furthermore, he considers the impact of changes in the organization and financing of medical care to be most appropriately reviewed at the level of medicine as an organized social and political entity rather than at the level of the practicing clinician. By stressing the nature of medicine as a highly organized and stratified special interest group rather than as a purely clinical body, Freidson marshals evidence that medicine is still very much in control of its professional destiny. By adopting this frame of reference (or unit of analysis), he clearly distances himself from those who, in concluding that medicine has lost its professional dominance, concentrate predominantly on what is happening to the practicing clinician.

Freidson can be challenged on his characterization of medicine as a corporate entity[7] or his selection of this particular unit of analysis, but recognizing that the professional dominance-deprofessionalization-proletarianization debate frequently is waged at different levels of analysis goes a long way towards clarifying areas of disagreement among the major players. Despite appearances to the contrary, substantial areas of agreement do, in fact, exist among the professional dominance, deprofessionalization, and proletarianization schools of thought (Hafferty 1988). All agree that health care has undergone massive changes in the past two decades. All agree that there has been an increasingly complex division of labor within medicine, accompanied by an increasingly complex administrative structure to coordinate that labor (including record systems and accounting practices covering both reimbursement and quality of care issues). All agree that medical work and services are becoming increasingly rationalized. All acknowledge the presence of increasingly sophisticated computer-based information systems, as well as the increased presence and demands of health care technologies accompanied by the demands of capital costs, the rise of legal and ethical maladies, and the further stratification of health care occupations. All concur that physicians are increasingly unable to carry out their clinical activities without reliance on services and goods that lie outside of their control. All acknowledge that an ever-increasing percentage of physicians are becoming salaried employees, and that the individual physician has suffered a loss of autonomy and perhaps even prestige. All agree that medicine's ability to control its own numbers (the issue of a physician surplus), as well as it's ability to maintain control over the entry of "outsiders" (alternative providers) into previously restricted areas of clinical activity, is critical to medicine's continued control over its own destiny.

In short, widespread agreement exists among the principles as to the number and kinds of changes in the organization of medicine and their impact on the individual practitioner. Where, then, do the differences lie? One critical difference is the aforementioned issue of level of analysis. Freidson consistently argues that the issue is not the computerization of clinical practice data, or even the development of computer-based algorithms to guide the diagnostic and treatment activities of individual practitioners per se, but rather who is in control of the input and interpretation of those data. For Freidson, these parameters remain in control of the medical profession—as a corporate entity—and thus medicine's professional dominance remains intact. Similarly, Freidson argues that the influx of a variety of new structures, protocols, and procedures for the review of clinical work may certainly restrict the autonomy of the individual practitioner but does not diminish medicine's autonomy or professional status—as long as medicine remains in control of establishing the criteria for review. Continuing, Freidson acknowledges that a variety of health care occupations including chiropractic, dentistry, optometry, and podiatry practice independently of medicine (and, in some cases, in spite of medicine's active opposition).[8] What is at issue for Freidson is that these other occupational groups must function within carefully limited spheres of activity which, in turn, are delineated by the control which medicine exercises over the essence of clinical work (that being the diagnosis, treatment, and discharge of patients). Focusing on employment status, Freidson defines the critical issue as the importance of that work in the labor market.

> If one's position in the labor market is strong, one can specify the terms and conditions of one's employment, granting little power to the employer (Freidson 1989, p. 187).

Similarly, Freidson (1985, p. 20) argues that one's focus should not be the increasing presence of rationalization per se, but rather the form that rationalization takes. Freidson rejects the notion that physicians will become "blue-collar workers," without voice or leverage to exert a meaningful choice in the work that they do or in how that work is carried out. Freidson (1989, p. 188) characterizes physicians not as "employees" but as "attendings" and insists that they are still able to exercise influence, in that hospitals remain critically dependent upon physicians for patients. In summary, Freidson (1989) rejects the proletarianization thesis by noting that

> neither the facts of employment nor of working in large, complex organizations constitute in and of themselves sufficiently persuasive evidence to support the use of the concept of proletarianization to characterize the position of physicians in a truly analytic fashion (p. 189).

Differences also exist with respect to the interpretation of data. For example, McKinlay (1988; McKinlay and Arches 1985) cites a decline in physician income as one indication that physicians have suffered a loss of professional status. Speaking in defense of the professional dominance perspective, Wolinsky (1988a) cites data to the contrary. Similarly, Freidson (1986b, 1989), in countering Haug's traditional claim that medicine has suffered a loss of social prestige, cites Harris polls to support his contention that there has been no relative loss to medicine in this arena. Navarro (1988, p. 60) cites unpublished data, again from Harris, which he maintains demonstrate just the opposite. In a third example, McKinlay (McKinlay and Arches 1985) cites the loss of the solo physician as an entrepreneur and the rise of the physician as a salaried employee to be evidence of medicine's loss of professional status. Freidson (1986b), in turn, presents data that there has been an increase in professional self-employment, not a decline. Subsequently, Freidson (1989) acknowledged the trend toward physicians becoming salaried workers, but characterizes labor statistics as flawed (in that the count of salaried physicians includes physicians serving as administrators, researchers, and teachers) and concluded by rejecting the general thesis that loss of self-employment status necessarily means loss of control over the economic terms and conditions of work. As noted earlier, Freidson unequivocally rejects the idea of employment status as a viable indicator. Freidson argues that the most meaningful focus rests on the value of the work performed and not on the nature of that work per se. Again, it is important to note that in these and similar circumstances, Freidson (1989, p. 190) is not referring to the state or status of individual physicians (even as a collectivity) but to medicine as an "organic social entity."

McKinlay (1977, 1988) also suggests that differences in the frame of reference (or unit of analysis) may result in alternative or contradictory conclusions being drawn about what is happening to the medical profession. Using the analogy of professional sports, McKinlay argues that differences in understanding are predicated on whether one views the "game" from the level of the "players," the "fans," the "owners," or the "State." McKinlay's analogy, although interesting, remains underdeveloped. For the most part, he fails to directly associate any of his four levels with the particular arguments advanced by the professional dominance, deprofessionalization, or proletarianization perspectives.[9] Furthermore, he does not indicate which level (either singularly or in concert) he considers the most useful in providing insights into the issue of change in the social position of physicians, and ultimately, whether or not physicians are losing their professional status. More by extrapolation than anything else, it appears that Freidson's primary attention is directed at the interface of McKinlay's level of the State (governmental activities) and the level of medicine itself. Most importantly, it appears that McKinlay's "medicine" and Freidson's "corporate medicine" do not represent the same entity. Freidson is consistent in his insistence that medicine at the level of an organic entity represents the proper unit of analysis. McKinlay (1988, p. 4), on the other hand, still appears to direct his primary analytical energies toward the players of the "game." If we are accurate in these two characterizations, then important differences remain between what Freidson refers to as "medicine" and the process of "doctoring" analyzed by McKinlay.[10]

Also basic to this discussion of units of analysis is a fundamental difference between Freidson and McKinlay regarding the general tenor of relationships among corporate, State, and professional interests. In taking the proletarianization literature as a whole, McKinlay appears to view these relationships as essentially strained and ultimately antagonistic. Freidson, on the other hand, is more prone to emphasize the amount of support (and thus stability) which exists between medicine and those institutions whose support Freidson considers to be vital to medicine's maintenance of its professional prerogatives. In short, McKinlay is more likely to perceive tension and dissolution where Freidson perceives evidence of continued support.

WHAT'S ON SECOND

Although Freidson has remained steadfast in rejecting the conclusion that medicine has already lost, or is in the process of losing, its dominant status, in some of his more recent writings he does suggest conditions under which such an outcome may be likely (see Freidson 1984, 1985, 1986a, 1986b, 1987). Freidson's thoughts center around the basic thesis that medical work is becoming increasingly rationalized and formalized. He concludes that, fueled by greater internal stratification, the control of medical work (including the critical aspect of standards setting) is moving out of the grasp of rank-and-file physicians and into the hands of elite practitioners and researchers. Specifically, Freidson foresees the rise of two elite groups within medicine: an administrative elite exerting economic and administrative power, and a knowledge elite wielding technical or cognitive power.[11]

Freidson considers the rise of these two elite groups within what has traditionally been a community of equals (see Goode 1957) to be a "critical change" in the organization of medicine, one with potentially dire consequences for medicine as a profession. Freidson perceives a growing rift between these new elite and the rank-and-file physicians, and foresees a growing tension between managers and managed, rule setters and rule followers, physicians as owners and physicians as employees, and those who review versus those who are reviewed. Within this process of increasing stratification, Freidson is particularly concerned with how medicine, as an organized entity, will adapt to the increasing formalization of professional controls. What had until recently been a largely informal and self-serving set of practices has evolved into a highly specific and formal set of procedures and protocols by which physicians judge the work of their colleagues. There also has been an increase in the number of activities subject to such review. Policing activities once limited to issues of "gross malpractice" now include contingencies such as test-ordering and duration of hospitalization, all driven by a new preoccupation with cost of care. In short, the issue of what is considered to be a "mistake" in medicine is changing. Correspondingly, Freidson also perceives the evolution of different groups within medicine, each with different perspectives, interests, and demands.

> When you have one elite setting the standards and another elite directing and controlling and other professions doing the work, you have altered the organization of the body and relations between its members which may have serious implications for its corporate character (Freidson 1984, p. 17).

Although Freidson obviously attaches much analytical importance to the rise of a technical and administrative elite, his overall handling of this dimension appears inconsistent at critical points. On the one hand, Freidson insists that as long as physician-insiders control the organization and content of medical work, medicine will retain its professional status. As such, the rise of an administrative and technical elite within the physician ranks will play a critical role in maintaining this control. On the other hand, as we have just noted, Freidson also argues that the rise of such elite groups threatens the internal cohesion that characterizes medicine as a profession and thus the corporate character so critical to Freidson's entire analysis of why medicine has been able to maintain its status as a profession.

How are we to reconcile these two perspectives or outcomes? If "reconciliation" is indeed the operative notion, then one possibility would be to characterize these two outcomes as occupying different stages in the evolution of medicine as a profession. By stressing the fundamentally dynamic nature of professions, we can assign the *emergence* of a knowledge and administrative elite to a stage early in medicine's struggle to *maintain* its professional status. By populating the ranks of the knowledge and administrative elite with physician "insiders," medicine seeks to maximize its continued influence over the process of formalization and rationalization, ultimately assuring its professional status. Unfortunately (for medicine), other (often countervailing) interests in the health care arena exist. The interests of capital and the State, for example, are not always in congruence with, or sympathetic to, medicine's desire to remain in control. Indeed, once outside the House of Medicine, very little consensus appears to exist among the players about who should control the nature, function, and scope of medical work. Certainly it is very much in the interest of capital and of the State to convince these new elite to advocate interests other than those of organized medicine. If these efforts prove successful, a different realm of organizational control will emerge. At this point, those occupying positions of leadership within the elite ranks begin to identify with the interests of capital or the State rather than with their "fellow" rank-and-file physicians. Analytically, such a shift in orientation or allegiance in medicine is not without precedence. Freidson (1970b, p. 42; 1988, p. 370) clearly documents how the element of autonomy, once so critical to medicine's assumption of a professional status, has come to have a dynamic of its own, with medicine increasingly unable to regulate itself in the public interest. If we postulate that the daily work of these administrative and knowledge elite occupationally differs from that of the practicing clinician, then Freidson's longstanding theoretical argument that explanations of human action are best derived from motivations and directions embedded in the institutional and economic structure of work (rather than individual knowledge, values, or attitudes) raises at least modest skepticism that any joint set of interest and values will emerge that tie together the interests of these elite to those of rank-and-file clinicians (Hafferty 1988).

How, then, do we assess the ongoing status of medicine as a professional community? If, as Freidson so convincingly argues, the nature of medical work is becoming more formalized and rationalized, then an increasing conflict and dissension within the House of Medicine is to be expected. Unfortunately, Freidson provides little further guidance on the matter. Does this identity (or status) derive from a similar background and training, or common *rites de passage?* Does it rest within the dictates of a more current and similar work environment? Freidson does not say. Wolinsky (1988a) suggests that physician administrators will lose their status as insiders only if they "fully and permanently divest themselves of all actual medical practice" (p. 43). According to Wolinsky, this will not happen as long as physician administrators move into that status by rising through the clinician ranks.

Besides giving greater specificity than Freidson to this issue, Wolinsky's criteria also provide an opportunity to compare the relative influence of prior socialization versus the present work setting on issues of identity and identification. Wolinsky's criteria give critical weight to past experiences; in particular, to values, norms, rationales, motives, and identities developed and nurtured within the process of medical school training and subsequent clinical experience. Of course, Freidson's insistence that background and training permit knowledge and administrative elites to remain insiders makes essentially the same point. Thus, both Wolinsky and Freidson appear to part company with Freidson's argument concerning the relative importance of current work setting versus prior training (or experiences). In contrast, McKinlay appears to more consistently highlight the influence of current work arrangements (and thus the interest of capital) in his analysis of physician allegiances. Nevertheless, it is not the image of physicians as laborers that should excite the proletarians. Rather, it is this image of physicians as managers. Medicine's loss of professional status may be driven less by the rank-and-file becoming similar to blue-collar workers as by the emerging elite adopting the values and allegiances of white-collar administrators. If true, the status of managers as agents of capital and the bourgeoisie class demands greater analytical attention by advocates of professional decay as well as by those who argue that medicine continues to maintain its professional dominance.

The issue of "trust" and its impact on the relationship between medicine and society at large remains to be addressed with respect to the issue of increasing stratification in medicine. Earlier, Freidson essentially (and we believe quite successfully) countered many of the specific challenges raised by the deprofessionalists and the proletarianists by framing his analysis at the level of medicine as a corporate entity. In turn, we noted that Freidson's arguments about medicine as a corporate entity were grounded in his insistence that critical areas of medical decision-making and autonomy still remain "within the profession." With the increasing hierarchical segmentation, however, the corporate body no longer remains as inviolate, intact, or homogeneous. Internally, divisive forces are at work. Medicine's very nature as an organized and organic social entity is being altered. It may well be true, as Freidson (1987, p. 144) insists, that the future "will be determined by the choices made by the new elites," but it is not as clear whether, in Freidson's words, these new elite will become "servants of capital or of the State," which would polarize the profession, or whether they will.

identify with the ideals of their profession and concern themselves with sustaining the integrity of the work for which they have taken responsibility. This [latter] choice would lead to an alliance with the professionally legitimate rather than merely self-interested demands of practitioners for resources adequate enough to permit good work for the benefit of the client (p.144).[12]

Although not explicitly stated, what Freidson is concerned about here is that empirically elusive entity "trust" which formed one of the cornerstones of medicine's ascension to professional power. As noted in both *Profession of Medicine* (1970a) and *Professional Dominance* (1970b), autonomy once achieved assumes its own dynamic; the work of the profession eventually diverges from what the State had initially expected and the profession becomes increasingly unable to regulate itself in the public interest. Freidson (1970a) saw autonomy as promoting a callousness and insincerity within itself, a "self-deceiving view of the objectivity and reliability of its knowledge and of the virtues of its members," the proliferation of "sanctimonious myths" about its own superior qualities, and an orientation which would be "at best patronizing and at worst contemptuous of its clientele" (p. 370). In sum, he perceived that medicine's "characteristics as a social institution lead it inevitably to have a distorted view of itself, its knowledge, and its mission" (1970b, p. 42).

Medicine's abuse of its trust and stewardship responsibilities has supported the rise of "external" regulatory activities concerning medical work. Although the critical battlefields may be in Congress, courts, and state legislatures, the issue and presence of trust remains fundamental to medicine's ability to retain (or regain) its professional prerogatives (see Reed and Evans 1987). Although the two authors of this paper disagree as to whether medicine still possesses the ability to direct or dictate its future in this regard, both of us consider the issue critical to any adequate understanding of profession as a socially dynamic entity. Medicine's ability to convince the public that it has recaptured its spirit of service and stewardship also depends, at least in part, on its ability to maintain the image (if not the reality) of possessing a cohesive identity, even in the face of increasing stratification and formalization of relations among physicians.[13]

As noted earlier, there is good reason to believe that the motives, values, and rationales of the emerging elite will not necessarily reflect those of the front-line rank and file. Similarly, we anticipate that the interests of the administrative and technical elite are also likely to be at odds (Hafferty and Light 1989). Finally, it is not clear how to operationalize the issues of professional identity and professional identification. On the one hand, we could advocate a structural approach and decide the issue of affiliation or identity on the basis of current work setting and the nature of the work being performed by these new elite. On the other hand, we could argue, at least with respect to the initial stages of any elite formation, that the issues of self-identity or self-identification are quite germane to the question of whether or not a previously homogeneous group is undergoing internal differentiation.

Although the issue of medicine's internal organization is critical to Freidson's overall theory of professions, this particular issue may not be the most appropriate stage upon which to argue his thesis that medicine retains its dominance in the medical division of labor. We could, for example, propose that regardless of whether or not medicine maintains an internal state of community, the key issue remains the presence or absence of institutional supports, the realm of licensing, the credentialing system, and the system of special laws and quasi-legal provisions that protect medicine from "outside" control. Should this be the case, Freidson can justifiably argue that the final battle will be fought at the level of medicine as a corporate entity and that issues of internal organization exert an indirect (and not a direct) influence on the nature of medicine as a profession. Nonetheless, it appears that this battle, like any military campaign, will depend more on the health, welfare, and spirit of its "soldiers" (as individuals or as collectivities) than Freidson has thus far been willing to formally acknowledge.

I DON'T KNOW'S ON THIRD

Although not as central as those detailed above, several other topics deserve mention with respect to the issue of profession (and also the professional dominance-deprofessionalization-proletarianization debate). This section will also include some suggestions for research on the future of medicine's professional dominance.

One unfortunate consequence of the professional dominance-deprofessionalization-proletarianization debate has been the tendency for participants to treat professional prerogatives in a dichotomous fashion. Discussions frequently treat professional dominance as something that is either present or absent, maintained or lost.[14] The consequence is a rather simplistic and essentially static portrayal of what is happening to medicine as a profession. What is subsequently underplayed is the dynamic and fluid nature of this form of organization.[15] For example, actions undertaken by medicine to successfully protect its professional interests may suggest that medicine is not losing its professional status. A different frame of reference, however, may identify these same successes as part of an increasing number of challenges to medicine's professional domain and thus a possible indication of medicine's loss of professional control. Conversely, the identification of areas where medicine has lost some of its professional prerogatives (prompting a conclusion of "deprofessionalization") may be re-evaluated when a broader or more historically grounded frame of analysis suggests that any such loss represents only a temporary downside in what is actually the re-emergence of profession (or some particular variation) as an influential form of organization. Both Haug (1988) and McKinlay (McKinlay and Arches 1985) suggest that history will be the final judge in deciding whose position best represents what is happening to medicine. Freidson, although not insisting that we wait this long for answers, appears to advance an image of medicine as an impervious megalith, essentially unaffected by virtually all that swirls around it. Neither position does full justice to the nature of profession as an ongoing dynamic social entity.

On yet another front, the professional dominance-deprofessionalization-proletarianization debate has been dominated by the case of the United States. Although yielding much insight into what is happening in this country's health care industry, one cost has been a rather provincialized understanding of profession. The viability of any profession is underscored by a rather complex interrelationship of forces radiating among relevant occupational groups, corporate entities, the State, and the public at large. Given the particular constellation of forces in this country, it is not likely that what is true for the United States will be generalizable to other nations.

This issue of external validity is illustrated in a supplementary issue of *The Milbank Quarterly* (see D. P. Willis 1988). Organized and edited by John McKinlay, and devoted to the changing character of the medical profession, this volume significantly advances the professional dominance-deprofessionalization-proletarianization debate by presenting a number of papers which focus on the nature of medicine as a profession in countries other than the United States. The countries covered are Canada (Coburn 1988), Britain (Larkin 1988), the Nordic Countries (Riska 1988), Italy (Krause 1988), Australia (E. Willis 1988), and the Soviet Union (Field 1988). Taken as a whole, these papers highlight the variety of forms or permutations that are possible in the organization of professional powers. The dominant status of medicine as a profession is not homogeneous across nation states, nor can it be taken for granted. Instead, "professional" configurations are markedly influenced by the particular interrelationships which have evolved among the above-mentioned constellations, but particularly between the State and organized medicine.

This brings us back to our earlier argument that professional dominance theory currently represents a more inclusive approach to the study of profession, given its focus on understanding the *rise* of professional powers. This attribute becomes relevant when we note, for example, that government by political party (*partitocrazia*) has severely hindered medicine's attainment of a professional status in Italy (Krause 1988). Larkin (1988) offers similar observations in the case of Britain and how medicine's historical lack of control over other health occupations has played an influential role in medicine's development of a professional status in that country. In short, a fully adequate theory of profession should be able to integrate issues of emergence, maintenance, and dissolution into an overall theory of professional powers. As long as the bulk of work emanating from the professional dominance, deprofessionalization, and proletarianization perspectives continues to focus on (1) the United States, and (2) the *loss* (or maintenance) of professional dominance, these three schools, as they stand today, will represent an incomplete approach to the study of profession.

The professional dominance-deprofessionalization-proletarianization debate has also suffered by being largely directed through Freidson's work on professional dominance. For example, when McKinlay advances his thesis of proletarianization, he often does so with the professional dominance perspective in mind. Haug is similarly preoccupied. Perhaps as a consequence, these two authors have little to say about each other's work. We know virtually nothing about how advocates of the deprofessionalization perspective view the proletarianization argument, and vice versa. This is unfortunate for several reasons. At minimum it limits the debate and tends to characterize both of these perspectives as secondary to the professional dominance model. Consequently, Freidson has come to occupy the role of theoretical arbiter. He is the only one of the "big three" who has consistently addressed the relative strengths and weaknesses of all three schools of thought in a focused and purposeful manner. The gatekeeping and interpretive roles played by Freidson and the relative lack of attention shown by Haug and McKinlay to each other's work also have resulted in some confusion over what actually differentiates the deprofessionalization perspective from that of proletarianization. Commentators often pair the two terms together ("deprofessionalization and proletarianization"), implying to the reader that they are synonymous or equivalent concepts. In other instances, the terms are substituted or shuffled, again suggesting that there is little difference between the two, at least when standing in the shadow of professional dominance theory.

Such conclusions or representations are unwarranted (Hafferty 1988). Not only do these two schools employ different variable sets, but the cross-substitution of these two terms obscures the possibility that deprofessionalization and proletarianization may also involve different *processes* which, in turn, may lead to fundamentally different *outcomes*. In other words, the social dynamics of deprofessionalization may well be quite different from the dynamics of proletarianization. Similarly, the outcomes evidenced during these two processes may differ as well. To the best of our knowledge, none of the principles have addressed these two theories with these issues in mind. While the theory of professional dominance currently offers observers a more fruitful framework for the analysis of professions,[16] this may not be true in the future.

Turning to directions for future research, two general topics clearly deserve more empirical attention. The first entails expanding our base of cross-national data. It is ludicrous to assume that a comprehensive theory of professions can be advanced without formally accounting for the nature of professional dynamics in other countries. With its traditional emphasis on the political economy as a major unit of analysis, proletarianization is well situated to make a substantial contribution in this area. Attention needs to be directed not only to other industrialized nations whose organization of health care delivery is different than ours (i.e., all of them), but also to developing nations. Regardless of Freidson's current focus on the *maintenance* of professional powers, his theory of the *rise* of professional prerogatives remains firmly embedded in the case of the United States. By focusing on developing nations, our understanding of profession as an emerging entity will be greatly enhanced. What differences exist remains to be seen. What is certain is that this broadened focus will allow us to better understand the complex role of State, corporate, and occupational relations, as well as to examine how variables such as sex, race, and age, all of which have been under-represented in the debate to date, will continue to influence the process of professional dynamics (Hafferty 1988).

The second area for research involves Freidson's hypothesized emergence of an administrative and technical elite within medicine. Although this topic may appear to primarily reflect Freidson's concern with the future of professional dominance, in this country it is actually quite broad-based and is relevant to the issues of professional attainment, maintenance, and dissolution. Once again drawing on *The Milbank Quarterly* supplemental issue (D. P. Willis 1988) and its wealth of cross-national materials, different chapters present evidence that an absence of internal cohesion within the provider ranks may function either as a barrier to the development of professional status or as a condition for a fall from professional dominance. It is, however, insufficient to simply note the presence or absence of any particular characteristic such as internal dissension without reference to the broader context in which it occurs. Professions, like other social entities, embody a dynamic in which events, situations, or indicators can have vastly different meanings or impact, depending upon where they occur during the "life course" of that profession. Thus, a certain degree of internal disequilibrium, which might prove fatal to an occupation in the early stages of professional development, may have a negligible effect on a mature profession. In summary, dissension per se is not the issue (as is also the case for rationalization or any other explanatory factor). Rather, it is the nature of the dissension, the degree to which it occurs, and the point in time where that internal divisiveness takes place. Despite these qualifications, it is important to remember that Freidson has accorded a central position to the issue of internal unity in his observations on professional disequilibrium. If it is true, as Freidson maintains, that the future of medicine as a profession will be determined by the choices made by these new elites, then it will be well worth our time to assess the professional identities and allegiances of those who are moving into such positions.

ACKNOWLEDGMENTS

We wish to express appreciation to Judith Levy and Bonnie Briest for their comments on earlier versions of this paper.

NOTES

1. Several earlier publications exist, including Freidson (1968) and Freidson and Rhea's (1963, 1965) articles on social control among professionals. Nevertheless, *Profession of Medicine* (1970a) and *Professional Dominance* (1970b) remain the most comprehensive and frequently cited sources of Freidson's early views on the nature of profession and professional dominance.

2. Although Haug and McKinlay are prominently identified with the deprofessionalization and proletarianization perspectives, respectively, they are not the only examples of social scientists working within such perspectives. Proletarianization, with its Marxist roots, commands a more numerous (if not always homogeneous) camp, which includes Krause (1977), Larson (1977, 1980), Navarro (1976, 1986, 1988), and Waitzkin (1983; Waitzkin and Waterman 1976). Social scientists commonly associated with the deprofessionalization perspective are more difficult to identify. A number of observers including Reiser (1978), Relman (1980), and Starr (1982) have made fruitful use of variable sets similar to those used by Haug (e.g., the consumer health movement and the rise of information technology) to advance their own arguments, but they are not closely identified with the deprofessionalization perspective.

3. Freidson's writings on profession may be viewed as falling into three broad stages (see Hafferty and Light 1989). The first stage includes Freidson's early work on profession culminating with his publication of *Profession of Medicine* (1970b) and *Professional Dominance* (1970b). The second stage covers the mid- to late 1970s and represents a period of restatement and consolidation with the publication of works such as *Doctoring Together* (1975). The third stage covers Freidson's writings in the 1980s and is characterized by his efforts to refute the arguments raised by these alternative models. Although there is reason to hope for yet a fourth stage in which Freidson more formally integrates his Stage One and Stage Three writings, he has yet to advance such a comprehensive statement of professional dominance.

4. Freidson's attention to how he believes medicine might lose its position of professional dominance is sketchy at best and is in no way integrated into his overall writings on professions (see Hafferty 1988; Hafferty and Light 1989).

5. In her use of the term "knowledge," Haug often appears to mean "information." To argue that the lay public continues to add it its storehouse of discrete pieces of technical information is not the same thing as asserting that such "facts" also exist within some systematic, theoretically grounded, and empirically based body of knowledge. The former claim is much more limited (and limiting) than the latter.

6. When Freidson does discuss the analytical appropriateness versus inappropriateness of certain variable sets, he appears to rest his case not so much on the grounds of analytical purity (what would be the best data in an abstract sense) but rather on the grounds of empirical pragmatism (what are the best available data). Thus, Freidson rejects the viability of exploring cultural hegemony as an indicator not because of its intrinsic inapplicability to the issue of professional dominance, but because he believes it difficult to imagine how such a factor would be unambiguously operationalized.

7. A more appropriately connotative term might be "collective" rather than "corporate." Nevertheless, when Freidson speaks of medicine as a profession, he is conceptualizing medicine as an organization or corporate body that employs institutions to shelter it in the political economy (see Freidson 1986b, p. 129).

8.   See as examples Johnson (1988) and Getzendanner (1988) on how organized medicine was found to violate federal antitrust laws by engaging in a conspiracy against chiropractors.

9.   In fairness to McKinlay, he does briefly outline how Freidson's arguments on medicine's attainment of a special and protected status are related to two of these four stages (see McKinlay 1977). McKinlay also criticizes Freidson for centering his analysis too exclusively within the level of medicine itself (which we assume to mean at the level of the game), and without adequate treatment of how medicine might be influenced by the interest of the financial or industrial capital (level one) or the State (level two). Freidson, in turn, charges that those who propose a decline of medicine as a profession ignore the institutions that *support* the position of professions within the political economy (see Friedson 1986b, p. 129).

10.   See Whitting (1989), whose comparative analysis of Japanese and American baseball demonstrates how cultural differences can produce a noticeably different game, even when based on an essentially similar rule structure.

11.   Although Freidson never says so explicitly, he does appear to consider the knowledge elite (or to be more analytically correct, an elite status based on knowledge) to be more central or critical than an elite status based on administrative skills. As an example, Freidson argues that an administrative elite lacks its own authority and expertise and therefore must rely upon the standards and guidelines of the knowledge elite in order to formulate and evaluate the work of the rank and file (see Friedson 1984, p. 1).

12.   Although Freidson does not specify which choice he saw as the more likely or why, he does express a value preference for the latter.

13.   An interesting analogy is the professional/technical schism within nursing and its impact on nursing's longstanding and yet unsuccessful efforts to achieve professional status. The lack of a common identity, identification, and ultimately cohesion among baccalaureate, diploma, and associate degree nurses is compounded by the "multiple subordination" (see Henry 1954) of nurses in hospital and large clinic settings to both physician/clinical and administrative/organizational demands (see Wolinsky 1988b). The fact that these two realms have undergone increasingly strained relations over the past several years has served to exacerbate the situation for nursing.

14.   The tendency to dichotomize objects, entities, or events is pervasive in Western societies and in Western science. Using computer sciences as an example, Aristotelian logic has long favored treating membership as either present or absent rather than as a matter of degree. Alternative models such as "fuzzy logic" (see Mandani and Gaines 1981; Smithson 1986) do use shadings in the assignment process with the hope of better simulating the uncertainties and ambiguities present in everyday life. Evidencing the role played by cultural factors, alternatives such as fuzzy logic enjoy considerably more popularity in Japan than in the United States (see Elmer-Dewitt 1989).

15.   Although some proponents claim that they are only advancing a "tendency toward," the thesis that medicine is "in the process of becoming" one thing or another still constitutes an argument defined in terms of the particular end state being advanced rather than one grounded in the process of change per se.

16.   This conclusion is supported by several of the cross-national authors in *The Milbank Quarterly* supplemental issue, including authors prominently associated with the proletarianization perspective.

REFERENCES

Anderson, O. 1985. *Health Services in the United States: A Growth Enterprise Since 1985*. Ann Arbor, MI: Ann Arbor Health Administration Press.

Bell, D. 1968. "The Measurement of Knowledge and Technology." Pp. 145-246 in *Indicators of Social Change*, edited by E.B. Sheldon and W. E. Moore. New York: Russell Sage Foundation.

_____. 1973. *The Coming of Post-Industrial Society.* New York: Basic Books.
Coburn, D. 1988. "Canadian Medicine: Dominance or Proletarianization?" *The Milbank Quarterly* 66(Supplement 2):92-116.
Elmer-Dewitt, P. 1989. "Some Time for Fuzzy Thinking." *Time Magazine* (September 25), p. 79.
Field, M.G. 1988. "The Position of the Soviet Physician: The Bureaucratic Professional." Milbank Quarterly 66(Supplement 2): 182-201.
Freidson, E. 1968. "The Impurity of Professional Authority." Pp. 25-34 in *Institutions and the Person,* edited by H.S. Becker, B. Geer, D. Riesman, and R.S. Weiss. Chicago: Aldine.
_____. 1970a. *Profession of Medicine: A Study of the Sociology of Applied Knowledge.* New York: Dodd, Mead.
_____. 1970b. *Professional Dominance: The Social Structure of Medical Care.* New York: Atherton Press.
_____. 1971a. "Editorial foreword." *American Behavioral Scientist* 14:467-474.
_____. ed. 1971b. *The Professions and Their Prospects.* Beverly Hills, CA: Sage.
_____. 1973. "Professionalization and Organization of Middle Class Labour in Post Industrial Society." *Sociological Review Monograph* 20:47-60.
_____. 1975. *Doctoring Together: A Study of Professional Social Control.* New York: Elsevier.
_____. 1976. "The Division of Labour as Social Interaction." *Social Problems* 23:304-313.
_____. 1977. "The Futures of Professionalization." Pp. 14-38 in *Health and the Division of Labour,* edited by M. Stacey, M. Reid, C. Heath, and R. Dingwall. London: Croom Helm.
_____. 1983. "The Theory of Professions: State of the Art." In *The Sociology of Professions: Lawyers, Doctors, and Others,* edited by R. Dingwall and P. Lewis. London: Macmillan.
_____. 1984. "The Changing Nature of Professional Control." *Annual Review of Sociology* 10:1-20.
_____. 1985. "The Reorganization of the Medical Profession." *Medical Care Review* 42:11-35.
_____. 1986a. "The Medical Profession in Transition." Pp. 63-79 in *Applications of Social Science to Clinical Medicine and Health Policy,* edited by L. Aiken and D. Mechanic. New Brunswick, NJ: Rutgers University Press.
_____. 1986b. *Professional Powers: A Study of the Institutionalization of Formal Knowledge.* Chicago: University of Chicago Press.
_____. 1987. "The Future of the Professions." *Journal of Dental Education* 53:140-144.
_____. 1988. *Profession of Medicine: A Study of the Sociology of Applied Knowledge,* 2nd ed. Chicago: University of Chicago Press.
_____. 1989. *Medical Work in America: Essays on Health Care.* New Haven, CT: Yale University Press.
Freidson, E., and B. Rhea. 1963. "Processes of Control in a Company of Equals." *Social Problems* 11:119-131.
_____. 1965. "Knowledge and Judgement in Professional Evaluations." *Administrative Science Quarterly* 10:107-124.
Getzendanner, S. 1988. "Special Communication." *Journal of the American Medical Association* 259(1):81-82.
Goode, W. J. 1957. "Community Within a Community: The Professions—Psychology, Sociology and Medicine." *American Sociological Review* 25:902-914.
Hafferty, F. W. 1988. "Theories at the Crossroads: A Discussion of Evolving Views on Medicine as a Profession." *Milbank Quarterly* 66(Supplement 2):202-225.
Hafferty, F. W., and D.W. Light. 1989. "The Evolution of Eliot Freidson's Theory of Professional Dominance: A Twenty-year Retrospective." Paper presented at the 53rd Annual Meeting of the Midwest Sociological Society, St. Louis, April 6-9.
Haug, M. R. 1973. "Deprofessionalization: An Alternate Hypothesis for the Future." *Sociological Review Monograph* 20:195-211.

_____. 1975. "The Deprofessionalization of Everyone?" *Sociological Focus* 3:197-213.

_____. 1976. "The Erosion of Professional Authority: A Cross-cultural Inquiry in the Case of the Physician." *Milbank Quarterly/Health and Society* 54(1):83-106.

_____. 1977. "Computer Technology and the Obsolescence of the Concept of Profession." Pp. 195-214 in *Work and Technology*, edited by M. Haug and J. Dofny. Beverly Hills, CA: Sage.

_____. 1988. "A Re-examination of the Hypothesis of Physician Deprofessionalization." *Milbank Quarterly* 66(Supplement 2):48-56.

Haug, M. R., and B. Lavin. 1978. "Method of Payment for Medical Care and Public Attitudes Toward Physician Authority." *Journal of Health and Social Behavior* 19:279-291.

_____. 1981. "Practitioner or Patient: Who's in Charge?" *Journal of Health and Social Behavior* 22:212-229.

_____. 1983. *Consumerism in Medicine: Challenging Physician Authority*. Beverly Hills, CA: Sage.

Henry, J. 1954. "The Formal Structure of a Psychiatric Hospital." *Psychiatry* 17:139-151.

Johnson, K. B. 1988. "Statement From AMA's General Council." *Journal of the American Medical Association* 259(1):83.

Krause, E. A. 1977. *Power and Illness: The Political Sociology of Health and Medical Care*. New York: Elsevier.

_____. 1988. "Doctors, Partitocrazia, and the Italian State." *Milbank Quarterly* 66(Supplement 2):148-166.

Larkin, G. V. 1988. "Medical Dominance in Britain: Image and Historical Reality." *Milbank Quarterly* 66(Supplement 2):117-132.

Larson, M. S. 1977. *The Rise of Professionalism: A Sociological Analysis*. Berkeley: University of California Press.

_____. 1980. "Proletarianization and Educated Labour." *Theory and Society* 9:131-175.

Light, D. W., and F.W. Hafferty. 1989. "The Theory of Professional Dominance Reconsidered." Paper delivered at the 84th Annual Meeting of the American Sociological Association, San Francisco, August 9-13.

Mandani, E. H., and B.R. Gaines. 1981. *Fuzzy Reasoning and Its Applications*. San Diego, CA: Academic Press.

McKinlay, J. B. 1973. "On the Professional Regulation of Change." *Sociological Review Monographs* 20:61-84.

_____. 1977. "The Business of Good Doctoring or Doctoring as Good Business: Reflections on Freidson's View of the Medical Game." *International Journal of Health Services* 7(30):459-487.

_____. 1978. "On the Medical-industrial Complex." *Monthly Review* 30(5):38-42.

_____. 1982. "Toward the Proletarianization of Physicians." Pp. 37-62 in *Professionals As Workers: Mental Labor in Advanced Capitalism*, edited by C. Derber. Boston, MA: G. K. Hall.

_____. 1984. *Issues in the Political Economy of Health Care*. London: Tavistock.

_____. 1986. "Proletarianization and the Social Transformation of Doctoring." Paper presented at the annual meeting of the American Sociological Association, New York, August.

_____. 1988. "The Changing Character of the Medical Profession: Introduction." *Milbank Quarterly* 66(Supplement 2):1-9.

McKinlay, J.B., and J. Arches. 1985. "Towards the Proletarianization of Physicians." *International Journal of Health Services* 15(2):161-195.

_____. 1986. "Historical Changes in Doctoring: A Reply to Milton Roemer." *International Journal of Health Services* 16:473-477.

McKinlay, J. B., and J.D. Stoeckle. 1987. "Corporatization and the Social Transformation of Doctoring." *Finnish Journal of Social Medicine* 24:73-84.

————. 1988. "Corporatization and the Social Transformation of Doctoring." *International Journal of Health Services* 18(2):191-205.

Navarro, V. 1976. *Medicine Under Capitalism.* New York: Prodist.

————. 1986. *Crisis, Health, and Medicine: A Social Critique.* New York: Tavistock.

————. 1988. "Professional Dominance or Proletarianization?: Neither." *Milbank Quarterly,* 66(Supplement 2):57-75.

Reed, R. R, and D. Evans. 1987. "The Deprofessionalization of Medicine: Causes, Effects, and Responses." *Journal of the American Medical Association* 258:3279-3282.

Reiser, S. J. 1978. *Medicine and the Reign of Technology.* New York: Cambridge University Press.

Relman, A. S. 1980. "The New Medical-industrial Complex." *New England Journal of Medicine* 303:963-970.

Riska, E. 1988. "The Professional Status of Physicians in the Nordic Countries." *Milbank Quarterly* 66(Supplement 2):133-147.

Smithson, M. 1986. *Fuzzy Set Analysis for Behavioral and Social Sciences.* New York: Springer-Verlag.

Starr, P. E. 1982. *The Social Transformation of American Medicine: The Rise of a Sovereign Profession and the Making of a Vast Industry.* New York: Basic Books.

Waitzkin, H. 1983. *The Second Sickness: Contradictions of Capitalist Health Care.* New York: Free Press.

Waitzkin, H., and B. Waterman. 1976. "Social Theory and Medicine." *International Journal of Health Services* 6(1):9-23.

Whitting, R. 1989. *You Gotta Have Wa.* New York: Macmillan.

Wilensky, H. 1964. "The Professionalization of Everyone?" *American Journal of Sociology* 70:137-158.

Willis, D. P., ed. 1988. "The Changing Character of the Medical Profession." *Milbank Quarterly* 66(Supplement 2).

Willis, E. 1988. "Doctoring in Australia: A View at the Bicentenary." *Milbank Quarterly* 66(Supplement 2):167-181.

Wolinsky, F. D. 1988a. "The Professional Dominance Perspective, Revisited." *Milbank Quarterly* 66(Supplement 2):33-47.

Wolinsky, F. D. 1988b. *The Sociology of Health: Principles, Practitioners, and Issues,* 2nd ed. Belmont, CA: Wadsworth.

GENERATIONAL MODEL OF ATTITUDINAL CHANGE IN MEDICAL PRACTICE

Pamela Dee Elkind

ABSTRACT

This paper argues that physicians who form a generational cohort have similar orientations toward their careers and environments. To examine this contention, the author considers professional autonomy versus control, an issue of major emphasis in the 1970s and 1980s. An historical model is constructed and then utilized to demonstrate similarities within, and differences between, physician generation units for a random sample of primary care physicians in Maryland. The project demonstrates that the ideas, attitudes, and modes of practice held by physicians often reflect the generation of the physicians. These are especially observable in an analysis of the issue of professional autonomy versus control.

INTRODUCTION

Physicians' early socialization in the medical profession is influenced by a number of factors: prevailing ideas about education; attitudes toward medical

Current Research on Occupations and Professions, Volume 6, pages 251-278.
Copyright © 1991 by JAI Press Inc.
All rights of reproduction in any form reserved.
ISBN: 1-55938-236-8

practice; social interactions with teachers, other health-care professionals, patients, and peers; and the environment of the medical school program. This all occurs within the context of a constantly changing global society. Influences such as family, friends, social situations, and social-political attitudes formed early in life have been internalized by the medical student effecting the process of socialization. However, due to the high degree of selectivity on the part of medical schools, students generally do not enter with ideologies that are in opposition to those of their potential mentors. Studies have shown a good deal of similarity in background and attitude between medical students and the clinical instructors who select them (Friedson 1970).

Throughout a physician's career, he or she treats patients, makes decisions, and pursues further education in light of a multitude of attitudes that were to some degree formed during the primary process of medical socialization (Becker, Geer, and Hughes 1968). Physicians who undergo their medical training during a given period are subjected to similar educational ideologies, share the same outside world situation, experience the same pressures to succeed, and are aware of the same attitudes toward medicine and medical practice. In this chapter we will demonstrate that these physicians who go through a generation together have similar orientations toward their careers and environments. Though their present practice situations may be quite different, and the attitudinal patterns they display may differ in some respects, they have developed very similar patterns as a result of their exposure to a range of allowable choices. Furthermore, we will look at these patterns, not only with respect to practice behavior and background characteristics, but also with respect to a particular issue of utmost importance to physicians in the late seventies and eighties. The issue is that of professional autonomy versus control. This issue took on major emphasis in unstructured interviews with physicians while designing the study. It reflects concerns about policing policies and agencies evaluating physicians, certification, case reviews, boards of review and the right to treat patients as one believes necessary.

Generation Units

Mannheim (1952), in "The Problem Generations," suggested that individuals in the same class, generation, or age group share a common "location" in the social and historical sense, which limits them to a certain characteristic mode of thought and range of experiences, as well as to a characteristic type of historically relevant action. There are certain tendencies in each of these "locations" that point the individual toward definite modes of behavior, feeling and self-expression. For any group of individuals who share a position in society, a generation, or an age group, there is available in society certain experiential, intellectual, and emotional data. In fact, according to Mannheim: "The concrete form of an existing behavior pattern of a cultural product does not derive from the history of a particular tradition but ultimately from the history of the location relationships in which it originally arose and hardened itself into a tradition" (p. 56). According to Mannheim, generation units are groups of individuals bonded together by integrative attitudes. They share experiences in different specific ways. These groups share a location, not only in time, but also in their collective ideologies by virtue of their experiences. To become assimilated into a group, one must be able to see things from a particular aspect and to endow the same meaning to experiences as others in the group. This commonality of thought enables individuals to deal with events in a fashion broadly predetermined by the group. The importance of these principles is that they form a link between spatially separated individuals who may never come into personal contact at all. Thus, within any given cross section of time, there are many generation units. Those young persons being "socialized into" the medical profession at any given time form one generation unit.

From the previous discussion, one may infer that attitudes, values, and expectations are shared by a particular medical school generation unit. In fact, we will demonstrate that generation units receiving their medical education at the same time exhibit similar values and attitudes toward their profession. These values have generally been formed prior to and during their medical education process. The gradual modification of these values and attitudes takes place at a time of similar world conditions. These values and attitudes later provide the basis for the physicians' patterns of behavior toward patients and toward the profession as a whole.

In this paper, we will build and utilize a model that demonstrates similarities within and differences between physician generation units. The demonstration will explore the generational differences in physicians' attitudes toward practice when educated between the early 1930s and the late 1970s.

The Model

Funkenstein (1978) completed a 17-year study of medical students at Harvard. He also gathered data on a sample of students from other medical schools throughout the nation. He compiled a variety of indicators of attitudes toward medical education and ideas about medical practice, including various primary data on attitudes of medical students from the 1940s to the 1970s. Based on the data, he has created several categories of physician-held perceptions of medical education and practice during specific periods in the twentieth century.

We have conducted an extensive search of the literature written by physicians and social scientists about the various medical educational and ideological orientations, from 1900 to 1980. The following is a brief summary of some of the reported happenings in medical education and practice, utilizing Funkenstein's time categories,[1] and a literature analysis summary.

THE GENERAL-PRACTICE ERA:
1910-1939

The General-Practice era of medicine was actually an era of turmoil, in which physicians were evaluating nineteenth-century medical practices and, in many cases, rejecting them. According to Slaby and Schwartz (1971), ever since the time of Hippocrates, physicians had been regarded with immense respect. The communities in which they served looked upon them as bastions of traditional values not given to the eccentricities of the moment. Many Americans today still believe that "the doctor" is rather conventional and predictable in attitudes and behavior.

In the early part of this era, people generally looked upon medicine as an art. Meara (1912) defined the general practitioner of this era as:

> The man who concerns himself with the art of medicine rather than the science of medicine. . . . This distinction of art from science of medicine is made with full appreciation that the former is absolutely dependent on the latter. . . . The art of medicine connotes much knowledge that is not contained in medical curriculum. . . . It is the knowledge of those spheres of man's activities other than those in which his bodily virtues are concerned . . . The physician knows his patient as a man and a friend, not as a commodity (p. 74).

In this era, a liberal humanistic education for physicians was being strongly urged, as one can see in a typical article by Alexander (1914). Alexander lists the primary elements of a good medical education: "These in reverse order of their importance are—information, mental culture, mental discipline, and the promotion of high ideals—I have placed information lowest in the scale . . . Personally, I would cut out much of the laboratory work."

As medical science became more complex during the 1920s, those whose orientation was artistic criticized the educational system for becoming too science-oriented. One criticism was:

> Modern medical instruction demands of the student that he accept fixed theories as explanations in themselves, that he make of his mind a mere store house of unrelated and oftentimes unimportant observations with little or no attempt at logical explanations. . . . and little time for freedom of scientific thought (Walker 1922, p. 1743).

The Flexner Report, published in 1910, was a turning point for modern medicine. Flexner evaluated nineteenth-century medicine and medical school training, pointing to blatant inadequacies in education and practice. Following the publication of this report, the traditional medical school curriculum of two years of preclinical sciences and then two years of clinical work became standard. The emphasis was more on science than on clinical medicine, but due to the orientation of those who believed that medicine was truly an art, the full impact of Flexner's ideas was not felt until the early 1930s, with the decline of inadequate medical schools and the increase of foundation support (Zinnser 1931).

The overall academic objective of medical schools during the 1910-1939 era was generalized medical education, qualifying students to enter general practice upon graduation. Medical school teachers themselves usually practiced medicine and taught only part time. By the 1930s, didactic lecturing was replacing some of the coursework that stressed clinical experience in medical school (Means 1932). Physicians were oriented to the art of medicine, which they defined as giving attention to the social, emotional, and family aspects of illness. Physicians used intuitive sense in applying to the patient's problems whatever scientific knowledge they had.

The widespread hardship and emotional as well as financial stress that resulted from World War II and the Great Depression inevitably influenced medical practice. Physicians became conscious of the financial burdens caused by war and depression in their practices and private lives as well. The need for a businesslike orientation in practice, facilities shared with other medical professionals, and prompt patient payment collection was observed by the physicians to be the only manner in which they could survive financially.

During this whole era, the social responsibility of the physician was to give the best care possible to patients and their families within the limits of medical knowledge. The role model for medical students was the general practitioner (Funkenstein 1978).

THE SPECIALTY ERA:
1940-1958

By the late thirties, physicians realized that a physician could not be competent in all areas of medicine. Skyrock (1947) expressed the physician's rising sense of insecurity in the face of a rapidly growing mass of technological information as:

> He came to fear the complete loss of his professional status, which involved not only his personal interest, but the quality of his service as well. An ancient and honorable guild seemed about to be forced into the employee status of modern industrial society (p. 391).

With the rise in the incidence of specialization in medicine, speciality boards had to be founded to judge the ability of specialists to deal with the vast volume of medical knowledge (Lehman 1945). World War II brought about the need for new drugs and highly specialized medical treatment. Thus, after their internships, medical school graduates began to take on specialized residencies. The objective of medical schools began to be to graduate highly competent specialists.

Toward the end of this era, medical schools' orientations began to change. Professors, instead of feeling that their teaching was of utmost importance to the student, began to emphasize the need for students to educate themselves throughout their careers. The education received in medical school was beginning to be considered "a phase of a lifelong education" (Rapplaye 1959, p. 687).

Those who graduated from medical school during this era did not purposefully turn away from careers as primary physicians or generalists. It was simply that the system itself did not encourage the enrollment of young people with such generalized psychological or personality orientations:

> The system, in fact, was a large psychological testing station that did not favor admission of people-oriented applicants. The pores in the sieve only fitted a certain candidate. His testing was polished by the faculty, but the selection system for 25 years, both at admission and at gatekeeping way stations, practically guaranteed the resultant heavily certified physician (Dimond 1974, p. 1118).

Foundation grants and federal support for research grew enormously during this era. Great medical centers were established, and medical treatment improved. Before this period, few full-time researchers or medical educators had existed, since the money to finance such positions was only now becoming available. However, a renewed concern that physicians were losing the art of medicine began to be evidenced (Gregg 1947).

The introduction of antibiotics and other wonder drugs during World War II and the expanded funding by the foundations for research and medical education led to the expansion of college departments of biochemistry, and this, too, greatly affected this era, which is called "the golden epic of American medicine" (Davidson 1954, p. 1716).

However, in the exercise of medicine, the physician was becoming, according to Gladstone (1954):

> . . . increasingly a middle-man between the patients and the diagnostic laboratory on the one hand, and the pharmaceutical houses on the other. Reflect on what changes have taken place in the task of diagnosing and treating such disorders as pulmonary tuberculosis, pneumonia and venereal diseases. It is not an exaggeration to affirm that it is not the physician but the laboratory that makes the diagnosis; it is the pharmaceutical house that provides the treatment.

The social responsibility of the physician during this era was competence in the particular medical discipline. The role model for medical students was the specialist (Funkenstein 1978).

THE SCIENTIFIC ERA:
1959-1968

The founding of the National Institutes of Health, the National Defense Education Act, and the National Aeronautics and Space Administration (NASA) in the late 1950s opened a new era in medicine. As in other areas of education, research took top priority in medical education. Especially after the Russians' launching of the first Sputnik in 1953, vast sums of money became available in the United States for scientific research and teaching. Medical school faculties began to be largely composed of full-time professors. These positions were held by scientists who were also physicians. Teaching hospitals became concerned with complicated and unusual illnesses. The orientation of these hospitals was toward national rather than community concerns. They wanted to make their presence felt in medical science as a whole rather than just the health of the community. People began to express concern about the effects of over-specialization, preoccupation with research, and deterioration of the doctor/patient relationship. They also began to be aware that there was a need for medical care for the poor and for programs of community health (Richmond 1969).

The social responsibility of the physician in this era was to be a research scientist, however. The average physician spent only about one-third of his or her time seeing hospitalized patients. Medical students' role model was now the full-time academic subspecialist (Funkenstein 1978).

THE COMMUNITY/FAMILY PRACTICE ERA:
1969-1979[2]

The seventies' physician changed in response to society's perception of its own needs:

> The young citizen entering medical school has accordingly interpreted this perception, and he is bringing a different set of values into medical school and is coming out aiming at a new image and purpose. The results are slow to appear, but the mass momentum will suddenly be here, and other large changes in the methods of provision of health care and of compensation will facilitate the education of this type of physician and multiply his importance to the society of his time . . . This dependable, stable professional will be the resource that combines the willingness to listen, the availability of confidential personal, private advice, and the huge resources of valuable, lifesaving, scientific knowledge in diagnosis, medicine and surgery (Dimond 1974, p. 1118).

During the late 1960s, in medical school as in other areas of education, many students were strong activists against elements of the system. There was a great deal of ideological strife between students and faculty; and, therefore, the students lacked heroes or role models (Funkenstein 1978). Students demanded that interest be shifted from research to solving the problem of bringing good health care to all the people. They believed the medical profession should place emphasis on the delivery of primary medical care to all segments of the population without regard to finances. They advocated community participation in health care policies; preferential attention to medical education for minority students; elimination of social factors that cause disease; preventive medicine; and more comprehensive social concern.

By the early 1970s, student activism was vastly reduced and a certain degree of apathy took its place. But there were definite changes that student activists brought about. One of the most practical demands of the activists was for the establishment of local community clinics for delivering health care to all persons. Such community clinics were indeed developed. There also remained a widespread movement to train minority students, which was not without its problems (as witness the Bakke case in California). In addition, there remained a trend toward increased community needs.

Medical educators who were themselves specialists began training family physicians and public-health specialists (McWhinney 1975). But, on the whole, medicine in the seventies remained the same as it was in the early 1960s. Basic attitudes of medical school faculty and of the medical establishment were unchanged, due in part to: (1) the lack of adequate financial support for the policies advocated by activists, and (2) previously developed networks that reinforced the established patterns of medical care.

Medical education had been affected by reductions in the amount of money available to improve it. Changes in society's attitudes toward medicine, coupled with high degrees of medical specialization, inhibited the further development of medical schools, and made it obvious that the end of the era of super specialization had come. During the 1970s, government and society both demanded an increase in primary care, especially in underserviced areas. Some medical faculty members, however, still hoped for the rebirth of specialization.

Family practice had grown since the establishment of a Board of Family Practice in 1969 (Geyman 1978). "Primary care," which was redefined as meaning "general family medical care," grew overwhelmingly in the 1970s. The reason is that the 1971 Manpower Act requires that schools, in order to receive federal funds, must guarantee that a certain percentage of students will enter primary care. Demands of society at large as well as government for reorienting of the medical profession in the direction of more and better primary care, especially family medicine, were reinforced by the realization that there were too many specialists in some fields. Some fields were actually overcrowded. This, of course, was in contradiction to the unchanged attitudes and, in many cases, patterns of teaching practiced by many medical school faculties. The faculty physicians were aware of society's demands for community general medicine but retained some speciality ideologies.

In the 1970s, medical students lacked faculty role models due to a renewed conflict between scientific specialization and the more humanistic concern for comprehensive primary medical care. In addition, the controversy between medicine as an art and medicine as a science was once again strengthened in the 1970s.[3]

Development of a Model: The Test-Case Approach

We shall now develop a model of generation units as this concept applies to physicians who have graduated from medical school roughly between 1930 and 1980, using as a test case an empirical body of data compiled by a research team from the University of Maryland Medical School and by the Sociology Department of the University of Maryland in the late 1970s. The research team conducted a statewide study of physicians' attitudes and self-reported behaviors. We shall disaggregate this data set according to the generation units described by Daniel Funkenstein.

On the basis of a socialization approach, we will build a framework that includes the University of Maryland data, reinforced by historical research, and epochs then shaped into generation units as defined by Mannheim (1952). Each unit will exhibit some similarity of attitudes and attitudinal clusters that differ from those of all other generation units. We will endeavor to demonstrate that the shared similarities and differences have a basis in the early socialization process which the physicians underwent during their medical training, and the milieus from which the members of the groups emerged. We shall seek the reasons for such variations from the literature on medical ideologies during the various eras.

Assuming that this model is applicable to the population of physicians of Maryland, it should also apply to physicians from other parts of the United States since persons practicing in Maryland represent a broad cross section of United States and foreign training programs and birthplaces. Clusters of attitudes should be similar within a given generation unit, but there should be a good deal of dissimilarity between generation units in the sample. Professional situational variables (that is, differences as between locale of practice, type of practice, and type of patient) should not significantly alter patterns of beliefs and attitudes of physicians in a given generation unit.

However, if the model is improper, the physicians' attitudes will be dispersed randomly within, as well as across, generation units. There will be very few statistically significant differences between generation units, there will be a similarity of attitude clusters within units only by chance.

Another possibility is that the variables scrutinized will vary by situational characteristics. In this instance, situational variables—as Becker, Geer, Hughes, and Strauss (1961), Bloom (1963), and Freidson (1970) believe—must have strong effects on the patterning of these clusters of attitudes.

The Data

In Phase One of the Maryland project, researchers conducted intensive open-ended interviews with groups of five or six physicians from the main geographic regions of Maryland: Baltimore, the suburban area bordering Washington, D.C., the rural southern part of the state, and the isolated rural eastern-shore region.

During the interviews, a good deal of information about the general concerns and attitudes of physicians came to light. The problems and issues raised and the solutions and recommendations offered during the 200 hours of talking with Maryland physicians during Phase One formed the basis of the questionnaire used in Phase Two of the data collection.

The questionnaire was divided into three parts. Part 1 sought information on the physicians' background and practice. Part 2 had questions about the physicians' probable degree of participation in continuing medical education programs, their preferences for certain kinds of programs, and perceived utility of continuing education programs. Part 3 probed physicians' attitudes and perceptions of the current state of the medical profession. In particular, it sought information about physicians' perceptions of the patients they see, their ideas about the role of government in the delivery of health care, about the threat to them posed by the current flurry of malpractice suits, and about other key issues that came out during the researchers' conversations with physicians in Phase One.

Questionnaires were sent to an 85% random sample of the primary care physicians in Maryland expecting a 25% response rate. Though appearing low, this response rate was derived from the general experience of researchers doing physician mailed questionnaires. They drew 15 samples and checked them for goodness of fit with the population in terms of physician specialties, urban versus rural, geographic location of training, and age. The samples "fit" the population on all these characteristics (X^2, $p < .05$).

The return rate of 28% yielded 651 usable questionnaires. Researchers analyzed the goodness-of-fit of the background characteristics of the sample and found that at the .01 level of significance the respondents were an acceptable representation of the population of primary care physicians in terms of the significance of summed X^2 of medical speciality, age of physician, and type of region in which they practice.

The goodness-of-fit suggests that the sample has a good deal of external validity and that the findings may be generalized to the population of physicians in Maryland. However, it says nothing about the internal reliability or validity of the measurements. To ensure the validity of the internal content, researchers based projective questions on the open-ended responses of the tape-recorded interviews in Phase One of the study. This assured the meaningfulness and authenticity of the questionnaire language to the physician group (Phillips 1973). It also meant that the content of the questions was relevant (Smith 1975).

The heterogeneity of the population, due to the selection process in medical schools, helped to provide a sample corresponding to the population of physicians with minimal possible bias in the responses resulting from differences in backgrounds. The vast majority of physicians in the state and, therefore, in the sample, are male, middle to upper class, and have similar levels of education.

Method

In preparing this study, we cross-tabulated all attitudinal and reported behavioral responses, except those that were pertinent only to the objective of the Maryland study, with generation units. We categorized generation units according to the dates on which the practicing physicians graduated from medical school. Of the 651 primary-practice physicians in the sample, data on the year of graduation were available for 621 respondents. These 621 respondents comprise the generation-unit variable.

Cross-tabulations that yielded statistically significant chi-square associations at the .05 level showed differences in eight areas or categories of response developed from a content analysis of the original Phase One interviews with physicians. One category was physicians' type of speciality practice and board certification. A second category was general attitudes toward patients, and a third was general attitudes toward continuing education. The fourth category concerned physicians' perceptions of the future of medicine. The remaining four categories of attitudes all concerned the quality of medical care and the judgement of who has responsibility for the quality and to what degree.

Judging from physicians' responses to questions on these four sets of attitudes, drawn from Phase One interviews, we found that by far the major area of concern for physicians was the judgement and policing aspects of control over the competence of physicians. In this main ideological controversy, if our model holds, generation units should differ from one another significantly, and there should be a good deal of cohesion within such units.

It is interesting to note that nearly half of the attitudes and behaviors differ significantly across generation units. This finding in itself appears to validate the claim that physicians in a given generation unit share a socialization process and, therefore, exhibit similar attitudes in their medical practice. Any more than 5% of the attitude clusters exhibited by physicians within a given generation unit differing by chance alone from attitudes exhibited by physicians in another generation would aid in the validation of this point.

Though cross-tabulations and the resulting measures of association show similarities and differences between generation units, they do not indicate within unit similarity. To show variation and conversely similarity with generation units, an "index of qualitative variation" approach was used (Mueller, Schuessler, and Costner 1977). All variables were dichotemized and the relative amount of variation in responses within generation units was determined by the ratio between the total number of observed differences and the hypothetical maximum:

$$(IQV = \underline{So})$$

Sm

The index varies between zero and unity. Index values between 0 and 1 represent some variation but less than the maximum. By determining the IQV scores on a cluster of attitudinal variables for each generation unit, it is possible to see how varied or conversely similar an attitude might be within the unit and how it compares to other generations of physicians.

To explore the ideologies that lie behind the differences in generation-unit responses by the Maryland physicians, we used a factor-analysis technique. The physicians' specific attitudes toward various questions showed idiosyncratic tendencies. Therefore, to better comprehend specific differences between generation units, we sought underlying constructs (Harmon 1967; Rummel 1967; Horst 1965; Kerling 1964).

In order not to impose a particular theoretical perspective on the analysis, we saw to it that all variables differing significantly between one generation unit and another were entered into the procedure. The initial procedure of considering a principal factor with interactions (Nie, Hull, Jenkins, Steinbrenner, and Bent 1975) produced seven uncorrelated factors in the total Maryland sample. To obtain a more readily interpretable pattern of factor loadings, we rotated these seven factors, using orthogonal rotation in order to keep the factors uncorrelated. In other words, we kept the factors at geometric right angles to ensure statistical independence. Rotated factors explain the same amount of variation as unrotated factors (Nunnally 1967). The varimax rotation method that was used maximized the sum of variances of squared loadings in the columns of the factor matrix.

Though the initial factor analysis produced seven uncorrelated factors, three had only one variable loading at .35 or more. Two other factors had two items each which were extremely similar and should have been highly correlated. The remaining two factors had eight times loading above .35 (Nunnally 1967).

We considered these eight items the most clearly apparent indicators of the uncorrelated factors, and produced a new factor structure including only these eight items. In the reproduced rotated matrix, two general factors emerged for the sample; one item did not load highly on either factor.

The 7-item analysis was rerun for each of the four generation units: those physicians who graduated from medical school before 1940, those who graduated between 1940 and 1958, those who graduated between 1959 and 1968, and those graduating between 1969 and 1979. Six of the seven variables loaded above .40 for at least three of the four generation units, showing a good deal of similarity of structure. The seventh item loaded highly for only one of the generation units. This was considered idiosyncratic for that unit, and required attention only as such.

In the next section, we present the varimax-rotated factor structure for the total sample and the 6-item analysis for the four generation units. The analysis shows the similarity of highly loaded variables and the dissimilarities of degree of loading and structure across generation units. Two factors are isolated for each generation unit, but the principal and secondary factors differ.

To help determine whether the two factors explained the ideology of most of the members of a given generation unit and to clarify the directions of the various patterns of beliefs, we constructed two linear composites by summing the positive item scores (Susmilch and Johnson 1975; Alwin 1973). We cross-tabulated the two composite scales according to generation units. The scale scores were significantly associated with generation units at the .001 level. The chi-square statistic (X^2), as well as Kendall's tau c, depicted significant differences between generation units for each of the two composite scales.

Analysis

First, because we felt that it was important not to impose any previously determined theoretical structure on the analysis by choosing specific variables, we included all 24 of the significant variables in the Maryland survey in our analysis of the factors.

Of the seven factors exhibited on the varimax-rotated matrix, five had only one or two variables loading higher than .35 on the factors (Nunnally 1967). The two remaining factors had a total of eight variables loading higher than .35 on the factors. For purposes of simplification, we reproduced this matrix of eight variables and two factors as they applied to all the physicians in the Maryland sample. Table 1 shows the eight variable totaled matrix. Although both factors appear to demonstrate the concept of individual autonomy versus external control, the two factors are slightly different. Factor 1 is physicians' need for self-motivation, and for freedom to make their own judgments on the basis of their practical experience. Factor 2 is physicians' concern about external control over them on the part of government and professional peers, as evidence by demands for periodic recertification and by requirements for continuing education. Hence, we call Factor 1 Autonomy and the other External Control. The statement, "Criticisms of the medical profession by the media are unjustified," does not load highly on either factor in this eight-variable rotated matrix. It has, thus, been eliminated from further analyses.

Table 1.   Varimax-Rotated Factor Matrix for Total Sample of
Maryland Physicians for Eight Variables

Variable	Factor 1: Autonomy	Factor 2: External Control
Government regulations increase cost of medical care	.52420	.19953
Practical experience is the most important factor in ensuring competence	.49534	.10034
Physicians must be free to make own clinical judgments	.44683	.18244
Only motivation physicians need is self-motivation	.42970	.13054
Criticisms of medical profession by media are unjustified	.28660	.17097
Competent physicians should not have to be periodically recertified	.16936	.75102
Public can demand recertification	−.14831	−.44978
Physicians should have right to determine amount of continuing medical education they need	.29937	.40009

Since our model deals with differences between generation units, let us compare the factor loadings across generation units to determine whether each group shares physicians' underlying concerns to the same degree. Of the seven variables loading .4 in Table 1, all but one, in terms of Factor 1, loaded highly in at least three of the four generation units. The exception was the variable, "The only motivation physicians need is self-motivation," which, when broken down by generation units, loaded differently for each generation unit. This variable was eliminated and the remaining six reflected two similar clusters of variables or factors for all generation units.

This similarity of the 6-variable rotated structure (Table 2) reveals the consistency of physicians' concerns across all generation units with respect to autonomy versus external control. This consistency is across six of the original items constituting a core but not total similarity. However, it reveals nothing about the direction of their concern or about the percentage of each generation unit that shares a given ideology.

Table 2.   Varimax-Rotated Factor Matrix for Total Sample of
Maryland Physicians for Six Variables
with Loadings Above .4

Variable	*Factor 1**: External Control	*Factor 2:* *Autonomy*
Practical experience is most important factor in ensuring competence	.12023	.44455
Government regulations increase cost of medical care	.18804	.59727
Physicians must be free to make own clinical judgments	.18233	.40816
Public can demand recertification	−.44510	−.16758
Competent physicians should not have to be periodically recertified	.75554	.15439

Physicians should have right to
    determine amount of continuing
    medical education they need
	.40317	.25258

Note: *Factors 1 and 2 differ from Table 1.

First, the direction of concern will be considered and later the percent will
be scrutinized. The factor analysis technique will be used to show the structure
of ideologies. We are locating generation units and comparing structure as well
as looking at the substance of indicators for concerns generalizable to all
physicians. From the size of the loading, we will see the correlation between
the item and the factor. We are attempting to get at the core concerns of each
generation unit as differing from other units though within the context of
concern by all physicians today. To accomplish this, factor loadings will be
analyzed as correlations.

We reproduced the matrices again for the six variables that loaded highly
on most generation units. Looking at the rotated factor matrices (Table 1),
you will note that, for the total sample, external control is the first factor and
autonomy is the second. The post-1969 generation unit does not exhibit any
clear split in their attitudes toward autonomy as opposed to external control
in Table 3, since two of the three items that indicate a greater degree of
autonomy load almost as highly as the external-control variables.[4]

Table 3.   Varimax-Rotated Factor Matrix Comparing Four Generation
Units with Respect to Concern About Autonomy

Variable	General Practice Era: Pre-1940	Specialty Era: 1940-1958	Scientific Era: 1959-1968	Community/ Family Practice Era: 1969-1980
Practical experience best	.41633	.10040	.14050	.40090
Government regulations increase cost	.48456	.22898	.05745	.75026
Physicians must be free in clinical judgments	.46372	.16938	.31693	.05337
Public can demand recertification	−.15681	−.46525	.60123	.46788
Competent physicians should not have to be recertified	−.02312	.73418	.75333	.87882
Physicians should have right to determine amount of CME	.08804	.49540	.37306	.40345

It is possible to see the difference between generation units in the consistency with which physicians of a given generation unit respond to questions about this controversial issue, which appears to be a dominant factor behind the attitudes of physicians in the mid-1970s. Table 3 demonstrates the strong bias toward autonomy of physicians educated in the General-Practice Era and the bias toward external control on the part of physicians educated in the Specialty and Scientific Eras. Although physicians educated in the Community/Family Practice Era (post-1969) also demonstrate a consistent favorable attitude toward external control, autonomy appears to be equally significant to them. Of the three variables loading highly in the external control factor, only two are correlated highly for the post-1969 unit. The .75 loading shows that their feelings that government regulations do not increase the cost of medical care is the most outstanding indicator.

In Table 4 concern about external control ranks second to concern about individual autonomy as a factor behind attitudes of the pre-1940 generation unit. Conversely, autonomy ranks second to external control in the two middle groups. As in the case of the first factor (Table 3), the attitudes of the post-1969 physicians show no clustering in one direction or another. In their case, the evidence points to a combination of desire for freedom of clinical judgment and respect for practical experience. For this group, the autonomy and external control issue is part of the same problem and, therefore, merely one factor.

Table 4.   Varimax-Rotated Factor Matrix Comparing Four
Generation Units with Respect to Concern About External Control

Variable	General Practice Era: Pre-1940	Specialty Era: 1940-1958	Scientific Era: 1959-1968	Community/ Family Practice Era: 1969-1980
Practical experience best	.03705	.33042	.72527	.68105
Government regulations increase cost	.10524	.71124	.39358	.26420
Physicians must be free in clinical judgments	.02919	.43461	.18749	.77187
Public can demand recertification	−.55183	−.21442	.03762	.28130
Competent physicians should not have to be recertified	.35413	.15249	.15915	−.03660
Physicians should have right to determine amount of CME	.21986	.21236	.24708	.20082

Using the variables in the autonomy and external-control factors separately, we devised two scales by a process of summation of factor items (Alwin 1973; Susmilch and Johnson 1975). The positive responses (coded as 1) for each item, in the direction of autonomy on one scale and in the direction of control on the other, were summed.[5] The scales run from 0 to 4, or from low to high on autonomy and on external control concerns. On the autonomy scale, only 3% of the cases fell into Category 0; we, therefore, combined it with Category 1. The concern about external-control scale has four categories, evenly distributed.

The two scales were broken down according to generation units. Cross-tabulations of the two scales show that there is a statistically significant difference in the amount of concern shown for autonomy and for external control within the generation units.

Table 5.   Factor Scale for Autonomy,
by Generation Units

Scale	General Practice Era: Pre-1940		Specialty Era: 1940-1958		Scientific Era: 1959-1968		Community/ Family Practice Era: 1969-1980		Total	
	%(N)		%(N)		%(N)		%(N)		%(N)	
Low 1	7.3	(8)	21.1	(64)	20.4	(28)	42.1	(8)		
2	25.7	(28)	28.0	(85)	29.2	(40)	21.1	(4)		
High 3	67.0	(73)	51.0	(155)	50.4	(69)	36.8	(7)		
Column total percentage/ total sample	19.2	(109)	53.4 (304)		24.1	(137)	3.3	(19)	100*	(569)

Notes: Subject to rounding errors. Chi square = 19.857, with 6 degrees of freedom; Significance = .0029; Kendall's tau c = −.11165; Significance = .0006; Gamma = −.20015.

Table 5 suggests that more than two-thirds of the pre-1940-era physicians score high on the scale of "concern for autonomy." While half of the middle two groups register deep concern for autonomy, only about one-third of the post-1969 generation unit do so ($X^2 = 19.857$, $p = .003$). Conversely, very few pre-1940 era physicians score low on the scale of "concern for autonomy" (7%). In the cases of the Specialty-Era and Scientific-Era generation units, this score increases. However, 42% of the post-1969 physicians indicate a low degree of concern for autonomy. This clearly demonstrates the difference between generation units. It also suggests that the medical profession has been changing, going from the era of the highly autonomous traditional physician, through the era of the physician who is nearly as autonomous as the predecessors but who is more technologically oriented and more attuned to science, to the latest era of more control or accountability oriented physicians. The most profound change seen in our data is in this last group, the post-1969 physicians who score low on the scale of concern for autonomy.

Table 6 illustrates the degree to which physicians of the various generation units express concern about external control. As might be expected, 43% of the post-1969-educated generation unit express little or no concern about external control. In fact, 81% of this group ranks low on the scale of concern, versus from 32-55% of the rest of the sample. The degree of concern increases as one moves backward through the generation units. Conversely, 68% of the pre-1940 generation unit, 55% of the Specialty-Era generation unit, 44% of the Scientific-Era generation unit, and only 19% of the post-1969 generation unit express a high degree of concern about external control over the medical

Table 6.   Factor Scale for Concern about External Control,
by Generation Units

Scale	General Practice Era: Pre-1940		Specialty Era: 1940-1958		Scientific Era: 1959-1968		Community/ Family Practice Era: 1969-1980		Total	
	%(N)		%(N)		%(N)		%(N)		%(N)	
Low 0	5.4	(6)	23.8	(73)	30.2	(42)	42.9	(9)		
1	26.1	(29)	21.5	(66)	25.2	(35)	38.1	(8)		
2	40.5	(45)	30.3	(93)	28.8	(40)	9.5	(2)		
High 3	27.9	(31)	24.4	(75)	15.8	(22)	9.5	(2)		
Column total percentage/ total sample	19.2	(111)	53.1 (307)		24.0	(139)	36.6	(21)	100*	(578)

Notes: *Within rounding error.
Chi square = 37.94025 with 9 degrees of freedom; Significance = .0000; Kendall's tau c = −.16476; Significance = .0000; Gamma = −26540.

profession. This is a significant relationship in that it shows the degree to which generation units differ on a controversial subject.

Summary of Factor Analysis

We have now isolated two main factors that seem to underlie the attitudes and behaviors reported by the sample of Maryland physicians. Both involve two opposing ideas: one, that physicians should have individual autonomy, and two, that there should be control over the medical profession by the public and by peer-group organizations.

Concern for physicians' autonomy is the key factor that underlies the attitudes of those physicians who graduated from medical school in the pre-1940 era. For physicians educated in the Specialist Era (1940-1958) and in the Scientific Era (1959-1968), it is the issue of external control of the medical profession that concerns them most. For the generation unit of physicians who have graduated during the 1970s, it is a combination of the two factors that gives them greatest concern. Again, it should be recalled that there were no practical differences in attitudes on many of the original questionnaire items; but in half the items where there were differences, the factors capture the core of these differences.

Although this analysis might at first glance appear to reflect considerable similarity among the last three generation units, if we scrutinize the direction and degree of concern in each generation unit, we find certain dissimilarities as well as similarities. Our analysis of the factors has merely served to hint at the main issues that color the thinking of physicians, and that, therefore, affect medical practice.

Scales developed from an analysis of physicians' scores on these factors enable us to see differences between their attitudes on these issues. Their opinions fall into certain patterns according to the era in which they attended medical school. We see, for example, the two-thirds of the physicians educated before 1940 give top priority to individual autonomy for the physician; and a similar percentage of them are deeply concerned over the issue of there being too much external control over the medical profession.

Scores of the Specialist-Era and Scientific-Era physicians reveal that half of them strongly favor individual autonomy for the physician; but 55% of the Specialty-Era physicians are concerned about too much external control, and 44% of the Scientific-Era physicians express great concern about not enough external control of the medical profession.

Only one-third of the physicians who had graduated from medical school in the years after 1969 expressed a deep concern for physicians' autonomy; and in the matter of external control over the medical profession, only 19% evinced a deep interest in it. This trend among scores not only demonstrates the differences between members of the various generation units, but also suggests that the medical professional has been gradually progressing over the past sixty years from very autonomous to a profession which is accountable to others.

Nearly half of the physicians' attitudes and reported behaviors analyzed showed differences between one generation unit and another. An "Index of Qualitative Variation" approach was used to determine variation of responses within generation units. The mean of categorical indicator means on the IQV index displayed a range of scores between .694 and .812 for the pre-1940 to post-1969 generation units. If the physicians were very varied in response, one could expect .999 or 1 for IQV scores. This would indicate, for example, that half of the physicians in any unit answered "yes" and half answered "no." Not only does this allow us to conclude that there is a lack of variation and conversely a good deal of similarity within generation units, it also suggests that the pre-1940 generation unit is very similar. The post-1969 unit is more varied than other units, and the two middle generations fall between but look very much alike in terms of variation of responses, as will be noted in Table 7.

The "Index of Qualitative Variation" indicates that members of the same generation unit often responded similarly. A good deal of the data appears to support the generation-unit socialization thesis.

Table 7.   Mean of Attitudinal Means of IQV

IQV Categorical Means	General Practice Era: Pre-1940	Specialty Era: 1940-1958	Scientific Era: 1959-1968	Community/ Family Practice Era: 1969-1980
Reported behavior	.730	.917	.769	.877
Continuing education	.705	.743	.735	.914
Attitudes toward patients	.614	.742	.892	.819
Feelings about the present and future practice of medicine	.938	.968	.916	.697
Competence and control	.529	.700	.725	.743
The role of government; public control	.648	.685	.650	.821
Mean of IQV attitudinal means	.694	.793	.781	.812

General Discussion

Though we have spent many pages in methodological analysis, many readers are looking for the substance of the findings. The following are some similarities within and differences between generation units. It results from the cross-tabulations, IQV summary, factor analyses, and literature reviews discussed previously. We know that these differences hold true with respect to Maryland physicians; if Maryland is representative of the United States, then we can assume, by extrapolation, that they may also hold true of physicians throughout the United States. We have taken the liberty of summarizing these findings in the form of an ideal typical categorization of each generation unit and will present it here. In that light, the reader is warned that these are only relative differences to other generation units.

Physicians educated in the so-called General-Practice Era (pre-1940) are more oriented toward general practice than others who came later. They are solo practitioners and generally have not been certified by a specialty board. More than half of this group believes that continuing medical education is of special benefit to older physicians. They tend to have faith in their patients. That is, when asked whether patients come to them with trivial complaints, or whether their patients think they know as much as physicians do, these pre-1940-era physicians answer "yes" less frequently than physicians from other generation units. Similarly, this group is slightly less likely to believe that their patients insist on inappropriate tests and medications or shop around for pliable physicians.

However, the major of the pre-1940-educated physicians believe that medicine is not as rewarding as it used to be, and feel that they might someday have to abandon their practice due to the increase in rates demanded by insurance companies to protect them against malpractice suits. With respect to recertification, they feel that many competent physicians would retire rather than take recertification exams.

These pre-1940-era physicians, when asked what they believe is most important for enhancing the quality of medical care, stress physicians' freedom to exercise their own judgment, and the great benefit that accrues from practical experience. More than three-fourths of them also consider new medical methods and ongoing research as being important components of high-quality medical care. They are in favor of strict professional standards, but believe that self-motivation is the only effective motivation. (This reveals a certain amount of contradictory thinking within this group.) They say that competent physicians should not have to be recertified, and that conformity to established medical standards should exempt physicians from malpractice suit. Overwhelmingly, they believe that individual physicians should determine the amount of continuing education they need. They feel that peer review should be on a local rather than national level. More than other groups, they tend to believe that material in recertification examinations should be determined by medical schools, but that tests of cognitive knowledge are not sufficient to reveal the level of competence of a physician.

The physicians educated before 1940 are less apt than other groups to believe that the public has a right to demand that physicians demonstrate their competence. They feel that the medical profession must be allowed to govern itself, and that government regulations are responsible for increasing medical costs.

In the factor analysis, we found that this pre-1940 generation unit held individual autonomy to be the most important factor underlying its attitudes. More than two-thirds of this group scored high on the scale "concern for individual autonomy," and 68% also scored high on the scale "concern about external control over the medical profession."

When we look at the 1940-1958 (Specialty Era) generation units, we find that they differ from the pre-1940-educated physicians in certain specific ways. In this group, most physicians call themselves specialists; half have been certified by specialty boards. This indicates that most of them believe in the principle of physicians having specialties, although in many cases they have not gone to the trouble of being certified by specialty boards themselves. Half the members of this group are solo practitioners. They attend lectures slightly more frequently than the pre-1940 generation unit, and are less apt to believe that continuing education especially benefits older physicians.

In terms of attitudes about patients, half of the 1940-1958 generation unit tend to believe, as do their predecessors, that most patients do have real complaints (that is, they do not feel their patients are hypochondriacs). They are slightly more prone to distrust their patients than the pre-1940 group distrusts theirs, however. Although physicians educated between 1940 and 1958 tend to resemble the pre-1940-educated group in many respects, in all areas in which they differed the difference was between 3% and 20% of the pre-1940-educated physicians.

In the factor analysis, we found that the generation units that graduated between 1940 and 1958 showed similarity in the most important factor underlying its attitudes. Half of these 1940-1958-educated physicians scored high on the scale "concern for individual autonomy," and 55% scored high on the scale "concern about external control over the medical profession."

Physicians educated in the so-called Scientific Era (1959-1968), like their slightly older colleagues in the 1940-1958 generation unit, are specialists.[6] Most of them have been certified by a specialty board. Most of them have joined forces with other physicians and maintain group practices. In addition, members of this generation unit see a larger number of patients than members of other generation units.

This group differs from the other two in certain significant respects. Due to their extremely busy schedules and resultant lack of time, according to our discussions with physicians, they find that reading certain selected medical journals is the most useful form of continuing their medical education. They attend lectures slightly less frequently than other groups, and are the least apt of all the groups to believe that continuing education especially benefits older physicians. This 1959-1968 generation unit also tends to have a slightly more jaded attitude toward their patients than the members of the previous groups; that is, they believe that they encounter a good many hypochondriacs and comparison shoppers among their patients. They resemble the specialty group in being more moderate in their beliefs about the importance of physicians exercising medical judgments, about the idea that practical experience is a physicians' most important asset, and especially about the importance of current medical research.

In most other areas of inquiry, physicians educated in the 1959-1968 era (the scientists) differ from those educated in the 1940-1958 era (the specialists), to a limited degree. The attitudes of this 1959-1968 group tend to be closer to those of the pre-1940-era group (the so-called general-practice physicians) than to the attitudes of the physicians educated in the 1940-1958 era (the specialists), however, with respect to the statements that "Tests of cognitive knowledge do not supply sufficient evidence for recertification of physicians," and that "The medical profession must be allowed to govern itself."

The scientists are similar to the specialists in many respects, however. For example, they are oriented even more definitely than the specialists toward having a subspecialty. They tend to believe in the same ideas as the specialists, though they are less unanimous in their attitudes.

In the factor analysis, we again found that the 1959-1968 generation unit resembled the group that preceded it, the 1940-1958 group. The major difference appeared in connection with the question as to whether the public should be able to demand that physicians demonstrate their competence. Both the 1940-1958 and 1959-1968 generation units load highly on this item. The correlations for both of the pre-1958 groups (pre-1940 and 1940-1958) are negative. However, the post-1959 group is positive.

The Scientific-Era physicians, like the Specialty-Era physicians, scored high on the questions that concerned the importance of physicians' individual autonomy. However, only 44% scored high on the questions having to do with external control over the medical profession. It appears that there are high correlations in the items relating to external control, but the Scientific-Era physicians register slightly less concern than the Specialty-Era physicians about the need for physicians to have individual autonomy, as evidenced by lower scores on the external control scale. They are apparently less concerned than earlier groups about external control over the medical profession.

Physicians educated in the post-1969 era (the so-called Community/Family Practice Era) differ from those in other groups in a progressive manner. In this era we see a reversal of the previous trend toward specialization; these physicians have returned to being generalists. However, more than half of them have been certified by specialty boards. They are, therefore, either certified specialists or acknowledged generalists. Group practice is the norm for 77% of them.

With respect to their preferences about methods of continuing their medical education, this group tends to favor the use of tapes and motion pictures, and to attend lectures slightly more frequently than members of other groups.

Although this generation of physicians is supposedly oriented toward the family and the community, there is some conflict in their beliefs about the patients they encounter in this community. Many of them feel that patients frequently come to them with trivial or nonexistent maladies, insisting on inappropriate tests and medications. Post-1969-era physicians are slightly more likely than physicians of any previous generation unit to believe that they frequently see patients "who think they know as much as the physician."

Post-1969-educated physicians feel that medicine is as rewarding as it ever was. They do not feel that they are likely to abandon their practices due to increasing rates of insurance against malpractice suits, nor would they retire rather than take recertification exams. The importance of practical experience and the need for freedom in making medical judgments tends to concern this group less than it does other physicians. This group does, however, like the earlier (pre-1940) generalists, attribute great importance to current methods and medical research.

The majority of physicians educated in the Community/Family Practice Era believe that physicians should periodically have to be recertified in order to prove their competence. They believe that certification boards, not individual physicians, should determine the amount of continuing medical education the physicians require, and that voluntary self-assessment tests are not effective measures of competence. More than one-fourth of this group, like the members of the specialist group, opts for peer review on a national rather than a local level.

Post-1969-educated physicians believe that the public has the right to demand that physicians periodically demonstrate their competence by means of recertification exams, and that government regulation is not responsible for increasing medical costs. One-third of them feel that the medical profession should not govern itself. More than one-third of them also believes that most criticisms of the medical profession by the media are justified. In sum, this group is more pro-public control than the others. They encompass the values of the scientist and those of the specialist, creating a new type of physician. But, in this process, many conflicting attitudes emerge.

In the factor analysis, we found that post-1969-educated physicians do not differentiate between autonomy and concern over control. In one factor, five of the six items of the two factors loaded above .35. On the autonomy scale, only approximately one-third of the post-1969-educated physicians scored highly, which shows their lack of orientation toward autonomy. Similarly, a mere 19% of these physicians evinced any great concern about external control over the medical profession. This was demonstrated by their scores on the external-control factor scale.

It is unlikely that this trend we have described is due to youth changing progressively with age. There is no evidence in the literature that physicians went through a period of increased social consciousness in any epoch prior to the late 1960s, nor were high degrees of subspecialization and scientifically oriented work evidenced in the middle-aged years of the pre-1940 group. Furthermore, physicians educated in the Specialty and Scientific Eras are not, as a general rule, as verbally concerned about patients as total human beings as are physicians educated in the 1970s. The total human being is what concerns the pre-1940 traditional general-practice physicians. In a different, more scientific way, this is also the chief concern voiced by the 1970s-educated physicians. These attitudes toward patients do not change observably with physicians' increasing age as measured by year of college graduation.

The Maryland research project revealed a high degree of correlation between the attitudes reflected in the literature of particular epochs and the present attitudes of physicians educated during those epochs. The ideas, attitudes, and modes of practice held by physicians reflect the generation of the physician.

Any particular generation in the Mannheimian sense maintains a degree of integrity over the time merely modified by the events and practical needs of the time. However, each generation comprehends these events and their meanings within a shared symbolic structure learned during early periods of socialization.

Thus, one possible explanation of the diversity of physician attitudes and behaviors is reflected in a generation unit model. Depending upon the historical time of early socialization and medical school training, each cohort of physicians has a degree of similarity which differs from other generation units. The generation units modify at differing rates and in diverse directions. This reflects the wide, yet bounded, range of attitudes and behavioral styles at any point in time in the history of medical practice.

ACKNOWLEDGMENTS

Support for this research was in part through two DHEW grants numbered 5R0ILM 02543-03 and ROILM 02456 from the National Library of Medicine. My gratitude to Peter Clepper of the NLM for all his encouragement. The data was gathered through an NLM project at the University of Maryland. Drs. Murray Koppelman and Carlton Hornung were most generous with that data. This chapter resulted from the work in my dissertation, "Socialization vs. Professional Adaptation: A Physician Generation Unit Analysis" (Northeastern University, 1979). I am grateful to Elliott Krause, Arnold Arluke, and Jeffrey Coleman Salloway for their outstanding aid in that process.

NOTES

1. The names of particular generation units are taken from Funkenstein (1978) except the 1969-to-1979 category. Funkenstein has subdivided this era into "The Student Activism Era: 1969-1970," "The Doldrums Era: 1971-1974," "The Primary Care and Increasing Governmental Control Era: 1975-1978."

2. As previously stated, Funkenstein (1978) subdivides this category into three subcategories. We believe the subdivision resulted from his imbeddedness in the historical period and have combined them into one category—Community/Family Practice.

3. According to Riesman (1939), "Art involves the idea of skill based on talent and long practice. It has an emotional content to which art gives expression. . . . Science knows, art does. Science is a body of connected facts, art is a set of directions. The facts of science are the same for all people, circumstances and occasions; the directions of art vary with the artist and the task. . . . [Medicine] is an art in the sense of skill based on practice and institution" (p. 14).

4. Tables 3 and 4 are both presented for purposes of exposition; obviously one factor structure is the reverse of the other.

5. Because many situational variables were only ordinal level and merely 2 or 3 categories, to maintain balance between the range of variables, the factor scores were designed in this manner.

6. Colombotos (1971), using a New York sample of practicing physicians in 1970, found that although younger and older physicians did not differ significantly in political ideology or in their attitudes toward the role of government in medical care, the younger physicians (scientists in our

sample) were more likely than older physicians to accept reviews of their work and to stress the "science" rather than the "art" of medicine. They were interested in "medicine as a 'work of special interest' rather than as a way of 'helping people.'"

REFERENCES

Alexander, D. 1914. "The Ideal Medical Education for the General Practitioner and the Specialist." *New York State Journal of Medicine* 11: 104-111.

Alwin, D.F. 1973. "The Use of Factor Analysis in the Construction of Linear Composites." *Sociological Methods and Research* 2(2):191-214.

Becker, H.S., B. Geer, and E.C. Hughes. 1968. *Making the Grade*. New York: Wiley.

Becker, H.S., B. Geer, E.C. Hughes, and A.K. Strauss. 1961. *Boys in White: Student Culture in Medical School*. Chicago: University of Chicago Press.

Bloom, S.W. 1963. "The Process of Becoming a Physician." *Annals of the American Academy of Political and Social Science* 346:77-87.

Colombotos, J. 1971. "Physicians' Responses to Changes in Health Care: Some Projections." *Inquiry* 8(1):20-26.

Davidson, W.C. 1954. "Changes in Medical Education and Patient Care." *Journal of the Florida Medical Association* 41:175-184.

Dimond, E. G. 1974. "The Physician and the Quality of Life." *The Journal of the American Medical Association* 228(9): 1117-1119.

Flexner, A. 1910. *Medical Education in the United States and Canada*. Boston: Updike.

Freidson, E. 1970. *Professional Dominance: The Social Structure of Medical Care*. New York: Allerton Press.

Funkenstein, D.H. 1978. *Medical Students, Medical Schools, and Society During Five Eras: Factors Affecting the Career Choices of Physicians 1958-1978*. Cambridge, MA: Ballinger.

Geyman, J.P. 1978. "Family Practice in Evolution." *New England Journal of Medicine* 299:593-601.

Gladstone, I. 1954. *The Meaning of Social Medicine*. Cambridge, MA: Harvard University Press.

Gregg, A. 1947. "Transition in Medical Education." *Journal of the Association of the Medical College* 22:226-232.

Harmon, H. 1967. *Modern Factor Analysis*. Chicago: University of Chicago Press.

Horst, P. 1965. *Factor Analysis of Data Matrices*. New York: Holt, Rinehart and Winston.

Kerlinger, F.N. 1964. *Foundations of Behavioral Research*. New York: Holt, Rinehart and Winston.

Lehman, E.P. 1945. "Cultural Values in Medical Education." *Southern Medical Journal* 38:356-360.

Mannheim, K. 1952. "The Problem of Generations." In *Essays on the Sociology of Knowledge*. London: Routledge & Kegan Paul.

McWhinney, O. R. 1975. "Family Medicine in Perspective." *New England Journal of Medicine* 29(July):176-181.

Means, J. H. 1932. "Didactic Versus Practical in the Teaching of Clinical Medicine." *Proceedings of the Annual Congress of Medical Education:* 39-43.

Meara, F.S. 1912. "The General Practitioner: An Idealization." *Boston Medical and Surgical Journal* 167:73-78.

Mueller, J.H., Schuessler, and Costner. 1977. *Statistical Reasoning in Sociology,* 3rd ed.

Nie, N.H., C.H. Hull, J.G. Jenkins, K. Steinbrenner, and D.H. Bent. 1975. *SPSS,* 2nd ed. New York: McGraw-Hill.

Nunally, J.C. 1967. *Psychometric Theory*. New York: McGraw-Hill.

Phillips, D.L. 1973. *Abandoning Method*. San Francisco: Jossey-Bass.

Rapplaye, W.C. 1959. "Major Changes in Medical Education During the Last Fifty Years."
     Journal of Medical Education 34 (July):683-689.
Richmond, J.B. 1969. *Currents in American Education.* Cambridge, MA: Harvard University
     Press.
Riesman, D. 1939. *Medicine in Modern Society.* Princeton, NJ: Princeton University Press.
Rummel, R. J. 1967. "Understanding Factor Analysis." *Conflict Resolution* 2:444-480.
Skyrock, R. H. 1947. *The Development of Modern Medicine: An Interpretation of the Social
     and Scientific Factors Involved,* New York: Knopf.
Slaby, A.E., and A.H. Schwartz. 1971. "Changing Attitudes and Patterns of Behavior Among
     Emerging Physicians." *Psychiatry in Medicine* 2:270-277.
Smith, H.W. 1975. *Strategies of Social Research.* Englewood Cliffs, NJ:Prentice-Hall.
Susmilch, C.E., and W.T. Johnson. 1975. "Factor Scores for Constructing Linear Composites."
     Sociological Methods and Research 4(2):166-188.
Walker, R.C. 1922. "Medical Education, A Student's Point of View." *Journal of the American
     Medical Association* 73(June):1743-1744.
Zinnser, H. 1931. "The Next Twenty Years." *Science* 74(October 23):397-404.

CONTROL OVER WORK IN
A PREPAID GROUP PRACTICE

Harriet Gross and Grace Budrys

ABSTRACT

Although declining physician autonomy is currently receiving a considerable amount of attention from sociologists, less is known about physicians' reactions to the decline. This paper reports what physicians affiliated with a pre-paid practice, a practice arrangement that is generally thought to allow for less autonomy than private practice, say about what attracted them to this form of practice. We go on to ask whether they found what they expected once they joined the practice. Their answers indicate that when they join they do not recognize the effect that administrative processes can have on their efforts "to do what they were trained to do," that is, patient care. With experience they come to appreciate more fully the effect that administrative decisions have on patient care. Those who stay do so because they consider the bargain they make to be a reasonable one. In their view, they give up components of the physicians' role which they value less in order to enhance those they value more.

Current Research on Occupations and Professions, Volume 6, pages 279-296.
ISBN: 1-55938-236-8

INTRODUCTION

Freidson's (1970a,1970b,1980,1984,1985,1986) thesis about medicine's professional dominance has been challenged by vast changes in health care delivery arrangements over the relatively short period of the last decade. Three alternative analyses have been offered to explain why medicine's dominance is waning: deprofessionalization (Haug 1973, 1976, 1988; Haug and Lavin 1981, 1983), proletarianization (Cheromas 1986; McKinlay 1982; McKinlay and Arches 1985; Navarro 1988) and corporationization (McKinlay and Stoeckle 1988; Roemer 1986). (For an extensive review of these arguments, see *Milbank Memorial Fund Quarterly* [supplement 2 1988].)

The degree to which such transformations in their roles have been attracting attention suggests that physicians must be experiencing significant changes in their everyday work lives. Yet, relatively little research has focused on physicians' perceptions of how much control they have over the work that they do (Stoeckle 1988, p. 83).

This analysis presents the views expressed by members of a prepaid group practice about their perceptions about how much autonomy and control they have over their work. The group practice is affiliated with a highly respected HMO (Health Maintenance Organization) that is also the oldest prepaid practice in its area. Physicians who work in large organizations rather than private practice settings are thought to be at greatest risk of losing their professional autonomy and by extension, their ability to exert control over their work.

We begin this paper by reviewing the literature on the changing nature of the physician's role. Implicit in this literature is the idea that physicians are passively accepting the loss of control over their work. By contrast, the physicians in this study were pleased to relinquish some aspects of the control that is traditionally associated with the physician's role. Their contractual bargain with the group practice permits them to do "what they were trained to do"—to practice medicine, while relieving them from having to assume responsibilities in which they have no interest. The identity they project is highly professionalized. They purposefully reject responsibility for the routine business practices that are usually associated with running an office. Their views about the trade-offs they make in choosing a prepaid practice setting become better defined with experience. With time, they develop a more complex and complete assessment of the advantages and disadvantages involved.

DIMENSIONS OF CONTROL
IDENTIFIED IN THE LITERATURE

The three arguments that challenge Friedson's professional dominance thesis (see Hafferty 1988; Light and Levine 1988; Wolinsky 1988) allege erosion of both the profession's collective autonomy and the individual physician's clinical autonomy. The deprofessionalization perspective argues that an increasingly informed and critical public, as well as greater dependence on nonphysician experts, limits physicians' control at the individual level with a resulting decline of professional dominance at the collective level (Haug 1988). Similarly, the proletarianization and corporatization perspectives point to evidence of change at the individual level to argue that such changes affect the profession as a whole. Thus, individual physicians, who are subject to organizational rules and corporate policies, are thought to be losing autonomy when they accept positions making them employees of hierarchical structures (McKinlay and Arches 1985; McKinlay and Stoeckle 1988; Navarro 1988).

Larson (1977) provides an early consideration of the dimensions of practicing physicians' autonomy. She identifies three dimensions of autonomy losses that she considers to be forms of alienation: economic, organizational and technical. The first two reflect physicians' realization that economic interests of health care delivery organizations often supersede their own, while technical alienation refers to physicians' loss of decision-making power over diagnosis and treatment.

Derber (1982, 1983) offers a more detailed analyses of potential loss of control that bureaucratically based clinicians confront. He posits four dimensions of control at stake when physicians work under conditions where, first, they do not control the market for their services and, second, they are not the proprietors of the institution where these services are performed— exactly the situation in which prepaid practice physicians find themselves. He identifies control over organizational policy and objectives as ideological control; control over auxiliary producers and their tasks as bureaucratic control; control over scheduling and workload as productivity control; control over technical skills as technical control. For Derber (1983, p. 122), unlike Friedson, the bureaucratic setting can be directly responsible for the decline in control.

Freidson (1980) acknowledges that physicians who affiliate with large bureaucratic organizations do lose some individual autonomy. He maintains, however, that this does not necessarily indicate a loss of power at the collective level. Instead he argues that increasing stratification within medicine accords an elite group of administrative physicians authority over rank and file physicians and, in doing so, insures that control over core issues remain within the bounds of the medical profession. Thus, because it is physicians who are making decisions that constrain other physicians, the potential threat to clinical discretion exists, but to a lesser degree than that imposed by nonphysician administrators. In his 1986 discussion of professional power and autonomy, Freidson argues that rank and file physicians are like other professionals employed in organizational settings who maintain interpersonal power over their clientele—they lack power over the allocation of the resources they need to exercise complete control. Thus, he says, "they are organizationally impotent even though technically autonomous" (1986, p. 178; also see Wolinsky 1988 for review).

More recently, Stoeckle (1988) focused on the trend toward the corporatization of medicine to show how proletarianization and deprofession-alization have begun to undermine physicians' control over the practice of medicine. He argues that corporatization is a threat to individual physicians' autonomy because the corporation controls powerful information systems and advanced medical technologies. Modern information systems, he notes, give corporations the ability to monitor "not only the clinical decisions of doctors but the doctor/patient relationship and the requests of patients" (1988, p. 82). With these capabilities patient care decisions, that have traditionally been the sole province of doctors, are now subject to monitoring and control by the corporation.

After reviewing research related to style of practice and physician satisfaction with autonomy, Luft (1987, p. 313) concludes that for physicians in group practice "the autonomy issue is largely a nonproblem." He argues that group, in contrast to solo, practices, offer clinical supports and function as physician-controlled intermediaries in dealings with third parties.

This literature review makes clear that what is meant by professional autonomy or control over work involves several dimensions. While the literature identifies a number of different forms of control, it does not differentiate the value attached to them. One is left with the impression that all are equally important. The physicians we interviewed expressed strong feelings about the aspects of control they value as well as those that they think are less important and may even detract from their image of the physician's role.

While their evaluation of the significance of various components of control does change with experience, we found that the physicians who had been affiliated with the prepaid group practice for more than a year or two were convinced that they had relinquished less important aspects of control in order to achieve greater control over those they valued more. Thus, our aim in this paper is, first, to examine the values that the physicians in this prepaid group practice attach to the components of control over work; and, second, to investigate how they go about constructing their work roles to match this definition.

DATA COLLECTION

We contacted all ($N = 61$) of the physicians who were affiliated with the group practice as of May 1987. Of those, 44 agreed to be interviewed (72%). The interviews were semi-structured, lasting 30 to 75 minutes. The interviews focused on why the physicians chose to join the group practice; whether or not they found what they expected; and, what they saw as the pros and cons of this form of practice in comparison to private practice. We probed for the kinds of changes the respondents wanted within the organization and the health care system. We also asked if they thought they needed other forms of representation in addition to those provided by existing professional associations. The interviews were recorded and transcribed. The data were coded independently by three persons: the two investigators and a graduate student responsible for managing the data.

The prepaid practice group was approximately 12 years old. During that time, it added 10 satellite practice sites. The prepaid practice group was established along side the HMO and its future was highly dependent on the latter's success. After the first few years of its existence, the HMO found itself in a hot and highly competitive HMO market. As a result, the group practice was confronted with financial difficulties. This organizational crisis resulted in some advantages and disadvantages for the research project. Because a number of physicians were being laid-off and others were leaving voluntarily, we were unable to interview everyone who was leaving. On the other hand, our questions were extremely salient as the physicians were in the process of self-reflection about their positions and career choices. Over the five months in which we actively conducted interviews, the group's financial position stabilized so that collective anxiety about the future abated and the atmosphere returned to near normal. Observing this organizational upheaval provided an opportunity to assess the physicians' views under both crisis and routine conditions.

CONTROL OVER WORK FROM
THE PHYSICIAN'S PERSPECTIVE

Affirming the importance of control issues to which current theory draws attention, the physicians we interviewed did register concern about their lack of control over various dimensions of their work. We found, however, that the physicians used terms somewhat differently from the way they are used in the literature. They used the terms "autonomy" and "control" interchangeably to refer to their ability to oversee their patients' medical management—what Derber (1983) refers to as technical control. But, they also used the term "autonomy," to express concern about being unable to pace themselves and to control their own workload and ancillary staff—Derber's referents for technical and bureaucratic control. They also reflected on their inability to influence organizational decision-making powers within the HMO, a concern which combines what Derber (1983, p. 122) calls administrative and bureaucratic control. One respondent put it this way:

I'd say the disadvantages are the lack of control over certain decisions and certain courses that my career or group (pediatrics) might take. I'd say that was a negative aspect: The ability to have control of certain situations and to be able to make some changes in your work environment. One of the disadvantages of working in a large organization like this is sometimes the blurriness of what the purpose of the organization is, and who's the authority, questions of who's working for whom, the nurses working for the doctors or working for the administration, or how the authority goes down.

Concern with control issues varied among individuals and seemed to increase over time and with the opportunity to assess and reassess the advantages and disadvantages of their work situations. Concerns about control over work increased after physicians had worked in the situation long enough to conclude that the problems they confronted were enduring. As the one physician who was leaving to set up his own practice put it:

It was lack of control over schedule and staff. They assigned us to a facility and that was it. If you needed more space, you could ask for it, but they wouldn't give it to us. It meant a fair amount of inconvenience to patients and to me. I typically had to work out of two (rooms) instead of three or four, which goes faster. So I had to see fewer patients. Yet, they still jammed in excess numbers of patients, so I had to stay later. And that was what finally got to me.

The history of this particular group practice accounts for the changing orientation to the organization voiced by some physicians. Because the pre-paid group practice was founded by physicians and administered by physicians, collegial relations initially were the norm. Thus, collective professional values permitted the members of the group to enjoy extensive control over the conditions of their work. With each passing year, however, the environment in which the HMO operated became increasingly competitive. As a result, the organization moved from its early "autonomous individualistic/reactive" structure to a "heteronomous/proactive" form of organization, where managed care contracts and the services offered were determined by nonphysician administrative decisions (Madison and Konrad 1988).

Because the physicians had been satisfied with their past work situation, they appeared more sensitive to the changes that were occurring than might otherwise have been the case. According to one physician:

One of the things that we often said was, "We're in control here. That's the thing that's different about us. We're still in a position of control here." And for the most part, for quite a while that was true. [The corporate headquarters of the HMO], you know they did their thing, but for the most part medical decisions were made by the physicians. And still are. Still that's the case. I mean that's why I have not felt any constraints about working here. The problem is that, you know, we thought we were in control, but we're not! I mean, when you get right down to it, you're in control as long as you're making money. That's why it's hard for me. I can't blame someone. you know say [the parent corporation] is terrible. Well if they're losing money, well you can't keep losing money. Can't blame them for that.

While they recognized a decline in their control over their work, we found that the relative strength of other factors (e.g., job security and income stability and/or the increased time with family permitted by this position) compensated for some loss of control. One physician put it this way:

I like practicing here. It is a lifestyle alternative that the HMO offers me. A lot of people stay with it for that reason. The pay is what it is; the benefits are great. Frankly it's one of the major reasons for being in this situation. It's great for women and men too, who want to work either part time or full time and still have a family life. There are different choices one can make. I know, my husband is a surgeon in private practice. He's not home yet (9 P.M.). He has no one to cover for him.

THE PRACTICE OF "GOOD MEDICINE"

While some gratifications and rewards associated with the physicians' role are unavailable to physicians who join a prepaid practice, the traditional reward of establishing a satisfying doctor/patient relationship remains (Luft 1987, pp. 309-311). Although "the service ideology" built into medical training assures that physicians value the rewards associated with successful doctor/patient encounters, in prepaid practice this becomes the most salient aspect of practice (Luft 1987, p. 308). In fact, according to the physicians associated with this group practice, the prepaid form of practice facilitates good doctor-patient relationships because it fosters the practice of "good medicine." A perspective invoked repeatedly was:

This allows me to practice medicine, to concentrate on what's best for the patient, and not worry about the business aspects and cost effectiveness. And there's no checkbook between you and the patient regarding the quality of care. Whatever the patient requires, you just do it. You don't have to bullshit everyone to do what you need to do.

Physicians join a prepaid practice setting understanding that they have agreed to forego alternative bases of accomplishment such as research proficiency or business acumen. The following statement illustrates an attitude expressed often:

I'm not interested in the business aspects of a medical practice. I'm not interested in choosing the carpeting or hiring a new receptionist. I prefer to do what I was trained to do.

In short, the relationship between the doctor as technical expert and patient who needs this expertise is the basic source of reward into which the practitioner puts all the eggs in his or her professional identity-basket. The following comment, which illustrates this theme, was made in the context of a physician explaining why he was having second thoughts about his situation. Until the recent financial problems in the HMO, he had been largely satisfied:

I would say, prior to this time, I've had a very good relationship with patients and that's obviously been a major source of satisfaction. Getting to establish relationships over five years is,—well you get to know people. And I have felt that I know my patients.

At the same time, the recent loss of colleagues with whom he had shared the workload caused him to review the pros and cons of the situation:

Right now at various times I feel I have a practice that's out of control. I can't manage it adequately. And one of the things that I resent the most is that I'm being put in the position where I'm giving less than the kind of care I want to give. And the thing I think I have come to realize through all this is that the most important thing I have is my professional reputation . . . . The thing I believe is the strongest thing I have is those patients who I've cared for and who want to continue as my patients. I mean ultimately it's the doctor/patient relation that's your strength.

Or as another physician concluded:

Most of my patients I actually have a very close relationship with. That's vital to me. I wouldn't continue practicing unless I had that kind of relationship.

As Luft reports (1987, pp. 313-314) in his review of factors associated with physicians' satisfaction, practicing "good medicine" is dependent on conditions that enable them to manage patient care well, which produces, in turn, the good relationship with patients that is a major source of reward. This is the aspect of practice over which the physicians we interviewed wanted to retain full discretionary control or autonomy.

ADMINISTRATIVE AND TECHNICAL CONTROL

It is only as they recognized that full control over the doctor/patient relationship required more than technical autonomy in the consulting room that they came to focus on the limited degree of the control they had over administratively determined practice patterns. Only then did they recognize the relationship between the administrative decision-making processes, which they willingly abandoned, and control over patient care decisions they believed they had maximized when joining the practice.

Whether or not they joined the prepaid practice because other options were unavailable (e.g., because they could not afford them, or no other positions were available) or had purposefully foregone other options (e.g., feeling as yet too insecure to practice solo), they defined the freedom from administrative responsibility as a major benefit. Repeatedly doctors proclaimed their distaste for the "administrative hassle" they acknowledged was required to manage a practice.

They mentioned a variety of examples of potential administrative roadblocks: the inability to control appointment scheduling which affected adversely their patient flow; their inability to control the flow of patients' records, which also backed up patient-flow; not having authority to reprimand subordinate staff for poor work performance, or not being able to get nurses to prepare patients for examination in ways they requested. The following doctor's irritation at being unable to get a nurse to set up a room for a procedure is illustrative:

> I had been trying to teach someone how to set up the room, so I didn't have to spend twenty minutes setting up in my own procedure room. That's a lot of time, to set up the room. It took twenty minutes and it was continually happening. But why was I doing it? I kept trying to teach them how to do it, but there was resistance. So I finally blew up and went to the Head Nurse and said, "This is ridiculous,"—to give the patient half an hour and spend twenty minutes setting up the room. The whole schedule's off for the rest of the day! And her answer to me was "you're not my boss."

Other exampes of a lack of authority over staff are captured by the following comments:

> I can't just snap my fingers and make changes. I could do that if I were in my own private practice. I could say, "We're going to do things differently now" and make the changes. You can't do that here.

And:

> There's a lack of autonomy here. I don't like to have to check with a nurse when I want to refer somebody or get something for a patient. You have to check for this or that.

Another respondent explained that her lack of control over the procedural aspects of her practice worried her more than anything she might do to a patient:

> I consider my major malpractice risk in practicing medicine here to be not what I actually do as a doctor to a patient, but the things that happen in the office that I can't control—like medical records, like triage. Like a lot of things, you know, incompetent staff.

One respondent connected even more graphically the aspects of control over work he had given up to practice in this setting to the problems he was now experiencing. By comparing himself to a traditional wife, he captures the essence of the pact one makes in joining a prepaid group practice:

> You feel like a housewife. You have little prerogative about how things are managed. You just have to take care of things the way they are. You don't get much of a say about it. You're taken care of, you're kept. The organization takes on a life of its own. The day-to-day frustrations go on and you don't have any say about it. For example, if you want to get rid of a receptionist because she is not doing a good job. Or if you want patients called every six months to remind them to have some things checked. There are 60,000 patients. It's cumbersome. It moves slowly. You have to deal with the administrators here. It has to go up the administrative line and down again. You just can't get things done easily.

Unlike this doctor, few were prepared to see the bargain they made when they joined a prepaid practice as Faustian (Derber 1982, p. 174). Given that so many identified freedom from administrative responsibility as a chief benefit of working in a prepaid practice, it may have been especially difficult for them to connect such responsibility with the constraints they were beginning to recognize. In fact, it took both time and experience to understand how much the constraints inherent in a prepaid group practice structure potentially impinge on the practice of "good medicine."

For some who had come to terms with the trade-off between control and job security, the HMO's growing economic precariousness just prior to our interviews caused them to re-evaluate the bargain they made in joining the group practice:

> All of a sudden decisions were being made by [the parent corporation] that had profound effects on my professional and personal life in terms of first, income, then hours, then workload, then co-workers, as people left. This basically changed the whole character of the job.

The threat to the conditions of work which were outlined in the contract they signed on joining the group meant that the trade-off, which had been satisfying in the past, was now out of balance. Some saw that they had relinquished control over an area of practice about which they now wanted to have some say. The working conditions that allowed them to "just practice medicine," free of administrative hassle, had been replaced with uncertainty and an inability to do much about them. Although he reverses Derber's referents for control dimensions, one pediatrician articulates this shift in perspective very well. He uses "autonomy" to mean administrative control and "power" to refer to what Derber (1983) calls technical control or autonomy:

> I felt very comfortable giving up my autonomy for the security of the organization. When the security wasn't there, then the autonomy became an issue. I didn't feel I needed autonomy—the hiring of the staff, the paying of the staff, worrying about overhead, all the headaches. But autonomy is not free. By giving up autonomy, you gain freedom. When you get more security, you give up power.

Here "autonomy" means freedom from the burdensomeness of administrative control or power in exchange for the security of having a stable practice, which this physician recognizes came at the price of his power to control the conditions of that practice.

It is interesting to consider the reactions of the physicians to the matter of administrative control in the context of Freidson's position that rank and file physicians' medical autonomy is not at risk as long as physician-administrators are responsible for administrative procedures (Freidson 1980, 1985, 1989). The physicians associated with this group practice, first, understood that the practice was being managed by physicians; and, second, believed that the administrative decisions these physician administrators were making did not much affect the care they were responsible for delivering. Both of these views were altered in response to the realities of the market place. When the parent corporation of the HMO put pressure on the physicians' group to cut costs, it became clear that the survival of the HMO depended on changes in administrative procedures that had noticeable effects on the physicians' working conditions and the practice patterns to which they had been accustomed.

PRODUCTIVITY, CLINICAL AUTONOMY, AND ADMINISTRATIVE CONTROL

For several years before this study was initiated, the physicians received utilization data—showing each physician's use of lab tests, x-rays, referrals, and so forth. These data could have been used by the administrators to limit doctors' use of procedures, what Derber (1983) calls "productivity control." This information could have been used to curtail the clinical autonomy they so valued. However, we found that none of the physicians believed that the data were being used to serve such a function. Again, it is well to recall that the decision to distribute utilization data was made by administrators who were also colleagues and fellow practitioners. Thus, the physicians had difficulty believing that their peers would use this information against them.

When we asked them if they felt that their work was monitored, virtually everyone replied negatively. They maintained this stance even when complaining about having their referrals questioned or denied—especially by subordinate staff (e.g., a nurse). When we pointed to the existence of the monthly review data, they acknowledged that they received figures showing each doctor's utilization but rejected the idea that the data had, in fact, been used for monitoring purposes. The following is a typical reaction:

> No, I really don't think so, which is a very special thing about this HMO. I think that most HMOs monitor you a lot more. We actually have quite a bit of freedom, and it's pretty rare that somebody questions what we're doing. Actually, we have utilization review people that monitor our patients who are in the hospital. Every now and then they'll call up and question why a patient is still in the hospital. And it typically is the patient that you are frustrated about, because, you know, you feel that they shouldn't be in the hospital. So, that's probably the closest monitoring that we have. We do try to keep track of all the lab tests that we order and referrals that we send out and various different things. And they actually at one point were trying to keep this all on a computer and were sending us printouts on how much each physician was spending each month on lab tests and things. Even in those cases where there are big financial differences in the ranges, nothing is ever said. People are allowed to practice in the way they feel is best.

In one instance, when asked whether or not the utilization records could have been used to intervene in patient care decisions, the physician first reiterated the commonly shared perception that they had not. Nevertheless, she followed this assertion by stating that she personally used the figures for this purpose. She had adjusted her behavior in comparing her own utilization record to others'. We found it interesting to consider the contradiction between her denial that the data were used for comparative purposes and her acknowledgment that she perceived the figures as a "pat on the back" which caused her to adjust her behavior.

> When you get patted on the back for doing something, it makes you think that you're doing okay. You start thinking that lowering those figures is something pretty good to do.

When asked the purpose of the monthly reports, if not for utilization control, a number of physicians answered that the data were distributed as a service to them. That is, they believed that these figures were made available for their own use, just so they could compare their work. Apparently, the organization was reaping the benefits of productivity monitoring without being perceived as doing so.

The point we make in focusing on this issue is that few of the respondents in this study cited infringments on their autonomy. They did not see the organizational/administrative procedures as interfering with patient care decisions, the dimension of control which we found to be the most central to their professional identities. Since most had only recently suspected that changes in organizational procedures might affect their clinical autonomy, few were prepared to connect the "administrative interference" about which they had some complaints to the release from administrative responsibility they sought in joining the prepaid group practice. Not feeling controlled in ways that they identified as critical, they continued to feel that being involved in administrative decision making was unnecessary. Only a few were prepared to recognize the implications of the insights they were developing, namely, that resolving concerns about loss of control over work required some acceptance of the burdens of administrative responsibility. As one physician put it, "getting involved" is the answer:

> I will be the Clinical Director at this office . . . and I am on the Board now. I had no desire to do this. But, if you don't get involved—you have no input.

RELATIONS WITH PATIENTS

Another aspect of control mentioned by the respondents centered on problems that result from dealing with a prepaid patient population: their limited ability to affect patient demandingness, patient allegiance and loyalty, and patients' respect for their expertise. Derber (1983) identifies such problems as consequences of employed physicians' lack of what he terms "market sponsorship" or control of the population they serve.

The belief among physicians in prepaid practice that patients over-utilize the system is well documented (Freidson 1973, 1985; Luft 1987, pp. 309-311). One of our respondents called it the "hangnail problem." Because prepayment takes the financial bite out of office visits and because patients feel they have paid for the services, they expect to utilize the system as much as they wish. What is pertinent to this discussion is that patient demandingness is regarded as an aspect of patient behavior difficult to control. One respondent described it this way:

> The patients' expectations are unrealistic. They won't tolerate a functional disorder or minor problem. They are often quite demanding when there's not

much that can be done. Sometimes its difficult. Especially in a small office, if you have a difficult patient, sometimes there isn't a good way to handle the patient. In a fee-for-service practice you potentially have more options. The patient is free to go elsewhere. The doctor can set limits, then the patient has a choice and the doctor has more control. Here there is no way to get a patient out of the practice. They don't have the freedom to go elsewhere. I don't have the freedom to set limits.

Some also complained about the limits of their ability to insure continued patient allegiance. That the circumstances of a patient's employment bring the doctor and the patient together means that both may view their relationship, in the words of one doctor, as "a forced marriage." Thus, the physicians cannot take satisfaction from "having been chosen" for their personal characteristics nor can they easily get rid of patients who are difficult. Although this problem bothers some physicians more than others, they all acknowledge its existence.

In a particularly illustrative case, a specialist expressed his acute disappointment that patients came to him as the only practitioner of that subspecialty in the HMO and not because they recognized his technical ability. He was frustrated at his inability to impress patients with what he saw as his exceptional skills:

I'm really doing good work. I may be one of the best people around in my area. The patients don't realize that. They come to me because I'm in the system, because they have to. They aren't coming to me because they selected me or because physicians in private practice are referring them to me.

An internist expressed similar regret about her inability to garner patients' respect by saying: "They're not my patients. They're the system's patients." Several others pointed to being unable to count on patient loyalty to build an equity in their practice as compared to their private-practice counterparts whom patients sought without the constraints of HMO enrollment. In sum, the points of dissatisfaction about their interactions with patients reflect the physicians' lack of "market control" over the population of patients being recruited to the practice (Derber 1983).

CONCLUSIONS

We began this paper by observing that everyone who is interested in the changes taking place in the health care delivery system agrees that physicians no longer occupy the position of dominance they occupied in the not too distant past. Yet, little consensus exists about the changes that have occured in physicians' roles; and, little is being said about physicians' views regarding the changes.

The physicians we interviewed painted a clear picture of their understandings about the conditions of practice to which they agreed when joining the prepaid group practice. They entered into a contractual arrangement which offered them a secure income, benefits, standardized hours of work, and so on. They understood that they were joining an established group practice and would not have to "build a practice," by recruiting patients. They were pleased to accept a position where they could "do what they were trained to do," that is, to practice medicine. They willingly, in fact, eagerly, relinquished what they consider to be the "administrative hassles" involved in setting up and managing a practice. They were satisfied to let someone else handle routine administrative tasks that they perceived as interfering with the practice of medicine rather than enhancing the physician's role.

From a theoretical perspective, it is clear that they assigned a high value to the dimension of control over work that theorists have called clinical autonomy (McKinlay and Stoeckle 1988, p. 5) or technical control (Derber 1983) or the practice of good medicine (Luft 1981, 1987). They assigned low value to what they saw as uninteresting, if not necessarily insignificant administrative tasks associated with the role. The latter are the dimensions of control that theorists have identified as organizational control (Larson 1977) or bureaucratic, productivity and market control (Derber 1983). Thus, we found these physicians saying that the core of their own sense of professional identity required that they deliver high quality patient care. They joined the prepaid group practice because they believed that this setting would permit them to do the work they were trained to do— unfettered by extraneous responsibilities, that is, without the need to do non-medical/administrative work. In their eyes, the prepaid group setting provided a more professionalized role rather than the deprofessionalized, proletarianized, or corporatized role being identified in the literature reviewed above.

We also found that once they joined the group and had time to experience this form of practice, they began to connect the one dimension of control they embraced above the others, (decision-making autonomy with regard to patient care) with the one that they had willingly rejected (control over administrative decisions). Once they began to practice, they found that administrative control includes the ability to give staff members orders, alter the standardized time alloted for patient appointments, introduce new procedures for contacting patients for return visits, and so on. In short, they discovered that administrative decisions do affect the structure of the doctor/ patient encounter and, consequently also may affect the quality of interaction that takes place between doctors and patients.

This is a significant discovery as physicians who join a prepaid practice group enter into a bargain that limits the traditional sources of reward associated with the physician's role such as a higher income and personal recognition for their work. The rewards they accrue come from practicing good medicine and the gratifications of a successful doctor/patient encounter. Accordingly, factors that threaten the quality or continuity of good doctor/patient relationships come to be seen as problematic. When the administrative decisions of the group practice organization threaten this relationship, the physicians have good reason to complain. We found it interesting, therefore, that the physicians we interviewed had not defined administrative procedures as problematic until the organization had violated the contractual bargain covering the conditions of work to which the physicians had agreed when they joined the practice.

The physicians, who had been associated with the organization for a number of years and had sufficient time to weigh the costs and benefits of the contractual bargain they made, clearly felt that it had been an acceptable arrangement. They concluded that the circumstances of their practice, while not perfect, constituted a fair exchange. They produced a lengthy list of pros and cons in assessing this form of practice, which, they argued, represented reasonable trade-offs.

An unanticipated aspect of the timing of this study was the sudden discovery that the HMO needed to be more cost conscious to be market competitive. As a result, the prepaid practice group underwent some financial difficulties. It was this change, which affected the conditions of the bargain into which they entered with the organization, that altered the balance of pros and cons of the work situation for many. From the perspective of some of our respondents, the group practice as an organization was not holding up its end of the bargain. In proposing to alter the conditions of the contractual arrangement (e.g., reduce income for a short period, increase hours, cut staff), the group practice was withdrawing certain benefits and offering nothing in compensation. Because of this, a number of physicians were considering alternative practice arrangements, while others had begun to look for new positions.

To conclude, when the arrangement between the physicians and the organization was viewed as stable, physicians did not feel they lacked control. Only on perceiving that the bargain into which they had entered had been violated did they miss the dimension of control giving them a greater voice in organizational decisions in response to the fiscal crisis. Even so, most hoped that things would stabilize, so they would not need to become involved in administrative control.

The large scale organization of medical practice is obviously relatively new; and, physicians' experience with it is limited. This form of practice has greatly expanded in recent years and this trend is expected to continue. Thus, the degree of control physicians have over their work can be expected to shift as the structures in which they work continue to evolve.

REFERENCES

Cheromas, R. 1986. "An Economic Basis for the Proletarianization of Physicians." *International Journal of Health Services* 16:669-674.

Derber, C. 1983. "Managing Professionals: Ideological Proletarianization and Mental Labor." In *Professionals as Workers: Mental Labor in Advanced Capitalism*, edited by C. Derber. Boston: G.K. Hall.

Friedson, E. 1970a. *Professional Dominance: The Social Structure of Medical Care.* New York: Atherton.

_____. 1970b. *Profession of Medicine.* New York: Dodd, Mead.

_____. 1973. "Prepaid Health Care and the New Demanding Patient." *Milbank Memorial Fund Quarterly* 51:473-488.

_____. 1980. *Doctoring Together.* Chicago: University of Chicago Press.

_____. 1984. "The Changing Nature of Professional Control." *Annual Review of Sociology* 10:1-20.

_____. 1985. "The Reorganization of the Medical Profession." *Medical Care Review* 42:11-35.

_____. 1986. *Professional Powers: A Study of the Institutionalization of Formal Knowledge.* Chicago: University of Chicago Press.

_____. 1989. *Medical Work in America.* New Haven: Yale University Press.

Hafferty, F.W. 1988. "Theories at the Crossroads: A Discussion of Evolving Views on Medicine as a Profession." *Milbank Memorial Fund Quarterly* 66 (Supplement 2):202-225.

Haug, M. 1973. "Deprofessionalization: An Alternate Hypothesis for the Future." *Sociological Review Monograph* 20:83-106.

_____. 1976. "The Erosion of Professional Authority: A Cross-Cultural Inquiry in the Case of the Physician." *Milbank Memorial Fund Quarterly* 54:83-106.

_____. 1988. "A Re-examination of the Hypothesis of Physician Deprofessionalization." *Milbank Memorial Fund Quarterly* 66 (Supplement 2):48-56.

Haug, M. and B. Lavin. 1981. "Practitioner and Patient: Who's in Charge?" *Journal of Health and Social Behavior* 22:212-229.

_____. 1983. *Consumerism in Medicine: Challenging Physician Authority.* Beverly Hills: Sage.

Larson, M.S. 1977. *The Rise of Professionalism.* Berkeley: University of California Press.

Light, D. 1986. "Corporate Medicine for Profit." *Scientific American* 255:38-45.

Light, D., and S. Levine. 1988. "The Changing Character of the Medical Profession: A Theoretical Overview." *Milbank Memorial Fund Quarterly* 66 (Supplement 2):10-32.

Luft, H. 1981. *Health Maintenance Organizations: Dimensions of Performance.* New York: Wiley.

_____. *Health Maintenance Organizations.* New Brunswick, NJ: Transaction Books.

Madison, D.L., and T.R. Konrad. 1988. "Larger Medical Group Practice Organizations and Employed Physicians: A Relationship Transaction." *Milbank Memorial Fund Quarterly* 66:240-282.

McKinlay, J. 1982. "Towards the Proletarianization of the Physician." In *Professionals as Workers*, edited by C. Derber. Boston: G.K. Hall.

McKinlay, J., and J. Arches. 1985. "Towards the Proletarianization of Physicians." *International Journal of Health Services* 18:191-205.

McKinlay, J., and J.D. Stoeckler. 1988. "Corporation and the Social Transformation of Doctoring." *International Journal of Health Services* 18:191-205.

Navarro, V. 1976. *Medicine Under Capitalism.* New York: Neale Watson.

_____. 1986. *Crisis, Health, and Medicine.* New York: Routledge & Kegan Paul.

_____. 1988. "Professional Dominance or Proletarianization? Neither." *Milbank Memorial Fund Quarterly* 66(Supplement 2):57-75.

Roemer, M.I. 1986. "Proletarianization of Physicians or Organization of Health Services?"

International Journal of Health Services 16:469-472.
Stoeckle, J.D. 1988. "Reflections on Modern Doctoring." *Milbank Memorial Fund Quarterly* 66 (Supplement 2):76-91.
Wolinsky, F.D. 1988. "The Professional Dominance Perspective, Revisited." *Milbank Memorial Fund Quarterly* 66(Supplement 2):33-47.

BIOGRAPHICAL SKETCHES OF THE CONTRIBUTORS

Arnold Arluke, after completing a Ph.D. in sociology at New York University, served as a postdoctoral fellow and research associate at Harvard Medical School. Since then he has been on the faculty of the Department of Sociology and Anthropology at Northeastern University where he is now an Associate Professor. His research has focused on the uses of knowledge in medical and everyday life.

Rosalind C. Barnett is Senior Research Associate at the Wellesley College Center for Research on Women and codirector of a longitudinal study of gender differences in work and family-role stress. She was codirector of a longitudinal study of stress and health professionals. She is the coauthor, with Grace K. Baruch, of *Beyond Sugar and Spices and Lifeprints: New Patterns of Love and Work for Today's Woman*, and coeditor, with Grace K. Baruch and Lois Beiner, of *Gender and Stress*.

Grace K. Baruch was an Associate Director of the Wellesley College for Research on Women and codirector of a longitudinal study of stress and health in women health professionals. She was the coauthor, with Rosaline C. Barnett, of *Beyond Sugar and Spice and Lifeprints: New Patterns of Love and Work for Today's Woman*.

Grace Budrys, Director of the Masters Degree Program in Public Services and Professor of Sociology at DePaul University in Chicago, has focused her research on medical occupations and organizations. Her recent book, *Planning for the Nation's Health* (1986) was concerned with evaluations of the successes and failures of the health care delivery system in the United States.

Pamela Dee Elkind is a Professor of Medical Sociology at Eastern Washington University. She has published several articles in the field of health occupations.

Her current interests lie in the environmental area where she has most recently researched and written about perceptions of health hazards at a nuclear repository and those of farm production in rural Washington. Dr. Elkind has served on a variety of state and federal boards dealing with the impact of environmental degradation.

Bernard Goldstein received his B.A. in 1946 from Sir George Williams College (now Concordia University) in Montreal. He earned an M.S.S.C. at the New School for Social Research in New York while working at Columbia University's Bureau of Applied Social Research. During 1948-49, he was a research fellow at Fisk University in Nashville, where he met Louis Wirth. The following year he started on his Ph.D. at Chicago, working as a research assistant for Wirth at the Committee on Race Relations, and then at the Industrial Relations Center of the University of Chicago, where he participated in an ongoing study of white collar unions. His dissertation, done under the guidance of Everett C. Hughes, concerned the unionized engineers at Western Electric.

Moving to New Jersey in 1956, he began his stay at Rutgers University with a joint apppointment at University College and the Research Program of the Institute of Management and Labor Relations, where he did research and published on engineering unions and in-plant medical programs. In the early 1960s, he moved to Rutgers' Urban Studies Center, where he helped to write the research components of numerous proposed poverty programs. With H.C. Bredemeier and others, he wrote *Low Income Youth in Urban Areas: A Critical Review of the Literature* published in 1967. During 1966-67 he was a Fulbright Scholar in India. On his return, he began, with Coralie Farlee, a five-year study of the introduction of a computerized health information system at a medical center. The study was designed to analyze the impact of the technological innovation on the social system. In addition to a final report, the study generated several articles. For five years, beginning in 1968, he was Chair of the Rutgers College Sociology Department, followed by another five-year stint as Chair of the Graduate Program. In 1979, the results of research by Jack Oldham and Goldstein were published in the monograph, *Children and Work: A Study in Socialization.* In 1987, he began his current collaboration with Howard Robboy to study the effects on patients, medical staff, and others of long-term, continuous attachment to ventilators. This research has produced a number of presented papers and this chapter. He retired on July 1, 1988, and now resides in Washington, D.C.

Harriet Engel Gross is University Professor of Sociology at Governor's State University, University Park, Illinois. She has studied work and family relationships and has written about commuter marriage among other topics in this area. Currently, she is working on a study of open adoption in addition to her work about physician responses to prepaid group practice.

Frederic W. Hafferty is an Associate Professor of Behavioral Sciences. Current research interests include medical specialization, occupations, and professions and disability studies. His book, *Into the Valley: Death and the Socialization of Medical Students,* is forthcoming from Yale University Press.

Michael I. Harrison is a Senior Lecturer in Sociology at Bar Ilan University (Ramat Gan, Israel) and head of the Graduate Program in Organizational Sociology. He received his doctorate from the University of Michigan, has taught at SUNY, Stony Brook and in the School of Management at Boston College, and was a visiting scholar at the Harvard Business School. His current research examines organizational change, social conflict, professional organizations, and consulting processes. His publications include *Diagnosing Organizations: Methods, Models and Processes* (1987, Sage), and he is an active organizational consultant.

Phyllis Ann Langton is Professor of Sociology at the George Washington University, Washington, D.C. She is currently completing a book, *Alcohol Use, Policy,* and *Institutional Relationships* for Allyn and Bacon, and a research monograph, *Health and Local Democracy in Scotland*, a fourteen-year study of public participation in health care decision making.

Judith A. Levy is Assistant Professor of Health Resources Management, School of Public Health, the University of Illinois at Chicago. Her research interests include social movements in medicine and chronic illness over the life course. Her most recent research examines the general public's knowledge, attitudes, and behavior toward AIDS.

Jacquelyn Litt is Assistant Professor of Sociology at Allegheny College, Meadville, PA. She is currently professor in the department of Sociology at Rutgers-New Brunswick. Her current work examines the meaning and implications for mothers of medical authority in child rearing.

Judith Lorber is Professor of Sociology at Brooklyn College and the Graduate School, City University of New York, where she is also Coordinator of Women's Studies Certificate Program. She is the author of *Women Physicians: Careers, Status and Power* (1984, Tavistock/Methuen) and numerous journal articles on gender and women in health care. Her current research is on the organization of in vitro fertilization clinics and couples' experiences with the new procreative technology. She is Founding Editor of *Gender and Society*, official publication of Sociologists for Women in Society.

Nancy L. Marshall is a Research Associate at the Wellesley College Center for Research on Women and codirector of a longitudinal study of the social ecology of infant child care. With her coauthors, she was codirector of a longitudinal study of stress and health in women health professionals. Her research interests include women and employment, the costs and benefits of social networks, and work and family roles of women and men.

Lorayn Olson is Director of the American Medical Association's Department of Survey Design and Analysis. She received her Ph.D. in sociology from the University of Chicago.

Joseph H. Pleck is the Henry R. Luce Professor of Families, Change and Society at Wheaton College. He was formerly an Associate Director at the Wellesley College Center for Research on Women and a codirector of a longitudinal study of stress and health in women and health professionals.

Howard Robboy is currently Associate Professor and Chair of the Department of Sociology & Anthropology at Trenton State College in New Jersey. His sociological training was obtained at Temple University (B.A., 1967) and Rutgers University (M.A., 1972; Ph.D., 1976). His dissertation, *They Work by Night: Temporal Adaptations in a Technological Society* a study of the impact of working steady nightshift on family life, was directed by Bernard Goldstein. He is the coeditor of *Social Interaction* (1979, 1983, 1988, St. Martin's Press) and the author of articles on minority group relations, the sociology of work, culture, social deviance, and the sociology of education. Since 1987, he has worked with Bernard Goldstein studying the long-term social effects of ventilator dependency on patients, their significant others, and medical caretakers.

Wendy Simonds is Assistant Professor of Sociology at Emory University. She coauthored *The Forgotten Cry: A History and Analysis of Maternal Consolidation Literature* (forthcoming, Temple University Press) with Barbara Katz Rothman. She is currently working on two projects: an analysis of women and self-help reading and a study of feminist abortion workers.

Howard Waitzkin is Professor of Medicine and Social Sciences at the University of California, Irvine. He received his M.D. and Ph.D. in sociology from Harvard University and has worked with several community-based health projects. His books include *The Exploitation of Illness in Capitalist Society* (coauthor), *The Second Sickness: Contradictions of Capitalist Health Care,* and *The Politics of Medical Encounters: How Patients and Doctors Deal with Social Problems* (Yale University Press). His interests focus on the micropolitics of professional-client encounters and on health policy.

Fredric D. Wolinsky is Professor of Medicine at Indiana University School of Medicine. His NIH-funded research program focuses on the health and health behaviors of elderly Americans.